"A superb and vivid biography . . . that brings the world of Francis I to life, skillfully delineating the moves and major players in both European and domestic politics . . . and also gives the reader wonderful glimpses of the often licentious court life of that time. . . . Ms. Frieda suggests that, under Francis I, France preserved its political power, greatly increased its cultural influence, and positioned itself for the Grand Siècle that his Bourbon successors would soon preside over." —John Steele Gordon, *Wall Street Journal*

"This book is a must for lovers of history, as Frieda provides a complex look at a leader who remains elusive despite being one of the most recognizable monarchs of the Renaissance period."

—*Brooklyn Digest*

"A thoroughgoing biography of the French ruler who allied with Islam. . . . Though a figure of major importance, Francis has been forgotten against better-known contemporaries such as England's Henry VIII. Frieda's work helps restore him to history."

—*Kirkus Reviews*

"In the lively colorful prose of this fast read . . . Leonie Frieda seeks context and truth for Francis I . . . who pulled his country together after . . . a time of great dissent caused by the Hundred Years' War and feudal infighting." —*New York Journal of Books*

"A thoughtful, vivid, and well-paced telling of a complex story, set against an even more complex background of European power politics, which Frieda picks apart with admirable skill."

—Noel Malcolm, *Sunday Telegraph*

FRANCIS I

The Maker of Modern France

LEONIE FRIEDA

HARPER  PERENNIAL

NEW YORK • LONDON • TORONTO • SYDNEY • NEW DELHI • AUCKLAND

HARPER ● PERENNIAL

Originally published in Great Britain in 2018 by Weidenfeld & Nicolson, an imprint of The Orion Publishing Group Ltd

A hardcover edition of this book was published in 2018 by HarperCollins Publishers.

HarperCollins books may be purchased for educational, business, or sales promotional use. For information, please email the Special Markets Department at SPsales@harpercollins.com.

FIRST HARPER PERENNIAL EDITION PUBLISHED 2019.

Library of Congress Cataloging-in-Publication Data has been applied for.

ISBN 978-0-06156311-9 (pbk.)

19 20 21 22 23   LSC   10 9 8 7 6 5 4 3 2 1

For Ion Trewin
1943–2015
Beloved teacher and friend

CONTENTS

LIST OF ILLUSTRATIONS

Francis I on horseback, French school (Superstock / The Art Archive)

The crowned salamander, symbol of Francis I (Shutterstock / Jose Ignacio Soto)

Manuscript miniature of Louise of Savoy (PVDE / Bridgeman)

Portrait of Marguerite of Angoulême, attr. to Jean Clouet (Walker Art Gallery, National Museums Liverpool / Bridgeman)

Portrait of Claude of France by Corneille de Lyon (Pushkin Museum, Moscow / Bridgeman)

Claude of France and her children, Italian school (Bibliothèque Nationale, Paris / Bridgeman)

Portrait of Anne de Pisseleu d'Heilly, attr. to Corneille de Lyon (Metropolitan Museum of Art / H. O. Havemeyer Collection, Bequest of Mrs H. O. Havemeyer, 1929)

The Field of the Cloth of Gold, English school (Royal Collection Trust © Her Majesty Queen Elizabeth II, 2017 / Bridgeman)

Charles V at Mühlberg by Titian (Prado, Madrid / Bridgeman)

Francis I and Suleiman I by Titian (World History Archive / Alamy)

MAPS

France

Holy Roman Empire

Italian Peninsula

France during the latter half of the sixteenth century

Acquisitions of Francis, 1515–7

Calais
Boulogne
FLANDERS
Antwer
BRUSSELS
NET
Cambrai
Cateau-
Cambré
PICARDY
Gui

Le Havre
Rouen
Rhei
NORMANDY
ALENÇON
St Denis
Chantilly
ILE-DE-
Meaux
Saint-Germain-en-Laye
Anet
PARIS
St-Maur-des-Foss
MAINE
FRANCE
Fontainebleau

BRITTANY
Cl
Orleans
Auxer
Angers
Amboise
Blois
R. Loire
Tours
Chenonceau
NIVERNAI
Nantes
ANJOU
TOURAINE
Moncontour
BERRY
Bourges
Nevers

POITOU
La Rochelle
Moulins
St-Jean-d'Angély
BOURBON
Cognac
SAINTONGE
ANGOU
LEME
LIMOUSIN
Angoulême
AUVERGNE

Bay of
Biscay
Coutras
PERIGORD
Bordeaux
Bergerac
GUYENNE

Nérac
Principality of
Bearn and
Kingdom of
Navarre
LANGUEDO
Bayonne
BASSE
NAVARRE
Toulouse
Montpellier
HAUTE
NAVARRE
R. Bidasoa
GASCONY

SPAIN

0   50   100   150 miles
0   50   100   150   200 km

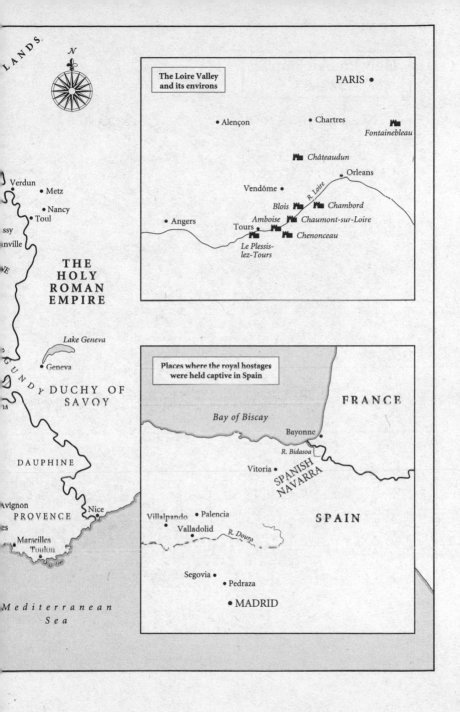

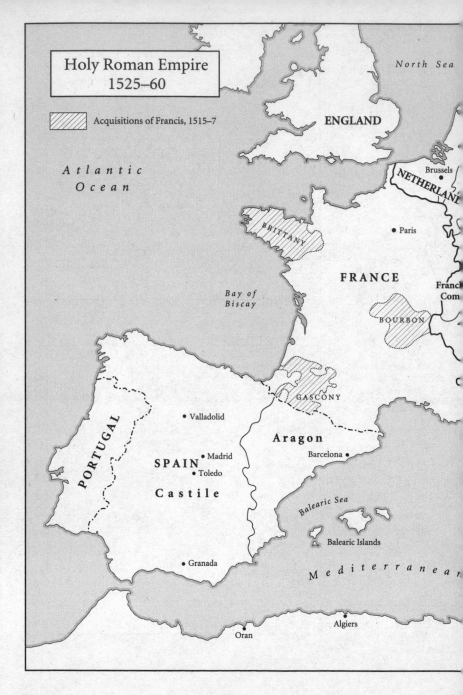

Holy Roman Empire
1525–60

Acquisitions of Francis, 1515–7

North Sea

ENGLAND

*Atlantic
Ocean*

Brussels

NETHERLAN

BRITTANY

Paris

FRANCE

*Bay of
Biscay*

Franc
Com

BOURBON

GASCONY

PORTUGAL

Valladolid

Aragon

SPAIN Madrid

Barcelona

Toledo

Castile

Balearic Sea

Balearic Islands

Granada

Mediterranean

Oran

Algiers

The Italian peninsula during the latter half of the sixteenth century

N

Monf. Monferrato (to Mantua)
G. Genoa
L. Lunigiana (Imperial fiefs)
Ist. Istria (to Venice)
C. Crema (to Venice)
Lan. Langhe (Imperial fiefs)
Gar. Garfagnana (to Lucca)
Sal. Saluzzo (to France)
Cas. Castro (to Parma)

HOLY ROMAN EMPIRE

Trento
(Austria)

DUCHY OF
SAVOY
(Piedmont)

DUCHY
OF   Marignano
Milan
MILAN
Pavia
(Spain)

Monf.

REPUBLIC
OF VENICE

MANTUA
Mantua

Venice   Ist.

PARMA

Sal.

Monf.

Lan.   Genoa
REPUBLIC
OF GENOA
(Spain)

Modena
(Ferrara)
L.
Gar.
Papal States

FERRARA

Finale
(Spain)   Massa

G.

G.

LUCCA   Florence

TUSCANY

URBINO

Piombino
(Spain)

Siena
(Tuscany)

Ligurian
Sea

Corsica
(Spain)

Presidial
State
(Spain)

PAPAL STATES

Adriatic Sea

• Rome

KINGDOM
OF NAPLES
(Spain)

SARDINIA
(Spain)

• Naples

Tyrrhenian
Sea

Mediterranean   Sea

SICILY

0   50   100 miles
0   50   100 150 kms

GENEALOGICAL TABLES

The House of Valois – senior line

The House of Valois – Valois-Orléans line

The House of Valois – Bourbon-Montpensier line

The House of Trastamara/Habsburg

CHARLES V = 1350, Joanna of Bourbon
'the Wise'   1338–78
1338–80
r. 1364–80

CHARLES VI = 1385, Isabeau of Bavaria
'the Mad'   1370–1435
1368–1422
r. 1380–1422

Isabella, Queen of England 1389–1409	Joan, Duchess of Brittany 1391–1438	Michelle, Duchess of Burgundy 1395–1422
= (1) 1396, **RICHARD II**, King of England	= 1396, John VI, Duke of Brittany	= 1409, Philip III, Duke of Burgundy
= (2) 1406, Charles, Duke of Orléans		

LOUIS XI 'the Prudent' 'the Spider King' 1423–83 r. 1461–1483	= (1) 1436, Margaret Stuart, Princess of Scotland 1424–45 = (2) 1451, Charlotte of Savoy 1441–83	Catherine 1428–46 = 1440, Charles, Duke of Burgundy	Yolande, Duchess of Savoy 1434–78 = 1452, Amadeus IX, Duke of Savoy

Anne of France, 'Madame la Grande', Duchess of Bourbon 1461–1522 Joint Regent for **CHARLES VIII** 1483–91	= 1473, Peter of Beaujeu, Duke of Bourbon 1438–1503 Joint Regent for **CHARLES VIII** 1483–91	Jeanne (Joan) Duchess of Orléans, Duchess of Berry, 'Saint Joan of Valois' 1464–1505 = 1476, **LOUIS XII**, Duke of Orléans 1462–1515 r. 1498–1515 marriage annulled in 1498 by **POPE ALEXANDER VI**

Suzanne, = 1505, Charles III, Duke
Duchess of Bourbon of Bourbon and Auvergne,
and Auvergne Count of Montpensier
1491–1521 1490–1527

three children,
died at infancy

✦ HOUSE OF VALOIS ✦
Senior line

Louis, = 1389, Valentine Visconti of Milan
Duke of Orléans   1371–1408
1372–1407

Valois-Orléans line

Louis,   Catherine,   **CHARLES VII** = 1422, Marie of Anjou
Dauphin of Viennois   Queen of England   'the Victorious'   1404–1463
1397–1415   1401–38   1403–61
     r. 1422–1461

= 1412, Marguerite   = (1) 1420, **HENRY V**,
of Burgundy   King of England

= (2) 1429, Owen Tudor

Joan,   Madeleine,   Charles,
Duchess of Bourbon   Princess of Viana   Duke of Berry,
1435–82   1443–86   Duke of Guyenne
     1446–72

= 1452, John II, Duke   = 1462, Gaston of Foix,
of Bourbon   Prince of Viana

CHARLES VIII — 1491, Anne,
'the Affable'   Duchess of Brittany
1470–98   1477–1514
r. 1483–98

four children,
died at infancy

The direct Valois line finishes

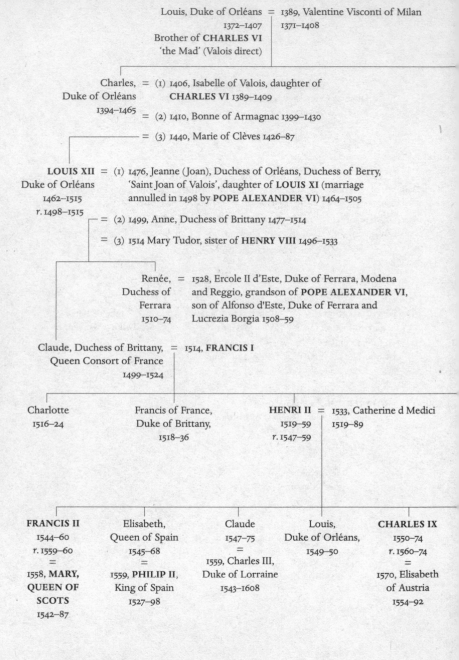

Louis, Duke of Orléans = 1389, Valentine Visconti of Milan
1372–1407 | 1371–1408
Brother of **CHARLES VI**
'the Mad' (Valois direct)

Charles, = (1) 1406, Isabelle of Valois, daughter of
Duke of Orléans | **CHARLES VI** 1389–1409
1394–1465
= (2) 1410, Bonne of Armagnac 1399–1430

= (3) 1440, Marie of Clèves 1426–87

LOUIS XII = (1) 1476, Jeanne (Joan), Duchess of Orléans, Duchess of Berry,
Duke of Orléans | 'Saint Joan of Valois', daughter of **LOUIS XI** (marriage
1462–1515 | annulled in 1498 by **POPE ALEXANDER VI**) 1464–1505
r. 1498–1515

= (2) 1499, Anne, Duchess of Brittany 1477–1514

= (3) 1514 Mary Tudor, sister of **HENRY VIII** 1496–1533

Renée, = 1528, Ercole II d'Este, Duke of Ferrara, Modena
Duchess of | and Reggio, grandson of **POPE ALEXANDER VI**,
Ferrara | son of Alfonso d'Este, Duke of Ferrara and
1510–74 | Lucrezia Borgia 1508–59

Claude, Duchess of Brittany, = 1514, **FRANCIS I**
Queen Consort of France
1499–1524

Charlotte
1516–24

Francis of France,
Duke of Brittany,
1518–36

HENRI II = 1533, Catherine d Medici
1519–59 | 1519–89
r. 1547–59

FRANCIS II
1544–60
r. 1559–60
=
1558, **MARY,
QUEEN OF
SCOTS**
1542–87

Elisabeth,
Queen of Spain
1545–68
=
1559, **PHILIP II**,
King of Spain
1527–98

Claude
1547–75
=
1559, Charles III,
Duke of Lorraine
1543–1608

Louis,
Duke of Orléans,
1549–50

CHARLES IX
1550–74
r. 1560–74
=
1570, Elisabeth
of Austria
1554–92

✦ VALOIS-ORLÉANS LINE ✦

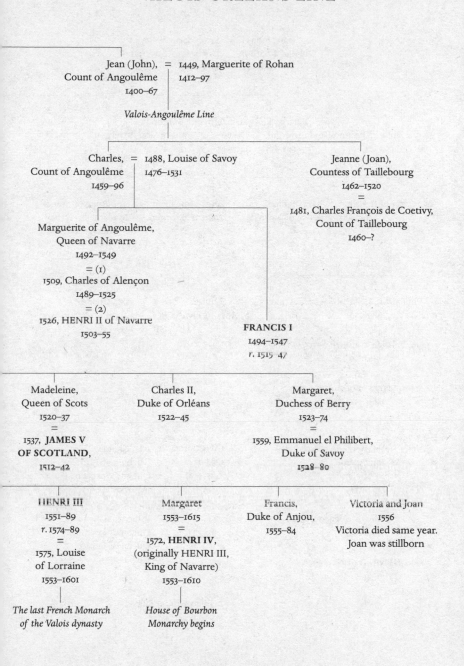

Jean (John), = 1449, Marguerite of Rohan
Count of Angoulême   1412–97
1400–67

Valois-Angoulême Line

Charles, = 1488, Louise of Savoy
Count of Angoulême   1476–1531
1459–96

Jeanne (Joan),
Countess of Taillebourg
1462–1520
=
1481, Charles François de Coetivy,
Count of Taillebourg
1460–?

Marguerite of Angoulême,
Queen of Navarre
1492–1549
= (1)
1509, Charles of Alençon
1489–1525
= (2)
1526, HENRI II of Navarre
1503–55

FRANCIS I
1494–1547
r. 1515–47

Madeleine,
Queen of Scots
1520–37
=
1537, **JAMES V
OF SCOTLAND**,
1512–42

Charles II,
Duke of Orléans
1522–45

Margaret,
Duchess of Berry
1523–74
=
1559, Emmanuel el Philibert,
Duke of Savoy
1528–80

HENRI III
1551–89
r. 1574–89
=
1575, Louise
of Lorraine
1553–1601

*The last French Monarch
of the Valois dynasty*

Margaret
1553–1615
=
1572, **HENRI IV**,
(originally HENRI III,
King of Navarre)
1553–1610

*House of Bourbon
Monarchy begins*

Francis,
Duke of Anjou,
1555–84

Victoria and Joan
1556
Victoria died same year.
Joan was stillborn

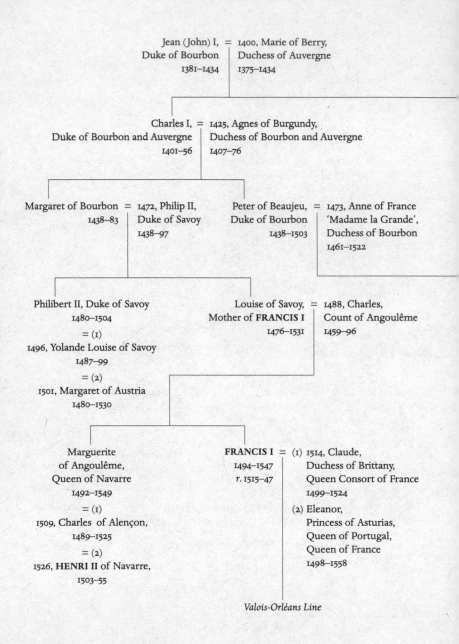

Jean (John) I, = 1400, Marie of Berry,
Duke of Bourbon | Duchess of Auvergne
1381–1434 | 1375–1434

Charles I, = 1425, Agnes of Burgundy,
Duke of Bourbon and Auvergne | Duchess of Bourbon and Auvergne
1401–56 | 1407–76

Margaret of Bourbon = 1472, Philip II,
1438–83 | Duke of Savoy
| 1438–97

Peter of Beaujeu, = 1473, Anne of France
Duke of Bourbon | 'Madame la Grande',
1438–1503 | Duchess of Bourbon
| 1461–1522

Philibert II, Duke of Savoy
1480–1504

= (1)
1496, Yolande Louise of Savoy
1487–99

= (2)
1501, Margaret of Austria
1480–1530

Louise of Savoy, = 1488, Charles,
Mother of **FRANCIS I** | Count of Angoulême
1476–1531 | 1459–96

Marguerite
of Angoulême,
Queen of Navarre
1492–1549

= (1)
1509, Charles of Alençon,
1489–1525

= (2)
1526, **HENRI II** of Navarre,
1503–55

FRANCIS I = (1) 1514, Claude,
1494–1547 | Duchess of Brittany,
r. 1515–47 | Queen Consort of France
| 1499–1524

(2) Eleanor,
Princess of Asturias,
Queen of Portugal,
Queen of France
1498–1558

Valois-Orléans Line

✦ BOURBON-MONTPENSIER LINE ✦

Louis I of Bourbon, = 1442, Gabrielle la Tour
Count of Montpensier   d. 1486
1405–86

Gilbert of Bourbon, = 1482, Clara Gonzaga of Mantua,
Count of Montpensier   Countess of Montpensier
1443–96   1464–1503

Suzanne, = 1505, Charles III,
Duchess of Bourbon   Duke of Bourbon
and Auvergne,   and Auvergne,
Countess of Montpensier   Count of Montpensier
1491–1521   1490–1527

FERDINAND II 'the Catholic' = 1469, **ISABELLA I**, Queen of Castile
1452–1516   1451–1504
King of Aragon (1479). King of Sicily (1468)   *r*. 1474–1504
King of Naples (1504). King of Navarre (1512)   = (2) 1505, Germaine of Foix
King of Castile (*jure uxoris* 1474)   1488–1538

Isabella,
Queen of Portugal
1470–98

= (1) 1490, Alfonso,
Prince of Portugal,
1475–91

= (2) 1497, **MANUEL I**,
King of Portugal,
'the Fortunate'
1469–1521

John,
Prince of Asturias
1478–97

= 1496, Margaret of Austria,
Princess of Asturias and
Duchess of Savoy, daughter
of **MAXIMILIAN I**,
Holy Roman Emperor, and
Mary of Burgundy
1480–1530

Eleanor,
Princess of Asturias,
Queen of Portugal,
Queen of France
1498–1558

= (1) 1518, **MANUEL I**, King
of Portugal, 'the Fortunate'
1469–1521

= (2) 1530, **FRANCIS I**,
King of France
1494–1547

CHARLES V,
Holy Roman
Emperor
1500–58
r. 1519–56
(voluntary abdication)

= 1526, Isabella of Portugal,
Holy Roman Empress,
daughter of Maria of
Aragon and **MANUEL I**
1503–39

Isabella,
Archduchess of Austria and
Infantana of Castile and Aragon,
Queen of Denmark, Sweden
and Norway
1501–26

= 1515, **CHRISTIAN II**,
King of Denmark, Sweden
and Norway. 'Christian the
Tyrant' (deposed)
1481–1559

PHILIP II = (1) 1543, Maria Manuela, daughter of **JOHN III**,
1527–98   King of Portugal, and Catherine of Austria
King of Spain (1556)   1527–45
King of Portugal (1581)
King of Naples and Sicily (1554)   = (2) 1554, **MARY I**, Queen of England
King of England (1554–58)   1516–58

= (3) 1559, Elisabeth of Valois, daughter of **HENRI II**,
King of France and Catherine de Medici
1545–68

= (4) 1570, Anne of Austria, daughter of

PHILIP III 'the Pious' = Margaret   **MAXIMILIAN II**, Holy Roman Emperor,
1578–1621   of Austria   and Maria of Spain
r. 1598–1621   1584–1611   1549–80
King of Spain (Philip III)
King of Portugal (Philip II)   had issue, Spanish royal line

JOANNA 'the Mad',
Queen of Castile and Aragon
1479–1555
Castile *r.* 1504–55
Aragon *r.* 1516–55

= 1496, **PHILIP I**, King of Castile by
jure uxoris, 'Philip the Handsome',
son of **MAXIMILIAN I**,
Holy Roman Emperor,
1478–1506

House of Habsburg

Maria,
Queen of Portugal
1482–1517

= 1500, **MANUEL I**,
King of Portugal,
'the Fortunate'
1469–1521

Catherine,
Queen of England
1485–1536

= (1) 1501, Arthur, Prince of
Wales, son of **HENRY VII**,
King of England
1486–1502

= (2) 1509, **HENRY VIII**,
King of England, brother of
Arthur, Prince of Wales
1491–1547

FERDINAND I,
Holy Roman Emperor
1503–64
r. 1558–64
King of Bohemia and Hungary
r. 1526–64

= 1521, Anne of Bohemia and
Hungary, Queen of the Romans
1503–47

had issue,
Holy Roman Emperor line

Mary,
Queen of Hungary and
Bohemia, Governor of
The Netherlands
1505–58

= 1522, **LOUIS II**,
King of Hungary,
Croatia and Bohemia
1506–26

Catherine,
Queen of Portugal
1507–78

= 1525, **JOHN III**,
King of Portugal and the
Algarves, son of Maria
and **MANUEL I**
1502–57

Maria of Spain,
Holy Roman Empress
1528–1603

= 1548, **MAXIMILIAN II**,
Holy Roman Emperor,
son of **FERDINAND I**
and Anne of Bohemia
1527–76

had issue,
Holy Roman Emperor line

Joanna
1535–73

= 1552, João Manuel,
Prince of Portugal
1537–54

LIST OF PRINCIPAL CHARACTERS

FRANCE – ROYAL FAMILY OF VALOIS-ANGOULÊME

The Angoulême belonged to the second branch of the royal house of Valois-Orléans. At the time of Francis's birth, the House of Valois-Orléans was led by Louis II, Duke of Orléans.

Francis I, King of France, born Francis of Angoulême, prince of the blood. Count of Angoulême after his father's death; elevated to Duke of Valois on becoming heir presumptive. He was Duke of Brittany by marriage to Claude of France and declared his right to the title Duke of Milan through his ancestress Valentina Visconti

Marguerite of Angoulême, also known as Duchess of Alençon, the king's sister and close adviser

Charles Orléans, Count of Angoulême and the king's father

Louise of Savoy, the king's mother

Claude of France, Queen Consort of France, daughter of Louis XII and Anne of Brittany

Francis of France, Duke of Brittany, Francis's eldest son; the dauphin

Henri of France, Duke of Orléans, Francis's second son and later Henri II

Madeleine of France, Francis's favourite daughter, married to James V of Scotland

Charles of France, Francis's youngest and favourite son, Count of Clermont

Marguerite of France, Duchess of Berry, Francis's youngest
daughter

Eleanor of Austria, Francis's second wife, Queen Consort of
France, sister of Charles V and Dowager Queen of Portugal

FRANCE – PREDECESSORS

Louis XI of France, known as 'The Cunning' or 'The Spider King'

Anne of France, eldest daughter of Louis XI and permitted to play
a role in carrying out his policies; she continued her father's
work after his death and at the same time, with her husband
Peter of Beaujeu, Duke of Bourbon, was her brother Charles
VIII's guardian

Charles VIII of France, known as 'Charles the Affable'

Louis XII, also known as Louis of Orléans; the only Valois-Orléans
King of France

Jeanne of France, Duchess of Berry and Louis XII's first wife; sister
of Anne of France and Charles VIII

Anne of Brittany, Sovereign Duchess of Brittany, wife of Emperor
Maximilian I, the Holy Roman Emperor; Charles VIII and
Louis XII

FRANCE – LEADING LIGHTS

Charles III, Duke of Bourbon-Montpensier (prince of the blood);
Bourbon's many titles included Count of Clermont-en-
Beauvaisis and La Marche. Constable of France. This office,
as well his own personal possessions, made the duke the most
powerful man in the country aside from the king.

Anne, Duke of Montmorency and Constable of France

Philippe of Chabot, Seigneur of Brion and Admiral of Brion

Antoine Duprat, Chancellor of France throughout Francis's reign
and Archbishop of Sens

Robert de La Marck, Seigneur of Fleuranges and Marshal of
France; a close friend of Francis

Pierre Terrail, Seigneur of Bayard, also known as Chevalier de
Bayard or 'The Good Knight'

Pierre de Rohan, Seigneur de Gié, governor to the young Francis

Anne d'Heilly, Duchess of Étampes. The so-called 'Madame d'Étampes' was the most significant of all Francis's mistresses.

Françoise de Foix, Countess of Châteaubriant, the king's first *maîtresse en titre*

Diane de Poitiers, Grand Seneschal of Normandy, mistress and mentor to Henri II

OVERSEAS – RULERS

Charles V, Holy Roman Emperor, also King of Spain, Archduke of Austria, Lord of the Netherlands, Duke of Burgundy; Francis's greatest nemesis

Henry VIII, King of England, occasional ally to both Francis and Charles

Suleiman I, known as 'The Magnificent', ruler of the Ottoman Empire

James V, King of Scotland, husband of Francis's daughter Madeleine and father with a second wife of Mary, Queen of Scots

Francesco II Sforza, Duke of Milan and the last of the Sforza family to rule Milan

OVERSEAS – LEADING LIGHTS

Pope Leo X (r. March 1513–December 1521), born Lorenzo de Medici; pope at the time of Francis's accession to the throne

Pope Adrian VI (r. January 1522–September 1523), born Adriaan Florensz Boeyens; the only non-Italian pope for centuries to come

Pope Clement VII (r. November 1523–September 1534), born Giulio de Medici; pope responsible both for the Sack of Rome and the English Reformation

Pope Paul III (r. October 1534–November 1549), born Alessandro Farnese; the final pope of Francis's reign

Catherine de Medici, daughter of Lorenzo II de Medici and Madeleine de La Tour d'Auvergne, and subsequently Queen of

France upon her marriage to Francis's son Henri II

Charles, Viceroy de Lannoy, soldier, statesman and Francis's one-time jailer and saviour

Cardinal Thomas Wolsey, Lord Chancellor of England and mastermind behind the Field of the Cloth of Gold

LIST OF MONARCHS OF FRANCE

Jean II
'The Good'
b. 1319
r. 1350–64

Charles V
'The Wise'
b. 1338
r. 1364–80

Charles VI
'The Beloved'
'The Mad'
b. 1368
r. 1380–1422

Charles VII
'The Victorious'
b. 1403
r. 1422–61

Louis XI
'The Prudent'
'The Spider King'
b. 1423
r. 1461–83

Charles VIII
'The Affable'
b. 1470
r. 1483–98

The direct line of Valois ends.

Louis XII
(Valois-Orléans)
b. 1462
r. 1498–1515

Francis I
(Valois-Angoulême)
b. 1494
r. 1515–47

Henri II
b. 1519
r. 1547–59

INTRODUCTION

For all the sobriquets that Francis I collected, and is still known by, there is one that was never coined. 'The Maker of Modern France' was 'The Renaissance Warrior', 'The Father of the French Language', 'The First Gentleman of France' and 'Le Grand Nez' (big nose). What he was not was Francis the Great. It is no exaggeration to say that he viewed himself as a man of the same calibre as Alexander or Charlemagne, and expected to be treated as such by his people and posterity alike. On his deathbed in 1547 his own assessment was that he had never treated any man unfairly, and that his conscience was clear. In death, as in life, he offered an optimism that was not borne out by action.

Insofar as he is remembered today, it is largely for his least attractive traits. He was a king of fleeting enthusiasms, and a capricious and impetuous figure who displayed short-lived passion rather than tenacity. He was ridiculed even during his lifetime as a time-waster whose single main obsession, to rule Milan and the Italian peninsula, dominated his reign without consummation. Since his demise, greater and lesser monarchs have sat upon the French throne, but there are few whose reputations have suffered such a decline. This book will explore why posterity has much diminished his legacy.

When I began researching my biography of Catherine de Medici in the late 1990s, the figure of Francis, Catherine's father-in-law and the great king of the day, informed much of my understanding of the period. He seemed to me to have been a vast and brilliant man, with a benign tendency that was frequently at odds with those of his contemporaries. Almost all the historic buildings that I visited during my research bore the mark of his personal emblem, the salamander: a recurring suggestion that this was a journey that I should take at greater length in due course.

Two decades later, Francis seems all but forgotten. The salamander remains the tantalising clue to the overwhelming impact he made during his reign. In England he is known, if at all, for being the other participant in the greatest Renaissance pageant between princes, the Field of the Cloth of Gold. For the more cosmopolitan, Victor Hugo's swingeing character assassination of him as a self-obsessed satyr in his 1832 play *Le Roi s'amuse*, banned after its first and only production, has mistakenly become his epitaph.* His achievements and influence have faded into undeserved obscurity. If ever there was a king who warrants rehabilitation, it is Francis.

This is not to exonerate his many mistakes. In addition to his time-wasting and mutability, he was a deeply flawed figure. He cannot be seen as his own man, so closely was his rise and early success tied to the influence of his mother, Louise of Savoy. She both inspired and indulged him, and some of the blame for his later poor decisions must lie with her. Likewise, it was his sister Marguerite, a woman comfortably his intellectual superior, to whom he often turned for much-needed advice, if only to clarify his own thoughts. They were the only people who could speak frankly to the king about his failings without fear of provoking an astonished and furious response. He was not a monarch who encouraged debate.

Neither sadistic nor cruel in the manner of many other rulers, and even lenient by contemporary standards, he was no proto-democrat. Instead, absolutist rule provided his greatest conviction and his guiding principle. He met any suggestion that his power might be checked with a fury that belied his otherwise charming reputation. He was given to paranoia, jealousy and a fickle attitude towards his favourites. In one particular instance, this led to a dispute that threatened his life and the integrity of France itself. His treatment of his wives, although unexceptional by the standards

---

* The play later became the basis for Verdi's *Rigoletto*.

of the day, was technically correct but with occasional outrageous public lapses. A womaniser all his life, he was not the first or last king to be guided by his baser carnal appetites. Nonetheless, some of his judgements were amongst the poorest made by any ruler; they were invariably made under the influence of powerful mistresses.

His achievements were extraordinary – and I shall return to them in a moment – but they could have been even greater. Much of the second half of his reign was misspent in over-elaborate stratagems, the whimsical making and then breaking of alliances, as well as pointless and expensive conflicts caused by his grotesquely inflated pride. Had he acknowledged his errors, and devoted himself to furthering the interests of his country, there is no doubt that he would now be regarded as among France's greatest kings.

Yet it is Francis's extraordinary charm that is key to understanding this most complex of monarchs. He succeeded to the throne following a time of great dissent largely caused by the Hundred Years War and feudal infighting. The country stood on the verge of being carved up into its constituent parts, with powerful magnates permanently on the verge of civil war. Just as the Italian peninsula was in a constant state of flux, and ambitious men plotted each other's destruction with the same ease with which they made their subsequent confession, so only the strong rule of Louis XI had avoided a similar fate for France. The failure of Louis XII to maintain the country's standing in Europe by losing its Italian possessions and parts of the north meant that Francis inherited a compromised kingdom. It would take the most remarkable of men to unite the country. Against the odds, Francis succeeded in this. The single largest nation in Europe was a formidable enemy and ally if led to maximum advantage.

For a man who was easily bored, it is a credit to Francis that he was able to muster the patience and tenacity to understand the disparate regions that made up his realm. With their many languages and dialects, to say nothing of their different laws and customs, it must at times have seemed as if he were attempting to rule Babel. Yet his response to the challenges he faced was an almost childlike enthusiasm for action. While many would have found the obstacles before him insurmountable, his belief in monarchical supremacy meant that he was unable to understand why things could not be done, for 'le Roi le veut', 'the king wills it', seemed quite sufficient.

This indomitable spirit permeated his reign both foreign and domestic. It was believed impossible that a French king could conquer the duchy of Milan, having successfully navigated one of the most treacherous passes in the Alps; Francis enjoyed proving the disbelievers wrong. When he faced his greatest downfall, his blithe willingness to behave in a dishonest and dishonourable fashion and abandon every treaty he had agreed shook Europe to its foundations, but also gave notice that his reign was cast in a new mould. For all his undoubted self-belief in his chivalric and gentlemanly qualities, he was prepared to break new ground in international relations that went against centuries of tradition and etiquette. And, in the most unlikely alliance that he eventually made, he forged an ecumenical sense of religious and social understanding, albeit for personal gain, that holds some valuable lessons for politicians and leaders today.

His aesthetic and artistic interests, again inspired by his mother, were genuine, and resulted in some of the most remarkable architecture, paintings and sculpture that his country had ever known. These remain an indisputable testament to him today. He wished to be a true Renaissance monarch in a way that his predecessors had not been, and the glorification of his own image through magnificent châteaux and splendid entertainments, exquisite and short-lived though they were, showed him to be unusually aware of the power of public manipulation. These great palaces included Fontainebleau, the inimitable Chambord and the refurbishment of the Louvre in Paris, which were worked upon by the likes of Primaticcio, Philibert de l'Orme and Giulio Romano.

Francis would rule as an absolute monarch, but he wanted to be loved and admired by his subjects; he made a point of travelling throughout his kingdom, showing himself to them. These royal progresses rarely comprised fewer than 10,000 people, with twice as many animals. The total expenditure was dramatic, costing both the locale visited and the nobles and royal exchequer a fortune. Although his final achievements did not match up to his giddy aims, few could have competed with him for showmanship. If his recruitment of an aged Leonardo da Vinci did not produce the late masterpiece that Francis had hoped for, it nonetheless proved to be a remarkable coup in terms of establishing his own credentials as a cultural patron for the nation. When da Vinci brought the *Mona Lisa* to France with him in 1516 it represented the imprimatur of the new French dominance of the international cultural scene. While an attempt to do the same with Cellini later in his reign was less successful, it had more to do with the growing factionalism at court, and the goldsmith's refusal to curry favour, than misplaced appreciation for talent.

Francis knew that he was a great bluffer rather than a great thinker. He surrounded himself with people more intelligent and adept than himself, and this paid dividends. Tellingly, most of the major failures of his reign took place when he placed an inappropriate faith in his own judgement and intelligence. His mother's death in 1531 can therefore be seen as a clear demarcation between his major achievements prior to it and the many blunders that occurred afterwards. Like many a little boy who has never quite grown up, it proved to be entirely true of Francis that 'Mummy knew best'. She gave him sound counsel, and when he ignored it the consequences were almost invariably regrettable. Yet when he did listen to her, or heeded his sister's advice later in life, he acted with a Machiavellian skill that put his peers to shame with his decisive and effective results.

He was the king that his country needed, if not the one that it might have wished for. In an age in which European relations were characterised by the emergence of great nations from small independent states, his cheerily forthright attitude towards the expansion of French territories overseas came at precisely the right time. A century before, he would have faced a near-endless number of local magnates and powerful prelates, meaning that, whatever small conquests he managed, he would have had no scope to develop the glory of France. If his people had an ambivalent attitude towards their king, especially later in his reign, greater civil disobedience was checked by their knowledge that he acted in both their interest and his own, which he considered one and the same.

An intriguingly magnetic and contradictory figure emerges

from a modern assessment of Francis. Perhaps the best point of comparison is with his contemporary and occasional ally-cum-enemy Henry VIII. Both men occupy an important symbolic position in their country's history, but for entirely different reasons. While Henry's influence was a destructive one, Francis furthered the glory of his kingdom. As Henry posed as a Renaissance man but without substance, Francis devoted his time and energy to the arts and to creativity. As men, their differences were as striking as their similarities. Despite his substantial nose, Francis was a handsome and dashing figure, as Henry had been in his youth, but the French monarch's acknowledged charm and accessibility endeared him to many. It was no wonder that he managed to seduce women, just as the blunter and more belligerent Henry executed them. Francis led his armies from the front, literally fighting until he was unable to do so any more; Henry's most notable military entanglement was the pointless accidental destruction of his flagship. It is not a comparison from which the English monarch emerges with any credit.

This book is not a hagiography of Francis. I have taken pains to expose his failings and inconsistencies, and I have little doubt that many will frequently find him as exasperatingly flawed as I have often done myself. Instead, I have attempted to use the historical and biographical facts of his life and reign as the basis on which the reader can make up his or her own mind about a man who, for all his foibles and drawbacks, was undoubtedly one of the most significant rulers in French history. Without him, there can be little doubt that his country would have risked taking a different and far less modern direction. He prevented the hegemony of Charles V, the Holy Roman Emperor, over the Continent, and reshaped territorial boundaries in a way that his successor and son Henri II would ultimately consolidate. Perhaps the most appropriate description of Francis, then, is as much 'The Maker of Modern Europe' as it is 'The Maker of Modern France'. This does credit to a king who, far from the obscurity in which he has undeservedly languished, merits a rigorous reassessment in our own, changeable, times.

CHAPTER I

A Prophecy Fulfilled

On Friday, 12 September 1494, the eighteen-year-old Louise of Savoy, Countess of Angoulême, went into labour at the Château of Cognac. The birth pains intensified, as did her prayers for the realisation of a prophecy. Four years earlier she had been told that she would bear a son. The seer who had revealed her destiny was the famed Calabrian hermit Francis of Paola, who had built an unparalleled reputation among nobles desperate for news of male heirs. He was much favoured by Louis XI, who brought him to the French court. Later, his son and successor, King Charles VIII, beguiled by the oracle, had refused to allow him to return home. It was ironic that the soothsayer had not foreseen his own, luxurious, captivity.

Louise, too, had travelled to him in search of comfort. At their meeting the friar had given her momentous news. He foretold that she would not only give birth to a boy, but that he would one day be King of France. This prediction had become her sacred truth, and would later justify her belief that she too had been chosen for greatness.

The marriage between eleven-year-old Louise and the twenty-eight-year-old Charles, Count of Angoulême, had taken place in Paris on 16 February 1488. The bride's extreme youth raised no eyebrows, for it was unexceptional in dynastic matches at the time. The couple had only begun living together as man and wife when Louise reached the age of fifteen. Angoulême, a prince of the blood, was first cousin of Louis II, Duke of Orléans. The Angoulême were the junior branch of the house of Valois-Orléans; after the ruling Valois dynasty, they were the most senior royal line. Louise of Savoy might not have married the immediate heir to the throne, but she had wed into the royal house of France. Charles of Valois-Orléans, Count of Angoulême, could hardly be described as a mismatch for the young Savoyard princess.

The union soon resulted in the birth of their first child, Marguerite, on 11 April 1492 at Count Charles's residence of the Château de Cognac, a vast fort that was much added to during the Hundred Years War to protect the town of Cognac, which it overlooked. Here, Louise and her husband presided over a royal court in miniature, with jesters, musicians and all the fanfare of a king's residence but without the same glamour.

Salic law in France dictated that only a male should inherit the dynastic rights that any great family could bestow upon their scions. The splendid future prophesied by the hermit for her as yet unborn son weighed upon the young countess as she felt the first birth pangs. Accompanied by the most trusted ladies of her household and a number of her female servants, Louise walked out into the park and sat down beneath the boughs of an ancient elm, which, according to Angoulême tradition, protected both mother and child. Here, the countess was safely delivered of a healthy boy, as foretold. The relieved parents had already agreed that if the child was male he would be named Francis in tribute to the man who had forecast both his birth and future greatness. Years later, Louise would write in her journal: 'Francis, by God's grace King of France and my own gentle Emperor had his first experience of this world's light at Cognac about ten o'clock of the afternoon, on the twelfth day of September, in 1494.'

Today Louise might be regarded as credulous, possibly even gullible. She was undoubtedly a deeply superstitious woman, with an obsessive terror of death and the dark. Many aristocrats were flattered by bogus fortune-tellers, but the Countess of Angoulême never doubted the hermit's claims. It seemed to her entirely unsurprising that her son would be destined to ascend to the throne of France, and her faith proved to be justified. A little over twenty years later, after a series of events that stemmed from agency either divine or more mundane, Louise would watch Francis proclaimed the first Valois-Angoulême King of France.

The country that Francis was born into had become embittered, scarred by both war and internal acrimony. The long conflict between France and England, the Hundred Years War, had ended with a French victory, though the cost in both financial and social terms had meant that such a triumph could only be the most Pyrrhic of successes. Widespread poverty, economic disaster and social misery blighted the kingdom. In the first half of the fifteenth century, the incursions of successive English kings into northern France meant that the unlovely duo of massacre and famine dominated the land. This desperate epoch reached its zenith when wild dogs and wolves roamed the streets of Paris; they came to eat the dead, whose bodies littered the streets like carrion.[1]

The young king, Charles VI, had been born in 1368 to Charles V, who rejoiced in the nickname of 'Le Sage', or 'The Wise'. He had inherited his throne aged eleven, but the true power lay with the king's four regents, who were also his uncles.* The ensuing civil unrest prevented him from ruling in his own right until 1388, when he finally managed to rid himself of his self-serving regents. His country was exhausted and bankrupt; the Crown exchequer lay virtually empty and a demoralised and afflicted people looked to their king for stability and prosperity.

Initially, Charles VI personified all that his subjects could have hoped, ruling with a mixture of compassion and strong leadership. He was helped by his appointment of a series of wise advisers known as the 'Marmosets', and soon became known as 'Le Bien Aimé', or 'The Beloved'. Unfortunately, the longed-for dawn of peace and plenty came to an end as Charles descended into madness. This took the form of severe delusions, which included failing to recognise his queen, Isabeau, his twelve children or his closest courtiers. At times he believed he was St George, and vainly tried to slay illusory dragons. His people once again had to reconcile themselves to an

---

* The so-called 'regent uncles' were Philip the Bold, Duke of Burgundy, Louis I, Duke of Anjou, John, Duke of Berry and Louis II, Duke of Bourbon.

unstable monarch, and Charles's sobriquet of 'The Beloved' was all too soon ditched in favour of 'Le Fou', or 'The Mad'.

The king endured cruel periods of lucidity, forcing him to confront his actions. Mercifully, these episodes of sanity gradually lessened in duration and occurrence. By the end of his life, Charles had become convinced that he was made of glass, and, despite special clothing designed to protect him from being smashed into royal smithereens, his anguished cries of 'No me le tangere! No me le tangere' ('Do not touch me! Do not touch me') were heard throughout the royal court. In 1422, to general relief, the poor wretch died.

He was succeeded by his son, Charles VII, whose reign was long, but compromised and undistinguished. He suffered the ignominy of being decisively outshone by one of his subjects, the young peasant girl Joan of Arc, whose supposedly divine charisma led to the English invaders being driven from the country by the mid-1450s. If he had hoped for some reflected glory, he was to be disappointed. Instead, he spent the last few years of his life wrangling with his ungovernable heir, Dauphin Louis, who had caused little but trouble from a young age. Eventually his father banished him from court after Louis defied his wishes and married Charlotte of Savoy, aunt to Louise of Savoy. He subsequently fled to Burgundy, where he lived in exile, broodingly waiting for the only news that could bring him satisfaction.

In 1461 that news arrived. With the announcement of Charles VII's death, the new king returned as Louis XI, and soon became known as 'The Spider King'. He proved to be one of the most brutal and Machiavellian rulers that France had ever seen. Austere and reclusive in his personal habits, he did not allow anyone around him to offer a credible threat to his power. It was typical of Louis that, when he became monarch, he repressed the power of the nobles who had helped him while in exile. Seizing their estates, he proceeded to neutralise his former supporters using a judicious mixture of imaginative forms of torture and, when necessary, execution. He was proud of his 'official' nickname of 'Le Prudent', which reflected his closeness with money, but the unofficial appellation of 'Le Ruse' or 'The Cunning' summed him up rather more accurately.

This desire to dominate every level of monarchical and state power extended to plotting the marriage of Charles, Count of Angoulême. The match that he chose was Louise, his niece by marriage and the daughter of Philip, Count of Bresse. Philip, the youngest son of Louis, Duke of Savoy, was better known as 'Sans Terre' or 'Lackland'; the nickname was mockingly bestowed in recognition of his lack of any substantial estate after he lost his *apanage* of Bresse, which was taken during hostilities between the warring neighbours France and Burgundy. In 1469 Philip's luck and nickname changed when he unexpectedly inherited the lucrative throne of Savoy. In 1472 he married Margaret of Bourbon; Louise of Savoy was born in 1476, but her mother was to die seven years later, three years after the birth of her son Philibert. As their father was far more interested in womanising than in his own children, Louise and Philibert were dispatched to live with Louis XI's daughter, Anne of France. Anne, who was known as 'Madame la Grande', was the elder of the young dauphin Charles's two sisters. Her father called her the least foolish woman in France, which proved a prophetic assessment of her worth when, shortly after Louise and Philibert arrived in France in 1483, Louis XI died. Before his death, he had appointed Anne and her husband Peter of Beaujeu as guardians to the young dauphin. When Louis of Orléans protested that, as senior male of the royal family of sufficient age, he should be made regent, the Estates General supported Madame la Grande and Peter. Consequently, upon the death of his childless elder brother, Louis became Duke of Bourbon.

Madame had little time for her ward Louise, whom she regarded as of secondary importance. The girl survived on a meagre and often inadequate allowance, dressed poorly and did not have the household or servants that her station would usually command. A small and anxious figure with thick brown hair and dark eyes, she seemed both highly strung and uncertain around others.[2] When Louis XI first commanded Charles of Angoulême to wed Louise, she offered little as a matrimonial prospect. The count took this as the insult it was intended to be; he had hoped to marry the more appealing Mary of Burgundy, a woman so well endowed with territories and money that the English simply referred to her as 'Mary the Rich'. After Louis XI's death, rather than embrace his matrimonial destiny,

Charles became involved in the so-called 'Mad War', a noble revolt led by his senior cousin Louis of Orléans against Anne of France's de facto regency during the minority of her brother, Charles VIII. The disorganised rebels had little chance of victory, and when a truce was eventually agreed upon in 1488, a condition of a royal pardon and the return of the seized Angoulême estates included compulsory marriage to Louise of Savoy. The union of Francis's parents took place with enormous reluctance and misgiving on his father's side, and presumably just as little relish or enjoyment on the part of the eleven-year-old bride.

It is therefore something of a surprise that the match proved to be a happier and more durable one than either party had expected. Louise quickly established herself as an efficient and capable administrator when it came to courtly matters, dealing with hierarchical and business details with brisk competence, but was also a worthy intellectual companion for her husband. Both shared a love of reading, and an appreciation of illuminated manuscripts, as well as the pleasures of literary discussion. Charles's enjoyment of masques and other entertainments was catered for by his wife, who ordered these feasts in an accomplished manner that might have been expected from one twice her age. Yet while Charles was amiable, he was also an indolent fellow who was content with his everyday pleasures.

Louise tolerated her husband's greatest enthusiasm: hunting, for both wild animals and women. His two most enduring mistresses, Antoinette de Polignac and Jeanne Comte, were attached to his household as permanent fixtures, and Louise treated the three daughters they bore as her own stepchildren. Rather than make rivals of the concubines, she appointed Antoinette head of her household, while Jeanne received an almost similarly exalted role, and the three women became friends. Louise needed their guidance as much as they needed her approval. By the time that Louise gave birth to Francis, both Antoinette and Jeanne were her closest companions as her labour progressed under the Angoulême elm; both women were also pregnant by Charles at the time. Francis was to grow up in a household dominated by women.

If her patience and tolerance seem at odds with the person she later became, it should be remembered that Louise, who was barely a teenage girl, had a different and greater ambition, both for herself and her offspring. Charles of Angoulême was ultimately a provincial prince who was unlikely to inherit the throne of France, and Louise might have nursed a hope that her fortunes would change. She understood that, if the childless Louis of Orléans became king, the chances of Count Charles becoming heir presumptive increased dramatically. Louise had developed a strong will from childhood, combined with an absence of sentimentality and a desire to fulfil her perceived purpose. As one chronicler described this avidity, '[it was] the most serious trait in her character, and, in the absence of worthier passions, often served to dignify it'.[3]

In winter 1496, a little more than a year after Francis's birth, tragedy visited the Angoulême household. Count Charles was riding to Paris to attend the funeral of the three-year-old dauphin Charles Orlande, the son of Charles VIII and Anne of Brittany, who had died of smallpox. Angoulême, intent upon reaching Paris in good time to attend the late dauphin's obsequies, did not take cover when a sudden rainstorm broke. Drenched and shivering, he took refuge at a nearby inn at Châteauneuf, but in the cramped and unsanitary conditions his chill turned into a fever, followed by pneumonia. The countess received news of her husband's illness and rode without resting until she had reached his bedside. Beside her were the best physicians in the area, but it was of little use. Despite their efforts, which included Louise looking after Charles 'as tenderly and humanely as the poorest wife might nurse her husband', he died on 1 January 1496.[4] One observer wrote that 'when, despite everything, my said Lord's malady worsened, it was necessary to take my said Lady out of the chamber, and indeed there was need to do so . . . otherwise, to speak truth, she would never have left it in this life, and certainly she seemed more dead than alive'.[5]

Louise was a widow at nineteen. While her marriage to Charles had begun inauspiciously, it had grown into a match of understanding and affection, if not true love. She now feared losing the guardianship of Francis and Marguerite, as French law stated that any guardian had to be aged at least twenty-five. It seemed as if the hermit's prophecy and her son's eventual destiny were further away from realisation than ever. Yet Louise remained a pragmatist. She lived in an age when futures changed without warning and beyond expectation, and when all seemed lost, the most unlikely of deliverances could restore her and her children's fortunes in an instant.

The first indication of good luck was in Charles VIII's choice of guardian for Francis and Marguerite. Louis, Duke of Orléans was Francis's closest male relative, as well as being heir presumptive to the royal throne, and as such exerted his right to claim the guardianship. However, the thirty-three-year-old Louis was an unimpressive figure, unhappy in his marriage to the crippled and unsightly Jeanne de France and incapable of exerting his authority in a sphere such as this. Louise invoked Angoulême law, which held that those who had reached the age of fifteen were considered competent to act on behalf of orphaned or fatherless children. Louise eventually took her case to the highest court in the land, the *Grand Conseil*, and a compromise was reached: she retained custody of her children, and Louis was accorded the senior guardianship. In truth, the only real check on the Countess of Angoulême's influence was that she was forbidden to carry out any important family business without Louis' permission, and, in the event of her remarrying, the duke would obtain full custody of the children. Such an occurrence was unlikely, given that Louise's priority remained her offspring. Personal happiness and fulfilment were to be obtained vicariously, rather than through another marriage.

She also had more significant adversaries to consider. Chief among these was Anne of France, who had grand territorial ambitions for both her brother Charles and for France. These were fulfilled when the king successfully invaded Brittany in 1490, annexing the territory. Part of the peace treaty was that Anne, the Sovereign Duchess of Brittany, was obliged to marry either Charles or his successor, should he die childless. The marriage took place in December 1491, and also ensured that Charles became the Breton Duke.

On 7 April 1498, an unfortunate accident occurred at Amboise. While hurrying to watch a game of tennis, 'Charles the Good', as his people called him, took a shortcut through the court latrine and cracked his head against the lintel. A little later the king was discovered lying face-down in the hay of that 'evil smelling gallery'; he fell into a coma and died in the early hours of the following day, at the age of twenty-seven. Philippe de Commynes, a royal adviser both to Louis XI and to his son Charles, summed up the late monarch's character in his memoirs: 'He was but a little man both in body and in understanding yet so good hearted that it was impossible to meet a better creature.'[6]

As Charles died without issue the throne passed to Louis, Duke of Orléans, who became Louis XII. It was typical of this gentle and unworldly man that, upon hearing the news of the young king's death and his own assumption of the throne, he burst into tears. One courtier wrote: 'I think no man ever died whom he so mourned. For he loved him with a great and perfect love, above all others, as nearest kinsman of his father's house, truest vassal and most loyal friend.'[7]

The rest of the Orléanist faction did not share this compassion, and Charles's fatal accident incited ridicule. Had Louise been able to turn cartwheels of joy, she would have done. However, Louis' relations assumed suitably sombre expressions in the weeks immediately after the late king's passing, during the period of deep mourning. Failure to observe the expected expressions of grief would have been impolitic, particularly as Louis had not expected to ascend the throne, and hoped to achieve a smooth transition of power. Nonetheless, the Orléanist dynasty, which had spent much of the past century jostling for position without success, rightly saw Charles's death as a stroke of good fortune, and Louis' kingship as a means of placing the junior branch of the royal family in power. The monarch had no children, and fulfilment of the hermit's prophecy that Francis would one day mount the throne drew closer. The three-year-old boy had become heir presumptive.

The king granted Francis an annuity of 8,000 *livres* a year, as well as creating him Duke of Valois. He was rarely known by this title, continuing to be referred to as the Count of Angoulême. As for the annuity, Louis drew this from his own pocket, or *apanage*, making it an impressively generous gift. His mother, an Orléanist

by marriage, had the continued guardianship of her children confirmed upon Louis' accession, and watched with wry amusement as
she became courted by those who wanted to be close to the centre
of power and influence. Louis had by now relegated his unfortunate wife Jeanne to a convent, dissolved the marriage and taken
Charles's widow Anne as his bride on 8 January 1499.

Once this was done, he summoned Louise and her children
from Cognac to his gloomy fortress and unprepossessing court at
Chinon, in the Loire Valley, where he greeted them with great affection; he had been looking forward to her arrival and that of the
children. It was a curious place to meet, being an eleventh-century
fortress and as much redolent of war and punishment as it was of
monarchical trappings, and so the assembled company soon moved
on to the more congenial setting of nearby Blois.

Louise had travelled to Chinon bringing with her a motley train
comprising her late husband's mistresses with their bastards, servants and various sycophants. Her retinue was only impressive insofar
as its colourful assortment of her various retainers made the whole
troupe appear as though it were part of a travelling circus. These
men and women included her household and nobles in attendance,
as well as priests, cooks, blacksmiths, laundresses, seers, fools and
musicians. An overwhelmed king, dismayed by the appearance of
the Angoulême caravanserai, was persuaded to give Francis (and
by extension Louise) the mighty Château of Amboise nearby as his
main residence, the traditional nursery of royal children. Amboise
was both larger and more pleasant than Blois, with a huge round
tower and great outdoor spaces where a young prince might cavort
with his new playmates.

Louis might have been a man of great sentimental feeling, but
he was by no means a fool. Aghast at the impression that Louise
had made, he realised that her influence needed to be checked, and
so appointed Anne of Brittany's cousin Pierre de Rohan, Seigneur
de Gié and Marshal of France, to act as a guardian to her and her
family. De Gié was one of Louis' closest advisers and, along with
the Cardinal of Amboise, the man with the greatest influence in
France. Here, de Gié was expected to fulfil the role of instructor
and spy on behalf of the king. He might have nursed ambitions to

marry the young widow; becoming stepfather to the heir presumptive and making himself regent would have been a wholly desirable outcome. However, there was not only no spark of warmth between the two, but de Gié's actions frequently angered Louise, as she chafed under his restrictions. Few other women in their early twenties would have been able to take on this forty-four-year-old widower and man of action, but Louise, toughened by experience and ambition, was not to be cowed. She would marry nobody; she was wed to her son's destiny, so closely coupled with her own.

Once de Gié was placed in a position of influence over the heir presumptive and his family, the manoeuvring began. His first move was to bring with him a military unit of twenty-five archers, under the command of the officer Roland de Ploret, whose task was to guard the Angoulême. Thus emboldened, he dismissed or banished most of Louise's household, which he regarded as dangerously subversive and liable to corrupt the young Francis. In de Gié's defence, this is likely to have been a direct order from the king, who was disconcerted by the free-living aspects of the household. Concerned that the boy was not growing up with the right manly values, de Gié then attempted to remove Francis from his mother's chamber, where she slept with both her children. Ploret, who was ordered to escort Francis to Mass every day, only had permission to venture as far as her door, an office that he respected, but his subordinate, a soldier named du Restal, became somewhat over-zealous and, perhaps misunderstanding his instructions, knocked down the door instead of knocking upon it. Although this resulted in du Restal's dismissal, it also meant that Francis was removed from Louise's quarters, on the feigned excuse that he needed the close attention of de Gié's men on a nightly basis.

Nonetheless, despite the privations that Louise felt had been heaped upon her, she continued to oversee the education of her children. She taught them Italian and Spanish and, following the grand traditions of a future monarch's education, she commissioned a globe, an impressive and unusual luxury in an early-sixteenth-century schoolroom. The countess also chose wisely in her appointment of tutors. The first of these, Christophe de Longueil, was a Humanist who had studied law for a time before exchanging it for classical literature, which the young prince enjoyed. The other, Francis Desmoulins de Rochefort, was one of Renaissance France's greatest scholars. Desmoulins de Rochefort remained a part of the Angoulême household for at least seven years from 1501 onwards, and featured in Francis's financial ledger as late as 1513, a little over a year before his pupil ascended the throne. He would eventually be given the title Grand Aumônier de France (Almoner), a role created by the king in honour of his mentor, which involved the administration of the ecclesiastical branch of the royal household.

Desmoulins de Rochefort taught Francis biblical history and some basic Latin, but he struggled to impart wisdom and knowledge to his august young charge, who was more interested in the many distractions that Amboise and its surroundings offered. It did not help that he was taught alongside his sister Marguerite, a far cleverer pupil whose intellectual and philosophical curiosity seemed to grow by the day and who threw her brother's scattered powers of attention into stark perspective. Nevertheless, the future king's intellectual curiosity and veneration for learning found their origins here.

This was partly down to Marguerite, who was perpetually anxious that he should make the most of his gifts, but others were impressed as well, such as the Italian nobleman Baldassare Castiglione, Count of Casatico. Castiglione hailed from Mantua, a small but vital city-state near Ferrara, between Venice and Milan. The Gonzaga, Mantua's ruling family, proved an unusually enlightened marquisate, and led the way for their local patrons in supporting young local artists. He also wrote a philosophical work, *Il Cortegiano* ('The Book of the Courtier'), which furnished aristocratic Europe with a guide to the etiquette of an ideal Renaissance court and was especially applicable to young Francis. In it, Castiglione wrote that 'if good fortune has it that Monsieur of Angoulême, as it is hoped, succeeds to the throne, then I believe that, just as the glory of arms flourishes and shines in France, so also with the greatest brilliance must that of letters. For when I was at that court not so long ago, I set eyes on this prince ... And among other things I was told that he greatly loved and esteemed learning and respected all men of letters, and that he condemned the French themselves for being so hostile to this profession.'[8]

As for the 'glory of arms', Francis was preparing for a future life of soldiering. He took great delight in pursuits such as hunting, hawking and mock battles, and Louis saw to it that he was provided with a number of noble playmates. One chronicler wrote: 'My said Lord of Angoulême, the self-styled "Young Adventurer" [Robert de La Marck, Seigneur of Fleurange, the Duke of Sedan's younger son], and other young noblemen built towers in which they fought, attacking and defending with strokes of the sword . . . and when they grew somewhat older they began to wear proper armour and to tilt in every sort of joust and tourney'. Francis had a natural talent in physical contests and required no hyperbole when describing his sporting accomplishments. Later Fleurange, who became one of the future king's closest friends and most valued courtiers, wrote, with an eye on diplomatic relations: 'I think no prince ever had more pastimes than did my said Lord or was better instructed, by the provision of my Lady his mother.'[9]

Louise stated that she loved her books second only to her off-spring, choosing the words 'Libris et Liberis' (Books and Children) as her personal motto, and proved dauntless in encouraging her son with his studies. Francis and his friends' favourite tales told of the lives of chivalrous knights, much in vogue at the time, and he himself spent a great deal of his time trying to emulate them. On one occasion, on 25 January 1502, a galloping horse carried Francis off. Although the steed threw him, the young man was unharmed by his ordeal; his survival was interpreted as miraculous, especially as it was the same date that St Paul had reputedly fallen from his own horse before embarking on his Damascene conversion.* Francis's mother and his tutors instilled in him a love of learning, as well as a reverence for scholarship.

When the boy turned ten, Louise had a medal struck to commemorate the occasion, with his noble profile on one side and a salamander surrounded by fire on the other. The implication was that he would be both enduring and heroic; the motto upon it, 'Notrisco al buono, stingo el reo', could be translated as 'I feed upon

---

* The same date would also be chosen for Francis's coronation in 1515.

the good fire, and extinguish the evil one'. It is a typical Humanist legend, and implies that the salamander is indestructible. The symbolism Louise desired is clear, and those who taught and formed Francis believed that the young prince in their charge was destined to become the next King of France.

CHAPTER 2

A Game of Thrones

While Francis sported with his fellow nobles and, occasionally, learnt from his tutors, the throne that he expected to inherit remained a prize coveted by a number of interested parties. Louis XII was doing his best to revive the country by living prudently and operating by example. Yet, faced with the ongoing situation in Europe, it was inevitable that the complex machinations that stretched over the final years of the fifteenth century and well into the sixteenth were dictated as much by circumstance as by determination.

Louis XII's marriage to Anne of Brittany in 1499 was one that had long and complex origins. Before she married Charles VIII, Anne had already been wed to the Habsburg prince, Maximilian I, who was also Holy Roman Emperor. As with many matches of the period, the actual ceremony had taken place by proxy, and although Maximilian and his lawyers had argued for its validity, French advocates managed to prove that it was not legally binding. As Maximilian was drawn into a war with King Matthias of Hungary, he had to turn his attention from matrimonial to military matters, and left Charles to marry Anne.

Unfortunately, Charles VIII was already married, to Margaret of Habsburg, Maximilian's daughter. Margaret had arrived at the court of France in 1483 when she was three years old, following the death of her mother, and her marriage to Charles was a direct result of the Treaty of Senlis, between Louis XI and Maximilian. The French king died almost immediately after Margaret's arrival,

and, due to the youth of both Charles and Margaret, the marriage
had never been consummated, which constituted grounds for annulment. Before she was later dispatched from France, Margaret
had considered the French court as her home. During her time as
Charles's wife she too had lived under the supervision of Madame la
Grande's aristocratic finishing school, along with Louise of Savoy,
where they were taught good manners and etiquette; the bond that
they formed proved crucial for European dynastic issues over the
following decades.

In 1499, once he was married to Anne of Brittany, Louis was free
to address the issue of succession. He was all too aware that his
uncle, the so-called 'Spider King' Louis XI, had loathed the Orléanist
faction and had schemed to dispose of the Valois-Orléans lines
through typically Machiavellian methods, namely the marriage of
Louis to his crippled younger daughter Jeanne, who was believed
(probably correctly) to be infertile. His uncle's reasoning was that
by forcing young Duke Louis, head of the house of Valois-Orléans,
into a sterile union with Jeanne, he would extinguish the Orléans
branch of the royal family. The loathing he felt for Duke Louis'
house brought out the king's coldest and most calculating side, and
his ingenious deviousness.

Despite the callousness of his manipulation of Jeanne, the future
Louis XI had remained dauphin and lived in Burgundian exile with
his wife Charlotte and two daughters. He considered his wife too
young and too stupid to be given the care of the couple's children,
and so, in order to ensure that Jeanne and her sister Anne received
an education fit for the daughters of a future King of France, he
placed the girls under the care of Francis de Linières and his wife.
They were a childless couple of gifted pedagogues who taught the
girls languages, the arts and mathematics, as well as the usual skills
that would be expected of them at court, such as the ability to sing,
read music and play the lute. Anne, whose stately bearing, fine features and white skin were made all the more regal by a pronounced
widow's peak, was married at the age of twelve to Peter of Beaujeu, younger brother of the childless Duke of Bourbon, the richest
duchy in France.

Shortly before his death in 1483, Louis XI made Madame la Grande and her husband Peter the official guardians of her brother Charles, the new King of France. Charged with care of the king's person, the couple became de facto co-regents. Challenged by Louis, Duke of Orléans, the Estates General confirmed the late king's wishes, which spurred him to lead an uprising. The war, described at best as a desultory series of skirmishes and minor battles, was named 'La Guerre Folle', 'The Mad War'. This was the conflict in which Charles of Angoulême had also participated, partly out of loyalty to his cousin, the leader of his house, and partly to register his protest against his betrothal to Louise of Savoy.

Upon its resolution, the Treaty of Sablé was signed, which also annexed Brittany to France. Louis of Orléans was imprisoned and his territories were forfeit, as were those of Count Charles of Angoulême. The couple ruled the kingdom for eight years, with Madame la Grande being the dominant figure in taking the decisions made by the French monarchy. One notable intercession in foreign policy was her support for Henry Tudor against King Richard III in England, whom she and many others believed to be nothing more than a usurper. She supplied Henry with troops and horses for his invasion of England in 1485, which resulted in Richard's defeat and death at the Battle of Bosworth and Henry's assumption of the title of Henry VII.

As the effective ruler of France, she attracted near-universal admiration and praise for her achievements. Even when her brother Charles became active as king, his sister continued to be the dominant power within the country. This was in part because the unfortunate monarch's attention proved all too easily distracted by a pretty girl or a new idea, and his physical appearance, consisting of an enormous head with vast bulging eyes and thick blubbery lips, was repellent: distinctly not what was expected from a ruler.

Madame la Grande's diplomatic triumphs, both domestic and overseas, had led to her late father describing her as 'the least foolish woman in France'. Upon his death, she would prove him right. Her successes included returning the estates of dissident Orléans nobles that had been confiscated under Louis XI, which benefited both Charles of Angoulême and Louise. Once their marriage contract was agreed, he was able to recover his former wealth and possessions. Yet after Charles VIII's death, when Louis XII inherited the throne, Madame la Grande found herself in a potentially compromised situation, not least because Louis lost little time in frustrating his uncle's plans to eliminate his bloodline by remarrying. His choice of Charles's widow, Anne of Brittany, was politically astute, as it would continue the links between the duchy of Brittany and the French Crown established through the Treaty of Sablé. It also allowed him to marry someone fabulously wealthy, thereby shoring him up financially. Accordingly, his existing wife had to be dispensed with, and as she was a princess this would require a delicate and carefully considered approach.

Anne of Brittany, meanwhile, was rid of her physically unprepossessing former husband, who had impregnated her repeatedly but without any of the children surviving. She had begun their marriage by bringing two beds with her, and the couple often lived apart, but his incursions into the marital bed seemed to result in a pregnancy roughly every year and a half. Charles was a priapic man; despite his ill-favoured appearance he had enjoyed a vast number of extramarital liaisons, which she had watched with the tolerance and forbearance expected of any royal wife.

Despite this, Anne had grown fond of her husband, and was hurt by his over-frequent infidelities. She knew that her role, as perceived by Madame la Grande, was to represent the union of Brittany and France, and she fulfilled it admirably (despite barely speaking a word of Breton). However, aware that the Treaty of Sablé forced her to marry her late husband's successor, or a man of his choice, she realised that as queen consort she would benefit Breton autonomy far more than any other marriage as dictated in the treaty, for Louis had the power to wed her to some lesser prince of the royal family. By agreeing to marry King Louis, she pursued her policy of Breton independence as far as she dared with a single-mindedness and a tough determination that belied her twenty-one years. She did not have the Humanist interests of Louise, and was closer to a medieval queen than a Renaissance figure, with a tough, unsentimental outlook and a determination to obtain her objectives. When she first saw Louis XII in 1498, following her late husband's death, Anne pertly ended their encounter with the words: 'Obtain the dissolution of your marriage to Jeanne of France, and I abandon my hand to you.'[1]

The unfortunate Jeanne now became entirely surplus to royal requirements. In most cases, disposing of a queen would have been no small undertaking, but, for all Jeanne's undiminished devotion to her husband, the couple had no children after more than two decades of marriage, leaving the new queen without any weapons with which to fight his decision to dissolve their union. In arguing for the annulment of his marriage, Louis could rely on the support of Pope Alexander VI, Rodrigo Borgia, since the Holy See needed French military aid in its armed resistance to Milan, Florence and Venice, which were casting covetous eyes towards the papal states.

Nonetheless, a certain process had to be followed which required Louis to advance reasons for the dissolution of his union with Jeanne. Two possible lines of argument presented themselves: consanguinity, which during this period could almost be guaranteed, or the prescribed legal age of consent to entering the contract of marriage. Unfortunately for the new king, his blood relationship to Jeanne proved unusually remote. French law, however, stated that the bride or groom had to be fourteen to agree to marry and Louis claimed that in 1476, the year of his marriage, he had been only twelve years old. However, no documentary evidence of his date of birth could be produced to support or refute this assertion; no doubt the appropriate records had been suppressed.

Louis, undeterred, blundered ahead and presented a third claim. He swore under oath that Jeanne suffered from a physical malformation preventing the consummation of their marriage. The graphic descriptions of his wife's disabilities caused a sensation. The king found himself unexpectedly contradicted by a number of witnesses, all of whom testified to Louis' boasts of having sex with his wife three or four times in the course of a single night. Despite general public disgust at the king's low argument, Jeanne had to endure a humiliating physical examination witnessed by no fewer than twenty-seven official observers, who proved the falseness of his claims.[2] Eventually, the Borgia pope's silken diplomacy finessed a solution to the chaotic proceedings. He decreed, with justification, that Louis had been forced into his marriage by Jeanne's father, Louis XI, who was also guardian to the Orléans groom, and thus the pontiff decreed the union null and void. Louis provided the expected quid pro quo by granting the French dukedom of Valentinois to the pope's bastard son, Cesare Borgia.

Losing her husband caused Jeanne intense sorrow, yet, as was her wont, she remained dignified and expressed her humility by bowing to God's will, and to that of the king. Jeanne felt no shame over exchanging the title Queen of France for that of Duchess of Berry and retired to Bourges, its capital. Here she concentrated upon establishing a religious order devoted to the Immaculate Conception of the Virgin Mary. She found her faith proved to be her salvation, as well as her final vocation. In November 1504 Jeanne took her religious vows and spent the last few months of her life as a nun in the order she had founded.*

With his former marriage annulled, no further obstacles remained to prevent the king's wedding to Anne of Brittany. Although the tide of popular opinion had turned back favourably towards the new monarch's marriage, it caused Louise of Savoy nothing but apprehension. She feared that her carefully calibrated plans to see her son obtain the kingdom of France faced potential ruin. Anne, a healthy young woman of twenty-two and Queen Consort of France for a second time, had every chance of bearing children. The Countess of Angoulême's worries seemed justified when Anne became pregnant almost immediately after her marriage in January 1499. However, to Louise's relief, Anne gave birth to a girl, Claude, on 13 October 1499 at the Château of Romorantin; while this did not preclude the chance of a male heir being born, it at least offered her some respite. Due to an outbreak of plague at Amboise, Louise and her children moved to the safety of Romorantin around the time of Claude's birth. A less confident or arrogant woman would have taken this opportunity to build an intimacy with Louis and his queen. However, Louise was unable to overcome her hatred for Anne and the ongoing threat she cast over her son's future position

---

* Jeanne attained a posthumous celebrity, with miracles being attributed to her powers of intercession, and she was canonised in 1950.

and did not attempt a closer understanding with her. The Countess of Angoulême had her eye on the ultimate prize alone; for her, nothing else mattered.

This led to a shift in relations between Louise and her family. The king had hitherto treated them with enormous kindness and generosity, but the queen poured distilled poison into his ear about Louise, including her claim that the latter had shown resentment at Claude's birth. This unsurprisingly caused the king to distance himself from the Angoulême family.

Louis had hoped that the arrival of his daughter would herald the birth of further children to fill the royal nursery, but he had also privately considered the idea that, were Anne to bear him no sons, Claude should be wed to Francis. The little girl's ill health proved a sad disappointment; she was distinctly fragile, with a serious curvature of the spine. This also caused the unfortunately named condition, claudication, which bloated her tiny legs and was especially evident when she tried to stand up. To add to her other health problems, Claude had a severe squint, leaving her unable to look at an object with both eyes at the same time. As Louis was preoccupied with his daughter's health, he reduced his visits to Amboise and Louise's satellite court shrank as he removed her most trusted courtiers.

Angry at this perceived act of aggression, the countess blamed Anne of Brittany as much as Louis, if not more so, for her privations. The two came to detest one another, which indicated an unusual failure of imagination on Louise's part; when it came to her rival, she had a surprising lacuna in her usually acute political instincts. She would not bend to Anne any more than courtly deference dictated, and their rivalry led to it being said that 'The Queen lived to thwart her [Louise] in all her affairs.' The only matter both agreed upon was that Francis and Claude should not – *could not* – be joined in marriage. The two enemies agreed with each other, but only in opposition. Anne did not wait long before she began diplomatic enquiries about her daughter marrying Charles of Habsburg, heir to Christendom's largest empire, to prevent a marriage with Francis and to remove Brittany from the French embrace.

Had the issue of the succession been removed, the tension

between the queen and the countess is unlikely to have existed. They were of a similar age and class, and both were far more accomplished than most women of their day. Anne was of an essentially gentle character and was able to change her opinions if she was convinced she had been wrong. She had a femininity that Louise lacked, and a more attractive mien, with a face that could be likened to a Gothic Madonna, although, as she suffered from a pronounced limp and a slight hunchback, it was not difficult for her rival to appear as regal as a queen, both in bearing and hauteur. Louise also proved a formidable adversary. Largely due to her lack of financial means and prospects, the Savoyard princess had been greatly underestimated by the opposite sex until her marriage. Becoming a widow at the age of nineteen had forced her to think and act like a man, and approach important matters as though going into battle. Like any great warrior, she knew that there could only be one victor.

It did not help that Anne of Brittany also openly disapproved of Louise's way of life, which she considered unbecoming in any woman of rank, let alone a royal princess. The countess enjoyed nothing better than a lively debate with musicians, scholars and witty courtiers, and her gatherings, fuelled by good food, wine and music, were animated by chatter and accompanying laughter that grew noisier as the nights wore on. It did not help that two brothers, Octavian de Saint-Gelais, a classics scholar and cleric, and Jean, Louise's valet, had been her familiars since her widowhood in Cognac. In the fourteenth and fifteenth centuries a royal valet was much more than a mere servant, fulfilling many different roles; they were 'raised socially from menial associations to a kind of convenient equality [with] . . . every opportunity for a free and easy friendship and it did not prevent their being thrown away at [their masters'] pleasure'.[3]

Inevitably, rumours grew that Jean was enjoying the countess's most intimate favours, although his lack of intellectual attainment made this gossip unlikely. A deeper relationship existed between her and Octavian, if not a sexual one; the cleric even inspired his patroness to write verse. Eventually, he would be rewarded with the bishopric of Angoulême. However, he remained, as one critic wrote, 'an author whose works were as heavy as his life was light'. As for his brother Jean, the rumours of scandal enabled Louis to dispatch him away from court. The king considered that marrying Louise off might have made matters easier for him, but the rumours over her relationship with Saint-Gelais did not make her a tempting prospect for matrimony. In any case, Louise categorically refused to consider remarriage. Her priority, as she would truthfully inform anyone who asked her, remained her children.

As Anne's frequent pregnancies continued, Louise watched with apprehension as the king and queen waited in hope. In her journal the countess wrote: 'Anne, Queen of France, at Blois, upon the day of St Agnes, the 21 January [1503], bore a son; but could not stop the exaltation of my Emperor, for he lacked life.' It would be hard to find a more chilling example of Louise's detached observation at the tragic result of Anne's frequent pregnancies. One commentator wrote: 'Louise's passions, whether of love or of hate were immoderate, though under the perfect outward control she knew no medium between cordial friendship or avowed hostility.'[4]

With Anne's fertility a constant threat to her family's advancement, Louise remained fixated on her son, no matter how uncertain his future position. However, she managed to turn her attention to Marguerite as a marriageable prospect. The countess's only daughter had grown up into an attractive girl, much taller than her thin and nervous mother, and with a quiet, searching and intelligent disposition. It was suggested that she could be a match either for the future Henry VIII or Charles of Habsburg, Emperor Maximilian's grandson and heir. The chance of her contracting a worthwhile union was increased by the intervention of Anne of Brittany, who decided that she would take charge of finding a good match for Marguerite, towards whom she felt a sincere attachment. The king, meanwhile, declared that he 'loved [Marguerite] with all his heart, and as dearly as if she were his own child'.[5]

Fate soon dictated that marriage to Henry, Prince of Wales, was not to be; his father, Henry VII, instead chose Catherine of Aragon, for predominantly financial reasons, but the couple did not marry until 1509, the same year that the Prince of Wales became Henry

VIII.* Louise felt disappointed that her daughter would not become Queen Consort of England, but Marguerite, who preferred her studies to the procession of worthies to whom she was being offered, remained philosophical. The uncertainty of Marguerite's situation did not help; had a potential suitor of great importance been sure that he was marrying the sister of the future King of France, her position on the royal marriage market would have been far stronger. As things stood, any potential husband seeking Marguerite's hand had to take into account that her brother might remain Francis, Count of Angoulême, for the rest of his life. Marguerite continued with her studies, and harboured no desire to live at a foreign court away from her mother and brother. She spoke Italian, Spanish and Latin, but had developed a keen interest in theology, although the subject that truly absorbed her above all others was her brother Francis. The papal legate Bernardo Dovizi, Cardinal Bibbiena, wrote to Rome from the French court and referred to Marguerite, Louise and the heir presumptive as 'a holy trinity'.

Had it not been for Marguerite's intense loyalty to her mother, this trinity might have been threatened by her close relationship with both the king and the queen. The most problematic aspect was Anne's fondness for Marguerite, which necessitated the latter's insightful diplomacy in order to avoid offending her mother. It was also strained by Louis suffering two serious illnesses, in 1504 and April 1505, which the Countess of Angoulême all but smacked her lips at, so little did she manage to conceal her hopes of the privately preferred outcome. The king realised that, faced with the prospect of dying without male issue, his formal consideration of the succession was urgently required. Much against Anne's wishes, Louis concentrated on a match between his daughter Claude and Francis. His queen had promised Claude's hand in marriage to Charles of Habsburg and she pursued Louis in an attempt to make him ratify a document to that effect. The king became unusually exasperated

---

* The Spanish Infanta had lived at the English court for most of her short life, and as Ferdinand had been clamouring for the return of his daughter's fabulous dowry, the proposed union would legitimately allow the treasure to remain in England's royal coffers.

with his wife and said to her: 'At the creation God had given horns to hinds as well as to stags, but finding they wanted to govern everybody, he took them away as a punishment.'[6] His actions were partly dictated by his own prudence; Louis had long since signed a secret document nullifying any betrothal made for Claude to the Habsburg heir, and since his daughter's birth he had always nurtured the belief that Claude and Francis should marry.

Both Anne and Louise were to receive satisfaction on one mutually agreeable matter. When Louis recovered from his first illness in 1504, servants of de Gié informed him that their master had attempted to make himself Regent of France. Louis reluctantly charged his formerly trusted lieutenant with high treason. According to the somewhat unreliable witnesses, who had been suborned by the queen, de Gié had plans to prevent Claude from being sent to Brittany and he had impounded two of Anne's royal barges, which she had filled with her silver and gold plate as well as other treasures, also on their way to Brittany. Louise then stepped in, adding her own claims. She accused de Gié of intending to seize Francis in order to have him locked up in the fortified castle of Angers. Further fictitious details were embroidered in the hope of making her testimony more convincing. De Gié admitted that he had feared some attempt would be made by Anne to escape with her daughter, but denied any plot against the heir presumptive. He claimed that all he wished for was the marriage between Francis and Claude to take place, and to prevent any attempt by Brittany to declare independence from France.

It is possible that some allegations against de Gié were partially true, but there was also an element of aggravation at a powerful man wishing to become more powerful still; it is not known to this day whether or not the barges filled with gold and silver plate had been stopped. Although he was not ultimately charged with high treason, de Gié paid dearly for his offences, whether imagined or real, against Anne and Louise. Found guilty of 'certain excesses and faults', he was stripped of his offices, banished to his estates for five years, and had to pay an enormous fine. He eventually died in 1513, a broken and forgotten figure. He served as a reminder of the perils of a surfeit of ambition and a willingness to be the secret scapegoat for his king.

Louis appointed a new governor for Francis in de Gié's stead, Artus Gouffier, Seigneur du Boissy, an accomplished diplomat who had travelled beside Louis on his Italian expeditions. He arrived with his younger brother, Guillaume, Seigneur du Bonnivet, who almost immediately became one of the young prince's closest friends. Du Boissy therefore not only had the advantage of being a trusted councillor to King Louis, but he enjoyed the unusual and not inconsiderable bonus of support from both the queen and Louise.

Following the king's second grave illness in 1505, he finally acted upon his earlier attempts to settle the future should he suffer a further, and fatal, attack of poor health in the near future. Louis therefore wrote a will stating that if he were to die before he could see Francis and Claude joined in marriage, they should become man and wife immediately. Little as either of them wished for it, he compelled both Anne and Louise to swear upon a shard of the Holy Cross that the nuptials would take place without any delay. Claude therefore became the official heiress to the Orléans patrimony, and Louis commanded that she was not to leave or be removed from the country under any circumstances.

Once the king had recovered, he travelled to Plessis-lez-Tours with Francis, where he assembled his council in order to witness his will and to swear their faithful allegiance to his wishes. The young heir presumptive was placed under 'the total administration' of Georges, Cardinal of Amboise, the most powerful man in the kingdom save his ruler, until the boy came of age. A year later, on 14 May 1506, the king called an assembly of French aristocrats at Tours. Their leader, Thomas Bricot, approached, addressing the king as 'Father of the People', and said: 'Sire . . . for the general welfare of your kingdom . . . Your humble subjects beg that it may please you to give your only daughter in marriage to my Lord Francis here present, who is *tout français* [France's son].'[7] This piece of stage management enabled Louis to argue that he was fulfilling the people's will as he broke the earlier promises that he had made to his queen and Charles of Habsburg. He feigned great emotion and promised that he would consider the matter carefully. In one of the least surprising moments in his country's history, the king announced five days later that he would agree to the marriage and called for the deputies to make a solemn oath to accept Francis as their king, should Louis die without leaving a son of his own, and to ensure that the marriage between the royal children took place once they had reached their majority. Thus, on 21 May 1506, at Plessis-lez-Tours, the deputies legally witnessed the betrothal between Princess Claude and Francis. As one commentator noted, 'At two o'clock on 22 May . . . Francis and Claude were therefore affianced, to the universal joy of France. Festivals and tournaments holden [sic] in the royal park of Plesis [sic] and elsewhere signified Louis' sympathy in the contentment for his people.'[8]

Anne was furious at being thwarted and did what little she could to register her anger; the queen 'carefully kept the young couple apart, and never permitted her daughter to spend a moment alone with her betrothed, or with his mother; and this system she pertinaciously pursued for the remaining eight years of her life'.[9] However, she now knew that, short of giving birth to a male heir, there was little more than these vexatious and impotent irritations that she could accomplish. Her daughter and her rival's son seemed destined to be the next ruling couple of France, and her own role shrank in consequence.

If Louise had reservations about the match on a personal level, she knew that it represented another step closer to the throne for her son, the heir presumptive, which satisfied her. It was around this time that she once again turned her attention to the question of Marguerite's potential marriage. She had grown into a young woman with a slender figure, remarkably long strawberry-blonde hair and striking violet-blue eyes, as well as the same long and bony nose as her brother. Witty and high-spirited by temperament, the princess carried herself with modesty, kept her own counsel and was the possessor of a mysterious and unusual charisma. In short, it was not difficult to understand why Louise regarded her daughter as capable of making another advantageous match, just as it was clear why Francis valued her candid counsel and advice in a manner only equalled by his mother.

In early 1507, Louis proposed the twenty-year-old Charles, Duke of Alençon and a prince of the blood, as a suitable match for the

eighteen-year-old Marguerite. The king's rationale was to attempt
to settle a territorial dispute about Armagnac, a valuable territory
in south-western France. It was felt by many that the match was
an unequal one: Marguerite had the potential to be an excellent
royal bride, while the duke was, for all his breeding, an insignificant
figure in comparison. Louis, however, decided to make the match a
lucrative one, offering to settle the county of Armagnac on Marguerite and the sum of 60,000 *livres tournois* in instalments, with the first
7,000 *livres* to be delivered by Francis to his future brother-in-law on
the day of the wedding. Louis felt pleased with his elegant solution
to the complex dynastic claims and counter-claims, but it was Marguerite who would pay the real price. Charles of Alençon was an
unsuitable candidate for his clever wife-to-be, 'naturally dull and
slow of comprehension' as well as 'reserved and unsocial from habit
and inclination'. Proud, bigoted and cowardly, Charles constantly
petitioned the king 'for offices that he was mentally and physically
unfitted to discharge'. Alençon's good looks and royal mien were
the sole reasons for his advancement.

The marriage between Charles and Marguerite took place shortly
after six in the evening on 9 October 1509 at the royal palace of Blois.
It was a lavish event, hosted by the king and queen; the feasting and
merriment lasted for four days. Louis led Marguerite to and from the
altar and treated her with 'the most marked distinction and affection'
throughout her marriage celebrations. Anne had personally paid for
the exceptionally grand wedding, and watched compassionately as
the young woman sobbed throughout the entire ceremony, which
joined her to a prince who 'had not the smallest credit at court'.
Louise, meanwhile, proudly claimed Marguerite wept with tears of
joy, which was doubtful; her brilliant daughter had been bartered like
a chattel for political expediency. At the end of the celebrations, the
new Duke and Duchess of Alençon set out for Normandy and the
Château of Argentans, where they soon learnt how miserable each
could make the other. It was, at least, a blessing that no children were
to result from the expedient and ill-fated union.*

---

* The man whom Marguerite would have preferred to marry, a young general
named Gaston de Foix, was not considered a suitable match.

*

While Marguerite suffered far away, Louise continued to watch the intertwined fortunes of her son and the king and queen. Francis, by now fifteen years old, had been regarded as a man since 1508 and had left his mother's side to take up a place at court. He was often referred to as 'Monsieur le Dauphin', although only the king's son could be thus named officially. Louis acted *in loco parentis* for the young man, explaining the role of his various councils, introducing the youth to his royal advisers and exploring other aspects of kingship, particularly the administrative roles. Francis's position was further endorsed when Louis made him a member of the King's Council. He had grown into a striking-looking figure, six feet tall, with a strong build, chestnut hair and large eyes of the same hue, which sometimes rolled up into his head. Although this was a nervous tic, it had the effect of disorienting those around him, something that he soon used to play to his advantage.

Even his long nose, a distinctive family feature, did not mar his looks; instead, his seductive charm proved irresistible to women. Marguerite recorded one of his earliest romantic adventures in her collection of short stories, *Le Heptaméron*, in which she described how her brother, who had hitherto preferred 'to ride and hunt than to behold the beauty of ladies', found his first sexual interest in a brown-haired girl who aroused 'an unaccustomed heat' inside his heart, even though she was a commoner. On this occasion, despite repeated entreaties and begging, he was unsuccessful in satisfying his desires, but this proved to be the exception; by 1512, his mother wrote in her journal that, due to his escapades, he had contracted a disease 'of the forbidden parts'. Louise remained the woman he was closest to and, until he married, he would remove his cap and kneel in her presence at all times, showing the respect undoubtedly due to his formidable mother.

However, it was fighting rather than the company of women that occupied him in these early years. It seemed a logical progression from playing at soldiering to experiencing the reality of warfare. Francis's first taste of war was as commander of the forces of Guyenne in September 1512. The aim was to recapture the neighbouring kingdom of Navarre by means of strong French ties, largely due to intermarriage with the French dynasties of Foix and Albret, both of which had distant connections with the royal house of France. King Ferdinand of Aragon had seized most of the Pyrenean kingdom; however, his appointment was a largely honorific one, and in November, following a disastrous campaign by the French commanders, Francis hurried back to Paris, while the army retreated in chaos. His actions made a mockery of the medal struck by his mother, in which he was depicted wearing the laurels of battle with the legend 'Maximus Francisus Francorum Dux, 1512'. It was unfortunate that his earliest participation in warfare coincided with a time of defeat for France. The following year, Henry VIII invaded Picardy in June with a combined force of 13,000 troops, and an early skirmish at Tournai, nicknamed 'the Battle of the Spurs' due to the speed with which the French forces fled the field, resulted in many noblemen being taken prisoner. Francis, who had been bathing in a river at the time, was not among them, but he was ignominiously compelled to flee without having the time to recover his armour, and certainly without the slightest sniff of the military success and honour for which he still longed.

As Francis failed to make any progress in the field of arms, Louise continued to fret over his prospects as heir presumptive. Louis and Anne welcomed the arrival of a second child, Renée, on 27 October 1510, but the birth of a healthy living son eluded the couple; a boy born in 1512 died almost immediately. This proved to be the final disappointment for Anne. Worn out and exhausted at the age of thirty-five, she was unable to recover. As her health visibly declined, she reflected on her many disappointments. Not only had she been unable to produce an heir to the French throne, but her loathed rival Louise would almost inevitably become queen mother. She also feared that the planned union between Francis and Claude would be an unhappy and difficult one for her daughter. She accepted defeat and nominated Louise as the executor of her will, responsible for the administration of her vast estate. Her kindness and decency had proved no match for Louise's tenacity and opportunism.

Anne died on 9 January 1514 aged thirty-seven. Francis's friend Fleurange noted that, while many mourned, 'he who had much ease by it was Monsieur d'Angoulême, for she was ever contrary to him in his business; there was never a moment when the two families were not at odds with one another'.[10] His lack of compassion was soon compounded following his marriage to Claude four months later at the chapel of Saint-Germain-en-Laye on 18 May 1514. The ceremony took place within a sombre atmosphere of lament – Francis sourly described it as a 'niggardly ceremony, without the pomp due to a royal marriage even in mourning', and another observer wrote: 'The wedding feast had been pared down to such an extreme degree no peasant would deign to taste that miser's repast.' As the tasteless joke did the rounds that, thanks to Claude's squint and semi-blindness and Francis's eye-rolling, husband and wife would never see eye to eye, the grief-stricken Louis was notable only for his wan and listless demeanour. Shattered by his wife's death, the king banished any levity from the court. He had the 'fiddlers, comedians, jugglers and buffoons' thrown out, and donned mourning dress of deep black as he closeted himself away and wept for a week.[11] He remained heartbroken and claimed that he would follow her to the grave within a year.

He did at least attend his daughter's wedding, which is more than could be said for the groom's mother. Louise, basking in the triumph that she had engineered, was nonetheless grieved that her son was marrying a fourteen-year-old girl, albeit the new Duchess of Brittany, who was 'very small and strangely fat'.[12] Claude's short-sightedness and hunchbacked appearance did not augur well for her ability to bear children. Not that the heir presumptive and new Duke of Brittany wasted any time mourning the situation. He spent the day following his wedding hunting, and barely bothered to speak to Claude. Francis and Louise now shared an increasing arrogance, as though it were a foregone conclusion that he would shortly be the King of France.

This manifested itself in distinctly unregal behaviour. Within four days of his marriage, he no longer hid his boredom at the monotonous routine at Saint-Germain-en-Laye. As though in conscious defiance of Louis and the prudent values for which he had earned the title 'Father of the People', Francis headed to Paris, where he spent extravagantly dissipated nights in whoring, gambling and drinking. His ostentation was such that even Louise, who blamed her daughter-in-law for her son's behaviour, started worrying about Francis's safety; she also feared that his prodigality had become too conspicuous. She knew that Louis had already noticed how much his son-in-law's spending had increased over the past months, lamenting it by saying, 'Ce gros garçon nous gâtera tout' (This great big boy will ruin everything). It was only a matter of time until he heard of Francis's exploits, as word had got around Paris as to who led the licentious band of noble roisterers.

Louis might have disciplined his son-in-law, or sent him off on a military expedition to keep him out of trouble. Instead, the ailing monarch decided upon one last stratagem, a decision that brought abject horror to the house of Angoulême.

CHAPTER 3

'The King Never Dies'

In 1514, Henry VIII's sister Mary Tudor was eighteen years old. Born at Sheen Palace on 18 March 1496, she had the advantage of a liberal education and enjoyed the honour of a large household of her own from the age of six 'with many gentlewomen to wait upon her'. Here she studied French and Latin as well as the traditional feminine arts of singing, embroidery and dancing. Mary enjoyed an unusually close relationship with her elder brother. Following the death of their father, Henry VII, on 21 April 1509, the new king indulged his favourite sister and offered her a great deal of freedom; she was thirteen years old at the time.* The Tudor princess resembled her brother in her high-spirited passion for hunting, as well as her love of dancing, masques and the many other games that kept easily jaded courtiers from more sinister distractions.

Mary not only appreciated the plentiful benefits that came with her exceptional position, but she also had a deserved reputation as one of the finest-looking young royals of her day. As well as a slim figure, golden hair and clear complexion, Mary had fine eyes, a pretty nose and a rosebud mouth that revealed her small white teeth when she smiled. It is hardly surprising that the royal houses of Europe viewed Henry's sister as one of the most exquisite and desirable young maidens to adorn their rarefied ranks; she presented a highly sought-after matrimonial prize on Europe's royal marriage market. Erasmus sighed that 'Nature never formed anything more beautiful.'¹ Mary was certainly expected to make a great match to

* Henry named his first surviving child, Mary I, after her.

one of the most powerful princes on the Continent.* Her dazzling looks suggested that her future husband should be as physically captivating as the Tudor princess. The fairy tale spun by romantic souls certainly did not include her marriage to the widowed, fifty-two-year-old Louis XII, a man riddled with gout, 'a decayed complexion' and one who desired a son and heir of his own, thereby disregarding his doctor's worry at the physical cost to the French king's fragile health.[2]

Whatever the princess's personal views, conventional realpolitik would dictate any nuptial union with a foreign prince. In concert with the arch-schemer Cardinal Wolsey, Louis had consented to a peace treaty with the English, in which it was agreed that they would retain the towns of Thérouanne and Tournai, and Henry's annual 100,000 *écus* pension from France, withheld during recent hostilities, would also be resumed if the parties reached an agreement. In order to strengthen his hope of maintaining a peace treaty, Louis decided to use the one trump card he still held up his regal sleeve. On 7 August 1514, the king signed two treaties of peace and friendship with the English Crown, which would become collectively known as the Treaty of London. Within these lay an unexpected and vitally important clause, and one that would quickly reverberate through the Angoulême and Tudor households, as Louis XII undertook marriage to Mary, thirty-four years his junior. It was an unpleasant surprise for the beauteous Mary, to say the least. After much weeping and pleading, the princess's hitherto carefree, untrammelled life in England seemed finished for ever. She wrote a short and perfunctory letter in her own hand, in which she humbly commended herself to Louis, who had become her husband by proxy marriage on 13 August 1514 at Greenwich Palace: 'bien humblement je me recommende a vostre bonne grace [*sic*]'. And the French Queen, as she would henceforth be known, signed the letter 'De la main vre bien humble compaigne [*sic*].** MARIE.'[3]

---

* The leading contender, Charles V, son of Philip I of Castile and later Holy Roman Emperor, would eventually become Francis I's greatest nemesis.

** 'With sincere humility I commend myself to you . . . from the true hand of your humble wife.'

Meanwhile, it would be hard to say who had taken the shock news of the king's nuptials worst: the bride, her beloved Duke of Suffolk, Francis the heir presumptive, who had but four months earlier become his son-in-law, or his mother. The results threatened to be catastrophic for many people, both personally and politically. With Louis revived and on the sexual prowl once more, Louise feared that all of her careful preparations for Francis's reign would be laid waste. She had presumptively planned her future household and the apartments she would occupy within the many royal palaces, for she wished to establish herself in the rooms closest to her son's to ensure that nobody could subvert her influence over Francis. She pictured herself standing beside the young king, guiding the fortunes of France; the crucial line between the national interest and her personal advantage had already become dangerously blurred. Her son, meanwhile, maintained an air of insouciance, and seemed unconcerned, as he stated: 'Even if the king should be foolish enough to marry again, he will not live long; any son he might have would be a child. This would necessitate a regency and in accordance with the constitution, I would be regent.'[4] These brave words sought to conceal the fact that the Angoulême triumvirate's fortunes seemed doomed; as for Claude, his new wife, she seemed quite forgotten by both her father and husband, even as she still mourned the death of her mother.

Mary of England seemed a picture of misery at the match, not least because she had already fallen for the handsome and courageous epitome of ideal manhood personified by Charles Brandon, Duke of Suffolk. Suffolk had served with great military distinction at the successful sieges of Thérouanne and Tournai in 1513. A strapping, hearty fellow, and probably the English king's closest intimate, he was the opposite of that sickly, diminished man to whom Mary had been joined by proxy. Henry knew of her deep affection for Suffolk, a hugely influential figure at court, but no royal blood flowed in his country squire's veins. It is said that Mary extracted a promise from her brother that, should Louis die before her, she would be allowed to marry whom she chose. The king is said to have readily agreed to her request, without any intention of holding to his royal word. As Dowager Queen of France, Mary would remain a rich marital prize for her brother to use as a political pawn. Henry, despite his affection for her, would have no qualms in manipulating her, as the price for being a princess at the time was a high one when it came to marriage; and being allowed to voice an opinion over the monarch's choice of groom would have been seen as provocative and rebellious.

With little time to consider her future, Mary had been accompanied to Dover by her brother and his Spanish-born queen, Catherine of Aragon, who waved the sobbing princess off, adding their own cheers to that of a huge crowd of spectators who gave the king's sister a rousing farewell. The onlookers crowding the streets and the quay were not just the local population, but many who had travelled long distances to enjoy the spectacle, proud of their beautiful princess. She in turn did not forget the esteem in which she was held by her countrymen as she left them, perhaps for ever. Mary boarded her ship, where she received further wedding presents of great value from her enthusiastic groom. The ship, along with further vessels for Mary's protection against marauders, cast off in the Channel. It bore a vast number of people, their possessions and animals; as well as Mary and her huge entourage of 2,000 ladies and gentlemen, she left her native shores laden with gems and gowns. Many of these formed part of her trousseau, but the most spectacular confections and glimmering jewels were those sent by Louis to his young bride.

In the weeks preceding her departure, Mary had already become aware of the honours due to her new rank as Queen of France; although she basked in her elevated status, all of the riches and trappings of wealth could not compensate her for losing the attentions of the handsome young Suffolk. It is little wonder that she wept copious tears as her ill-fated journey began. As if her misery were not bad enough, the crossing from Dover to France on 22 September proved exceptionally stormy, as the rough seas claimed at least one of the escorting ships and its crew. Carrying on the unlucky run of fortune, Mary's own vessel ran aground off Boulogne, where she had to be carried ashore, and the 2,000 courtiers accompanying her struggled to safety. They were greeted by Francis, acting in the sickly king's stead, who suavely offered her all the honour due to the new Queen of France. He gallantly escorted Mary towards Abbeville through the rain and stormy weather.

The downpour continued, and by the time the French and English parties arrived outside Abbeville, Mary's striking ensemble of crimson and gold had become a sodden mess. As for the beautiful pert crimson hat which she had worn at a jaunty angle, topping off her rich costume to perfection, by the time the company had reached their destination it called to mind nothing more than a miserable dead bird. As Mary reached the outskirts of the town she was greeted by the king. As he approached, Mary was unable to take her eyes off her new husband, although less out of admiration than horror. The gouty king, described sardonically as 'very antique',[5] wore a short and unflattering jacket of red cloth and, with a gleam in his eye, he rode over and kissed his new bride with all the lecherous passion of a teenage boy. This departed slightly from the usual protocol whereby a groom met his foreign bride upon arrival, as if by chance, which had become a tradition throughout the Italian peninsula and was commonplace during the Renaissance throughout most of the Continent. It is doubtful that the overwhelmed queen was able to make a full curtsey to her new husband and sovereign, for the soaked and freezing brocades had become a deadweight and rising required help.

Unsurprisingly, given the circumstances, it was remarked upon that people thronged the streets and, ignoring the deluge, sat perched upon the rooftops eager to catch a glimpse of their new queen, even as the rain poured down with increased intensity. There were fires manically lit in celebration, despite the wet weather, and thirteen houses burned to the ground on the night of Mary's arrival – hardly an auspicious start to married life.

On 9 October 1514, the day following this eventful advent, the royal nuptials took place with almost unseemly haste. For a miserable few weeks, the issue of the succession became fraught with uncertainty. As his mother fretted Francis adopted a relaxed posture, telling his friend Fleurange that he had never felt as happy or as relaxed before, and that he had nothing to fear. This might have been because a spy had reported that 'it is not possible for the King and the Queen to beget children'. This intelligence was soon proved

accurate; although Louis' boasts about his conjugal performance, as
he had made before during his marriage to Jeanne, may have been
true – he claimed that he had 'done marvels' and 'crossed the river
three times' – his bedroom antics, regardless of their success, were
visibly harming his health. Mary might have felt some relief at this,
even as he called for more.

In his single-minded desire to produce an heir, the king ignored
his councillors' pleas for caution. It is possible that this stemmed
in part from a bizarre belief that his young wife, far from being
repelled by the goat-like satyr who tormented her in bed, instead
relished her husband's attentions and her new position of Queen of
France. The last part, at least, bore some relation to the truth. Her
coronation took place on 5 November 1514, at Saint-Denis, and Francis carried the consort's crown, in acknowledgement of his status.
When Mary made her first official entry into Paris her grace and
beauty were widely acknowledged, and a month-long fête was declared in celebration of the match. Meanwhile it continued to rain,
as it would for the rest of their marriage.

The wedding entertainments consisted of jousting, wrestling
and other sports, including the demanding and dangerous 'combat
at the barrier', a feat of strength involving swords, maces and axes.
These were then followed by lavish banquets and dancing at night.
It would have been exhausting and demanding, but Francis, seeking
to redeem himself from the reputation of being a roistering playboy,
threw himself into the excitements with verve. He never ceased to
dazzle when it came to his appearance, wearing sumptuous clothes
made of crimson velvet and embroidered with silver and gold, and
surrounded by a retinue of men and horses clad in the same colours.
Although the English proved themselves superior in the games of
jousting and physical skill, Francis acquitted himself admirably.
The contrast between the young, vigorous heir presumptive and
the by now disintegrating king, forced by the vigour of his noctur-
nal antics into a supine slump on a day bed in order to attempt to
watch the sports, could not have been clearer.

Francis's confidence that there would be no child born from the
union between Louis and Mary proved well placed; as Christmas
approached, Louis fell seriously ill, plagued by gout and fatigue.

Had he had a greater amount of rest he might have recovered, but he was still priapic, although the intent had long since outweighed the execution. Knowing that another kind of end was imminent, he was still capable of some black humour: he promised Mary a present that would make her happiest, and when asked what, replied 'My death', with a grim half-smile. Her reaction is not recorded, but it is unlikely to have been a sorrowful one, as she contemplated a blessed deliverance from her intimate torments.

She had another, more attractive prospect as well. Francis, who rivalled Louis for sexual vitality but to rather greater effect, sought to engage in a love affair with the beautiful queen, who openly encouraged his advances while her unbeloved husband was ailing. He undoubtedly would have cuckolded his monarch until a wise courtier, Antoine de Grignaux, pointed out that, should she become pregnant, he would remain merely Count of Angoulême and never be King of France; however, it took a final warning from his mother in the form of a furious letter for him to curtail his behaviour. It was said that he trembled after he read it. The other threat to Francis's ultimate goal, besides his rampant libido, was the presence of the Duke of Suffolk, who had accompanied Mary to France as 'special emissary'. Francis, aware of the possibility of intimacy between the two developing, gave instruction that they be constantly watched, and Louise ordered Claude, who was acting as Mary's lady-in-waiting, to ensure that she was never left alone unless the king was with her.

Whether these preparations were necessary or over-cautious, they paid off handsomely. Louis suffered a further and final attack on New Year's Eve at the Palace of Tournelles, near Paris. Summoning Francis to his bedside, he embraced him tenderly and told him his time had come, and that as his heir the young man must prepare to take Louis' place on the French throne within the next few hours. Francis, who despite everything retained a deep affection for Louis, attempted to comfort his monarch, but the old king repeated the words, 'I am dying.' As, in Fleurange's words, 'the most horrible weather ever seen' raged outside the palace, the king started vomiting, as if in counterpoint to the deluge outside.[6] He died in hideous agony in the early hours of 1 January 1515, and, as

Louise wrote in her journal, 'on the first day of January, my son was King of France'. Fleurange, unmoved by Louis' final indignities, described the whole affair as 'a splendid New Year's gift, for he was not the king's son . . . the said Seigneur of Angoulême was born on New Year's Day and acquired the kingdom of France on New Year's Day.' He was wrong about the birthday, but entirely correct about everything else.

The greatest prize of all was finally Francis's. Yet he did not inherit a united country. Powerful local rulers, such as the Duke of Lorraine, divided their loyalty and homages between France and the Holy Roman Empire, and different areas of France had different laws, traditions and languages; although by 1515 this was largely extinct, only a few areas in the south-west of the country still spoke the dialect *langue d'oc* rather than the more commonly adopted *langue d'oïl*. The country had a population of around fifteen million, but one prone to depletion through regular outbreaks of plague, although none on the scale of the pandemics of the fourteenth and early fifteenth centuries. The major towns, such as Paris, Rouen and Lyons, were leading European centres, but many more were small, poverty-stricken and deficient in the production of the food and goods that were the lifeblood of a successful country's trade. In short, the France of which its near-namesake had become monarch was a nation desperately in need of a reforming king who could drag the country out of the semi-Dark Ages into a new age of culture, civilisation and prosperity. Francis, a man not given to self-doubt or lack of confidence, believed that he was that ruler, but events would soon challenge his grandiose self-assurance. His country adhered to the maxim that 'the king never dies', and, as Mary was not pregnant with either his or Suffolk's child, he had no obstacles to his long-cherished prize.

At the death of a king, the usual protocols had to be observed; although his successor to the throne became monarch automatically, the sacerdotal aspect of being anointed with holy oil was considered vital, even more so than the crowning. His mother was at Romorantin in central France when she received the news of Louis' death from Francis, who asked that she hurry to Paris 'to aid him by her counsels'.[7] Marguerite also received a similarly urgent summons, and she, her husband and Louise arrived in Paris on Wednesday, 3 January 1515. Louis' body had been embalmed immediately after his death, and now lay in state inside the chapel of the royal palace of Les Tournelles, clad in his royal robes, the sceptre placed in one hand and the *Main de Justice* (hand of justice) in the other. Les Tournelles had been transformed into a place of mourning, with the walls of the Great Hall dressed in black taffeta and the windows covered in the same sumptuous silk, all in preparation for Louis' funeral ceremony.[8]

The old king was buried at Saint-Denis on 12 January 1515, the last in a succession of down-at-heel and often sickly men. Francis was determined to make a symbolic break with the past, but it was not to the approval of all. A Venetian envoy described how 'the King attended Mass for the obsequies of the late King attired in a purple mantle with a long train'. Clearly unimpressed by what seemed the opposite of the traditional black mourning dress, the envoy sneered: 'he resembled the Devil'.[9] Demon or angel, there could be little doubt that Francis, young, charismatic and ambitious, was an altogether more contemporary monarch.

From the beginning, the new king was at the centre of intense activity. Francis was a ruler of both the sacred and potentially profane, not only ruling over his physical kingdom, but also acting as the vessel of the Church's authority. Additionally, he was expected to discriminate between undeserving sycophants and deserving opportunists petitioning for favours, to act as a glorious military leader, a careful domestic strategist and a canny manager of the powerful. The role of king was not, to put it mildly, an easy or relaxing one, but with the right man in charge, the early days and weeks could offer the basis on which to define the beginning of a reign.

Many of the administrative matters that Francis had to deal with were routine. He reappointed the members of the *parlement* of Paris, a court of law rather than a representative assembly, as well as their provincial equivalents. He offered stability and reassurance, and erred on the side of conservatism, keeping several members of the old regime in post; chief among these was Florimond Robertet, of whom Fleurange wrote: 'He governed the entire kingdom . . .

he was the man closest to his master . . . he was undoubtedly one of the most intelligent and able men I have ever seen and it is to his credit that, as long as he was in charge of the affairs of France, they fared marvellously.'[10]

However, emboldened by his new powers, Francis was also an innovator. He made Antoine Duprat, a fifty-two-year-old bureaucrat, Chancellor, which placed him in charge of the French judicial system; this merchant's son had previously impressed both Louise and Anne of Brittany in his prosecution of the bumptious de Gié, and Louise had taken him into her service after Anne's death. With decades of experience of the tortuous and difficult world of legal administration, Duprat would be a useful mentor to the king. However, his ruthlessness and perceived grasping nature would eventually render him hugely unpopular in the country at large.

Francis's greatest interest, perhaps more so than any legal or bureaucratic matters, lay in the military appointments that he made. The most crucial office was that of Constable of France, the First Officer of the Crown, responsible for the administration and supply of the country's army, and the most jealously guarded honour of all was the constable's right to lead the vanguard of the army in the monarch's absence. It was appropriate that Francis appointed possibly the leading figure in France after the king to this position. Charles III, Duke of Bourbon, was the twenty-five-year-old son-in-law of Anne of France, the former regent known as Madame la Grande. Bourbon had already proved himself both brave and competent, and on 12 January the duke's new office was officially ratified. The constable was an enormously important symbolic role, and from that point onwards Charles of Bourbon would bear the king's unsheathed sword on all ceremonial occasions, demonstrating that he was the ruler's trusted knight. The new constable was presented with his badge of office, named the *Joyeuse* after the great sword of Charlemagne. This beautiful object was made up of all the swords that had been used at the coronation of a French king since 1271, and sheathed in a blue scabbard covered in fleurs-de-lys from hilt to point.

To show his appreciation, and to indicate his adherence to the new regime, Duke Charles and his duchess Suzanne invited Francis and Queen Claude, as well as the most important members of their court, to a lavish celebration at his splendid Hôtel de Bourbon in Paris. The purpose of the event was twofold: it both served as a symbol of his gratitude, and honoured the marriage between fifteen-year-old Diane de Poitiers and Louis de Brézé, a man more than thirty-five years his bride's senior, and reputedly both the richest and the ugliest man in France. At this grand gathering, ties of family and rank were strengthened as Diane was honoured with the office of lady-in-waiting to both Claude and Louise. No expense was spared; the guests ate their food off gold plate, and every footman wore a gold chain of such size and weight that it could be looped two or three times round his neck.[11]

The message from all this pageantry was clear: this was to be a new monarchy, with a new style of approach and behaviour. Nonetheless, some things had not changed. Nepotism remained a widespread issue at court: Louise, for instance, was granted the duchy of Anjou, the county of Maine and the barony of Amboise, among others, in recognition of her extraordinary achievements in placing her son on the throne rather more than because she deserved the honours. While token attempts were made at handing out posts with real responsibilities to the most capable family members and friends, nepotism often trumped experience, meaning that it was often the deputies who found themselves making the crucial decisions of which their over-appointed superiors were incapable. Bribery, for want of a better name, was rife: officials paid large fees when their roles were reconfirmed and these substantial sums were much appreciated by both Francis and, in turn, Louise, who often benefited from her grateful son's generosity. To call this an expected obligation would be cynical, but probably accurate. Yet this was nothing exceptional or scandalous at the time: Francis's predecessors would have acted in the same way, as would any other major European ruler.

Nonetheless, it was the coronation and subsequent pageantry that proved the event that would define Francis in the eyes of the public. It was not just a sacred rite, imbued with immense religious and dynastic significance, as it had been since the tenth century; it was also a public relations exercise without peer. On the evening before the coronation, 24 January, Francis, following tradition, had undertaken a vigil of meditation and prayer in the vast Gothic cathedral of Rheims, an event that he approached with utmost seriousness. He might have prayed that he be a wise and noble ruler, or, more selfishly, that he be showered with fame and glory like his great forebear Charlemagne. In either case, he was mere hours away from a consummation that he had wished for all his life, which duly took place the following day. Francis was anointed the fifty-seventh ruler of France by Archbishop Robert de Lenoncourt, making him both the defender of Christendom and King of France, imbued with priestly powers of his own. These included a belief, dating back to ancient times, that the king could heal the sick, and 'touching' the afflicted was an unenjoyable but necessary duty that was bound up with the symbolism that any ruler of France had supernatural powers. The inability of Louis and Charles VIII to heal themselves, let alone others, was tactfully overlooked. As he was crowned, the archbishop shouted 'Vivat Rex in aeternum!', to which the congregation called 'Vive le Roi!' The king had never died; he had simply been reborn.

After the coronation, Francis headed to the shrine of Notre-Dame de Liesse, a popular destination for pilgrims, before once again revisiting the Abbey of Saint-Denis, scene of his predecessor's funeral a mere couple of weeks before. The abbey's monks had played a vital role in the development of royal administration during the Middle Ages, and it was symbolically important therefore to show that Francis enjoyed the support of this major centre of learning. Having confirmed the abbey in its privileges and rights, he was once again crowned. However, all of this was but a preamble to his grand entry into Paris. The previous year, he and his boon companions had drunk, wenched and roared in the streets. Now he revisited the same roads, but his arrival and bearing could not have been a greater contrast.

Precedent dictated the exact way that a new French king made his ceremonial entry into the capital. On the morning of 15 February 1515, the mayor and aldermen of Paris, accompanied by senior representatives of the seventeen trade guilds that regulated the city's commercial life and members of the *parlement*, made their way to

Saint-Denis in order to greet the king. These civic dignitaries then re-entered Paris at the head of the procession, followed by the king's highest-ranking generals, the four *Maréchals de France*, bedecked in their gold and silver uniforms. The sizeable personage of Chancellor Duprat, the senior figure in civilian government, brought up the considerable rear as the assembled dignitaries poured through the city's northern gate, the Porte Saint-Denis. The Great Seal needed for the king to approve important documents travelled separately by horse. Heralds and various members of the royal household followed, among them the four *gens du roi* who carried Francis's helmet, sword, cloak and hat. And then, finally, came the king in all his impressive majesty.

Francis was mounted on horseback and the canopy that was held above him could barely contain the monarch as he leant out to throw coins of gold and silver into the crowds of his adoring, delighted subjects. He wore an elegant suit of silver cloth with a white hat bejewelled with precious stones. The senior aristocracy and other male members of the royal family, similarly attired to majestic effect, rode behind their king. At the rear of the procession, and as a constant reminder of the security precautions required even in peacetime whenever the monarch was travelling, 400 archers followed behind. It was reputed to have been the most impressive entrance ever made by a sovereign.

The grand procession, both good-hearted and momentous, made its way across the city and ended with a service of thanksgiving at Notre-Dame Cathedral. There was a minor stir caused by Francis's decision to take the new Pont Nôtre-Dame, designed by the Veronese architect and engineer Fra Giocondo, rather than the old but rickety Pont au Change, but this was done for both practical and symbolic reasons. The young king wished to embrace a new and modern style of ruling. The implicit contrast with his predecessor would not have been lost upon the crowd, many of whom were present just a few months ago to witness Queen Mary's coronation at Saint-Denis. Now, though, the service in which Francis participated in Notre-Dame was of an altogether different order. The archbishop gave thanks for the divine providence that had guided the young king to his throne and the congregation echoed the clergy's effusive prayers. Afterwards, the celebrations continued with a lavish banquet at the royal palace, the Louvre, followed by dancing and several days of jousting and tournaments. Confidence and excitement filled the air, reflecting the public mood throughout the city and indeed the country.

Francis would need all the confidence and excitement from his people that he could muster. He had long ago decided to be a strong king, both at home and abroad. Therefore, with a sense of inevitability, he was set upon his first major action as ruler of France. He would go to war and recapture Milan, an action that would define him for ever as either a glorious warrior king or a tragic failure. It was the greatest gamble that he had yet taken but, as ever, he was nothing if not ready for a mighty challenge.

CHAPTER 4

Swimming in French Blood

As Francis started to prepare for war against Milan in the first days
of his reign, he was continuing a tradition begun by his predecessor. A French claim to the duchy had been established by Louis'
grandmother (and great-grandmother to Francis), Valentina Visconti of Milan's former ruling dynasty. The duchy continued to be
important for strategic reasons as a geographical gateway to the
Italian peninsula; the successful conquest of Milan would make an
invasion of Naples considerably easier. As a territorial acquisition,
the duchy was one of the largest and most prosperous in Italy, enjoying extensive political and diplomatic influence throughout the
Continent. Italy's wealth had provided a lifeline to many bankrupt
monarchs, to say nothing of their courtiers. The Italian states had
maintained an uneasy peace among themselves since the middle
of the fifteenth century, and the unspoken fear was the arrival of a
powerful foreign king with territorial ambitions. This fear had been
realised in 1494 when Charles VIII and his distant cousin Louis XII
led a massive French army into the peninsula; they reached Milan
after a secret arrangement with Duke Ludovico Sforza that allowed
them to enter the city without a fight. Before long, Charles VIII sat
in the royal palace of Naples, his ambitions fulfilled.

However, by 1515 Milan had been conquered, lost, reconquered
and then lost once again, with the various reversals of military fortune taking place at near-dizzying speed. These machinations had
also, at one time or another, made enemies of the Venetians, the
Spanish and mercenaries in the pay of the pope, in a comprehensive

display of diplomatic failure. Shortly before the death of Louis XII, the humiliating peace treaty of Saint-Germain-en-Laye in 1514 had expelled the French from Italy altogether. Francis understood that a swift and complete victory recapturing the duchy of Milan would raise his country's morale and establish him as a mighty warrior king. Having never served with any real responsibility or proximity to the action, for Louis considered the risk of losing his heir far too great, Francis believed that he had been given no chance to acquire a military reputation. He saw the forthcoming campaign as a heaven-sent opportunity to act decisively and heroically. His bellicose plans would not disappoint him.

Going to war was an expensive and time-consuming affair. Louis' ill-fated foreign expeditions had meant that the exchequer was now running with a deficit of almost two million *livres*, and Francis nearly doubled this figure in preparation for his Italian campaign. He was also leading a life of cheerful extravagance. The Venetian observer Marc' Antonio Contarini, observing his antics at the end of March, wrote: 'The king is most handsome, so much so that it's impossible to convey. And generous too – in two months he has given away 300,000 crowns, including pensions of 60,000.'[1] The campaign ahead needed to be a conclusive triumph. If Francis and his top commanders managed to inflict a decisive defeat upon their enemies, the concomitant victory would establish him as a military genius whose cunning and courage on the battlefield made him a figure to be feared as well as admired. It would also place him in a position of great strength when, during the aftermath, accommodations needed to be reached with his new neighbours, whose future support would be required in order to hold on to the duchy. The French treatment of a comprehensively beaten enemy would be important for establishing strong international relations in the future, but the outcome needed to be a lucrative one in order for the king to maintain his current generous rate of patronage and spending.

He had, however, made a prudent appointment in his Superin-tendent of Finances. Jacques de Beaune, Baron de Semblançay, had been retained from Louis XII's reign, and he kept his office at the express request of Louise, for whom he had done many favours.

Semblançay was in the unenviable position of having to produce money as though he were a magician. The baron was fortunately at the peak of his financial wizardry and by levying extra taxes and applying special fiscal expedients, such as the sale of offices far in excess of the number required, fines, loans and the sale of titles of nobility, Semblançay raised the revenue required. This in turn bought the most up-to-date arms and armour and secured supplies to keep the army housed, fed and watered. Francis spent a great deal of time planning; his schemes and stratagems were designed to see him securing either a tactical advantage over France's enemies, or, better yet, outright victory.

The King's Council, the *Curia Regis*, was a crucial part of these preparations, in times of war and peace alike. It was they who ensured the smooth running of the country, and that the king's will was obeyed. The councillors were a prestigious group, including members of the royal family and the higher aristocracy, holders of the great offices of state such as the Chancellor and Constable, senior churchmen and major figures involved in the administration of provincial France. The *Curia* therefore consisted of a large body of influential and opinionated men, all of whom had been personally appointed by Francis and were trusted by him implicitly; perhaps because the king's trust often waned, their term in office rarely lasted more than a few years.

In early 1515, as the much-anticipated war approached, Francis's officials sent couriers to each *bailliage*, or bailiwick, in the kingdom in order to raise troops for the conflict. Each local magnate or lord was relied upon to supply a certain quota of men, as the king had neither the means nor the money to raise and maintain an army himself. Thus Francis depended upon the soldiers sent by the nobles, all the while knowing that, if the monarch was weak and the time uncertain, a powerful feudal lord could either retreat behind his high castle walls and refuse to help, or, in extremis, use his own men in armed revolt. Therefore, Francis knew that he needed the support of his aristocrats, but trust – on either side – was a commodity less easily obtained. Many of these lords were spending a great deal of their time at court by the beginning of the king's reign, where they were feasted, entertained – and watched.

As Francis remarked, their presence served 'to prevent them from making worse mischief'.

The most significant local figure that had to be dealt with, and handled extremely carefully, was the provincial governor. It was his responsibility to ensure that the monarch could head off to war well equipped, not only with all the men and arms he needed, but secure in the knowledge that any hint of rebellion at home could be stamped upon brutally and immediately. It was an office normally given to a high-ranking aristocrat, and there were eleven governors at any given time, their loyalty to the king being considered absolute.

When he was not on a military campaign, the governor normally spent his time at the royal court, but enjoyed the privilege of having a fully staffed local household and high standing in the region, as well as his own military company, paid for out of the royal treasury. The importance of maintaining a close relationship with these governors was crucial to a king's success; without it, revolt and disquiet were inevitable. Any great monarch had to be the most skilful and charming of diplomats if he wished to avoid disaster.

The king's diplomacy began with his choice of allies, or at least coming to an understanding with those whom he hoped would remain neutral. He knew that the two European rulers who posed the greatest threat to him, either directly or as a result of their alliances, were Charles V of Spain and Henry VIII of England. Charles would eventually become his greatest nemesis but, in 1515, the fifteen-year-old Habsburg was a novice in the world of European statecraft and the labyrinthine manoeuvres required in order to gain the desired objectives. As for war, Charles had even less experience than Francis, being little more than an observer during any military action. Through the good offices of spies or sympathetic allies at Charles's court, Francis was informed that the young ruler's greatest desire was to regain the duchy of Burgundy.

Burgundy posed a complex problem in 1515. Its recent history had seen the rich and fertile duchy flourish, to become one of the most important in Europe, and it had allowed for development of thought, art and general sophistication. Lost to Louis XI on

5 January 1477, the duchy was then incorporated into France, but it continued to be challenged by Charles V, who had a claim via his great-grandmother, Mary the Rich. Francis considered Burgundy far too valuable to cede, but he understood the necessity of keeping Charles neutral. Accordingly a treaty was agreed in Paris on 24 March 1515 as a result of which Renée, the younger daughter of Louis XII, became betrothed to the future emperor; this would, at least unofficially, buy Charles's neutrality, if not his military assistance.

Relations with Henry VIII remained somewhat delicate for Francis, largely due to the continued presence at the French court of his favourite sister, the recently widowed Dowager Queen Mary. While Francis had continued to pursue his amorous intentions towards her in an opportunistic fashion – she complained that he had been 'importunate with her in divers matters not to her honour' – the complaint can at best be described as disingenuous, for Mary's fascination with Charles Brandon, the dashing Duke of Suffolk, had if anything grown since the death of her late husband a few months earlier. However, it was unlikely to have been consummated, as Brandon's ardour was kept in check by his terror at the thought of infuriating Henry and ending up with his head on the executioner's block. Despite their friendship, the English king had made Brandon swear an oath that he would not marry his sister, and openly planned to use her to form an alliance with another useful ruler. Francis, by now fully immersed in the Machiavellian world of underhand diplomacy, realised that Mary was a valuable asset, but one who could easily be neutralised. Hearing a rumour that Henry would have liked to see her marry the future Charles V, he adopted a pose of *naïveté* and said to Brandon: 'My Lord of Suffolk, there is a rumour you have come to marry the Queen, your master's sister.'[2]

Francis was helped by Mary's distrust of her brother; he might have promised her that she could choose her next husband, but she knew his untrustworthiness better than most. Therefore the French king played pander, promising Mary that he would use his diplomatic sway with Henry, and falsely assuring both Suffolk and Mary that they had nothing to fear from the English king's wrath. His efforts were undoubtedly persuasive, as they contracted a marriage

in Paris at the Hôtel de Cluny on 3 March 1515. However, Francis
had underestimated how poorly Henry would receive the news. For
Suffolk, no matter how close he was to Henry, marriage to a royal
princess without the king's permission was an act of *lèse-majesté*.
Once the news reached England, Cardinal Wolsey wrote to the
terrified bridegroom, not without relish, that 'the King has taken
the news grievously and displeasantly [*sic*]'. Brandon attempted to
offer his own defence, claiming, 'Sir, I never saw a woman so weep
. . . and the Queen would never let me rest till I had granted her to
be married.' It was possibly less tactful to announce that 'to be plain
with you I have married her heartily, and has [*sic*] lain with her, in
so much I fear me lest she be with child'. Henry's fury at the insult
that had been paid to both his house and his sister led to Wolsey
reporting back to Brandon with grim pleasure that 'You are in the
greatest danger that ever man was in.' Mary was now no longer
a marriageable prospect; no prince would want a twice-married
woman, especially if one of her husbands was a mere member of
the gentry. Anne of Brittany was very much the exception to this.

Francis therefore found himself in a position where he had to
be conciliatory to both parties, especially because he wished once
again to regain the territory of Tournai that had been lost to the
English in 1513. His own interests, such as they were, also involved
retaining some valuable jewels that Louis had given to Mary upon
their union, and which now once again lay in his possession. He informed Henry, tongue in cheek, that he was shocked that Mary, the
Dowager Queen of France, had taken 'a man of low condition' as her
husband, and that in consequence she had forfeited the jewels given
to her by Louis. However, Francis also agreed to pay a significant
part of Mary's dowry due after her marriage to Louis; her miserable
and degrading experiences with the grim old lecher meant that
few had earned that money in such personally humiliating circumstances. Henry, gratified by Francis's willingness to compromise,
made it known that he would therefore offer no opposition to his
counterpart's Milanese ambitions.

As for the transgressing couple, they had decided to return to
England. Matters did not go entirely as Francis had expected during
their departure. Mary proved herself the equal of the men she was

surrounded by when it came to cunning behaviour; she liberated several of the most prized pieces of the French crown jewels, including the legendary 'Mirror of Naples', one of the largest diamonds in the world. She sent it to Henry as a peace offering, and it worked; on 15 May 1515, Mary and Suffolk were formally married at Greenwich before Henry and the whole court. Francis, furious at the theft, demanded the return of the 'mirror', but Henry, claiming it was but 'a small thing', demanded an extortionate 60,000 crowns for its return, leaving the French king fuming at having been outmanoeuvred in this small but crucial way. As for the woman who might have borne the boy who would have supplanted him, for the rest of her life she was known as 'The French Queen'; her use of that title is likely to have been the only thing of any value that she gained from her brief and demeaning marriage.

By the early summer of 1515, Francis had completed his preparations for war, and was ready to lead his men across the border and into Lombardy. He appointed his mother as regent in his stead on 15 July, although she did not have total authority over the kingdom; her power was checked by the removal of the Great Seal, which travelled with the chancellor and meant that no government business could take place in its absence. Three days before, the king had arrived in Lyons to a spectacular welcome, as the city spared no expense or effort to welcome the new monarch. Arriving to find a ship being towed across the River Saône by a white stag, he entered the city beneath a gate bedecked with his personal emblem of the salamander. Entertainments on offer to his majesty included tableaux that showed him battling the Duke of Milan, Maximilian Sforza, and triumphing over him and his Swiss allies. Francis, still a young man, took delight in the colourful and costly pageantry, as well as many of the city's available women, some of whom had greeted him upon his entrance by standing on columns holding a letter of his name. This frivolity was all a distraction from the serious task at hand: invasion, and victory over a formidable foe.

His careful preparations for battle meant that he boasted a force of extraordinary size, namely an army that would be composed of nearly 40,000 men. It was comfortably the largest in Europe at the time, at least if everyone appeared at the right moment. His forces were traditionally strong in cavalry, especially the *compagnies d'ordonnance*, comprising heavily armoured men-at-arms, lightly clad archers and auxiliaries. However, these were supplemented by the infantry who had been 'volunteered' by the various nobles around his country; these men, the *aventuriers*, made up approximately half his forces, together with some 15,000 *Landsknechts* or mercenaries. They hailed from Germany and were known both for their extreme viciousness on the battlefield and their disreputable and unsoldierly behaviour off it. Francis was not in a position to be discerning in choosing who would fight on his side, and he was confident in the loyalty and efficiency of his troops. He was also proud of the artillery that his army possessed, consisting of around sixty guns of various calibres. Even if, by later standards, these were heavy and slow-moving, they were sure to inflict a remarkable degree of damage on the enemy, to say nothing of the psychological advantage they gave their own side.

He was not fighting alone. Venice and Genoa were both willing to come to his assistance and wage war upon their neighbour, the former because a history of difficult relations with the duchy of Milan and a pledge of French support sufficed to ally them with Francis, and the latter was a traditionally subservient French state because of its geographical position. However, Francis also faced an unexpected and unwelcome adversary in the form of 15,000 Swiss mercenaries. These soldiers were reputed to be the best in Europe because of their excellent training and state-of-the-art fighting equipment, and also could be bought by the highest bidder: there was a well-known saying, 'no money, no Swiss'.[3] There remained a lingering national grudge against Louis XII and his refusal to honour a peace treaty he had signed at Dijon, and when promised extensive land rights by the duchy, the mercenaries were only too happy to join the opposing side. This now consisted of Sforza, the Emperor Maximilian, Ferdinand of Aragon and Pope Leo X, all of whom formed a defensive alliance to uphold the legitimacy of the Sforza dynasty's claim to rule in Milan.

Of these, Ferdinand was motivated by his fear of Francis threatening the security of the decade-long Aragonese administration in

Naples. The others, meanwhile, took arms against their traditional enemy, the Republic of Venice, in equal measure to the French. There was also a personal grudge on the part of the pope, who was an altogether more difficult enemy because of the power he could yield.

Leo X, formerly Cardinal Giovanni de Medici, had been forced into exile during Charles VIII's 1494 invasion of Italy. In 1512, the Medici were firmly back in power, supported by the Italian states that had belonged to the Holy League against Louis XII. Giovanni's brother Giuliano was duly made ruler of Florence, and the next year Giovanni was elected to the papal throne in the conclave of 11 March 1513, following Julius II's death, and moved into the altogether more congenial surroundings of the Vatican, having first created his illegitimate cousin, Giulio, his chief administrator.

Francis understood that the alliance against him of the Emperor Maximilian, King Ferdinand of Aragon and the Medici pope with Sforza meant that a strenuous campaign lay ahead. Thus, his strategy was an innovative one. It was expected that, as was traditional, the French king would cross the Alps using either the Mont-Genèvre or the Mont-Cenis pass, and accordingly Swiss mercenaries heavily defended both. Instead, after he amassed his army at Grenoble on 30 July, Francis took the advice of his senior generals and headed instead for the far more obscure Col de Larche, which was mainly used by the braver local farmers when they drove their sheep and cattle between the lowlands and the highlands. Its perilous nature, due to frequent rockfalls, meant that few travellers chose it as their route to Piedmont, and so the Milanese and their allies had discounted it as a potential means of entry. Francis dispatched over 1,000 sappers to remove any rocks and boulders that might halt the advance of the cavalry and artillery, and their engineering skills ensured that they could construct crude wooden bridges to traverse rivers and streams. Nonetheless, embarking on this exceptionally difficult journey, Francis found it as challenging and tiring as his men did. He wrote to Louise that 'we are in the strangest country that any of us has ever seen, but I hope to reach the plain of Piedmont with my army tomorrow'. It proved difficult to wear protective armour since its weight impeded his soldiers' progress, and 'most of the time we have to go on foot, leading our horses by the bridle'.[4]

Arduous and terrifying though the odyssey undeniably was, complete with loss of valuable horses and soldiers, it also had heroic antecedents. One Venetian observer believed that the only historical event that might be compared to it was Hannibal's traverse of the Alps, and even as Francis cajoled and bullied his troops, he was aware of his own self-mythology, following in the footsteps of both Hannibal and Charlemagne.* An imminent victory would only further his reputation throughout Europe. Therefore, he was prepared to go without provisions and comforts for a short time; an especial privation was that he had to pass an entire two days without wine.

As he had sent some of the heavier artillery via the Mount-Genèvre pass, the Milanese and Swiss were fooled into believing that he was taking the traditional route. They were soon disabused of this when, in the third week of August, the army's vanguard had finished their alpine descent and led a surprise attack on the papal cavalry's base camp at Villafranca. With surprise on their side, the French captured 300 enemy soldiers and their cavalry as well as their commander, Prospero Colonna, an ageing feudal lord who at least retained his sense of humour in the face of adversity. When informed that he would be kept prisoner in France and held for ransom, he quipped: 'It is a country that I have always wanted to visit.' His men might have found the joke a hollow one. From now on the Swiss army would be composed exclusively of artillery and infantry, without any cavalry to support them.

Once Francis's entire army had reassembled at Piedmont, the king led his men on a rapid progress eastwards, with only a brief pause at Turin. He demanded that his troops behave with the utmost courtesy to the locals, any transgressions being punished by swift summary execution; his intention was to engender the trust of what he hoped would be his new people. Meanwhile, the Swiss, now outflanked and demoralised by the loss of their cavalry, retreated to Lake Maggiore. Francis, scenting capitulation, sent a peace emissary, led by his uncle René, 'The Great Bastard of Savoy'.

---

* As there was only room for one horse at a time, any beast that fell tumbled 'half a league'.

He offered the Swiss money, future military subsidy and an alliance, as long as they would aid him in his fight against the Milanese; in an unenviable situation, they agreed to begin negotiations. As an opening gesture of his sincerity, he sent the Swiss all the plate and money that he could find in the camp, amounting to a value of around 150,000 crowns. It was a gamble atop a gamble, but Francis had already wagered everything he owned; another speculation made little difference.

As the king continued his eastward advance, he united with the Venetian army at Lodi, to the south of Milan. He found himself sued for peace by the Ghibelline faction in the city, who were traditionally anti-papacy; however, their more powerful rivals, the pro-papist Guelfs, were not prepared to submit to any kind of invasion or deal, and they remained the dominant force within Milan. An easy and peaceful solution would not, it seemed, be reached. This contrasted with the Swiss, who, on 9 September 1515, agreed a deal that went beyond a simple treaty. In return for one million *écus* from the French, 150,000 of which was payable immediately, Francis would be allowed to raise as many Swiss troops as he wanted, provided that he undertook to assist his new allies with artillery and cavalry and gave a subsidy to each canton. The Swiss also stipulated that, given that it looked likely that Sforza would lose Milan without their support, he should receive the duchy of Nemours, a company of men-at-arms and a French royal princess as his bride. The deal was offered with a day's grace; if it lapsed, the opportunity would not be renewed. Not for nothing did Machiavelli refer to the Swiss as 'brutal, arrogant and victorious'.

These were steep terms; steeper, in fact, than a conquering king would have liked. However, Francis was intelligent enough to know that, despite his early military successes, he still faced a tough fight when it came to the capture of Milan, and only Swiss support could guarantee victory. And, of course, agreements and treaties seldom were worth more than the paper that they were written on. The king agreed to these conditions, and within a few hours he had collected 150,000 *écus* from those around him, to be sent within the agreed day's span to French officials who had been negotiating on his behalf.

To add to the confusion, only some of the Swiss accepted the peace terms. The Confederacy was a complex place and the negotiators were not able to impose the peace with any degree of uniformity across the cantons, meaning that those from the west accepted the deal and returned home, whereas those from the centre and east headed out to meet Francis in open combat. At midday on 13 September 1515 they left Milan under the command of Cardinal Matthäus Schiner, Bishop of Sion and leader of the aggressively militaristic Swiss faction. That morning the cardinal preached a rabble-rousing sermon in front of Milan Cathedral, in which he made the ungodly vow that 'I want to wash my hands and swim in French blood.'[5] No prisoners would be taken, save the king. They planned a surprise attack, and travelled swiftly and silently, with minimal fuss. An observer noted that 'most were without bonnets or shoes or armour'.[6]

Three days previously, Francis established his camp not far from the town of Marignano and Louis d'Ars, one of his senior commanders, was ordered to occupy Pavia. French military intelligence had meanwhile been engaged in a reconnaissance of the terrain and the king received a warning that the combined papal-Spanish army which had assembled at Piacenza was well placed to attack his forces from the rear. The battle royal that he had expected – even longed for – was now upon him, and its result would be decisive.

The remaining Swiss had the advantage of surprise, but as Thursday, 13 September, was an especially hot and dusty day, their footfall had the effect of scattering dust clouds, which meant that the French were given more notice than anticipated. As it happened, they had formed a defensive strategy in formation on a plain just outside Marignano, complete with light and heavy horse, artillery and massed infantry. A deep ditch and a line of sharp-shooting marksmen protected the artillery at its front and some 10,000 infantry did the same job at the flanks and to the rear. Francis's 10,000 *Landsknechts* were positioned to the rear and organised in a square formation in order to repel attacks from all directions. Their ranks included pikemen, halberdiers, two-handed swordsmen and those equipped with an arquebus capable of firing arrows at deadly speed. Just under 1,000 men-at-arms, cavalrymen in full body armour, were positioned behind the *Landsknechts*. France's royal standing army, collectively known as the *gendarmerie*, usually came under the king's direct command. On this bloody September day they had assembled, together with another group of *Landsknechts* numbering some 9,000, half a mile behind the front and at a point that became the central battlefield. Further to the south, one and a half miles to the rear, Francis's brother-in-law, Charles, Duke of Alençon, commander of the cavalry, waited for the signal to proceed to the battlefield. The end would soon come, one way or the other. Even with depleted numbers, the Swiss were still formidable adversaries.

The Battle of Marignano finally started at four o'clock in the afternoon. The first of three units of Swiss pikemen, each of which consisted of 7,000 men moving in a square formation, crossed the ditch and broke through the line of marksmen who were covering the artillery. The speed and viciousness of the enemy advance disorientated the French infantry utterly, and the Swiss captured fifteen guns almost immediately. Had their advance continued, they might well have taken the day. Yet they had reckoned without the bravery and ability of the *Landsknechts*, who advanced and engaged with the vicious Swiss. As 30,000 pikes clashed, the only sounds that could be heard above the noise of battle were the screams of the dying and wounded.

Some monarchs might have held back in their first major engagement and allowed their generals and captains to lead the charge. Not Francis. He knew that his moment had come, and that death or glory awaited. He donned steel armour from head to toe and led his army into battle himself, on an enormous warhorse with a blue and gold saddle, just as the Swiss sent their second column into the fray. Over and over again, the king's adversaries repelled cavalry attacks, never flagging or stopping; Francis later estimated that his troops had made thirty charges, but they were well matched by the grim indefatigability of the Swiss. Francis himself fought valiantly on horseback; it was said of him that he was 'an excellent man-at-arms and could handle a lance very well'.[7] His army needed every man they could muster, from royalty to the commonest peasant.

Nightfall did nothing to cease the fighting, as neither side was able to claim anything like victory, or even obvious superiority. By eleven in the evening the combat had descended into a confusing pell-mell of slaughter, the heavy dust meaning that each side was finding it hard to see whom they were hacking away at. Francis was magnificent in adversity, leading cavalry charges to save his artillery and fighting as if his life depended on it: which, in most regards, it did. Fleurange, although hardly an unbiased observer, wrote: 'The King was one of the finest captains in the whole army, and never left the artillery, rallying as many men as he could.'[8]

By midnight it became obvious that both sides were too exhausted to continue, and the moon had disappeared. Trumpets summoned the French-led force back to their camp and roaring horns recalled the Swiss from the battlefield, which was now a sodden mass of corpses and fatally wounded soldiers. In the confusion, soldiers on both sides blundered into the enemy camps to sleep alongside their foes. Many were too full of adrenaline to sleep, and some of the hardiest souls even attempted their own freelance engagements with the enemy as they waited for dawn and the resumption of wholesale slaughter.

Francis, too, was unable to rest. He had distinguished himself as both a military leader and a man-at-arms, but he knew that all his valour meant nothing unless it resulted in a decisive victory the following day. As he later wrote, 'We stayed by our horses, helmeted, lance in hand, all night long, the Landsknechts drawn up in battle order.'[9] As he leant against a nearby cannon for support, he concentrated on organising all his men into a single extended line, including those who had originally been positioned at the rear. He took no refreshment, spurning a proffered drink of water in a helmet as it was full of mud and blood. Instead, the king hoped and prayed for the arrival of the Venetian forces, led by Bartolomeo d'Alviano, the next day, as without them he feared that the Swiss would take the field. Meanwhile, Chancellor Duprat, perhaps understandably given the viciousness of the enemy, sent messengers to his officials ordering them not to hand over the agreed 150,000 écus to the Swiss negotiators since they had failed to deliver a comprehensive peace package. Francis also prepared for the possibility of defeat. He sent word to Louis d'Ars at nearby Pavia to continue to enforce its occupation, and to prepare in case a sudden retreat had to be made; even as he gave the order, he knew that the likelihood of leaving the battlefield was slim.

The battle resumed at daybreak on Friday, 14 September, with the competing sounds of horns and trumpets summoning the combatants to the fighting. The Swiss had 8,000 pikemen, divided into three squares, and two mounted cannon, which they flung at the French line with unparalleled intensity. Even one of the French squires allowed that 'no men ever fought better'.[10] After an hour of fighting, the Swiss had crossed the defensive ditch the French had constructed and then overwhelmed the infantry, prompting Francis to fight on foot, armed with a pike. Even the *Landsknechts* were challenged by the enemy at this dangerous stage, and news arrived that the left of the French line, commanded by the Duke of Alençon, was perilously close to collapsing. The infantry had scattered and the artillery was being threatened by the seemingly unstoppable Swiss. For a brief, panicked moment it seemed as if defeat was imminent. Alençon suffered a further indignity: his men began to retreat to Marignano, attempting to save themselves as the tide looked as if it was turning.

And then, as if in a great saga, events turned in Francis's favour. At eight o'clock, two hours after fighting had begun that day, a great cry of 'Marco! Marco!' was heard, striking terror into the Swiss and joy into the French and their allies. The Venetian forces of infantry and heavy cavalry, all 12,000 of them, had arrived in the nick of time, commanded by Bartolomeo d'Alviano. The combined forces of the French, Venetians and *Landsknechts* outnumbered the Swiss nearly three to one, and the end of the battle was imminent. Many of the adversaries were brave to the last, standing their ground until they were wiped out by cannon fire; others gathered their wounded and fled into Milan, unpursued by the French and Venetians who, weary of fighting, knew that their victory could now be finished by diplomatic means. By midday the fighting was finally over, and had resulted in a spectacular victory for Francis.

As the battle ended, a piece of theatre took place. Francis knelt before the Chevalier de Bayard and handed him his sword. Bayard was probably Francis's greatest hero, both as a soldier and as a knight of the chivalric ideal, who had distinguished himself in battle with typical dignity and courage.* Victorious and elated, the king asked his gallant warrior to knight him. Bayard protested that the King of France 'and the Church's eldest son' surely did not need to be knighted. Francis repeated the request and asked Bayard to make greater haste. The soldier knighted his kneeling sovereign, with various graceful references to Charlemagne's paladins. Those present, deeply moved, thought that the chevalier acted with great honour. They were even more touched by Francis's humility. The man who, a year ago, had been roistering in Paris taverns had now distinguished himself as a great military leader; his crown had been earned through his legendary victory. It was entirely deserved, then, that it would be with one of Milan's finest courtesans that he celebrated his victory that night.

Louise, Marguerite and Queen Claude had waited at home in agonised suspense until finally they received a letter from Francis, written the day after his victory. Proudly he announced: 'There has not been so fierce and cruel a battle these last 2,000 years.' He credited the royal *gendarmerie* and men-at-arms with their vital role in the victory, and saw this as their redemption, after being ridiculed for their retreat at the Battle of the Spurs in 1513, saying: 'never again [will they] be called "hares in armour"'.[11] Gravediggers reported that they buried over 16,000 bodies, and one general, Trivulzio, called Marignano 'a battle of giants', saying that every other of the seventeen battles he had fought in were 'children's games' by comparison.

As for France's opponents, the remaining Swiss marched back to their home country, and the defeated Cardinal Schiner took refuge with the emperor. The Duke of Milan, Maximilian Sforza, knew that all was lost, but Francis offered him extremely generous terms to surrender his duchy, namely an indemnity of 94,000 crowns, an

---

* Pierre Terrail, Chevalier de Bayard. Born in 1476 to a family of the lesser nobility of Dauphiné. A tactical genius and soldier of unswerving courage, Bayard probably lived his life closest to the Arthurian ideals of chivalry. He had a reputation for protecting the weak, courage, fidelity to his king and all the other lofty ideals that formed part of the chivalric model. Bayard had a well-known disdain for money and comforts, sleeping on a stone floor throughout the year.

annual pension of 36,000 crowns and a grand residence in France. It was certainly preferable to the terror and humiliation of a public execution and so, on 16 September 1515, Sforza surrendered the city and duchy of Milan to Francis. The relieved duke commented: 'I count myself the most fortunate of my family. When I was called Duke I was really only a slave to the Swiss, my masters, who did whatever they liked with me.'[12] Sforza lived in luxury for the next fifteen years, finally dying peacefully in 1530. Few other conquered lords could expect such generous treatment.

Yet it was in Francis's interests to exhibit both mercy and generosity. He had won a remarkable victory, a triumph of internal and external diplomacy that had established him as a military visionary and a wise and far-sighted ruler. He entered Milan on 16 October in a joyful and proud procession, adorned in blue velvet with decorations of fleurs-de-lys. Heading to the cathedral to give thanks, the contrast between his peaceful, regal exterior and the deranged and bloodthirsty frothing of Cardinal Schiner was noted by the Milanese, who seemed delighted with their new ruler. One commentator noted, possibly not without a touch of irony, that 'there was never prince in Italy who was better feasted by lords and ladies'.

The peace settlement that followed was as generous as could be expected. A substantial fine was imposed and every member of Milan's citizen body had to contribute towards its payment. This was levied on the grounds that the Milanese, in rejecting the legitimacy of Francis's right to rule, had been guilty of rebellion and disobedience. Although this was essentially nonsense, and made no distinction between the pro-peace Ghibellines and more aggressive Guelfs, the fine was paid; nobody wanted further bloodshed, especially not in the city streets. As for the Swiss, Francis needed to be far more circumspect, since their mercenary services would be required in future French campaigns. Having observed their fighting skills, he did not want to face them in battle again. With this in mind, he offered all the canton leaders subsidies, irrespective of their former loyalties. By 10 November, ten Swiss cantons had signed peace treaties with the French; the others remained loyal to the emperor, who offered them more money. Cash trumped principles when it came to these negotiations.

On a domestic note, Francis received the news that Claude had given birth to a daughter, whom the couple named Louise in honour of her grandmother. It was a disappointment that she had not produced the longed-for son and heir that he desired, but at least it proved that his unsightly wife was at least capable of childbirth. Typically of any monarch of the day, he did not bother to write to his queen, nor send her any gift or congratulation; it is unlikely that she would have expected any, especially given that she had failed to deliver the next French king.

If this was a disappointment, plenty more glad tidings awaited. The Doge of Genoa, hugely impressed by the victory, sent a deputation informing the king that he intended to surrender the Genovese Republic to Francis. In the year of 1515, the new arrival among European monarchs had become the toast of the leaders on the political stage. The king was generous to acknowledge the assistance of those around him, especially the canny Duprat, who was created Chancellor of Milan. The city's senate was revived, to include both French and Italian members, although this was largely a piece of theatre, and a nod in the direction of the great Roman emperors. Francis was flattered by comparisons of him to Caesar, which had once been made privately by his mother but now seemed to be on everyone's lips.

Appropriately enough, a medal was struck to celebrate the great occasion. It shows the twenty-one-year-old Francis in profile, looking regal and handsome, and wearing a plumed hat. It bore the legend: 'Françis I, King of the French and tamer of the Swiss.' A march was commissioned, and all France resounded with its stirring words: 'Victory to the noble King Francis! Victory to the gentleman of Valois!'

Francis's gamble had been successful, and assured his reputation. Yet he knew that one victory was not enough to maintain the status quo. There would be more battles and more wars, and it would take all his military and strategic prowess to win them, as well as luck. And, as every king was aware, sometimes good fortune was the hardest commodity of all to find. Had he known that Marignano was to be the high point of his military career – perhaps even of his reign – Francis might have been less inclined to celebrate.

CHAPTER 5

A Good and Honest Man

After his magnificent victory at Marignano, Francis lingered in Italy for the rest of 1515. Not only did he have administrative and logistical matters to settle, but he also wished to enjoy the full splendour of his triumph, rejoicing in his nickname of 'Le Roi Chevalier', or 'The Knight King'. It was preferable to his other, unofficial, nickname of 'François au Grand Nez', or 'Francis of the Big Nose'. As Louise, Claude and Marguerite, desperate to see their victorious Caesar once more, besieged him with requests for his return, Francis indulged them while continuing to see the best of what his new city could offer both him and France.

Although the king did not have the intellectual curiosity of his sister, he was anything but a stupid man, and the time that he spent in Italy from 1515 onwards coincided with the birth in France of what would become known as the Renaissance. Francis could see that a new strain of culture and thought was manifesting itself in southern Europe, and he began to realise that he could enhance his own prestige by cultivating the scholars, artists and great thinkers of the day. Not only did this offer him the thrill of novelty and the glamour of fashion, but it meant that he could reinvent himself as a ruler. His military success and reputation in battle were assured, and remained dear to him. Yet he understood that kingship was not merely a matter of swinging weapons around until they collided with the nearest unfortunate torso. Instead, he decided that his reign would be one that encompassed both the body's strength and the mind's art, reinventing his country in the process.

Key to this mixture of intellect and force was the complex relationship that Francis had to maintain with other European leaders.
One of these figures was Pope Leo X, hitherto his opponent in battle.
The head of the Medici family, Leo was a shrewdly practical man
who feared that Francis would seek to capitalise on his Milanese
conquest by marching on Florence with the intention of occupying
it and unseating the Medici. However, the king had no intention
of doing this, not least because Leo was in a considerably stronger
position than Sforza had been. The pope was both a spiritual and
military leader who was not just Christ's representative on earth,
but possessed the powers of a monarch in his guise as ruler of the
papal states. Not only did this mean that the pope's papal tiara
placed him above kings and emperors, and ensured that he was the
possessor of a vast amount of land, but he also had the right to legal
jurisdiction throughout Catholic countries, whose citizens bent the
knee to the Ecclesiastical Court. Therefore, Leo knew that monarchs across Europe required papal support for their legitimate rule
if they were to have any chance of long-term success.

As Francis basked in his new prestige as ruler of Milan, he knew
that a single victory, however magnificent, did not answer the question of his territorial ambitions. The slaughter of their countrymen
meant that large numbers of the Swiss, who had buried brothers,
fathers and sons, remained hostile. As for Henry VIII, matters
with Mary and her marriage had only been uneasily resolved, if
at all, and the English king, who was jealous of Francis's military
success and given to rash and impetuous acts, might easily forge an
alliance with the Emperor Maximilian. Therefore a concord with
the papacy, especially if it might assist with Francis's further Italian
ambitions, needed to be reached, and quickly, before a decidedly
unholy alliance of France's enemies could unite against him.

The question of Naples was an especially pressing one. Ferdinand
of Aragon, the aged and ailing ruler of the city, had become 'apoplec-
tic and tremulous' upon receiving the news of Francis's capture of
Milan. His victory had unsettled the entire peninsula, which now
feverishly speculated on who would be the next man in charge. It
was not, however, simply a question of choice. For centuries the
papacy had exercised complete, if at times notional, suzerainty over

Naples and the decision as to who should become the next ruler of the kingdom would fall to Pope Leo. Francis, who wished to expand his conquests, realised that he needed to charm the pope, rather than wage war upon him, in order to achieve his desired goals.

Thus the two men, each of whom wanted something significant from the other, engaged in a process of diplomatic niceties that saw relations between them conducted with an unusual amount of goodwill and courtesy; they might have been planning a marriage settlement, so intricate was the flattery involved. It worked, and a deal was reached. Firstly, a treaty was agreed, and then Francis promised the duchy of Nemours, along with a large pension, to Leo's brother Giuliano, as well as the hand in marriage of the king's aunt, Philiberta of Savoy. The pope's nephew Lorenzo II de Medici, a feckless and spoilt youth, was also to receive a substantial annual pension from the French treasury, as well as marriage to the orphaned Bourbon heiress Madeleine de La Tour d'Auvergne. In return Leo awarded Parma and Piacenza to Francis. Both sides professed themselves happy with this arrangement, but two issues remained. The first was what would happen to Naples, and the second, more complex, one was the Pragmatic Sanction of Bourges. The Sanction, which had been in place since 1438, limited the papacy's influence within France in favour of the monarchy; the top ecclesiastical offices were in the gift of the king, who also had the right to impose and collect taxes upon the Church.

Francis, who took the attitude that the Church was his domain as much as anything else in his country, was following the belief of Gallicanism, which held that an autonomous Church of France was the desirable outcome for both country and ruler. However, the papacy, fearing the waning of its own influence in a major territory, was opposed to such a development. In less than two decades, events in England would lead to even greater trouble for the Catholic Church but, for the time being, an amicable compromise of sorts seemed the only option. A meeting was arranged in Bologna, which lay within the papal territories, and Francis arrived in the city on 11 December 1515. He lodged at the Palazzo Pubblico, beneath the papal apartments, in an arrangement designed to show stability and trust on both sides.

The usual lavish preparations for welcoming a monarch had been made for Francis's entry into the city. Streets and buildings were richly festooned with hanging garlands and tapestries, and colourful carpets hung from the windows as he passed by. As if to show the full pageantry and ceremony of the Church, the cardinals sported their crimson capes, standing on the balconies and waving, even as they privately wondered who this man was. Francis, by now quite a fashionable figure, donned an impressive outfit of black velvet and silver brocade, but he was no fop. His personal body-guard of 300 archers saw to it that those around him had no doubt that he was a man of action, above all other things. The Bishop of Worcester, who was present, described the event in a letter to Henry VIII. Mindful of his master's jealousy of the French king,* he took pains to make the grand entrance sound unimpressive; he wrote that Francis's arrival created no more stir than that of a re-turning city official, and described the royal bodyguard as 'looking like bargees wearing greasy, threadbare coats'. However, the day could only be fictionalised so much. As Francis dismounted, even the bishop had to admit that, 'like waves of the sea', the surging crowds nearly engulfed the king, who, flanked by several cardinals, hastened into the papal palace.[1]

The next day, Francis and Leo met for the first time. Even though the French monarch was clad in a sable-lined gown of gold brocade, he was no match in sartorial splendour for the pope, whose papal tiara, festooned with jewels, and lavish gem-studded golden surcoat made him look near-divine. This was, of course, the intention, and served to compensate for his unprepossessing physical appearance; not only was he grossly overweight, but he was afflicted by a stom-ach ulcer and anal fistula, which caused him to emit unsavoury odours, to the consternation and barely concealed disgust of those around him.

Introduced to Leo sitting upon his throne, surrounded by his

---

* When Henry heard of Francis's victory at Marignano, a French envoy, Mon-sieur. Baupaume, recounted that 'it seemed tears would flow from his eyes, so red were they with the pain he suffered on hearing of the King's good tidings and success'.

cardinals, Francis genuflected three times and kissed the papal toe, only for Leo to respond by affectionately kissing the Frenchman on the mouth, startling him and causing him to step backwards. The sheer weight of both man and garb nearly made Leo topple over, but Francis, with customary speed and dexterity, rescued the pope and restored him to his throne. What might have been either a disastrous or farcical first encounter was thus saved, and the cheers that arose came as much out of relief as expected courtesy. Fleurange later wrote that the pope 'looked like a truly good and honest man . . . and he gave the King wonderfully good cheer'.

It seemed as if the meeting of the two leaders was a propitious one, both men being equally delighted with each other's company. Francis's emerging aesthetic and artistic interests found their obvious match in the Medici pope, who was a cultured man of enormous sophistication, belying his gross appearance. Nonetheless, Leo had a lighter side that encompassed practical jokes and displays of levity, such as banquets in which tiny birds flew out of pies. The lavishness of the welcome was both a grand show and a sincere expression of the papal sensibilities; in this Leo resembled his father, the great Medici ruler Lorenzo the Magnificent, who had nicknamed his son 'The Wise'. Leo was a worthy heir to him in both an appreciation of beauty and sharpness of mind. The talks between the pope and Francis consisted of witty repartee, deep Humanist and intellectual discussion and simple realpolitik. History does not record which topic dominated.

Due in part to the warmth of the relationship between the king and pope, an agreement was reached by 14 December on how the Church in France should be run in future. The Pragmatic Sanction was to be repealed and would be replaced by a Concordat whose terms limited the French monarchy's role in appointing the higher clergy. Francis assented to this, and also to lending his support for a papal crusade against the Turks; the expenses were to be raised by a special levy upon the French clergy of a tenth of their income. Finally, the most pressing issue, the question of Naples, was dealt with mainly in euphemism and hints. Leo suggested, without committing himself to any action, that Francis might be given Naples after the death of Ferdinand of Aragon, in return for his

continued support of the Medici family in Florence. It was thus tac-
itly suggested that French territorial ambitions would never include
crossing the Medici.

Francis agreed to these conditions, promising to assist the pope's
brother, Giuliano de Medici, whom he had just created Duke of
Nemours, in maintaining his rule over Florence. In addition to this
commitment, Francis, with rather less enthusiasm, pledged to help
the pontiff's indolent nephew Lorenzo II de Medici in his efforts to
seize Urbino and become duke of the small but strategically important state perched in the Apennine mountain range. If Francis felt
that this lay beneath his dignity – he privately referred to Lorenzo
as 'only a tradesman'² – he could at least console himself with the
knowledge that he had behaved both regally and diplomatically, and
that a potential enemy had now become a useful ally. The strength
of the bond, as well as the potential for future difficulty, could be
seen by their parting exchange. Leo proposed as a gift to the king a
diamond reliquary, containing one of the many supposed fragments
of the True Cross, but Francis instead requested an antique Baroque
sculpture of the Laocoön, depicting a Trojan priest and his two sons
gripped in the terrible coils of a mighty serpent*, before each bestowed on the other their own brand of religious favour. The pope
offered the king absolution, but asked in turn that he might 'touch'
for the king's evil – a power, Leo noted, that not even he possessed.

Francis left Bologna on 15 December, pleased with what had been
achieved and what he had been given. The pope's entourage noted
that the royal gifts had been less generous, including a comparatively
trifling 100 crowns for the papal master of ceremonies. While Francis had not been confirmed as Duke of Naples, Ferdinand remained
alive and it would have been diplomatically indecent to make a grab
for the duchy. Given that Naples was a highly contested prize, it
seemed better to ascertain the strength of the competition first while

---

* This sculpture, which was hugely expensive, was chosen by Francis, and left
Leo in a state of some distress at its loss. The first craftsman whom he asked to
make a copy of it was a sixty-three-year-old painter who refused the commission:
none other than Leonardo da Vinci. Eventually an inferior copy was made, and
conflicting accounts exist as to whether this was sent to Francis or retained by
Leo.

trusting in the pope's tacit support in the long term. Milan had been a swift, highly effective victory. Now it was time for Francis to exhibit patience and to consolidate his existing power. In an excellent humour, he returned to his new possession, where he surprised and delighted the populace by remitting the fine he had levied on them, released the hostages from gaol and summoned the exiles home, offering a pardon for any wrongs committed. As the relieved Milanese swore allegiance to him, Francis placed his loyal general Charles de Bourbon as lieutenant-general in his stead. This was a wise choice, as Bourbon combined military intelligence with administrative prowess, and was well placed to suppress any trouble that might arise. The king, satisfied with the totality of his victory, prepared to meet those whom he loved best: his sister and his mother.

Louise and Marguerite, along with the less significant figure of the king's wife, Queen Claude, were frustrated at not being able to see the conquering hero. They therefore decided to travel south in the autumn with a suitably grand retinue, with the intention of giving Francis the welcome that he deserved. They departed Amboise on 20 October 1515, eventually arriving at Sisteron in Provence on 13 January 1516. Before the long-looked-for reunion the royal women made a pilgrimage to Saint-Maximin-la-Sainte-Baume, near Lyons, where Lazarus, Martha and Mary Magdalene were said to have lived out their last days in a dank cave. The symbolism of their visit there was no less compelling than that of Francis taking absolution from Pope Leo X.

The eventual reunion between the four was as happy and celebratory as could be imagined. Louise poured out her feelings of relief at seeing her son again and wrote in her journal: 'God knows how I, a poor mother, was comforted to see my son safe and sound after all the hardship he had suffered and endured for the common good.'[3] The reunion of Claude and her husband, meanwhile, resulted in another pregnancy, and the birth of another daughter, Charlotte, on 23 October 1516. Inspired by his family's journey, Francis set out on 21 January 1516 to make his own pilgrimage to Saint-Maximin, although stories were whispered of his ungodly behaviour. It was rumoured that, in the small town of Manosque, he chanced his arm

with the daughter of one of the leading citizens and she, desperate
to fend him off, defaced her beautiful face with a hot dish. Yet his
reception elsewhere was a warmer one, and his entry into Marseilles later in the month, when he was greeted by 2,000 white-clad
children and 4,000 men-at-arms, was nothing less than he seemed
to deserve.

It would be the beginning of October before Francis and his
court were back in Paris; he and his men were based at Lyons from
the end of February before they travelled throughout the Loire over
the summer months. Since his departure, French governmental
business had all but ground to a standstill, and the king's arrival
both delighted his subjects and showed them that it was once again
to be business as usual. Yet the king had not been idle, but was instead preoccupied by international developments, most notably the
longed-for death of Ferdinand of Aragon on 23 January 1516. It was
rumoured that his demise occurred because of 'dropsy occasioned
by a beverage which Germaine, his wife, had given him, to enable
him to beget children',[4] but whatever the old king's cause of dying,
the issue of the succession to Naples now arose.

Ferdinand's grandson, the Archduke Charles, was nominated
in his will to be his heir, thereby inheriting his grandfather's kingdoms of Castile, Aragon and Naples. Allied to his existing kingdoms
of the Netherlands and Franche-Comté on the French-Swiss border,
he would be a significant figure, not least because he was France's
most powerful neighbour. Francis, seeing the potential both for
trouble and for obtaining the coveted territories, set about reminding Leo of their agreement and his implied obligations. Charles
was the nominated heir of a dead king, but Francis believed he had
found a solution that would benefit his own ambitions.

The benefit of advantageous marriages contracted for political
gain could continue long beyond the death of one or both of the
partners. Louis XII had ceded his own claim to the Neapolitan kingdom to his niece, Germaine de Foix, Ferdinand's second wife, but
with a condition attached: the marriage had to produce children.
As none were sired, Francis, as Louis' nearest male relative, therefore reasserted the French claim to Naples. He hoped that his new
friend Leo would now publicly endorse his right to do so, and acted

accordingly, releasing the Italian general Prospero Colonna from captivity on the understanding that Colonna would show support for Francis's claim.

Francis had no wish to make an enemy of Charles, who in turn was aware that his own situation was a precarious one, especially when it came to the territories of Castile and Aragon. These favoured a return to self-government, and patrician revolt seemed imminent in many of the Castilian towns, so Charles had to head south of the Pyrenean border in order to quell these separatist murmurings and demonstrate both his right to rule and his potential kingship. He knew that he was a comparative novice when it came to matters of state in Europe, and in order to make a success of his territorial ambitions he needed French support. This would be offered in the usual conditional fashion: upon a marriage.

On 13 August, at Noyon, the two rulers signed a treaty. Louise, Francis and Claude's infant daughter, was promised in marriage to Charles (as a substitute for Louis XII's younger daughter Renée) and it was agreed that Naples would form part of her dowry. Before then, Charles had undertaken to pay Francis an annual tribute of 100,000 *écus* in respect of Naples, thereby implicitly agreeing to his claim. Francis had also advanced the case of Jean d'Albret, King of Spanish Navarre, who had lost his territory in Ferdinand's military offensive of 1512. It suited Francis for Navarre to be independent – and favourably disposed towards him – and he had promised d'Albret that 'the hour has come when you must exercise extreme diligence to recover your kingdom, and I for my part wish to help you in every possible way'.[5] D'Albret had since died, but the beleaguered Charles agreed to make a compensation payment to his widow, Catherine.

Francis was also fortunate in his choice of enemies. The bloodthirsty Cardinal Schiner, who had been plotting in Vienna, convinced Emperor Maximilian that the population of Milan was ready to rebel against its French rulers, aided by the defeated Swiss cantons and Henry VIII, who remained furious at Francis's success. This was mere fantasy, and although Maximilian duly led an army into Lombardy in March 1516 and forced the French to flee to Milan, 8,000 Swiss mercenaries, who had previously signed a peace agreement with Francis, arrived in typically belligerent

mood. Maximilian, frightened at the prospect of a second Marignano, fled, his tail between his legs. This led to the ratification of a
treaty, agreed in Fribourg in 1516, of 'perpetual peace', whereby, in
exchange for a total of a million *écus* and an annual pension of 2,000
écus per canton, the Swiss would not support France's enemies in
France itself or in Milan, and Francis would be able to levy any
troops that he wished, with the proviso that they were not called
upon to fight the Holy Roman Emperor.

As 1517 dawned, Francis's reputation seemed assured. The
strength of his relationship with Leo was well known throughout
Europe; there was a saying, muttered by the English envoys, that
'the Pope is French [as is] everything from Rome to Calais'. Raphael
and his pupils completed a fresco, *The Oath of Leo III*, which showed
Leo III with the face of his successor being rewarded for his piety,
while a figure carrying a crown behind him was none other than
Francis. There were other, more scurrilous rumours that touched
upon the perceived sexual preferences of the pope, but Francis's
dedication to heterosexuality in all its many forms meant that
nobody but a fool would have dared to suggest any sodomitical
inclinations on his part.

Even his former adversary Maximilian seemed to acknowledge
that there was little to be achieved by opposing the force of nature
that was the French king. Besides, there was much to be gained by
fooling Henry VIII into thinking that he was planning an attack
on Francis, not least an advance of 75,000 crowns. As he later said
to Charles, 'You're going to fool the French and I'm going to fool
the English.'[6] On 11 March 1517 he, along with Francis and Charles
V, signed the Treaty of Cambrai. Although this was theoretically
an equal partnership, the momentum remained with France, and
the tokenistic nature of the agreement was indicated by the secret
clauses. As the main treaty made the usual claims about mutual
support in the event of an attack and a joint commitment to an
anti-Turkish crusade, to satisfy Leo's persistent urgings,* there was

---

* While they conceded that there would eventually have to be a coordinated
response to the Turkish aggression, domestic priorities remained the overwhelming ones.

skulduggery in the shape of an agreement to divide up the Italian peninsula between the three great powers, largely at Venice's expense. How seriously Francis took this was shown when he renewed his alliance with the Venetians in October that year.

The French king could have been forgiven for feeling hubristic. Still only twenty-three, he had restored French national pride, conquered Milan, was occupying Genoa and had every chance of inheriting Naples. After Cambrai, he had a formal peace treaty with his two greatest potential adversaries, to say nothing of a warm personal relationship with the pope. The only European monarch of any stature who was not content with the status quo was Henry VIII, but Francis knew that his canny cardinal, Thomas Wolsey, was unwilling to let the king drag the country into an expensive and fruitless foreign war, and was instead exploring back-channels that would see a peace treaty negotiated the following year in London. This mood of confidence and happiness had spread throughout France; Duprat's secretary, Jean Barillon, wrote that 'there was great peace and tranquillity in the kingdom of France, and no noise or rumour of war, division of partisanship . . . this was a great favour bestowed by Christendom'.

However, Francis had made one critical error which would come to define the rest of his reign: this was to underestimate Charles V. In 1517 the newly crowned King of Spain was merely a boy who often seemed out of his depth. He had run into financial difficulties almost straight away, being unable to pay Francis the annual tribute to Naples agreed at the Treaty of Noyon, and with the ongoing question of the Navarre possession unresolved. He neither could nor would pay Catherine d'Albret her compensation, but had to tread lightly between the northern kingdom's dispossessed ruling class, who wished for a restoration of Navarre's independence, and the Castilian aristocracy, who believed that the loss of Navarre would endanger the security of all Spain. Charles needed to exert the greatest diplomatic skill to retain his throne, which he began to do by prevailing upon Ferdinand of Aragon's widow, Germaine de Foix, to cede her claim to Navarre over to him in August 1518. This answered the immediate question of his dynastic right to rule in Navarre, but support for Charles among the political elite in Castile and Aragon remained at best lukewarm. This meant that it was important for him to maintain good diplomatic relations with Francis: the alternative, namely a war in defence of his right to Navarre, would be both expensive and potentially catastrophic, as a military defeat would embolden his courtiers to attempt to overthrow him. Therefore Francis had to be kept amenable, and, in a masterstroke of diplomacy, Charles asked to be allowed to marry his and Claude's infant daughter Charlotte; his previous fiancée, their eldest daughter Louise, had died at the age of two in September 1517. The request was granted, purely for diplomatic reasons.

Francis was an intelligent man, and skilled in the ways of the world. Yet his indulgence of Charles proved, in retrospect, to be his great undoing. He would have a great deal of time to muse upon the folly of his actions in due course, in circumstances that he, at the peak of his success, could scarcely have imagined.

CHAPTER 6

A New King of France

As Francis hoped to establish himself as one of France's greatest kings, there was much interest in both his appearance and character. As befitted a military hero, he was a large man of muscular standing, although his prominent nose and surprisingly bandy legs seemed incongruent with such a physique. One visitor to the French court, Antonio de Beatis, wrote of him in August 1517: 'The King is very tall, well featured and has a pleasant disposition, cheerful and most engaging, though he has a large nose, and in the opinion of many . . . his legs are too thin for so big a body.'[1]

Francis took great delight in dressing sumptuously, whether he was participating in a grand ceremonial event or simply preparing for an everyday occurrence. He could be likened to a magnificent bird, given that he loved colour and splendour in all their forms; his rich cloaks of ermine were trimmed with gold and lined with herons' feathers. He embellished his clothing, which was fastened with gold buckles and brooches, with a dazzling array of pearls and diamonds; his love of ornamentation and the eye-catching could be seen in the rich jewels that festooned his body at all times. The impression that he wished to give was that of a man who not only caught the eye, but sparkled while he did so, even extending to his personal effects. His writing desk was set in gold, he carried mirrors and looking glasses made of crystal and studded with emeralds, and the books in his library were clasped with silver and bound in velvet.

Yet, despite this love of ostentation, it was Francis's cheerful and engaging character that served him well. He was given to expressions of bawdy humour, especially as a younger man; it was reported without pleasure that Francis and his followers would speed 'daily disguised through Paris, throwing eggs, stones and other foolish trifles at the people, which light demeanour of a king was much discommended and jested at'. Yet he could also be subtle in his wit, with a satirical edge; de Beatis reported, with some surprise, that Francis claimed that he dared not visit Brittany because of the ferocity of its inhabitants. The implied joke was probably a dig at the mild-mannered Queen Claude, but it was one that de Beatis did not fully appreciate. Yet underneath the humour and eloquence lurked a surprising initial shyness; the English courtier Sir Thomas Cheney said of him: 'If a man speak not to him first, he will not likely begin to speak to him, but when he is once entered, he is as good a man to speak to as I ever saw.'[2]

Perhaps to compensate for this shyness, he displayed itinerant habits, which saw him travel throughout his kingdom restlessly, never lingering in any one place for more than a few months at a time. One Venetian ambassador wrote that 'Never, during the whole of my embassy, was the court in the same place for fifteen consecutive days'.[3] Some of the places visited early in his reign included Normandy and Picardy in 1517, Anjou and Brittany in 1518 and Cognac and his ancestral domain, Angoulême, in 1519. He travelled with a sizeable court that comprised as many as 10,000 people, including everyone from troops, merchants and court officials to mistresses, private secretaries and, of course, the royal family, to say nothing of their animals. French tradition had it that the capital of the country was wherever the king was resident, which meant that humble places could be elevated by the royal presence. As the goldsmith, writer and artist Benvenuto Cellini wrote in 1540, 'We sometimes danced attendance in places where there were hardly two houses, were often under the necessity of pitching inconvenient tents, and lived like gypsies.'[4] These gypsies were unusually well catered for, thanks to the dozens of supply wagons that travelled in the wake of the royal entourage, carrying wine, food and all the luxuries of the day. As Pierre de Bourdeille, Seigneur de Brantôme, put it, the travellers suffered no hardship, even if the accommodation that anyone other than the king and his ladies could expect was basic: '[the tables] were very well supplied, and lacked nothing . . . whether in a village or in the forest, the assembly was served as well as if one had been in Paris'. Francis was not a man who would happily stint on creature comforts.

Although he did not possess Marguerite's towering intellect, he was far from stupid, either in terms of diplomacy or in his appreciation of the arts and literature. Not only was he a fluent and witty correspondent, especially as far as his mother was concerned, but he wrote a number of poems in ballad form and as shorter *épitaphes*, although, given the difficulty of correct attribution, it is likely that many other contemporary poems have been erroneously ascribed to him. He was not publicly recognised as a poet in his lifetime (no collection of his work was published until the nineteenth century, and then inaccurately), but some of his verses were set to music by the royal composers of the day, such as Claudin de Sermisy and Clément Janequin.

Yet although his own artistic achievements were essentially modest, he was a man who was keen to present himself as a patron of the intellectual arts. Before Francis's accession, French kings had shown little interest in Renaissance and Humanist culture. It was he who saw how an artistic revival could be channelled in a way that would bring glory and prestige to the monarchy. The first opportunity for this took place in 1517, when Europe was temporarily (and unusually) at peace. Inspired by his travels throughout Italy, particularly his visits to Medici-ruled Florence and papal Rome, he attempted to move beyond his traditional image of *le roi chevalier* and to embrace the Italian concept of *l'uomo universale*. Not for nothing had he adopted his mother's adoring description of him as 'my Caesar'. He would be a new kind of French monarch, one as much influenced by Humanism and philosophical ideas as by battle strategies and complex diplomacy, and to this end he set about making the French court a place where the arts and learning were not just tolerated, but encouraged in all their forms.

His ambition was boundless. Inspired by his early lessons with Christophe de Longueil and Francis Desmoulins de Rochefort, he attempted to gather Europe's greatest minds at his court and to employ them in various capacities, whether as tutors, gentlemen-in-waiting or general scholars. Sometimes Francis's interests verged on the esoteric, even the crankish. He was intrigued by the occult sciences, such as alchemy and Kabbalah, which were held to contain the secrets of the universe, and was almost childishly impressed by anyone who claimed to be able to unlock them. When the Italian philosopher Giulio Camillo visited Paris, Francis was fascinated by his so-called 'theatre of memory', which seemed to offer an explanation for the world's conscious and unconscious workings alike. The king paid Camillo 500 crowns to divulge his secrets to him, but it has not been recorded whether Francis subsequently reached a higher plane of consciousness.

Likewise, Francis's enthusiasm could sometimes get the better of him. When, in 1518, he asked the philosopher Jean Thenaud to explain the secrets of Kabbalah to him in a treatise, Thenaud refused, later acidly commenting in his 1519 work *La Cabale métrifiée* (The Composition of Kabbalah) that 'it is far better to be ignorant than to ask or look for what cannot be known without sinning'. Even the king's ample gifts could only go so far in his quest for intellectual enlightenment; another disappointment was the philosopher Erasmus's refusal to become chancellor of a college for the study of classical languages, to be founded in Paris, although Erasmus was tactful enough to decline on the grounds of his age and wish to remain in his home of the Netherlands. He wrote to Francis that 'France has always smiled on me, but so far I have been detained by any number of obstacles.'[5]

Nonetheless, other brilliant minds were happier presences at court. His secretary, former tutor and eventual Master of the King's Library, Guillaume Budé, was an especially important influence. Budé was a former lawyer and bon viveur who had abandoned the bottle for books; on intimate terms with the greatest minds within Europe, including Rabelais, Thomas More and Erasmus; he wrote on a dazzling variety of subjects, including mathematics, law and history. Unlike Francis, Budé had no interest in esoteric religious cults, being a committed Christian; instead he impressed upon his master the importance of 'arms and letters', by which he meant that no king without deep classical and scriptural learning could hope to be a true monarch. This was revelatory, even subversive thinking, but Francis was sufficiently impressed to have Budé remain a central figure at his court, and trusted him enough to use him on several diplomatic missions that required an intellectual's finesse.

It was a mark of royal prestige to attract great men of other nations to one's country, and Francis scored a spectacular coup by wooing to France none other than Leonardo da Vinci. Da Vinci had been resident at the court of Giuliano de Medici, the less-impressive brother of Giovanni, Pope Leo X, but after Giuliano's death in 1516 the then sixty-three-year-old polymath faced an uncertain future. Francis, who had been captivated by his painting *The Last Supper*, which he saw at the Friary of Santa Maria delle Grazie in Milan, probably first encountered da Vinci when he visited Pavia in 1515, after the Battle of Marignano. He had tried to acquire da Vinci's painting at enormous expense and inconvenience, but the impossibility of removing it from a wall meant that it had to remain in Milan. Nonetheless, if he could not have the art, he would do his very best to have the artist instead.

Francis initially asked da Vinci to 'devise some unusual entertainment' to impress him, and so the great man 'constructed a lion, which, after walking a few steps, opened its breast to reveal a cluster of lilies'.[6] This piece of ingenuity had the desired effect, and so Francis offered the artist an annual pension of 700 gold crowns, the use of the Château du Clos Lucé, near the royal palace of Amboise, and the admiration of the court. Da Vinci was both flattered and wary, and 'for a long time put [Francis] off with more words'.[7] In the end, professional jealousy swayed him; believing that his rival Michelangelo was in greater favour with the pope, he agreed to travel to France, taking with him his servants, notebooks and some of his greatest paintings, including none other than the *Mona Lisa*.

Once Leonardo arrived in late 1516, Francis lost no time in honouring him. The king said: 'No one in the world knows so much as Leonardo',[8] and gave him the honorific title of 'First Painter, Engineer and Architect to the King'. He had no official responsibilities other than to make daily conversation with Francis. While the monarch might have hoped for another *Last Supper*, it was apparent that da Vinci, by now paralysed in his right arm, was no longer capable of any complex works of art – as de Beatis wrote, 'No more masterpieces can be expected' – although his ability to produce architectural sketches and ideas remained unimpaired. His thoughts and opinions about painting and sculpture enthralled and delighted Francis, who considered that his investment in the great man had been highly worthwhile; as he later reported to Benvenuto Cellini, da Vinci knew more about art and architectural design than any other man alive.

The artist spent his last years in contented retirement in Amboise, eventually dying at Clos on 2 May 1519. There is a fine story about how he died in Francis's arms, da Vinci breathing his last words into the enraptured and sorrowful king's breast, but unfortunately the tale is a fiction: Francis was celebrating the arrival of his much-anticipated second son, Henri, at nearby Saint-Germain-en-Laye at the time. His response to da Vinci's death would undoubtedly have been one of sorrow, but also of pragmatism; he set about acquiring many of Leonardo's masterpieces, including *The Virgin of the Rocks*, *St John* and, of course, the *Mona Lisa*, which soon joined the royal collection. There they were displayed alongside such diplomatic gifts as Raphael's *St Michael Slaying the Demon* and *Joanna of Aragon*, by Raphael and his pupil Giulio Michael.

Other artists were invited to join the royal court, such as Michelangelo and Fra Bartolommeo, but were less tempted by the munificent pensions and annuities offered. One who was lured by lucre was the young Italian artist Andrea del Sarto, whose painting *Christ Being Supported by Angels* had deeply impressed Francis. Shortly after da Vinci's death, in 1518 del Sarto was offered the role of royal painter, along with a substantial allowance. Many courtiers, noting that he stood in the king's favour and wishing to be in the vanguard of fashionable opinion, decided that they needed a del Sarto canvas commissioned. His earnings (which included being paid 300 gold crowns to paint the recently-born Dauphin Francis) were considerable, but then so were his debts: his wife was a legendarily extravagant woman and, tiring of her husband's absence, summoned him home to Florence. Del Sarto promised Francis that he would return to the French court in the near future, accompanied by his wife, but once he was in Italy he squandered the money that Francis had given him in order to buy Italian paintings and sculptures intended for the French court, and never returned. A furious Francis, chastened by this betrayal of his hospitality, 'for a long time looked askance at Florentine painters, and he swore that if Andrea ever fell into his hands he would have more pain than pleasure, in spite of all his ability'.

An area in which Francis was able to exert greater authority, with no danger of its practitioners fleeing to Italy and to their wives, was architecture. He had grown up in the grand châteaux of Amboise and Blois in the Loire Valley, and commissioned a great deal of rebuilding work, following in the footsteps of Louis XII and Charles VIII; his improvements would be seen by posterity as the most significant. At Amboise, these mainly took the form of decorative enhancements, but at Blois, which he had given to Queen Claude upon becoming king, he decided to build a new wing, and commissioned the work in June 1515. Blois had been a royal château ever since 1391 and, as Louis XII's favourite residence, it became a focus for the exercise of political power; therefore Francis's decision was as much a practical demonstration of his strength as a desire to be uxorious.

The new wing was influenced, as was much of the king's taste, by Italian design, albeit more in terms of decoration than in structure. The edifice looked out onto the gardens, which had been designed by the Italian Fra Pacello da Mercogliano and were lavishly decorated with fountains and pavilions; its dual-storeyed loggias gave the façade an appearance that would not have been out of place in Rome. Yet the French medieval tradition remained in the narrow doorways and tiny windows, occasionally interspersed with enormous fireplaces. The most famous and noteworthy feature was the open octagonal staircase, emblazoned with the royal salamander and crests, which simultaneously nodded to the Gothic traditions of previous French architecture and to the new Renaissance ideas that were gaining popularity in the country.

Blois was also the place where Francis's bibliophile leanings could be indulged. Since beginning his reign, he had amassed a vast collection of books which were initially housed in the library at Blois, before later being moved to Fontainebleau. An inventory of the royal library compiled in 1518 itemised just over 1,600 volumes. Budé, as Master of the King's Library from 1522, took a special interest in the 500 or so Greek manuscripts acquired by Francis's agents in Venice and Rome during the early to mid 1520s. The king's literary enthusiasms were not confined to acquiring rare manuscripts and commissioning printed books; he also read widely and thoughtfully, in a range of languages, and enjoyed little more than to discuss philosophical or historical issues with those around him.

Yet Francis was not content with mere additions to an existing building, especially as he saw Blois as his wife's château. He sought to construct a new palace altogether that would be a fitting testament to both him and his reign. He found a suitable location in a forest in which he enjoyed hunting, at Chambord, and in 1519 commissioned the construction of what was intended to be 'a beautiful and sumptuous edifice'.[9] The architect was Bernabei Domenico da Cortona, who designed a château in the traditional medieval French style, but with some innovative additions, not least a double spiral staircase at the centre of the keep, which meant that one could pass someone else without ever meeting them. Such was the brilliance of these designs that it has long been suggested that da Cortona took inspiration from da Vinci. Although the great man died in the year in which construction began at Chambord, many of his late designs and sketches indicate that, had he lived, he would have planned something very similar; and it seems unlikely that, da Vinci being such an integral part of Francis's intellectual and artistic scene in the years that they spent together, the king would not have wished to take advantage of his ideas. If the description sometimes voiced of da Vinci as 'the architect of Chambord' seems hyperbolic, it is likely that he was a key influence in its design.

Although Chambord was not completed in Francis's lifetime, it was sufficiently advanced by the end of his reign for the Venetian bishop Luigi Lippomano to say: 'I have seen many magnificent buildings in my life, but never one so beautiful or so rich as this.' Chambord, like the other châteaux in which Francis spent time, was cheerfully and richly decorated with bright tapestries, gold and silver plate on the tables and great collections of Venetian glass, painted cloth and even scented logs.

'A court without ladies is like a garden without beautiful flowers,' Francis was once reputed to have said, and Brantôme recorded that 'King Francis believed that the entire ornament of a court lay in its ladies . . . I myself have seen chests and wardrobes, belonging to old ladies of those days, filled with dresses which the King had given them . . . which were worth a fortune.'[10] It was undoubtedly the case that Francis had two great loves: hunting and women. In both fields he displayed remarkable courage, physical fortitude and stamina, as well as a dedication to his goal that left bystanders both astonished and envious.

The stories about Francis's love affairs have conflated a healthy dose of salaciousness with undeniable accuracy. It is unlikely, for instance, that he lost his virginity at the age of ten to his mother's lady-in-waiting, Jeanne de Polignac, and even less possible that he maintained a mistress at that tender age. A series of misinterpreted letters caused eighteenth-century scholars to believe that he had had an incestuous love affair with Marguerite, and, while there is no evidence to support this, it has added lustre to the image of the king as a libertine of strong, and sometimes shocking, sexual appetites.

This is an exaggeration, although based at least partially in documented fact.* One biographer described him as being 'as amorous as a cat, amorous and inconstant'.[11] It is true that Francis enjoyed both casual liaisons and a string of more significant mistresses, who included Françoise de Foix, Madame de Châteaubriant; her husband, who took his wife's infidelity in his stride, was Jean de Laval, Sire de Châteaubriant. Françoise was a demanding and spoilt woman, whose requirements both sexual and political were considerable. She made the king work for her affections, and only agreed to become his *maîtresse en titre* in 1518. Boasting dark hair and a tall, slender figure, she was attractive, naturally, but with a steeliness and strength that made her the opposite of the demure Queen Claude. She had been educated and shared Francis's cultural and aesthetic

---

* See Chapter 2 for Francis's first forays into sex, and their consequences.

interests and, like him, was seldom content with the status quo. She was by no means faithful, at one point sleeping not only with Francis but also with the Admiral of France, Guillaume Gouffier, Seigneur de Bonnivet. In an effort to make the king jealous, or possibly to excite him, she described their encounter in sexually graphic terms. On another occasion, Bonnivet was obliged to hide in the fireplace under some green boughs after sleeping with Françoise when the king arrived, only to suffer the indignity of being urinated upon by the monarch relieving himself before having his way with his mistress. She also wrote Francis love poems, one of which extolled the virtues of the dark over the fair. Perhaps she had heard rumours about his great intimacy with his sister and wished to dissuade him from finding another mistress reminiscent of her.

One reason why de Laval remained sanguine about being cuckolded by his monarch is because he was a beneficiary of the king's largesse. Not only did he receive many expensive and lavish gifts, courtesy of his wife, but he became a commander of a company: a lucrative position because of the potential for back-handers and bribery. It is unsurprising, then, that when de Laval was sent by Francis to Brittany in December 1519 to negotiate a tax, he did not mention the other circumstances that bound him and his monarch. Françoise was also able to provide favours for her brothers: Thomas de Lescun, Odet de Foix, Viscount of Lautrec, and André de Lesparre all found themselves promoted to similar positions commanding companies, but their inefficiency meant that this particular example of nepotism had backfired.

Françoise was by no means the king's only significant mistress. Instead, the monarch maintained a loose harem which was known as 'la petite bande'. These included Anne de Pisseleu d'Heilly, whom he called 'the most beautiful of the scholars, the most scholarly of the beauties';[12] she was both well read and extremely well favoured in her looks, and eventually became Duchesse d'Étampes in gratitude for her many favours. Others, such as Marie de Langeac, Marie de Canaples and Marie de Montchenu – the latter being the wife of Francis's close friend Marin de Montchenu, his first minister – all joined his seraglio, and benefited from the king's generosity and often impulsive favours. Many of these women were procured by the dissolute Jean, Cardinal of Lorraine; Brantôme described the all-night revels that the cardinal threw, many of which were attended by the king, as debauched ones, in which 'rarely or never did any maid or wife leave that court chaste', although at least they could expect riches in compensation: 'You would have found their coffers and their wardrobes more full of gowns and petticoats of cloth of gold or silver, and of silk, than those of our Queens and great princesses today.'[13]

Francis grew careless in his licentiousness, once again acting out the swashbuckling fancies of his time when 'merely' heir apparent. He would don a disguise of cloak and mask and wander the Parisian streets anonymously, a state of affairs that could easily have led to his being attacked or even killed by street robbers. Likewise, not all husbands behaved with equanimity at the prospect of becoming cuckolds. The ever-knowledgeable Brantôme recounts the story of how the king wished to sleep with a great lady, only to find her husband standing in front of her bedchamber, sword at the ready. The ever-resourceful Francis 'pointed his own sword at the gentleman's throat and commanded him, on his life, to do her no harm, adding that if the gentleman hurt her at all, he himself would kill him or have somebody else cut his head off'. The power that the king wielded proved unassailable; the unsurprising sequel was that 'that night, he sent the gentleman outside and took his place'.[14] Such were the perks of monarchy.

Yet, despite his dedication to the pleasures of the flesh, Francis retained an affection for his wife that went beyond the necessary incursions into the bedchamber designed to produce an heir. Claude was no beauty, but she was charming, good-natured, unfailingly kind to all around her and, crucially, not prone to jealousy; she accepted her husband's philandering with equanimity and never offered any hint of dissatisfaction with her lot. When she was crowned Queen of France on 10 May 1517, she was dressed magnificently in a silver robe, with a cap of white satin trimmed with gold, and made an appropriately grand entrance into Paris flanked by sixteen princesses. Although it was not obligatory for queen consorts to receive such an honour, Francis wished to demonstrate his respect for Claude in as public a fashion as possible, and was following the recent tradition of both her mother Anne of Brittany and her stepmother Mary Tudor in having their own coronation.

It seemed fitting that, nine months later, Claude finally delivered Francis his much-longed-for son, also named Francis, on 28 February 1518; when he was born, she said: 'Tell the king that he is even more beautiful than himself.' The delighted monarch described his tiny namesake as 'a beautiful Dauphin who is the most beautiful and puissant child one could imagine, and who will be the easiest to bring up'.[15]

Although Francis was a kind and devoted father to his daughters, he had made little secret of his longing for a son, not least because it would avoid the issues of dynastic succession that had made his own inheritance of the throne possible, complex and tense a process though that had been. When the christening took place at Amboise on 25 April 1518, it was accomplished with all the glittering pageantry that might be expected upon the arrival of a new royal prince. Drums and trumpeters announced the procession of the royal family and all the leading courtiers, while the influential godparents included Lorenzo de Medici, acting as representative for his uncle Pope Leo, and the Count of Guise. The courtyard of the château was transformed into a series of magnificent pavilions hung with great tapestries and lit by thousands of candles. A covered bridge with carved dolphins as pillars, and further dolphins painted on the roof, led direct from the castle to the chapel. After the baby was baptised there were banquets, celebrations and cheering of 'Vive Monsieur le Dauphin!' beyond measure, before Francis's young son was knighted, in preparation for what was expected to be his own glorious reign. The spectacle was created by none other than Francis's most distinguished subject of patronage, da Vinci, although the great man, close to the end of his life, had duplicated a *mise-en-scène* that he had used earlier for another patron in Milan. It did not matter; the desired effect was achieved. The message sent out to the world was clear: the dauphin was to be the most splendid representative of a forward-looking and magnificent country, second only to its king.

*

Perhaps inevitably, Francis followed a fixed routine that combined business, pleasure and a keen eye for the trappings of royalty and ritual. When he was not travelling between his dominions, he liked to rise late in the morning, at around ten o'clock, and hear Mass upon waking. This was a much-cherished time for him as it was the only period of the day when he was able to be truly alone, un-bothered by the blandishments and ministrations of court life. He took his main meal of the day at around eleven o'clock, surrounded by courtiers and the learned. Brantôme, who was sometimes pres-ent at his king's table, called it 'a real school as he discussed every subject, not just war . . . but also the sciences, high and low'.[16] This was echoed by the nobleman and chronicler Martin du Bellay, who noted, perhaps with just a touch of irony, that Francis's wide accumulation of superficial knowledge meant that 'many learned men who had been much in his company admitted that they learnt more from him than he did from them'. After the meal there was a lengthy reading from a book such as the chivalric romance *Le Ro-maunt de la Rose* or a French translation of Justinian, to keep Francis informed about Roman law, and then, at last, there was time for outdoor pursuits.

The king's favourite sporting pastime, one that he had practised since youth, was hunting, and great importance was attached to it. It was regarded as the best of all aristocratic pursuits as it kept the participants alert and fit, sharpened their reflexes and ended in a satisfyingly bloody fashion. Around 150,000 gold crowns a year were spent on maintaining the royal hunt, which fielded a mini-mum of twenty-five hounds, twelve huntsmen, dozens of grooms and running footmen and held one of the great offices of state, the Grand Huntsman of France. Francis preferred *vénerie*, or hunting with hounds, to *fauconnerie*, the art of using birds of prey; this was largely because it offered a greater spectacle and resembled nothing so much as a great battle.

This grand pursuit was taken enormously seriously, and the animals hunted (which included boar, wolves, deer and even otters) were pursued and slaughtered with great pomp and ceremony with a gilded sword or spear, to the accompaniment of ritualistic horn music and whooping. Francis saw hunting as a pastime to be enjoyed whatever the season, and galloped fast and recklessly through his preferred terrain of forest, such as those at Blois and Fontainebleau, hacking away at any branches that obstructed his progress. It was a hazardous, thrilling occasion, and one that could potentially have been fatal; one time he lost his way completely and had to take shelter in a cave on a winter night, nearly freezing to death before he was discovered.

The English ambassador, Sir Richard Wingfield, supplied Henry VIII with a rich and detailed account of what a typical hunt involved in April 1520. It would normally begin at around three o'clock, with Francis heading off to hunt wild boar and bidding all his courtiers to attend him. Wingfield wrote, in bloodthirsty detail, that 'when he came to the place in which the boar lay, there was cast off one hound only to him, the which inconveniently had him at the bay, and then immediately was thrown off upon a twenty couple [sic] of hounds, with three or four brace of mastiffs let slip, all which drew to the bay, and then plucked down the poor boar, and the king, with divers others, being afoot, with their boar spears had dispatched him shortly; and then the king himself, after their fashion, cut off the right foot of the said boar.'

There then followed a return to court for rather less strenuous activity, such as a game of tennis, some dancing of a jig or a galliard, or a concert or masque. There were also evenings in which verse was performed, including Francis's own efforts, although these were not greeted with anything other than dutiful applause. The more successful and acclaimed poems were written by the courtier-poet Clément Marot, who was a great favourite of Marguerite's, occasionally leading to whispered speculation that she had been inappropriately moved by his fine words and finer sentiments. Nonetheless, Francis was a great admirer of Marot too, and nobody would dare accuse him – let alone the king's sister – of any unbecoming behaviour.

Eventually the mood would become less restrained. As the evening wore on wine would be taken, and a royal jester encouraged to cavort and mock the assembled dignitaries. The most famous of these, Triboulet, frequently made jokes that would have had him executed, were it not for the fact that Francis found many of his bawdier sallies amusing. On one occasion Triboulet slapped the king upon his noble behind, a liberty that went too far, even for the jester. Francis was furious, threatening to execute him, but, after a moment's pause, calmed down enough to offer Triboulet a deal: if he could come up with an apology that was more insulting than the original slight, he would go free. The jester responded swiftly and brilliantly: 'I'm so sorry, Your Majesty, but I didn't recognise you. I mistook you for the Queen.'

It was, of course, not Claude who partook of regal pleasures when the king finally retired to his vast canopied bed at around midnight. In addition to the royal mistresses who frequented this bed, there was also a group of royal courtesans – the unkind might call them prostitutes – who roamed the court, watched over by an official Madam. These women were known as 'les filles de joie', and their keeper as 'la dame'. Ritual dictated that they were given presents on the first day of January, and in return they offered the king flowers on May Day. Their favours went beyond this floral tribute, however, and many of these young and highly attractive women valued the opportunity to be close to the king, who was well known for his generosity to his favourites. Although they were not high-born enough to be regarded as official mistresses, they could expect to receive significant gifts and patronage, and their position was highly sought after.

However, despite all of his many accomplishments in the fields of warfare, the arts and the bedroom, Francis's life was not without its own sorrows and difficulties. His eldest daughter Louise died on 21 September 1517 at the age of two, thereby coincidentally ending her engagement to Charles I of Spain. As Brantôme wrote, 'Pretty rosebuds [are] carried off by the wind as well as flowers full blown, and children snatched away are mourned a hundred times more than the old who die.'[17]

Francis was undeniably a new kind of monarch. Influenced both by his mother and by the philosophers and scholars who acted as his tutors and companions, he could be described as France's first Humanist king, possessed of an inquisitive and impatient spirit that was keen to seek out new ideas. This was a conscious effort by Francis, who saw himself as a modern and enlightened figure who cast off the tired superstitions and threadbare traditions of his medieval predecessors, even though he was a traditional and conscientious Christian, attended Mass daily and took great interest in the latest religious debates. In this he was undeniably the right monarch for the time. Doctrines that had previously been proposed by only a tiny minority were increasingly voiced by people who considered themselves part of the vanguard of contemporary and enlightened opinion, and could express themselves without fear of being denounced as heretics.

To blame Francis for hubris and arrogance, in view of what would occur later in his reign, is unfair. Yet it was ironic that religion and its representatives on earth would be his greatest challenge.

CHAPTER 7

The End of Ambition

In order to examine what would later cause Francis's downfall one must give consideration to events that, at the time, must have seemed little more than unfortunate accidents or simple occurrences of fate. One of these was the death of the Holy Roman Emperor, Maximilian I, on 12 January 1519, at the age of fifty-nine. Throughout most of his lengthy and successful reign, Maximilian had been an effective moderniser. Unfortunately he had been struck by a debilitating form of senility during the last two years of his life, which led him to make absurd and meaningless statements. He grandly informed his daughter, Margaret of Austria, that he planned to abdicate, after which he would become pope; following his death he would be canonised, 'and then you will pray to me for intercession with the Almighty'. He then tried to sell his crown to his occasional ally Henry VIII, who, realising that the emperor's growing insanity would nullify such an appointment, regretfully turned down the offer. Not being able to sell the title as if it were an indulgence, Maximilian decided to ensure that his own choice would succeed him as Holy Roman Emperor: his grandson, Charles of Habsburg.

The position of emperor was no mere sinecure. Its holder was an international figure rather than just a national one, and the title itself could be traced back hundreds of years to 962 AD when Otto I, King of Eastern Francia – a territory roughly equivalent to the modern German state – had been crowned emperor by the pope. Although the old joke that the Holy Roman Empire was neither

holy, Roman nor an empire had some basis in fact, by 1518 it still occupied a substantial portion of Europe that included Germany, the
Low Countries, Burgundy, Savoy and a good deal of northern Italy.
Although ramshackle, the empire was far from being a backward-
looking institution obsessed by its own importance. A series of
reforming measures streamlined some of its bureaucracy in the
fifteenth century, and its diplomatic prestige was only matched by
the power and influence that the emperor could expect to wield.
Therefore it was unsurprising that, upon his death, Maximilian's
own wishes would be ignored and that many major European kings
would frantically jockey for position to further their own power.
One of these, inevitably, was Francis.

The French king's motives in attempting to have himself
elected Holy Roman Emperor were twofold. Initially, he wished to
strengthen his own position, which, after the successful territorial
acquisitions of the previous years, seemed like a fitting continu-
ation of his ambitions, particularly in Italy, both for himself and
for France. Afterwards he knew that, if Charles were to become
emperor, it would consolidate the powerbase of an impressive and
potentially dangerous adversary. The acquisition of an extra layer
of prestige by a rival who already ruled much of western Europe
was not something Francis relished. During the second half of the
fifteenth century Christendom's balance of power had shifted from
local coalitions of small states to formidable emerging nations,
whose jostling for power would dominate world politics for the next
500 years. Whoever ruled Christendom could establish himself as a
peerless leader. It was time, Francis believed, to flex his muscles and
prove to Europe, and the world, that he was pre-eminent among
temporal rulers.

He was far from subtle in his ambitions. The fact that a meeting
of the seven imperial electors in late 1518 at the Reichstag in Augsburg had been inconclusive and fell short of the anticipated election
of Charles, meant that Francis's diplomatic horse-trading had begun
while Maximilian still breathed, much to the contempt of some,
who considered it undignified; Henry VIII's spies reported that
'[Francis] goeth about covertly and layeth many baits to attain the
empire.'[1] After Maximilian's death Francis lost little time in setting

out his stall. At the former emperor's Requiem Mass, which was held at Notre-Dame on 21 February 1519, Francis began to see the possibility of reigning as a European emperor on the scale of Charlemagne, if not greater. He confessed to Sir Thomas Boleyn, while leaning out of a window to frustrate eavesdroppers, that 'he would have the empire if it cost him three million crowns, and that three years after his election he would be in Constantinople or his grave'.[2] Although there was no precedent that allowed a non-German to be elected as emperor, Francis was hopeful about his chances, despite the fact that it had long been traditional for the electors to nominate a Habsburg to fill the vacancy; it would take a great deal, in terms of both diplomacy and simple bribery, to set that precedent aside.

Maximilian's wish that his grandson should succeed him would, in normal circumstances, have been enough to ensure Charles's uncontested election. Yet there were various reasons why the electors were queasy at the idea of Charles becoming Holy Roman Emperor. Nobody had any clear idea who this eighteen-year-old was, and there was little understanding of what he was capable of. As he had already acquired a whole set of major titles, senior European figures feared that the election of a man who had already attained international stature as ruler of Spain, Naples and the Netherlands would give him an unholy amount of power and influence. There were also rumours about his mental health, given that his mother, Joanna of Castile, had been certified insane and confined to a nunnery.

Therefore Francis could rely on some influential support, including that of the Archbishops of Trier and Mainz, who were much influenced by Pope Leo's advocacy of the French monarch. In the summer of 1517 the Margrave of Brandenburg, a corrupt figure known as 'the father of all greediness', and the Elector Palatine stated publicly that they too would support Francis, meaning that he now had a majority of four out of seven electors – albeit four bound together more by anti-Habsburg sentiment and greed than by any particular enthusiasm for the French king. They wanted a contested election, with its attendant financial benefits, and Francis's candidature ensured that one would take place.

Unsurprisingly, the months between Maximilian's death and the gathering of the electors saw a feverish spate of skulduggery take place. At times this was simply farcical, as when Admiral Bonnivet was found behind a tapestry, dressed as a *Landsknecht*, listening in on a conversation between an English emissary and the Margrave of Brandenburg. Given the unfortunate and humiliating incident that had occurred when he had concealed himself while bedding Françoise de Foix, the good admiral might have been well advised to avoid such instances of concealment altogether. Nonetheless, Francis attempted to present himself as rising above the grubby machinations in which his courtiers were engaging, graciously writing to Charles to inform him that their close friendship must not be compromised by their both desiring the same prize; as he put it, 'Sire, we are both courting the same lady.'[3] The implied condescension in his letter indicated that he was confident of victory.

As for the electors, they were delighted at the antagonism that had developed in the contest, especially as it seemed that Henry VIII, encouraged by the prospect of a deadlocked vote, was considering his own candidacy as well. Whoever was victorious would benefit them on a personal level, as their private finances received a huge fillip from the substantial bribes willingly offered by each candidate. This was by no means unusual; Maximilian had done exactly the same thing in order to secure his own election as emperor in 1493. Yet the potential addition of Henry briefly excited the greed of the electors beyond measure, and the Archbishop of Trier, previously a supporter of Francis, now let it be known that he considered Henry's candidacy a strong one. The English king dispatched his diplomatic envoy, Richard Pace, Dean of St Paul's, to Germany in May 1519 to see what the situation was; Pace could only report that success was unlikely without huge expenditure, leading Henry to withdraw his interest.

Charles, meanwhile, saw himself as the frontrunner throughout, not least because, in August 1518, five electors had privately declared for him, and the only two who had not, namely the Archbishop of Trier and the Duke of Saxony, had held out for financial reasons rather than principles. Therefore he did not feel the need to match Francis's lavish bribes, but was likewise prepared to offer politically advantageous marriages; the Margrave of Brandenburg was presented, in turn, with the choice of the Dowager Queen of Spain, Louis XII's daughter Renée and Charles's sister Catherine. Money and pensions were also dangled in front of the electors with aplomb. Francis's representatives shamelessly promised the relevant parties huge sums if they supported his candidacy, with 407,000 crowns being sent to the King of Poland, who would be casting a vote on behalf of another elector, the King of Bohemia, who was still in his minority.

Francis's campaign was undoubtedly expensive, costing him every crown of the three million that he had so rashly promised to spend. In order to raise the cash he again resorted to the selling of government posts, just as he had done in order to finance the invasion of Milan in 1515; thus many of the newly created posts were essentially meaningless. He was not helped by the banking system of the time, which was administered by the Fuggers of Augsburg, the leading bankers of the day; they backed Charles without hesitation and refused bills of exchange issued by the French government. The French money therefore had to be sent in cash and by road – an extremely hazardous, even foolhardy, enterprise given the poor state of the highways and the likelihood of robbery. Many bribes thus ended up in the pockets of rather more obviously criminal individuals.

The French king was not a stupid man, and even in the frenzy of ambition retained his pragmatism and at least a vestige of his earlier prudence. Many of his most generous offers to the electors were promises of what they would get if they actually voted for him on the day, rather than bribes dispensed willy nilly. Both Charles and Francis attempted to advance their candidacy by using broadsheets that extolled their suitability for the role while castigating the other: so much for Francis's disingenuous comments to Charles that he hoped for a lasting friendship, whatever the result. Although the only people who could directly vote in the election were the seven electors, both sides recognised that the opinions of literate people mattered, since readers and writers could help to promote their cause.

At last, the offers of advancement came to an end when the electors convened in Frankfurt on 8 June 1519; home to many imperial institutions, it was also the centre of much of the public interest in the result of the imperial election. Such occasions were inevitably momentous events in German public life, but this particular, highly personalised contest had generated unprecedented patriotic feeling, not least because a related campaign to keep the imperial title in Habsburg hands had encouraged a great deal of anti-French sentiment. By this point, despite the Herculean efforts that Francis had made, it was almost inconceivable that the electors should opt for anyone other than Charles. The announcement of the result, which came on 28 June, reaffirmed the Holy Roman Empire's essentially German identity and saw to it that Charles supplanted Francis as the most powerful figure in Europe, possessing a great empire that stretched as far as Africa and Jerusalem. He had gone from being a strong, if slightly naïve, young king to potentially the greatest threat that a monarch bent on his own idea of expansion might face. It had cost him dearly – a rumoured 850,000 crowns, and many obligations to the electors – but Charles was now supreme.

When Francis heard the unwelcome news he was at his palace of Fontainebleau. His first response, both petulant and stunned, was to say, 'I am well pleased not to have the Empire's cares',[4] before disappearing off into the forest to hunt. He might have attempted to feign a lack of concern but he fooled nobody, especially his most trusted courtiers, many of whom had been intimately involved in the preparations for the planned empire. It was the first serious setback that he had faced, both as a monarch and as a man, since becoming King of France, and he knew that many of his erstwhile supporters would now flock to Charles, demonstrating how fickle the great men of Europe could be when it came to the display of power.

Francis's concentration on his political jockeying meant that he was less focused on affairs closer to home at this time. He paid scant attention to the marriage of Pope Leo's nephew Lorenzo II de Medici to Madeleine de La Tour d'Auvergne. Lorenzo had been possessed of an erratic and petulant temperament ever since his mother, Alfonsina, an Orsini princess from the Neapolitan branch, had led him to believe that he was entitled to the obligations due to any prince. On his previous visits to Florence, which had been mercifully short in duration, he had managed to offend the notionally republican Florentine people, who found their natural tolerance strained to the limit.

However, it was considered diplomatically vital not only to maintain good relations with Lorenzo, but to ensure that he was happy in his choice of bride. Francis had gone so far as to write to him on 26 September 1517, while congratulating him on his appointment as Duke of Urbino, to say: 'I intend to help you with all my power. I also wish to marry you off to some beautiful and good lady of noble birth and of my kin, so that the love which I bear you may grow and be strengthened.'[5] He was being more than usually disingenuous, but knew that few marital prospects were more glittering than Madeleine, who was both a royal orphan and one of the greatest heiresses in Europe; her parents had been hugely wealthy magnates who owned vast territories including the counties of Clermont and Auvergne, the baronies of La Tour and La Chaise, as well as seigneuries in Lauraguais, Castres, Limousin and Berry. Any child born to the two would thus inherit extraordinary wealth and privilege, to say nothing of royal lineage.

Lorenzo and Madeleine were married shortly after the dauphin's christening, on 28 April 1518, before a company that included Leonardo da Vinci. The wedding was followed by ten days of banquets, masked balls and ballets, as well as the usual opportunities for the men to show off their masculine skills of violence. Tournaments and a mock battle were held; although the latter usually incurred fatalities, as only two people died on this occasion the lack of further slaughter was considered a good outcome. He was twenty-six, she sixteen, and onlookers commented that the two, unusually for an arranged marriage, seemed very much in love. Some tongues wagged, not without jealousy, that it had been an unequal match: she, a countess of royal blood, wed to a man descending from nouveaux-riches merchants.

Lorenzo, who had arrived in such magnificent state and splendour that he resembled a great emperor rather than the grandson of a merchant banker, wooed the court by lavishing gifts on those present. From the highest courtier to the lowest, he ensured that he curried favour by distributing mementoes of the occasion. A particularly impressive treasure was a vast bed made of tortoiseshell decorated with gems and mother-of-pearl; he made it entirely clear that he intended to consummate his marriage on this bed, and it was little surprise that, by the time that Lorenzo and Madeleine set out for Florence, he was able to inform his patron with some pride that his wife was already pregnant. The news sent Leo and Francis into raptures of delight.[6] The arrival of an heir to this great union of dynasties seemed a holy blessing.

Shortly after the birth of Francis and Claude's second son Henri, Madeleine was delivered of her own child on 13 April 1519: not the desired son, but instead a daughter, who was christened Catherine. Nonetheless, it was put about that her arrival made Lorenzo and Madeleine 'as pleased as if it had been a boy',[7] a piece of public relations spin designed to make up for the ducal disappointment. It was unfortunate that, despite the wealth and status that she was born into, both of her parents were in very poor health. Lorenzo, who had overindulged himself in a life of excess to the extent that he had contracted both syphilis and consumption, had been confined to his bed for the second half of his wife's pregnancy, and she suffered from a severe postpartum infection. Their daughter was christened Caterina Maria Romula on 16 April 1519 at San Lorenzo in Florence, and Madeleine died just twelve days later. An ailing Lorenzo dictated a letter to Francis in which he bemoaned how 'I am in bed with a little fever, catarrh and many other bad symptoms, and for my evil fortune there has come upon me in addition this sad blow to lose my most beloved wife.'[8]

His own end came on 4 May 1519, leaving Catherine de Medici a fabulously rich orphan. In August she became seriously ill as well, and for several weeks the possibility existed that she, too, would die; it was only in October that she recovered. The duke's friend, the poet Ariosto, had arrived to offer his condolences upon the death of Madeleine, and now found himself mourning a double sorrow: possibly a treble, if one considered the fact that Catherine was no male heir. His poem 'Verdeggia un solo ramo' was dedicated to this young remnant of two great dynasties:

> A single branch, buds and lo,
> I am distraught with hope and fear,
> Whether winter will let it blow,
> Or blight it on the growing bier.[9]

After the deaths of Lorenzo and Madeleine and Catherine's own severe illness, Francis's first impulse was to have her brought up at the French court. However, Pope Leo denied him this opportunity on the grounds that the girl, whom he affectionately called 'duchessina', belonged in Rome, and that he intended to marry her off to Ippolito, the bastard son of Giuliano, Duke of Nemours, thereby establishing them as the rulers of Florence. This was at least partially a spurious reason, and one invented for the sake of convenience. Instead, the death of Lorenzo meant that Leo's grandest strategy, namely establishing French support for a Medici dynasty in Florence, had come to an end, which in turn meant that his previously warm attitude towards Francis now cooled. After the failure of his attempt to become Holy Roman Emperor, the French king was now being seen as yesterday's man. Europe's attention instead turned to Charles V as the more desirable ruler with whom to ingratiate oneself, less than half a decade after the Battle of Marignano and subsequent conquest of Milan. Leo had no desire to offer up his beloved great-niece as an apparent hostage against the promises that he had made to Francis earlier, for he was well aware that he was now in a position where he had to break them. The amity that the two men had had was real enough, but now other concerns had to intrude.

However, although Francis's wish that Catherine join his court was frustrated, she would reappear in his life in a crucial way and become a figure of enormous influence and importance: a remarkable change of fortune from her early days as an orphaned child shuttled about Italy.

Disappointed by his various failures, Francis threw himself into distractions and games, the more adventurous and violent the better. An especially elaborate mock battle had taken place at Amboise in April 1518 when 600 men, commanded by the king with his

lieutenant, the Duke of Alençon, by his side, attempted to defend
a model town, which itself was besieged by an equally-sized force
commanded by the Dukes of Bourbon and Vendôme. As Fleurange
described it, 'It was the finest battle ever seen, and the nearest to
real warfare, but the entertainment did not please everyone, for
some were killed and others frightened.'[10] Even so-called 'pretend'
battles were fought as if they were matters of honour, which in a
sense they were; the fact that the 'honour' at stake was Francis's ego
did not mean that any of his lieutenants fought any less vigorously.

Without a military campaign to pursue, nor the funds to finance
it, there was an inertia at court that frustrated the king. This in
turn led to displays of strength and impatience, such as an incident
when, showing Cardinal Federico Gonzaga around his château at
Blois, he found himself unable to open a door, and so hurled his
considerable weight against it, breaking it open. As one in Gonzaga's retinue later wrote, 'He then wished to show him the library,
but the key-holder could not be found, so he wanted to break down
the door; Monsignor told him that he would see to it the next day,
urging and begging him not to give himself so much trouble.'

Maintaining a reputation as a strongman was not easy. On one
occasion, in September 1519, Francis was nearly blinded when, while
riding pell-mell in pursuit of a boar, he was struck on the head by a
branch and thrown off his horse. He was fortunate not to have been
incapacitated, as he had serious and pressing international matters
to contend with. Italy, although distant geographically, was rarely
absent from the king's thoughts in the years immediately after the
acquisition of Milan. Francis had obtained an undoubtedly magnificent prize thanks to his military efforts, but the occupying force
faced a real challenge in maintaining control of a situation never
less than precarious, which was equally true of the civilian administration that had been put in place by the French. Milan's long and
proud history of independence meant that the local citizens were
bound to resent a government imposed on them from the outside
and, despite the lavishness of their initial welcome, no Milanese
ever thought of the French as being anything other than foreign
invaders.

There were also other concerns, not least the kingdom of Naples;

it was a hugely desirable expanse of land, which included the island of Sicily, and whose territories extended across the entire southern half of the Italian peninsula. Once it had been part of the Aragonese royal domain, but it looked as if it would now be subsumed into the new Holy Roman Emperor's dominion, not least because Charles had been ruling it since his grandfather's death in 1519. He had already implicitly conceded the French dynastic claim to the kingdom, since he had undertaken to pay tribute money to Francis as a condition of his being allowed to continue to rule in Naples; but these were interim arrangements contingent on the decision of the papacy, as Pope Leo continued to have the final word on who was allowed the territory.

Even after Charles was confirmed as Holy Roman Emperor, Leo made no public announcement about an investiture. This was due less to a desire to be enigmatic than to uncertainty about the best course of action. On the one hand, the papacy could hardly disinherit Charles since he was his uncle's heir and Naples's legitimate de facto ruler. Yet Leo also wished to keep his options open. If, at some stage, Charles should be invested, he would thereby enjoy the added security of a papal affirmation. On the other hand, a papal judgement favouring the investiture of the French Crown would affirm Francis's own claim. In that event Charles would continue to rule in Naples, but only because the King of France granted him the right to do so.

Shortly after the victory at Marignano in 1515, Leo had allowed Francis to hope that, when the time came, the Neapolitan ratification would be made in his favour. However, casting aside earlier reservations, Leo now stated that the Crown of Naples could be united with that of the empire; he had therefore made his decision to support Charles's claim, leading Francis to fear for his Italian prospects. His campaign for the imperial title, seductive though it might have been, was insignificant compared to his desire to maintain his rights in Italy. Now, Leo's adjudication and the electors' decision pointed towards a formidable consolidation of Habsburg power both north and south of the Alps. Until the summer of 1519 there had been four significant powers in western Europe. Henceforth Charles would solely represent Spain, the Netherlands and the

Habsburg Empire. Nearly eighty years later, Francis Bacon wrote: 'During that Triumvirate of Kings, King Henry VIII of England, Francis I, King of France, and Charles V, Emperor, there was such a good watch kept that none of the three could win a palm of ground, but the other two would straightways [*sic*] balance it, either by confederation, or, if need were, by war, and would not in any wise take up peace at interest.'[11]

This left Francis in search of an ally. Charles was now apparently all-powerful; only one candidate remained, and a former enemy at that. Henceforth French foreign policy was to lean in a more Anglophile direction.

CHAPTER 8

The Field of the Cloth of Gold

Henry VIII needed a barber. He had made a rash vow, around the time of the imperial election, that he would not shave until he had finally met Francis I; this was similarly reciprocated, perhaps with tongue faintly in cheek, by his French counterpart. This promise had been made in the expectation that they would encounter one another for the first time in the early summer of 1519, but the wearisome saga of the election of the Holy Roman Emperor and other business meant that Henry's beard grew shaggier, and bushier, and ever more repellent to his wife, Catherine of Aragon. She 'daily made him great instance and desired him to put it off for her sake',[1] until, without any sign of a meeting, he was prevailed upon to summon the barber, and the beard came off.

The king's facial hair might seem a triviality, but in the game of diplomacy that the European rulers practised it was a small but significant detail that showed a lack of faith. However, the potential slight was quickly smoothed over, as it was put about by both countries' diplomats that the real love between Francis and Henry lay 'not in the beards, but in the hearts'.[2] At the beginning of 1520 Cardinal Wolsey finally began to make plans for the two monarchs to meet. It would be a great occasion full of pageantry, diplomatic manoeuvring and barely concealed rivalry. The consequences were not to be entirely as either ruler had planned.

By 1520 the relationship between Henry and Francis was one of enmity, although not overt hostility. Wolsey's Treaty of London, a non-aggression pact between the two countries brokered in July 1518, had seen Bonnivet and eighty 'young fresh gallants of the court of France'[3] arrive in England for a season of roistering and, when the drinking and merriment paused for a moment, diplomacy; in return, the French court received a similar embassy later that year. The treaty had made it clear that an English visit to France was desirable, because 'the said serene princes of England and France be like in force corporal, beauty and gifts of nature right expert, and having knowledge in the art militant, right chivalrous in arms, and in the flower and vigour of youth'.[4] At this point Francis was fresh from his success at Milan and still a figure to be courted and admired. Treaties signed in October 1518 provided for the return of Tournai to the French in exchange for a total payment, spread over twelve years, of 600,000 gold *écus*; of these, 12,000 were to be paid in compensation to Wolsey. Mary Tudor, Henry VIII's two-year old daughter, was meanwhile promised in marriage to the Dauphin Francis, the French king's eldest son, heir and namesake. A meeting between Francis and Henry was anticipated before the end of July 1519, and on 9 February that year Tournai was finally returned to France, six years after its capture.

The reason why both Henry and Wolsey were so keen to arrange a meeting with Francis was that, as Spain and the Holy Roman Empire were now the joint dominion of Charles, power was unequally distributed across Europe, despite France's current strength. England liked to regard herself as a kingmaker of sorts; 'her alliance would bestow dominance, while her neutrality could, in theory, guarantee peace'.[5] It was in this spirit that further negotiations took place, resulting in a draft treaty in early 1520, and in March that year the document, largely the result of the work done by Wolsey and his officials, was ratified by the two kings. The treaty declared that the monarchs would meet near Guînes, within the English-controlled Pale of Calais, in June and that the site chosen would afford both sovereigns an opportunity to display the chivalric refinement and aesthetic sophistication of their respective courts, as well as taking part in a 'feat of arms', the term used in contemporary guidebooks to chivalry when describing the most comprehensive display of knightly prowess.

Before Henry travelled to France to meet Francis, he encountered Charles while the emperor was returning from Spain. This ended up being a three-day event conducted in Kent, mainly at Dover and Canterbury, and with a great deal of banqueting and dancing. The achievements of the meeting were to be more symbolic than practical, but the two rulers spent Whitsun together at Canterbury, within sight of Thomas Becket's shrine, and had, as their courtiers were informed afterwards, a most agreeable discussion. The Treaty of Canterbury, signed on 29 May, reconfirmed the alliance that had existed between the English king and Ferdinand of Aragon. Charles and Henry agreed, before the emperor elect's departure on the 31st, that they would meet again before long, with both parties keeping their diplomatic options open.

Meanwhile, Wolsey's officials had found a location for the historic Anglo-French encounter. The requirements had been specific: there should be enough room for the 'feat of arms', which was intended to include traditional jousting between two knights mounted on horseback, a 'tournament' or confrontation between pairs of mounted challengers, and man-to-man combat on foot. In the latter sport swords were, for the most part, deployed but spears could also be used. Opponents were allowed to inflict physical harm on each other but no fatalities were allowed, for fear of a diplomatic crisis. A 'tree of honour' was also erected, on which the victors' shields were to be hung. It was made abundantly clear that, despite the lavish spectacle arranged for the Field, there could be no *mano a mano* competition between the two monarchs. Neither Francis nor Henry could afford to be seen in public as anything other than a successful and heroic king. Losing either fight or face would have been a diplomatic disaster and negated the basis on which the entire colloquy took place.

The site chosen was a shallow valley that lay between Guînes and Ardres, a region rich in English associations as a domain of the Crown, and the labourers started on the heavy lifting required in order to ensure that traditional requirement for fairness: a literal level playing field. The area was poorly favoured in terms of potential accommodation for the expected multitudes, as Ardres had been sacked in the 1513–14 Anglo-French conflict, and the castle of Guînes was partially ruined and largely uninhabitable, which meant that they would have to sleep and live in tents, if they were lucky; one lawyer who was present, Edward Hall, said how 'both knights and ladies that were come to see the nobleness were fain to lie in hay and straw'.[6] Turning necessity into opportunity, both the French and English set to work transforming the dull earth into a spectacle that would transform the site's original name – 'the golden valley' – into 'the Field of the Cloth of Gold'.

When Charles arrived in England on 26 May 1520, he was surprised by the spectacle that greeted him at Dover. An enormous expedition seemed bound for France, as if about to invade, but these men and women were finely clad in anything but warrior attire, instead wearing hugely expensive garments made out of velvet, satin and gold cloth, as well as the finest boots and cloaks. Around 5,000 of England's greatest grandees were to travel with the king and queen, making the short but inevitably perilous journey over the water to Calais, from where they would head to Guînes. Here their quarters had been prepared at great expense and with fine attention to detail by thousands of masons, carpenters and glaziers, who had begun work as early as March. The assembled flock included practically the entire nobility, the knights chosen to represent all the counties of England, senior office holders of state who were members of the King's Council, and bureaucrats such as the clerks of the Privy Seal, as well as archbishops, bishops and abbots. A surprise attack would have destroyed England's ruling class.

However, Wolsey had left little to chance in his arrangements. He saw to it that temporary accommodation was constructed that was quite literally fit for a king, with a palace made out of timber, brick and canvas that was in turn connected to many of the other grand tents to form a pavilion, complete with banners painted by Holbein. Herein lay all the necessary accoutrements of majesty, including a banqueting hall, wine cellar, chapel and pantry to accommodate the vast quantities of victuals that were being brought over from England. These included whole herds of deer, sheep and pigs that had been shipped across the Channel, and would soon be slaughtered to provide cooked meats for the feasting to come. Catering requirements were immense on both sides, given the numbers of stomachs to be filled. Arrangements were made for the English to depart on 31 May, and by 5 June Henry was in Guînes, awaiting the arrival of Francis for a historic and long-anticipated encounter.

The French king, meanwhile, was not to be outdone when it came to glittering trappings of wealth and power. He arrived at the small town of Ardres with his own mighty entourage of 5,000 courtiers, which included aristocracy, clergymen and, inevitably, the bureaucrats charged with ensuring that there would be enough rabbits, quails and cheese to eat, to say nothing of the rivers of beer and wine that the assembled company would drink over the coming weeks. The challenge in this regard had been laid down by the English, who had installed two fountains which 'ran to all people plenteously with red, white and claret wine',[7] and which soon attracted all comers for the free, strong drink.

The 300 tents in which the French contingent were accommodated gave their name to the Field of the Cloth of Gold, thanks to the glittering material that covered so much of the camp. These were of an order of magnificence never previously seen in the history of Renaissance showmanship. Chivalric spectacle had always made much use of such structures and, at their most ostentatious, they would be covered with velvets and other precious cloth. Coats of arms could then be affixed to the tents' surface. Their shields identified their occupants, and emblazoned detail specified the ancestral nature of familial glory; Francis's own pavilion was sixty feet high, covered in cloth of gold, supported by two ships' masts lashed together and topped by a life-sized statue of St Michael. It is impossible to think of a showier display of wealth and power short of observing a great army preparing for battle. Fleurange described how 'when they were in the sunlight, [they] were wonderfully fine to look on',[8] and one eyewitness called the French camp, with only a faint touch of hyperbole, greater than 'the miracles of the Egyptian pyramids and the Roman amphitheatres'.[9]

Beneath the spectacle there were tensions. Francis was wary of Henry's loyalties, especially given the recent visit of Charles to England, and the question of whether he was likely to support France or the Holy Roman Empire remained unanswered. And, for all the expense and spectacle, the idea behind the encounter was anachronistic. The large scale and progressively more mechanised demands of early modern European warfare made the whole concept of individual chivalry increasingly redundant; the display of chivalric history recreated on the Field during those days in June 1520 must have seemed quaintly remote, even perhaps fantastical. The fashion of the time was to hark back to an imaginary bygone age of honour and the protection of virtue; what really mattered was the symbolism of two sovereign princes, surrounded by the nobility and knights of their realms, striving to outdo each other in self-consciously regal bearing. This was a Renaissance scene like no other.

Before the encounter between Francis and Henry there was the usual haggling, related to matters matrimonial and financial. A treaty signed on 6 June 1520 restated France's obligation to pay Henry a million gold crowns in two instalments, in recognition of the betrothal of the Princess Mary to the dauphin. Were the marriage finally to take place, half a million gold crowns would be payable annually during the period of their union. These terms had already been agreed weeks beforehand and no further serious negotiations took place between the parties during the festivities that formally began the following day. It was also agreed that the two people who were the great powers behind the thrones – Wolsey and Louise – were to be united in an attempt to settle Anglo-Scottish problems, a diplomatic endeavour that would almost certainly be expected to stray far beyond its stated brief. The two dined together at least twice during the summit; doubtless their observations about obtaining and using power were invaluable.

Francis and Henry had their first meeting on 7 June, the feast day of Corpus Christi. After they departed from their respective camps, with 500 horsemen and 3,000 foot soldiers, the two kings came to a halt at opposite sides of the Val Doré, then riding to a space indicated by a spear at the bottom of the valley. Both men were dressed magnificently; Francis in particular stood out in a doublet of cloth of silver and gold studded with diamonds, pearls and rubies, covered by a gold satin cloak. Even his horse was festooned with gold and jewellery. Henry, meanwhile, was attired in an outfit of silver and rubies, with an enormous gold belt around his already substantial waist. They were accompanied by many of their most trusted lords, including Bonnivet and Bourbon on the French side and Wolsey and the Master of Horse, Sir Henry Guildford, on the English wing.

They rode towards each other slowly at first, but, when they were nearly at the agreed spot, the kings spurred their mounts, as if they were about to do battle with one another. Both seemed uncharacteristically nervous, each suspecting that the other had highly trained bodyguards on hand in case anything unexpected should occur. The assembled onlookers were briefly silent and anxious, alarmed lest something was amiss. Yet any fears were soon assuaged, as Francis and Henry lowered their hats to each other before embracing in the full amity of fraternal fellowship. A celebratory drink of a spiced wine cup was served, and a toast drunk – 'English and French – good friends!'[10]

The two men had more in common than they might have acknowledged, as the treaty of 1518 had made clear. Both did indeed have 'the flower and vigour of youth': Henry was twenty-eight, Francis twenty-five. Both had inherited countries that were essentially stable, thanks to their predecessors, but had imperial ambitions far beyond their own borders. Both were good-humoured, charismatic and athletic men who enjoyed the pleasures of food, drink and sex, but who also had erudite and aesthetic interests in music, art and literature. Both were largely popular in their home countries thanks to early military successes, and both, inevitably, knew that the other had to be watched carefully, lest their rival ambitions should clash.

There then followed a brief meeting between Wolsey and Bonnivet in the royal pavilion, in which some dull but necessary business was conducted, not least an almost ritualistic argument that took place about Henry's perceived claims to the French throne. It was reported by Fleurange – albeit a far from impartial witness – that when a herald made the proclamation, 'I, Henry, King of France', Henry interrupted, saying: 'I cannot be while you are here, for I would be a liar', and instructed the herald instead to call him 'Henry, King of England'. Once the necessities had been taken care of, the two monarchs emerged arm in arm, to public acclaim, and the serious business of celebrating began in earnest.

The preliminary 'feat of arms' began two days later, on 9 June 1520, with 300 riders involved in some jousting. By the standards of the occasion, this was nothing more than a little light relief before the proper business of the next fortnight began, but it was still taken seriously; shields of 'challengers' were presented at the 'tree of honour', with those of the 'comers' or stars of the tournament at its base. The next day, being a Sunday, contained no violent encounters, but instead witnessed a courtly ritual in which each king dined with the other's queen, both of whom were heavily pregnant; Francis headed to the wooden palace at Guînes to entertain Catherine, and others, for the evening, while Henry made the journey to Andres to amuse Claude.

Francis spent the evening in a typical display of chivalry and almost exaggerated courtesy; arriving on a mule, he seemed less interested in the musical entertainment, provided by the Gentlemen of the Chapel Royal, than he did in finding 130 of the finest ladies at court dining in the nearby hall. He removed his bonnet and kissed and embraced every single one of them, 'saving four or five that were old and not fair, standing together'.[11] A few hurt feelings did not bother a king. After much dancing and merriment, including an encounter with the beautiful noblewoman Anne Browne, he finally took his leave, although not before kissing each of the women of the court once more as his farewell. Historians, even Fleurange, do not record whether his courtesy extended to leaving with Miss Browne, but he certainly danced with her several more times over the coming days.

The mood of good cheer and amity lasted for the next fortnight, despite some unwelcome outbreaks of poor weather. The jousting continued, except on one day when the rain made it impossible. This ceremonial event began with the queens arriving on the field in lavishly decorated litters, complete with ladies-in-waiting and their servants, and declaring the field open. Claude, who was pregnant with her fifth child, was seen in a silver-cloth gown, over which she wore a gold petticoat. Her sartorial splendour was reflected by her countrywomen, who epitomised the best of French femininity;

by way of contrast, the ambassador to Mantua, who was present, was dismissive of the Englishwomen, whom he considered neither attractive nor well dressed, in addition to being far too fond of drinking.

After the women had fulfilled their decorative purpose, it was time to allow the men to engage in the bloodthirsty act of jousting, which both countries did with aplomb. Both Francis and Henry participated vigorously in the tournaments, splintering lances and shields alike with royal authority, and did not escape unscathed; Francis received a black eye and a bloody nose while in competition with the Earl of Devon, while Henry conducted himself with such kingly excitement that he ended up killing one of his finest horses.

In the evenings, a different kind of Anglo-French cordiality was also evident. Formal post-prandial dancing was performed to the accompaniment of tabor, pipe and viols. These dances, termed 'masques', involved a lot of dressing-up and were a distinctively Italianate element in the festivities. Francis had come across the masque for the first time in Milan during the recent occupation of the city, and after his return to France it became a regular feature of entertainment at the royal court. Participants would often dress up as characters from history or mythology, and during the festiv-ities of the Field the masque could itself be good for establishing some basic diplomacy. Apart from a handful of senior courtiers and aristocrats, very few of the Field's participants were at all fluent in each other's native tongues and translation difficulties often arose. Laughter during a masque was doubtless one way of establishing some kind of communication, as was the brio encouraged by the ever-flowing fountains of wine.

There were also a few surprises. A couple of unusual members of Henry's retinue, a pair of monkeys covered in gold leaf, gave the bemused but enchanted Francis much pleasure. Cardinal Wolsey wrote later that 'the French King was overcome with much curi-osity playing with those little knaves that did all they could to steal and pester his advisers, yet he willed them to be present at every banquet'. At times, Francis may well have found the relative stiff-ness of the English and the formality of the proceedings something of a trial, and wished to liven things up. His readiness to break with accepted protocol is illustrated by two further incidents. On the evening of Wednesday, 13 June 1520, after a particularly large amount of wine had been drunk, wrestling had replaced jousting due to the inclement weather, and some Bretons were sparring with the Yeomen of the Guard. Whether he was drunk or caught up in the adrenaline of the moment, Henry decided to challenge Francis to a match. A competition between the two monarchs contravened the rules set down for the duration of the Field, established so that neither would feel that they had been dishonoured, and Henry, a large and vigorous man, probably envisaged nothing more than a friendly exercise in male grappling. But Francis was master of an especially effective technique called *tour de Bretagne* and within seconds the English king had been thrown onto the floor in a 'wonderful fall'. This particular episode did not appear in contemporary English accounts of the pageantry and Henry, who considered himself an expert wrestler, could not conceal his annoyance, although he swiftly laughed it off to maintain the amicable mood and asked for another bout; Francis, who knew the value of quitting while ahead, graciously declined.

A more explicit, and potentially dangerous, breach of royal etiquette took place on the morning of Sunday, 17 June. Francis got up early and rode, without giving any advance notice, to the English encampment at Guînes, accompanied only by two royal gentlemen. He burst into Henry's chamber while the English king still slept and, in an elaborate charade, declared himself to be his prisoner, before insisting on acting as a valet, begging Henry's permission to help him put on his shirt. This piece of theatre was both a bold jest and a symbolic gesture; by describing himself as a 'prisoner', Francis had in fact made a direct challenge to Henry's competence. His insistence on being allowed to dress the English king showed that, far from being a supplicant, he was Henry's sovereign equal. The stratagem worked; Henry professed himself amused by the ploy, referred to Francis as 'Brother' and, calling it 'the best trick ever played', gifted him an expensive ruby collar, only to be given a doubly valuable bracelet before the French king departed, all before breakfast.

The story shows Francis at his best and worst. His boldness and impetuosity are a tribute to his courage, and the less-than-subtle gesture demanding that Henry respect his sovereignty proved entirely successful; so much so that the English monarch repaid the favour by doing exactly the same thing to his French counterpart a few days later, by which time the novelty had perhaps worn off a little. Yet it was a decision made instinctively, with no heed for the careful and patient diplomatic achievements that had been made over the previous days. Had the prank offended Henry, the outcome would have been embarrassing and undone all the previous good work; had an over-cautious English soldier attempted to confront Francis, the result might have been deadly.

As the pageantry drew to a close there were especially warm public declarations of mutual esteem, appreciation of progress made and expectation of future joint projects. On 23 June Wolsey celebrated High Mass at an altar that had been set up in the middle of the tournament field – an impressive achievement at any time, but all the more so now as it was believed that he had not performed a Mass for many years. As Claude and Catherine embraced during the sign of the peace, real warmth seemed evident amidst the formality and trappings of pageantry, and this was strengthened by the handing over of gifts on 24 June; Wolsey, for example, gave Louise a fragment of the True Cross, while she bestowed a hugely expensive jewelled Cross upon him. There were prizes for the jousting, great promises of amity and much embracing. Louise informed the foreign ambassadors that, after the closing ceremonies on the following Monday, the two kings had agreed to build a special chapel on the Field of the Cloth of Gold. It would, apparently, be dedicated to Our Lady of Friendship. The whole event, said Francis and Henry to each other with great sincerity, had been most remarkable. With tears in their eyes, they vowed to return annually in order to commemorate two and a half successful weeks. Observers might have been forgiven for thinking that they were in the presence of something very wonderful indeed, to say nothing of a potential breakthrough in European diplomacy: a permanent *entente cordiale* between two great kingdoms.

And then reality intruded in its usual prosaic way. In the space of a day, it was all over. The grand golden tents were dismantled and the wine-dispensing fountains had dried up. The excitements of the sport and the riches of the pageantry must suddenly have seemed quite insubstantial. One English aristocrat, who had been seen embracing Frenchmen and women alike, returned to England and announced: 'If I had a drop of French blood in my body, I would cut myself open and get rid of it.'[12] Promises of eternal friendship were to prove just as flimsy as the makeshift city of gold. Francis was back at court by the evening of 25 June. As for Henry, he rode east and, having crossed the French border, arrived at Gravelines in Flanders, where he met Charles V once again. The English king and the emperor decided to hold a conference in Calais and agreed that it should take place in approximately twelve months' time. There they would have a chance to further their own mutual understanding and agreed interests. Meanwhile, the pair concluded that it would be best if neither of them signed an independent treaty with the King of France. Henry did nothing to disown the treaties that he had signed previously with Francis, but nor did recent events result in a new treaty. The chapel of Our Lady of Friendship remained unbuilt.

The Field of the Cloth of Gold was a triumph, both aesthetically and in bringing together two opposed nations in the spirit of friendship and peace, if only for a short time and in an artificial situation. And the affection between Francis and Henry was real; probably far more so than any personal relationship that existed between Henry and Charles. Yet ultimately the huge, expensive entertainments that had taken place remained as transitory and ultimately expendable as the King of England's unkempt beard.

CHAPTER 9

Consequences

In June 1520, Francis was in his pomp. The extravaganza of the Field of the Cloth of Gold might have been costly, of little lasting diplomatic value and, at times, potentially dangerous to many of those involved, but one area in which it undeniably succeeded was to show the French ruler, five years into his reign, as a great king, adept at feats of strength and gallant love-making alike. He was a man conscious of his image and the value of a good report being made of it, and he considered that the first half-decade in which he had held power reflected well upon him both as monarch and man. Yet, as autumn followed summer, the unstable and uneasy peace that currently held in Europe could not last, and the repercussions of many of Francis's former actions would soon return to haunt him. The next decade was once referred to as 'the time of tears and sorrows',[1] and would bring unimaginable shame and humiliation.

The major problem was, of course, the new Holy Roman Emperor. By the autumn of 1520 Francis was faced with the unpleasant but undeniable fact that the increasing consolidation of Habsburg power was growing more formidable by the day. He needed to counter this, and considered his options, both military and diplomatic. He was helped by the geographical distribution of Charles V's main territories, namely the Spanish kingdom, Naples, the Netherlands and his Germanic empire; none of them adjoined any other. This fundamental issue militated against their consolidation as a centre of European power, giving Francis an advantage. Yet it was still undeniably the case that Charles V possessed an empire, with the young Habsburg at the apex as its sovereign lord.

Charles was already known as 'King of the Romans', an interim title bestowed on the emperor elect following his coronation at Aachen on 23 October 1520. Yet something far greater awaited him in the near future, when the pope would preside over the planned imperial coronation in Rome. It would be then, and only then, that the crown of the Holy Roman Empire – one descended from Char-lemagne, no less – would adorn the young emperor's brow for the very first time. In the meantime, Pope Leo allowed Charles to use the title 'Roman Emperor elect'. As luck would have it, the coron-ation in Rome never took place. Instead, Charles had to wait over a decade and the reign of two popes before his *sacre* in Bologna. On a personal level this was an irritation, but it also had a serious practical implication when it came to the sharp end of international politics. From whichever direction he travelled, Charles could not conceivably arrive in central Italy without an army. All of this made it highly likely that the emperor elect would use that power to attack French-occupied Milan, and thereby establish his own power without further competition. Italy was widely believed to be key to any serious attempt to rule Europe; conquer it, and glory was there for the taking.

Francis was entirely aware of the difficulties that he faced but, for the first time, he was unable to deal with his enemies swiftly and decisively. The obvious move was for him to lead his own force in a defensive capacity, advancing south from the garrison in Milan and towards Rome before the end of 1520. Such a show of strength might have kept the Habsburg at bay, and might even have led to further conquests. Unfortunately, Francis was distracted by some serious domestic problems. His military campaigns had been hugely ex-pensive, and even by 1519, rumours had circulated that Francis and Louise were misusing public funds for their own ends; the Venetian ambassador, Sebastiano Giustiniani, had reported to his masters that 'King Francis and his mother the Duchess are very unpopular all over France. The Duchess is believed to have amassed monies throughout the kingdom with the object, people say, of helping the King in any sudden need.'[2] While this was good common sense, it also felt as if the royal pair were filling their hugely expensive boots without any discernible benefit to their subjects. It did not help the country's parlous financial situation that the pageantry of the Field of the Cloth of Gold was obtained on credit, which would take a decade to repay.

The king was also worried about his mother's health, which had become poor by 1520 and therefore made her potential regency in his absence hazardous. Although she had been an excellent and efficient regent while her son was away fighting his Marignano campaign of 1515, she had been something of a figurehead working within the narrow proscriptions imposed upon her power, not least because the Great Seal was not in her keeping. Now forty-four years old, the duchess was no longer a young woman, and had fallen prey to ill health. She had developed gout, probably due to her sedentary and protein-enriched existence at court; Louise lived in agony caused by the dreaded malady. A gouty regent in permanent pain would be rendered incapable of devoting her full attention to affairs of state, which meant that it was inadvisable for her to perform this task on Francis's behalf once again. It did not help that Chancellor Duprat, who was the only other person with the executive ability needed to run a regency administration, was expected to be at the king's side were he to leave for Italy.

Another concern was that Francis's continued devotion to strenuous physical exercise almost cost him his life, after a series of accidents. These included his being set ablaze during a series of revels and, bizarrely, being struck on the head by a firebrand, which knocked him unconscious. He took the ailment in relatively good humour, saying: 'Don't try to find out who threw the torch – if I play the fool, I must take the consequences.'[3] His hair had to be cropped short as a result of his injury, inspiring a fashion among the nobility for closely shorn scalps.

Such instances of misfortune caused by carelessness would continue. In the early months of 1521 Francis sustained a serious leg injury during one of his beloved mock battles. These games had been devised to tire out the young nobles and had become a feature of the almost ceaseless court amusements, not least because they kept soldiers active in preparation for a real war. The wound was sufficiently serious for the king to take two months' enforced rest; it was a deliverance that the injury was not a fatal one. Therefore, when he considered the necessity of embarking on a prolonged military campaign, the king had to contend with his mother's gout, his own infirmity, potentially treacherous allies, a lack of money in the exchequer and a people who were starting to lose faith in his judgement. Whatever happened next would make the hard-won Marignano campaign look as easy and pleasant as a night spent with a royal mistress.

Francis's solution, and a less than ideal one, was to wage war by proxy. In order to do this he turned to a *condottiere*, a mercenary who was in charge of his own private army. These figures were vital in the military campaigns of Renaissance Europe, serving their master without discrimination in return for a substantial fee. The *condottiere* and his men could therefore be relied upon to advance a ruler's strategic and military interests in his stead. Although usually associated with northern Italy, other excellent mercenaries were also to be found in the French-speaking territories and Robert de La Marck, lord of Sedan, had accrued an enviable reputation on account of his military prowess. In February 1521 de La Marck visited Francis while he was convalescing at Romorantin and agreed his terms. In return for a cash payment of 10,000 *écus* – one that Francis could ill afford – an annuity and the services of twenty-five of the king's best men-at-arms, La Marck agreed to declare war on Charles. He lost little time in fulfilling his master's orders, and in March 1521 invaded Luxembourg, part of the ancestral Habsburg domain.

At the same time, a further diversionary move came from the ruler of Navarre, Henri d'Albret. As a result of Francis's financial generosity, d'Albret led his men out of his kingdom's northern lands in an attempt at recovering the southern Navarrese territories that had been occupied by the Castilian army in 1512. Although it would obviously be an advantage if the outcome were successful, this was not the primary objective. Instead the king hoped that Charles's forces, inconvenienced by the need to open these fronts to his west, would therefore be unable to plan and execute an Italian campaign, thereby removing Milan from any danger. It was another gamble, played for high stakes, but for a few weeks it looked as if Francis's ploys might succeed; his money certainly bought him time to recover from his injuries.

The momentum was not with him for long. Charles was not a stupid or gullible man, and in early April Francis received his ambassador, Naturelli, who accused the French king of having paid for these mercenaries and warned of dire consequences if they continued. Francis, disingenuously, denied having anything to do with either party, even going so far as to claim that he had forbidden any subjects of his to help La Marck; as for d'Albret, it was his own business whatever course of action he pursued. The lies did not convince, but it was soon irrelevant. By the end of the month a 6,000-strong contingent of the imperial army commanded by the brilliant general Henry, Count of Nassau, had expelled La Marck and his men from Luxembourg and forced their retreat to Sedan, which Nassau subsequently occupied. Thus, instead of improving his situation, Francis had a hostile armed force encamped on his kingdom's north-eastern frontier. As if this was not bad enough, a military debacle soon followed in the south.

D'Albret and his Navarrese army enjoyed notable initial success in regaining the Spanish-occupied territories of Navarre, so, drunk with bloodlust and ambition, the army's commanders, including André de Foix, Lord of Lesparre, decided to continue the campaign beyond what they had agreed. Their new objective was to press on beyond the border and into Castile itself. This was an insane miscalculation since the Castilian army, with its superb military equipment and well-trained troops, was one of Europe's most formidable fighting units.

In early 1520 it was distracted while suppressing a local revolt, allowing the Navarrese force mistakenly to believe that they enjoyed a superiority. Once the Castilian army was able to concentrate on the invading force, having crushed the internal dissent with especial brutality, it steamrollered the Navarrese into submission at a battle fought at Esquiroz on 30 June, during which Lesparre lost an eye. The status quo was restored, and Spanish rule in occupied southern Navarre appeared as secure as ever. On both his southern and north-eastern frontiers, therefore, Francis's actions had imperilled French safety. Both of these ill-fated expeditions gave Charles the opportunity to portray Francis as a duplicitous ruler, conniving at an invasion of territories where the emperor exercised sovereignty. The Holy Roman Emperor had a maxim that he was especially fond of quoting: 'Fortune usually favours not only the brave, but also the young.'[4] War by stealth had turned out to be a very poor idea indeed.

If these problems were serious for Francis, then what occurred in Italy was to be even more catastrophic, directly prefiguring his downfall. After the deaths of Lorenzo de Medici and his French wife Madeleine, the alliance contracted between Francis and Pope Leo X was of little military value to the papacy, and so Leo decided instead to pledge his allegiance to a stronger and more valuable ally. His courtship of Charles V had begun the previous Christmas, when he sent the emperor elect a valuable white horse – a traditional sign of papal favour which paved the way for a more formal alliance in due course. This followed sooner than expected, in part because of Francis's territorial manoeuvring. After Naturelli's protest, and the king's lies, Charles and Leo signed a secret treaty on 29 May 1521. This affirmed Charles's right to be crowned emperor when he was in Rome, and also promised him the succession to Naples. The existence of their alliance was to be made public when Leo had a suitable pretext for breaking his existing treaty with Francis, but both parties knew that the increasingly volatile behaviour of the French king would provide the necessary excuse.

In fact, it took mere weeks for a reason to be found. In early June, French commanders based in Milan led by the Seigneur de Lescun crossed the border into the papal states while pursuing the instigators of anti-French protests within the duchy. This was an easy mistake to make due to the porous nature of the border, and the terrain gave few clues as to where one jurisdiction ended and another might begin. Under any normal circumstances, a blind eye would have been turned, especially as a supposed ally was involved, but Leo saw his opportunity. Swiftly, the pope turned a minor infringement into a major diplomatic incident, one that could be used to herald an imminent realignment as dictated by papal self-interest.

It seemed as if Francis and the French were cursed, as other incidents of ill fortune soon visited them. On 28 June, the building that housed the French garrison in Milan was struck by lightning and caught fire; just over 300 French soldiers died as a result of an explosion in the garrison's arsenal. It proved a portent for Leo, who promptly acclaimed the disaster as a positive indication of divine discontent. God too, it seemed, was anti-French and the pope's alliance with Charles became public knowledge on the following day, after which the two of them formed a new treaty with the Marquis of Mantua and the Florentines.

Initially, the French king believed that the personal relationship between himself and Leo might lead to a rapprochement, but he was soon disabused of this. The new treaty fortified French anti-papal sentiment and so, on 13 July, a furious and resentful Francis retaliated by announcing that the French would therefore retain any ecclesiastical revenues rather than dispatch them to Rome; he went on to claim that 'he would ere long enter Rome and impose laws on the pope'.[5] This tit-for-tat diplomacy was in line with previous quarrels between the French monarchy and the Church. Francis also seized the initiative by demanding substantial sums from the Florentine bankers currently living in France, which were quickly paid; the Lyons chapter alone contributed 100,000 *livres*. For a court living well beyond its means, this money was, quite literally, a godsend.

In June 1520 there had been protestations at the Field of the Cloth of Gold that the celebrations would become an annual event. Just over a year later, many of the participants of those revels were indeed reunited at Calais, but the mood was altogether more sombre. Previous diplomatic machinations had taken place at a time of peace; now war seemed imminent. The victory at Marignano had become an increasingly distant memory and Francis was beginning to realise that the throne of Naples seemed unlikely to be his; it was all he could do to maintain his army and administration in Milan, where the empire now wished to assert its power to enjoy the huge symbolic value of establishing an important presence in Italy. It did not help that the pope was also against him.

In the early summer of 1521, Henry VIII, who was entertained rather than threatened by the conflict between Charles and Francis, let it be known that he was available to act as a suitably regal mediator – one whose experiences in the business of kingship qualified him to adjudicate on the issues underlying the quarrels of his fellow monarchs. He was helped by his ambassador, Sir William Fitzwilliam, who could see the chaos that was breaking out in the French court; as Fitzwilliam put it, 'For about half a year past, they would by their words have overrun all the world, and cared for nothing save our master; and by as much as I can see, they would now have peace with all their hearts.' The role of Solomon was an unusual one for Henry to play, and so he decided that his trusted cardinal would act in his stead, providing arbitration and balm in equal measure.

Wolsey therefore presided at an international conference held in Calais on 20 July. Duprat led the French negotiating team and Charles had sent Mercurino di Gattinara, head of the imperial chancery, to speak for him. Duprat explained that Francis's motives were to obtain lasting peace, not simply a transitory truce; he did not mention that this was a financial necessity rather than an ideological decision. He was out of luck. The emperor, it turned out, did not want peace. Indeed, as di Gattinara explained to the conference, the pursuit of war might well be the policy that best advanced the interests of the empire. After all, he argued, Francis had started all the trouble by backing two underhand initiatives whose consequences undermined general peace and security in Europe. The King of France could best be described as a deceitful and unregal character with a taste for jingoistic military adventures conducted by soldiers with neither brains nor judgement. Therefore, he concluded, Francis deserved to be taught a lesson. Would Henry like to join him, he mused, in forming a grand alliance against France?

The cunning Wolsey kept his counsel. To this day, it is uncertain whether he arrived in Calais looking for a peaceful settlement among all the parties involved, or whether he hoped to take the opportunity to ally with Charles after proving that Francis was unworthy of diplomatic respect. Certainly, his instructions from

Henry were clear: whatever he entered into, the crucial necessity was that England be given the time to prepare for what could be a long and expensive campaign. In the event, it might have been the persuasive powers of di Gattinara that impressed Wolsey in their private conversations, or perhaps it was the suggestion that he would be made pope. By mid-August the cardinal had left Calais for Bruges and on 23 August he signed a treaty, on behalf of Henry VIII, with Charles V. This treaty of alliance was subsequently described as 'a monument to perfidy worthy of Ferdinand the Catholic'.[6] The terms agreed were that, should Franco-imperial difficulties remain unresolved at the end of the autumn, England would declare war on France and the emperor would mount a campaign against the French army from Spain in the spring of 1523. Each was committed to a sizeable force of 40,000 men.

Di Gattinara, and by extension Charles, had argued for the almost immediate launch of a joint military expedition but Wolsey got the delay that he wanted. He appreciated the emperor's strong position and considered the Anglo-imperial alliance by far the best for England; Francis had been eclipsed and Charles, the shining new addition to the galaxy of European potentates, was undoubtedly the coming man. Yet Wolsey appreciated the time to observe and consider all that occurred. After all, before the Battle of Marignano and the subsequent capture of Milan, Francis had not been taken seriously as a great European ruler. There remained dynastic complications; Francis's daughter Charlotte had been promised in marriage to Charles, but then so had Henry's daughter Mary, and whichever one of the two girls ended up in ever closer union with the emperor dictated her country's fortunes. The arrangement could be described as highly provisional, at best, like all such deals contracted on behalf of children who were barely out of their swaddling clothes, and other events almost invariably intervened; nevertheless, Princess Mary seemed destined for Charles's bed at some point in the future, as part of an Anglo-imperial alliance.

Initially, it appeared as if some kind of peace deal might be obtained. Charles let it be known via his emissaries that he was prepared to negotiate a truce with France which would end the intermittent hostilities by November. If this had been the case, it would have been an enormous relief for Francis, who was on the ropes when it came to his country's finances, as his adversaries were aware. Fitzwilliam had reported in February that 'both horse meat and man's meat are growing dear as they do in England', and soon he would say: 'as for money, the French king maketh all shift he can to borrow of every man still . . . [I have seldom seen] such poverty as is now.' For their own sake, the French hoped that a general and lasting European peace was at hand, something that Francis would surely have accepted in exchange for the dilution of his territorial ambitions.

Charles, however, had other ideas, meaning that the treaty was worthless even before it was signed. His army, under the gallant command of Nassau, attacked the north-eastern border of France on 20 August 1521 and besieged Mézières for three weeks. The resistance, led by the equally noble Bayard, was spirited and valiantly fought, but it was of little use as bombs and mortars destroyed what remained of the town. On 9 September the imperial army over-ran Ardres, scene of Francis's makeshift court the previous year, which offered proof to the outraged French emissaries, if any more was needed, that further negotiation at Calais was useless. Duprat tried what little he could to prolong the talks in the hope of a resolution, but it was clear that there was nothing to be done; Marguerite remarked to Fitzwilliam, scornfully, 'See ye not how the cardinal is ever treating for peace almost to the day of battle?'[7] With civility extinguished between the participants at Calais, relations descended into lies and abuse; Duprat wagered his head that Francis had not been involved with La Marck, only for di Gattinara, observing Duprat's porcine form, to request a pig's head instead, on the grounds that it would be easier to eat.

Francis, in desperation, raised a large army at Rheims in order to relieve the siege at Mézières. His first stroke of luck for a considerable time came when a small advance force supplied the besieged town with much-needed supplies on 23 September, and, when Francis's army was sighted three days later, Nassau and the imperial army considered it prudent to retreat, prompting Francis to write in triumph to his mother that 'God has shown he is a good Frenchman'.[8] He did not know that Nassau had decided to lay waste to every town that he encountered on his withdrawal; the French poet Joachim du Bellay described the sack of Aubenton, in which few were spared, as 'the origin of the great cruelties committed in wars for the next thirty years'.[9]

The king had not forgotten his abilities as a military leader and, gravely imperilled, fought with vigour and authority, remembering the lessons that he had learnt in his previous campaigns. Consequently, what began as a defensive manoeuvre began to evolve into a steady stream of successes. In northern Italy his army, led by Lautrec, regained control of Parma, and French support for the rump kingdom of Navarre kept the Spanish at bay; on 19 October Bonnivet even captured Fuenterrabía, which had been regarded as 'the key to Spain'. The tide appeared to be turning in his favour.

It seemed for a brief instant as if he would be in a position to march against Charles, who, panicked by his opponent's success, was prepared to agree to a peace treaty with rather more alacrity than he had hitherto displayed. Francis's negotiators at Calais took heart at Wolsey's shifting position; his aim was to ensure that the English supported the winning side, not to be involved in a complex and expensive European war. On 4 October, having consulted the emperor, the cardinal announced that the envisaged truce was now offered without further conditions: Charles and the pope were ready to sign. In theory, at least, Francis had won.

As before, the French king was unable to leave the gambling table with his winnings intact. Once again he was experiencing military success and, with a rush of blood to his royal head, he wanted more of it. Having gone to the considerable bother of raising an army in order to repel Nassau, he wished his soldiers to be kept occupied, telling Fitzwilliam: 'Ye see what charge I am at, and also how my men eat up my subjects, wherefore I will march on straight, and live upon their countries as they have done on mine.' His aim now was no longer defence, but revenge against those who he believed had wronged him. He had finally over-reached himself.

To go into battle at the head of one's army was, for many monarchs, an honour and a privilege rather than a military obligation. The pageantry involved was considerable, and its symbolic and patriotic effects incalculable. The sight of a king leading his men onto the field of battle reminded everybody – including monarchs themselves – of kingship's glorious and martial origins. For a man of action such as Francis, it made all the tedious aspects of kingship – the lawyers, the courtiers, the political skulduggery – seem trivial in comparison. His objective was to relieve Tournai, which was being besieged by the imperial army. On 4 October he advanced with his forces, including a good number of Swiss mercenaries, with his pike literally in his hand, but appalling weather ceased his progress and caused enormous difficulty for his men. Fitzwilliam complained: 'Their horses waste sore about by stabling [outside], and men weary and sick very fast; and for my part, I had never worse journey in all the wars that ever I had been in.'[10]

Disaster soon replaced triumph. As October drew to a close, Francis lost his military advantage and failed to relieve the siege of Tournai. On 1 November he ordered a retreat and, against Duprat's advice, disbanded his army nine days later. The chancellor had favoured a war of attrition which would wear down Charles's resources, but Francis remained obstinate. At this news Tournai's defenders lost all hope and surrendered at the end of November. The king initially ignored Wolsey's increasingly desperate attempts to broker a truce, believing that it was a feint by Charles to regroup his forces before resuming war, but he was unable to take advantage of an opportunity to seize victory on 23 October at Bouchain, leading du Bellay to lament that 'God placed the enemy in our hands and our refusal to accept him has since cost us dear; he who refuses what God offers through good fortune cannot get it back when he asks.'[11] In a petulant fit Francis ordered his army to lay waste to nearby countryside, an act that was described as 'the most piteous destruction of towns and spoiling of so fair a country as never have been seen among Christian men.'[12] Imperial propaganda accused Francis of all kinds of outrage, including severing the fingers of small children. Although this was almost certainly an exaggeration, there was no doubt that the sour, acrid taste of defeat was poisoning both the morale and the honour of the French forces.

When sorrows come, they come not single spies, but in battalions, and Francis's own battalions were finding themselves under unbearable pressure in northern Italy, where November witnessed a series of catastrophes. A lack of money and the perceived cruelty of the French occupiers meant that there was no affection towards them from the Milanese, and when the imperial army broke through the fortifications that surrounded Milan on 19 November, they were greeted as conquering heroes. The unloved French administrators, led by Lautrec, were forced to join the erstwhile army of occupation as it retreated to the north. By the end of the year, the French had been expelled from all the cities that they had occupied in the duchy of Milan. It was ironic that the Italian army was commanded by Prospero Colonna, who had been captured by the French after the seizure of Milan; the old general was once more in the ascendant. A matter of weeks after he had resisted Wolsey's urgings, Francis was now prepared to sign a truce. This time it was Charles who, exulting in his mighty victories, had no interest in seeking peace. The talks at Calais concluded, fruitlessly, three days after the French lost control of Milan. On 24 November, at Bruges, Wolsey signed a treaty committing English troops to a campaign that would be launched by the empire at some time in the following spring. Francis was therefore facing a coalition of Europe's two most powerful forces, with no money, a disaffected people and an army worn down by repeated defeats. It was either to his credit or to his shame that he remained undaunted.

At the beginning of December 1521, Francis learnt of the death of Pope Leo X. The pope had perished shortly after hearing the news of the relief of Milan, which gave him great joy. After he had had an operation on his persistently troublesome anal fistula, he went out hunting, caught a chill and fell ill with pneumonia shortly afterwards on 1 December and died so suddenly that he could not be given the last rites; rumours of poisoning circulated, but were never proved. It was expected that another Medici, Leo's illegitimate cousin Giulio, would be elected pope; as he was the leader of the imperial group, Francis threatened to withdraw his allegiance to Rome if this came to pass. However, to the surprise of both Charles and Francis, Cardinal Adrian of Utrecht was elected as Pope Adrian VI – a rarity for a non-Italian.

Adrian had been the emperor's tutor and could be expected to have a degree of loyalty to a pupil of whom he was genuinely fond;

Charles wrote to the new pope that his appointment meant that 'God had wished to make a sign to them that His will was to set in order the affairs of Christendom and to enable them together to spread the Christian faith.' Francis was as appalled as he would have been at Giulio's election, initially refusing to recognise him and sneering that he was nothing more than 'the Emperor's school-master'. His mother, meanwhile, believed that Charles might as well call himself pope, so absolute did his dominance appear to be.

Nonetheless, Pope Adrian soon proved to be his own man and no imperial puppet, somewhat to Francis's relief. Adrian refused to join the anti-French coalition and instead concentrated his efforts on uniting Europe in a new religious crusade against the Turks, who were threatening Rhodes; the last Christian outpost in the eastern Mediterranean looked likely to be invaded at any moment. Francis, who had never had any great interest in crusades, none-theless knew that he had to remain in Adrian's favour, and so he informed the pope that he was certainly prepared 'to come with great power against the Turk, provided Milan which is our patri-mony is returned to us'.[13] Old convictions never died.

By January 1522 the king was ready to strike back against his ene-mies. The 16,000 Swiss troops he had asked the cantons to deliver had marched across the Alpine passes and were descending into Italy. Knowing that he was about to fight a major campaign against the empire meant that Francis had to maintain good relations with Henry VIII, so as to avoid waging a war on two fronts. Francis han-dled Henry in a masterly fashion. He declared that, as the English king was now the emperor's ally and therefore an enemy of France, it was inappropriate that he should continue to receive a pension. He therefore ordered it to be cancelled but feigned ignorance when Henry complained, swearing, doubtless with tongue firmly in cheek, that the money would eventually get there but had been delayed and that all would be well before long.

Another, more subtle act of retaliation also followed, which brought the Franco-Scottish 'Auld Alliance' into play. John Stuart, Duke of Albany and illegitimate grandson of James II of Scotland, had been born and raised in France after his father Alexander had fled there after quarrelling with his brother, James III. Albany was an experienced military commander who had seen action with Francis's armies throughout his reign. In early 1522 Francis dispatched Albany from Paris to southern Scotland, from where he took delight in bothering and frustrating the English army. Once again, Francis shrugged his shoulders at Henry's protests. Albany, he swore, had not sought the French king's permission, as he should have done, before leaving the country, and therefore his actions were not sanctioned by Francis. Louise, meanwhile, declared that she would rather never see her son again than have his alliance with England broken. Although Henry was unconvinced by the veracity of these evasions, he had no desire to embark upon a war with France, and so the dreaded alliance between England and the imperial army remained an abstract one, rather than a real threat.

Once again it was Italy, and the dream of dominion, that inspired Francis. In March 1522 his commander Lautrec had started well. At the head of an army reinforced by Swiss mercenaries he had begun to restore French control in parts of Lombardy despite the intensity of anti-French sentiment in the region. Yet Milan represented a considerably greater prize, and recapturing it was crucial for French morale. Lautrec faced Colonna's army and the Duke of Milan, Francesco II Sforza, who had returned to the city the previous year. Sforza could rely on local loyalty, and this, along with some cash payments, allowed him to reinforce Colonna's own troops, meaning that Lautrec was unable to capture the garrison as he had planned. When Francis heard this he was furious; blaming his captains for their failure to be decisive, he threatened to take charge of operations himself, but events soon made this impossible.

Lautrec decided to save face by attempting a siege of Pavia but Colonna, emboldened by victory, commanded his army out of Milan and based his force at the Charterhouse of Pavia, a monastery five miles to the north of the city, from which he launched attacks on the rear of the French army. Lautrec, unnerved by this unwelcome development, ordered his troops to lift the siege of Pavia and to march north towards Monza. Colonna followed his trail and after establishing his camp at La Bicocca, a substantial manor house, he ordered his men to start digging. The field entrenchments that emerged, incorporating deep ditches and raised platforms for the artillery divisions, were an impressive feat; it was folly to consider attacking them.

Lautrec, however, had no alternative. Faced with a tired and mutinous group of Swiss mercenaries, who demanded either that they went into action or that they be allowed to go home, he presented them with the promise of a swift, victorious engagement and then a triumphant return home to Switzerland. The Swiss eventually agreed, which led to their near-immediate downfall. Adopting their usual style of frontal assault on 27 April, they were massacred by the imperial army's artillery. Some 3,000 men, over 20 per cent of the total force, were killed, and the remainder fled to Switzerland, honour lost. As the statesman Francesco Guicciardini said, 'They returned to their mountains diminished in number, but much more in audacity; for it is certain that the loss they received at Bicocca humbled them to that degree that for several years afterwards they did not show their accustomed vigour.' It was a lasting humiliation that the word *bicocca*, meaning 'something acquired at little cost', subsequently entered the Spanish language.

Without the Swiss, little could be done. Lautrec returned to France, where Francis reproached him for his failure. His commander tartly replied that 'not he but the king lost it, that he had warned the king many times that were he not supplied with money, he would be unable to keep the *gendarmerie* who had had to serve without pay, and that the Swiss had made him fight against his better judgement which they would not have done had they been paid'.[14] It soon transpired, farcically, that 400,000 crowns that Francis believed he had sent to pay for the Swiss troops had never been received, but were instead requisitioned by Louise. When her son, 'his face contorted', confronted her and accused her of being directly responsible for the loss of the duchy of Milan, she pertly claimed that the money was hers by right, being 'her savings from her revenues'.[15] Lautrec left the court for his estates in Guyenne in disgrace, as Francis contemplated the end of his power and influence. Genoa, which had withstood the imperial onslaught for so long, surrendered on 30 May. A French-dominated northern Italy, once an achieved reality, had disappeared from the map. It seemed, finally, that Francis had been defeated. Yet the reason for his failure lay less with his enemies than it did with himself. Like Icarus, he had flown too close to the sun, and his subsequent plummet to earth could only shatter his dreams.

CHAPTER 10

The Enemy Within

Henry VIII and Wolsey were nothing if not self-serving when it came to backing the winning side. After the debacle in Italy in April 1522, it was inevitable that the English would wish to remain allied with the empire, and so, after Charles paid another visit to England in late May, it was once again agreed that they would plan a joint invasion of France before May 1523. It therefore seemed an inevitable occurrence when a herald arrived at the French court in Lyons on 29 May 1522 to issue a formal declaration of Anglo-imperial hostilities in the name of Henry. Louise – by no means an impartial observer – noted that the herald seemed terrified as he stammered out his message, while Francis replied to him at length with withering scorn. The cynical might have speculated that he had plenty of time to prepare his fine words.

Although no formal invasion took place, the Earl of Surrey led an opportunistic raid in July on Morlaix, on the northern coast of Brittany, followed by some further military activity in the following month. The town of Calais, which was still a possession of the English Crown, allowed soldiers from the nearby military garrison to lay waste to large areas of the countryside in adjacent Picardy, before they tried to occupy the town of Hesdin. The French were less concerned about this offensive than the English initially expected, the Duke of Vendôme decrying the 'foul warfare' that their opponents were practising. Without supplies or further backing the English forces lacked momentum, and a vigorous counter-offensive soon forced the aggressors to retreat to the security of Calais.

It now seemed a good opportunity for the Franco-Scottish alliance to bear fruit, and accordingly it was with some delight that Francis heard of the Duke of Albany's plans to attack northern England. Albany had been busy recruiting soldiers in Scotland and in September 1522 he led a large force over the border, intending to capture Carlisle. However, Albany's army were weary and had little interest in fighting a long, vainglorious campaign, and so were happy to accept a truce offered by Lord Dacre, Warden of the Marches, meaning that Albany had to disband his army and flee to the French court. Here Albany persuaded Francis of the merits of a full-scale expeditionary force and, cash-strapped though he was, the French king agreed to give Albany and his cohort Richard de la Pole, Edward IV's nephew, 200,000 *livres* to facilitate an invasion. By June 1523 some 500 French soldiers had arrived in southern Scotland, where they were joined three months later by a contingent of over 1,000 men led by Albany.

The possibility also emerged of some sympathetic help from across the Irish Sea. During the summer of 1523 James FitzGerald, whose earldom of Desmond stretched across most of south-west Ireland, indicated his support for an attack on the 'Pale', the English colony centred on Dublin whose territories encircled the town. Dublin's defenders had every reason to feel alarmed, since Desmond's army posed a considerable military threat. His retainers could go into battle equipped with full body armour, and his mounted warriors, many of whom scorned the use of saddle and stirrups, formed a fierce and near-feral cavalry unit. Had this occurred it would have been highly advantageous for Francis, but, unfortunately for the French, Desmond's energies were soon diverted into launching forays against neighbouring Irish tribal leaders. His motivations were always more anti-English than pro-French in any case; a few years later, in the winter of 1528–9, he would be talking about allegiance to Charles V since by then it was the emperor, rather than Francis, who was Henry's enemy. Although Desmond died in June 1529, the intrigues of his successors continued to challenge the authority of the English Crown in Ireland during the 1530s.

*

Yet in 1522 the most pressing issue for Francis remained the recapture of Milan. Unfortunately, what few allies he still had were
scattered in March 1523 by the revelation of a series of incriminating
letters written by Cardinal Francesco Soderini, leader of the pro-
French faction in the College of Cardinals, which came into the
possession of his fellow cardinal, Giulio de Medici, no friend of
France or of Francis. Soderini was a member of the traditional Florentine patriciate, which dictated his opposition to the Medici clan;
he had attempted to maintain this in a surreptitious manner, especially since Giovanni de Medici's election to the papacy as Leo X in
March 1513, but he remained unreconciled to the Medici hegemony.
Rumours circulated of his involvement in a 1517 plot, hatched by an
anti-Medicean group of cardinals, to kill Leo X, which resulted in
the ringleader, Cardinal Alfonso Petrucci, being executed after a
papal court found him guilty of conspiracy to murder Leo. Soderini
escaped for lack of evidence to bring him to trial.

While some would have left the country, Soderini was instead
implicated in a French plot to invade the kingdom of Naples; as bad
luck would have it, the correspondence detailing his involvement
fell into the hands of Cardinal Medici. Adrian ordered that Soderini
be arrested, and Cardinal Medici, who had been cooling his heels
in Florence since his cousin Pope Leo's death in December 1521,
returned triumphantly to Rome. As he was wholly in favour of the
Anglo-imperial alliance, he took delight in informing Wolsey that
they should petition Pope Adrian to punish Soderini.* He passed the
evidence to the Duke of Sessa, Charles V's newly appointed ambassador to the Holy See, and the seventy-year-old Soderini, following
an interview with the pope in Giulio's presence, was imprisoned
in the Castel Sant'Angelo while awaiting trial. Perhaps unsurprisingly, Wolsey was delighted at this turn of events, describing the
arrested cardinal as 'the chief cause of the present disturbance
in Italy'.

With good reason, Francis regarded Cardinal Medici's actions
as hostile, and was also offended when Adrian, clinging to the

* Giulio de Medici was the illegitimate son of Lorenzo the Magnificent's younger
brother Giuliano de Medici, murdered in 1478.

papacy's vestigial authority as an international arbiter of war and peace, declared in a papal bull that Europe's Christian sovereigns had to agree to a truce. If they did not comply, he would retaliate with spiritual censure. Although he did not specify the nature of the punishment, Adrian was probably referring to a swingeing papal interdict that forbade priests from celebrating Mass and officiating at the sacraments within territories that came under the jurisdiction of a ruler who had offended the papacy. This was a considerable threat, and Francis accused him of breaking canon law. He cited the unfortunate fate of Adrian's early-fourteenth-century predecessor Boniface VIII who, after claiming a universal authority in matters temporal as well as spiritual, was imprisoned by his aristocratic enemies, viciously beaten, and died of his injuries a few days after his release. The establishment of an antipope on French soil had happened before, wrote Francis, and he was perfectly happy to see it happen again.

Adrian was a less politically driven and therefore less divisive pope than his predecessor, Leo X, but he also lacked the latter's flair for diplomacy and worldliness; it did not help that he had never so much as visited Rome before he was elected pope. His desire to remain on good terms with all parties stemmed from reasons as much to do with cash as Christianity; as he said, 'I shall not declare myself against France, because such a step would be immediately followed by the stoppage of all supplies of money from that kingdom, on which I chiefly depend for the maintenance of my court.'[1] He also stated that he believed that, without his spiritual guidance, Francis would lapse into Lutheran heresy. It was of little use; on 18 June 1523 the French king banned the dispatch of money from his court to Rome and, for good measure, expelled the papal nuncio. If he had wished to antagonise Adrian, he could not have done a more effective job. The pope found himself forced into a corner, and on 3 August 1523 he formally joined the Anglo-imperial alliance which, supplemented by the support of Venice, pledged itself to defend Italy against any French attack.

While future events make Francis's actions look reckless, it was clear that he was bent on war against his many enemies, preferably at the same time. His options were limited. Charles V was asking for the territories of Burgundy, Champagne, Provence, Languedoc and Dauphiné to be restored to him, while Henry would apparently only be satisfied by the Crown of France itself. Coupled with the enormous deficit that the country faced – nearly four million *livres* by 1523 – there was little that could be done, save attempting to resolve matters with military might. The country's poverty was such that Francis was reduced to selling sacred plate and jewels, yet more offices and titles, and demanding extortionate taxes from the clergy. It gave the impression of desperation, not kingship.

Nevertheless, on 23 July Francis made the brief journey north to Saint-Denis Abbey where he attended Mass and, in accordance with tradition, placed the saint's relics on the high altar. Prayers asking for St Denis's intercession were considered especially necessary when peril threatened the kingdom. Throughout the campaign to come, his bones would remain exposed as objects of prayer for the faithful. Afterwards, Francis formally took leave of the citizens of Paris and then, accompanied by almost the entire court, moved south and towards the town of Gien in the Loire Valley. Here, in a ceremony conducted on 12 August, Louise was once again named regent with powers to act while her son was out of the country. Her health problems and infirmity were not mentioned. Accompanied by Queen Claude, Louise then made for Blois, the centre of the regency administration. Francis continued on his own journey towards Lyons where, as in 1520, he planned to cross the Alps into northern Italy. Unfortunately, his progress was checked on 16 August by some surprising and distressing news of treason.

Francis's popularity had been waning over the previous years, and so whisperings of insurrection were inevitable. However, a greater blow was that the plot to depose him was led by one of his closest and most trusted allies, Charles III, Duke of Bourbon. Together with his fellow conspirators, the Constable of France now stood ready to launch an armed rebellion and form an alliance with none other than Charles V. The reasons for this decision were complex, and stretched back many years; they also reflected a surprising personal connection between the two men that gave Bourbon's decision an added animosity.

It was said that, in a moment of candour at the Field of the Cloth of Gold, Henry VIII informed Francis that, had he had a subject like Bourbon in his retinue, he would have seen to it that his head would not have remained on his shoulders for long. This was no idle boast; in 1521 Henry had executed Edward Stafford, Constable of England and Duke of Buckingham, out of fear that his subject was over-powerful and lacked sufficient respect for his king. He might have been right, or even over-reacting in a paranoid fashion, but it was nonetheless a mark of regal power that showed where authority lay in decidedly definite terms.

Bourbon was a vastly significant figure in France, and came from a cadet branch of the royal family that had dominated politics for at least the previous century. Their landholdings extended across a huge swathe of central-eastern France and, being contiguous rather than scattered, gave Charles a significant advantage over all other French magnates. The absolute nature of the duke's authority also extended to matters military and legal, financial and political. He had a retinue of soldiers that was a private army in all but name and the duchy's courts of law operated independently of the French Crown's judicial system. Bourbon's extensive fiscal powers included the right to levy his own taxes, and the local representative estates, consisting of the clergy and the nobility, assembled at a time of the duke's choosing. Having convened the estates, it was Charles who presided over their formal deliberations. In truth, little set him apart from the ranks of Europe's sovereign, independent princes. He ruled from the Château of Chantelles and had a court to rival the king's, complete with a captain of the guard, pages, gentlemen in-waiting and even a herald. He was an invaluable ally but a dangerous enemy.

On a personal level, it had always rankled with Francis that Bourbon had the more convincing dynastic claim to the French throne. Founded by Louis IX's younger son Robert de Clermont, the house of Bourbon was richer and, until Francis's accession, considerably more influential than that of Angoulême. Holders of the ducal title stood in a line of direct succession from the royal founder, whereas Francis's claim to the throne was derived from his father, who had only been Louis XII's cousin. The king's lineage was therefore less illustrious than that of the Bourbon duke who, in addition to being a prince of the blood, possessed titles that included being Duke of Auvergne, Dauphin of Auvergne, Prince of Dombes and lord of Beaujolais, among many others. Francis's comparatively humble upbringing offered few points of comparison with the opulence of the ducal establishment. The splendour of the Bourbon estate was certainly enviable, but its ability to arouse the jealousy of both the king and his mother also led to the reign's first political showdown.

Francis's relations with Bourbon, four years his senior, were diplomatically correct rather than close. The older man had conducted his military career with undeniable distinction and few contested his right to be regarded as the kingdom's greatest tactician when it came to waging war. He had been the obvious – perhaps the only – choice to be appointed Constable of France upon Francis's accession in 1515. Bourbon had played a key role in securing the victory at Marignano and in January 1516 he was appointed Lieutenant-General of Milan. An excellent administrator, Bourbon's organisation of the city's defensive system meant that Maximilian's forces were repelled with comparative ease when the emperor tried to eject the French occupying force, all of which in turn strengthened Francis's own position as king. After establishing the French regime in Milan, Bourbon was succeeded there by Lautrec in 1517, and returned to the French court where his diplomatic skills and administrative experience were highly valued by both the royal family and the inner circle of courtiers.

Bourbon was married to Suzanne de Bourbon, Charles VIII's niece; her mother Anne of France, the Dowager Duchess of Bourbon, had ruled France as its regent between 1483 and 1491. Although he was far from poor in his own right, Suzanne's enormous wealth was an invaluable asset when it came to controlling his own domain. Therefore her death on 28 April 1521, as well as being a personal tragedy for Charles, led to a bitter dispute about who owned what within the Bourbon domain. The duke and duchess's first-born child, named Francis after the king, who also served as his godfather, had died in infancy. Their twin sons had similarly not survived for long after being born, and as a result the constable had no male heir.

By the autumn of 1521 there had been a noticeable cooling of relations between the duke and the king, largely because of military matters. Francis's decision to appoint his brother-in-law Charles IV, Duke of Alençon, as commander of the vanguard of the army fighting the imperial forces in the Low Countries went against all known precedents. This particular command had traditionally been a prerogative accorded to the Constable of France, the kingdom's leading general. The duke, despite a habitual tendency to hauteur, managed to conceal his anger, although the English ambassador Fitzwilliam noted that 'some say that Monsieur de Bourbon is not contented that he hath not the award'.[2]

Some observers nonetheless noticed the emergence of a rift between Francis and his supreme military commander. The king's handling of the complex issues surrounding the Bourbon possessions, together with his mother's machinations in that regard, was leading both of them into a bitter public quarrel with the duke, not least because two separate lawsuits were submitted to the *parlement* following the Duchess of Bourbon's death. Louise believed she had a legitimate claim to many of the Bourbon lands as she was Suzanne's first cousin and nearest relative, and therefore, on 7 October 1523, Francis decided that his mother should be entitled to inherit the Bourbonnais territories that had formed part of the late duchess's patrimony. These included Auvergne, Beaujolais, Clermont and others. The king, meanwhile, laid claim to other Bourbon lands on the grounds that, in the event of there being no male heir, they were supposed to revert to the Crown. Although these rights had been showily and publicly renounced by Louis XII, using all available legal means and with the support of France's leading nobles, it was now both financially and politically practical to assert them once more.

Louise also sought to achieve her territorial goal by other, more intimate means. Fourteen years older than Bourbon, the king's mother decided that, in order to achieve true supremacy, she ought to marry him. This has been construed either as an expression of her passionate feelings for him, or as an opportunity to restrain his power and to ensure that his lands reverted to the French king.

Perhaps unsurprisingly, the opportunity of marriage to the gout-ridden forty-four-year-old Louise did not appeal to Bourbon. One, admittedly colourful, account had the duke announce, upon hearing of her interest in him from a mutual friend, 'Is it worthy of our friendship to bring me such an offer from such a woman? You are counselling me, to whom the best woman in the entire kingdom of France belonged, to marry the worst woman in the world. I will not do it, not even for all Christendom.'[3]

It seems unlikely, however, that Louise heard of his reaction, and that her reputed response – 'by the creator of our souls, those words will cost him dear'[4] – was ever uttered. Publicly, the constable handled the situation with extreme caution. Charles V had contacted him soon after Suzanne's death and offered one of his sisters in marriage. Bourbon knew that that option, however, tempting though it might have been in terms of retaining his territory, would be considered treason. Yet while he knew that marriage to a young French princess was a politically expedient option, he did not meet anyone to whom he felt sufficiently drawn. Compared to Louise, however, virtually anyone else was a more appealing prospect. As for her, she was acting out of political calculation, rather than any great feeling of affection. Certainly, the chances of her producing an heir by the summer of 1521 were negligible, meaning that there would be no Bourbon-Savoy union or issue. Had Louise married the constable, the Bourbon lands that she regarded as her own would have reverted to the French Crown following her death.

Louise, who was used to getting her own way, was reduced to fury by the failure of her marital scheme. In the wake of that rejection she took matters into legal realms, with the certain knowledge that, even if the courts ruled against her, her son would use royal privilege to obtain the desired objective, by force if need be. Unsurprisingly, Bourbon was less than impressed by the scheme to break up his domain but, in November 1522, following his mother-in-law Anne of Brittany's death, Francis transferred to Louise the lands that Anne had bequeathed in her will to her son-in-law. The duke was by now incensed, and so the king offered some token conciliation, in the form of marriage to Claude's younger sister Renée and a military command in Italy. If Bourbon had accepted these all might have been salvaged, but Francis became atypically paranoid about the constable's loyalties at the beginning of 1523, convincing himself that Bourbon was about to marry a Habsburg princess. He therefore confronted the bemused duke, who happened to be lunching with Queen Claude at the time, saying: 'Senyor, it is shown to us that you be or shall be married; is it true?' Bourbon denied the charge but Francis repeated his baseless insistence. At this the constable responded, with dignity, 'You menace and threaten me; I have deserved no such cause';[5] any hope he might have had that his reputation at court was intact was now dashed.

Francis's paranoia soon proved to be justified, although the cause lay mainly with him and his mother. After he left court, accompanied by his gentlemen-in-waiting, Bourbon returned home to his château in Moulins to decide upon his next move. By May 1523 the constable told his friend the Bishop of Le Puy that he could no longer expect fair treatment from Francis. He would instead return the constable's sword and the ceremonial collar of St Michael and head to Germany. There, more than 1,000 members of the French nobility would join him. It was time to consider what his next move should be, and he remembered the words of his mother-in-law Anne to him in November 1522: 'I beg and command you to make an alliance with the Emperor.' Once, he had been a master tactician in the field of battle, but now, faced with the possibility of losing everything, he turned this tactical genius into self-preservation; by playing off Francis against the emperor, he saw that he could stand to gain everything.

In May 1523 Charles became aware of Bourbon's intentions and sought a treaty with him, which was negotiated on 11 July at Montbrison in central France. If Bourbon were to sell his soul to the emperor, he would be well rewarded; Charles repeated his offer of marriage to one of his sisters, whether Eleanor or Catherine, with a dowry of 100,000 écus. In exchange for this, Bourbon was expected to spearhead a major domestic rebellion against the French Crown. An imperial army, with the emperor Charles at its head, would invade Languedoc from the south and Bourbon's own military force would be supplemented by 10,000 imperial *Landsknechts*. It was also anticipated that Henry VIII would assist this invasion from the north, in Normandy, and that he would offer Bourbon a subsidy of 100,000 crowns, although England was absent from these negotiations; once again, the royal emissary had failed to arrive at Montbrison in time to sign the treaty.

If there had been any hope that Bourbon would not betray his king and country, it was dispelled by the *parlement*'s report of August 1523, delivered at a time when Louise was embarking on her second regency. The judgement delivered, reflecting her influence, was that the constable's lands be sequestrated. Hell, indeed, hath no fury like a woman scorned. Chancellor Duprat, ever eager to support his benefactors, had gone a step further, claiming, despite the case being *sub judice*, that the constable should be stripped of all his lands and assets, save a token squire's allowance of 4,000 *livres* or so. The judgement meant that little stood between Bourbon and the Anglo-imperial alliance that now seemed poised to intervene militarily on his behalf.

Francis's military intentions would make it easy for the planned uprising to take place. The emperor and Henry VIII, invading from the south and north respectively, would act once the French king was heading towards the Alps in pursuit of his Milanese ambitions. Bourbon still retained a wish for a settlement with Francis, whether out of a lingering sense of residual loyalty or because he was keen to improve his bargaining power with Charles V. This was in contrast to some of his co-conspirators, who wished for action rather than further discussion. Their mistake was to approach two Norman noblemen, Jacques de Matignon and Jean d'Argouges, who, it was thought, might be induced to support the proposed rebellion. De Matignon and d'Argouges were given a detailed account of the conspiracy, which proved to be a fatal miscalculation; the terrified men revealed the plans in the course of a confession they made to the Bishop of Lisieux, who then ignored the sacramental secrecy of the confessional booth and passed the information on to Louis de Brézé, Normandy's supreme seneschal, a relative of the king's and one of his most loyal confidants. It was symptomatic of most contemporary plots that any request for secrecy guaranteed public exposure. De Brézé wrote to Francis on 10 August to inform him of the planned treason. This placed the king in an unenviable position.

If he did nothing he looked weak and allowed the possibility of a rebellion taking place when he left the country; if he attempted to deal with Bourbon in the fashion that Henry VIII had once suggested, Francis ran the risk of creating a martyr and appearing an unjust bully.

There seemed little option than to confront Bourbon; as the ducal palace of Moulins happened to be nearby, Francis headed there with his retinue. He was greeted by a bed-bound Bourbon, suffering from an unnamed illness that might possibly have been nerves after his plot was discovered. Yet Francis, rather than shouting threats or being violent, displayed his considerable charm. Letting Bourbon know that he had received a report of treasonous plotting by the duke, he stated that he believed that it had no authority. Nonetheless, it had made him realise that perhaps he had been a trifle harsh in his dealings with his loyal – very loyal – subordinate, and so not only did he promise to settle the legal suits in the duke's favour, but would raise him up in honour 'as far as it was possible for him to go'.[6] All that he required in return was that the constable should join him on the Italian campaign, without a moment's delay. After all, he had made a great success of the last invasion of Italy, and could do the same once more.

Francis had outplayed Bourbon magnificently. If he refused to accompany the king he might as well have admitted his part in the rebellion. Yet if he accepted, his carefully planned campaign would amount to nothing. Playing desperately for time, the duke asked Francis if he might be permitted a week's grace, citing his ill health and claiming that he needed to recover before he could be of any use in northern Italy. Francis, satisfied that the duke's illness was real rather than a sham, therefore resumed his journey to Lyons, but not before sending his envoy Perrot de Warty to Moulins on 22 August to keep Bourbon mindful of his royal obligations. A frantic duke met with Henry VIII's emissary, Sir John Russell, on 6 September and informed him that he would be quite content to allow an imperial court to decide the issue of the English claim to the French Crown. He had chosen his path, and it was one of conflict.

As Francis suspected, Bourbon's failure to turn up at Lyons within the agreed seven days indicated where his true allegiances lay. Three of his senior advisers were arrested by the king's men in Lyons on 5 September and the duke's servants in Moulins were taken into custody. And yet, despite the self-evident facts, Francis continued to offer Bourbon olive branches, promising that all would be well if the duke could explain his conduct. Unsurprisingly, an explanation was not forthcoming. Bourbon withdrew to the Chantelle, a region where he could hide in one of his grand mansions, and on 7 September severed his allegiance to Francis by informing Charles V that he would appeal to him for redress. He was in a dire position, as the promised imperial *Landsknechts* had failed to arrive and there was no sign of an invasion of France from either the north or the south, and Francis's forces were closing in on him. As for the promised uprising of his fellow magnates, it never materialised, proving that Francis had succeeded in stabilising the situation within his kingdom. Bourbon had little choice but to make a getaway, but not before writing several letters; one of these was to Louise, begging her to intercede on his behalf with her son, despite his actions. On the night of 8 September he fled Chantelle, with 30,000 crowns and disguised as a servant. A few days later he crossed the Rhône. As he left the country he heard heralds proclaiming him a traitor and a wanted man in each town he passed through. By early October he was settled at Sainte-Claude, a mountainous district that lay within the Jura region and safely inside the empire. His treason was complete.

Francis's actions in retaliation were swift and ruthless. It was said that 'no one ever saw any man so overcome by rage'.[7] On 11 September thirty of the constable's accomplices were arrested, and the king announced that a reward of 10,000 *écus* would be paid to whoever captured Bourbon. It was soon clear that the rebellion was less widespread than he had feared, but Francis wished to make a very public example of any of the conspirators, ordering that anyone found guilty of conspiring with Bourbon was to be tortured to elicit the names of their accomplices, who would promptly be arrested. Two of the most notable figures arrested were Jean de Poitiers, Seigneur de Saint-Vallier, and the Bishop of Autun. Meanwhile, Francis commanded that the army should proceed across the Alpine passes but without him at its head; the details of the treachery would have to be rooted out before the sovereign could leave his kingdom. The French forces, under the command of Admiral Bonnivet, forced the retreat of the imperial army towards Milan; unfortunately for the French, their former city's defences remained in good repair and the imperial army, led by Prospero Colonna, repelled the attacking force.

At home, the anticipated Anglo-imperial-Bourbon invasion did not take place as anticipated. In Picardy a 12,000-strong English army under the command of the Duke of Suffolk marched through the countryside in the third week of September. His objective was Paris, and by late October Suffolk's men were just fifty miles from the capital. The Duke of Vendôme was placed in charge of the city's defences, in anticipation of a last-ditch and desperate battle, but the imperial forces that should have arrived to assist the English failed to appear, in part because the weather was bitterly cold, which led to a loss of morale among the English force. The Parisians were aggrieved at having been exposed to disaster, and blamed the king, who had done little to help them. Street poets and satirical musicians composed songs mocking Francis for abandoning his people in order to pursue glory abroad; many in the city believed that, given the king's greed, Bourbon's treachery was quite understandable, and he was regarded as a man of 'wisdom, virtue and valour'.

Meanwhile the wise, virtuous and valorous duke's plans to invade eastern France never materialised; the imperial *Landsknechts* proved worse than useless, many having deserted and the remainder being routed by French loyalists after an unsuccessful invasion of Champagne. For all his fine words, the perennially cash-strapped emperor Charles V had been forced to abandon his planned invasion of the Languedoc, meaning that Suffolk and his men were back in Calais by mid-December and Bourbon was compelled to flee to Italy.

Given the widespread national sympathy towards Bourbon, whom many lauded as a hero, Francis wished to ensure judicial compliancy by appointing a special commission of four *parlementaires* with wide-reaching powers to examine and then sentence the conspirators. However, the *parlement* insisted that it had to meet in full session in order to try the cases, to which Francis reluctantly agreed, and the proceedings against Bourbon's arrested accomplices began in late December. On 16 January 1524 the most high-profile of the conspirators, Jean de Poitiers, father of Diane de Poitiers, was stripped of his knighthood and received the death sentence; he was also to have been tortured, but his ill health meant that it was unlikely that he would have survived this. He was hauled to the Place de la Grève in the centre of Lyons, the traditional site for public executions, before a large and silent crowd on 17 February. However, literally seconds before he was to be beheaded, a royal messenger arrived and cried out that he bore a reprieve. De Poitiers was instead to be taken back to prison.

These showy last-minute pardons were occasionally used to flaunt royal clemency, and to remind the prisoner that he owed his life to the king. It did not hurt that they offered the spectacle of a public execution without the ill-feeling that normally arose among the condemned man's friends and family. It had, after all, been de Brézé, de Poitiers' own son-in-in law, who had revealed the plot to Francis, and it is likely that the king spared the prisoner in recognition of the service that de Brézé had performed. It is debatable how grateful de Poitiers might have been for his actions. The reprieved man would spend the next two years in prison before his eventual release in 1526. His case was the most serious since he had refused to divulge any information about the plot to his interrogators. It was also rumoured that there had been a very personal aspect to his rebellion, namely that de Poitiers wished for revenge on Francis because the king had raped his daughter, Diane. This version of events is unlikely for numerous reasons, both practical and ideological; Francis, first gentleman of France and a man used to having his own way with the *crème de la crème* of court, had no reason to rape any woman, especially not the wife of one of his closest and most honoured advisers. Nonetheless, that the tale even made its way into circulation indicates how low the king's standing was.

The other conspirators received lenient sentences: perhaps surprisingly lenient, given the circumstances. Aymar de Prie was placed under house arrest and two other leading conspirators, Antoine d'Esguières and Bertrand Simon de Brion, were each sentenced to three years in prison. Hector d'Angeray received an outright pardon. The lightness of the sentences seems to have been dictated by the popular pro-Bourbon sentiment that the *parlement* felt. Yet, although there was universal disdain for Francis, Louise and Duprat, all of whom were perceived to have behaved avariciously, Bourbon's insurrection had few overt supporters among the nobility, the people who really mattered when it came to the maintenance of power. Bourbon had a justified grievance to pursue, but it was a specific one, rather than representative of a cause that might have inspired a great noble revolt. If anything, the rebellion had shown the relative strength of Francis's position; by distributing largesse in the form of jobs, titles and lands, he had ensured that the wider French nobility was dependent on his continued good graces.

Even if he had managed to keep order at home, Francis's foreign policy had become increasingly chaotic. In the winter of 1523–4, Francis remained in France to deal with the conspiracy's aftermath, while his army in northern Italy had a huge task before them, all the more grievous since they lacked both their king's inspirational leadership and that of Bourbon. The latter, one of the greatest military commanders of the age, no longer rallied French troops but stood against them in the service of Charles V and had pledged to defend Milan against all-comers. One minor relief was that Pope Adrian had died on 14 September 1523, at the age of sixty-four, before he had even served two years; rumours circulated that his end had come about by means of the decidedly earthly form of poisoning. His replacement, Clement VII, the former Giulio de Medici, launched a peace initiative; although he had formerly been an imperial supporter, as pope he now pursued a policy of neutrality. Yet this was not enough to save an increasingly doomed campaign.

Peace between Francis and Charles seemed an impossibility. The emperor's key demand was that he be given Burgundy in exchange for Milan; this was, unsurprisingly, unacceptable to the French since it would have placed an imperial power at the heart of eastern France. Yet Francis's demands – that he would only make peace if the emperor handed Bourbon over to him – were treated with equal scorn. Bourbon had thrown himself wholeheartedly into the service of the emperor, and Charles V was hardly likely to hand over a rebel who had now become one of his chief partisans. Thus the fighting continued, disastrously for the French by early 1524. Another severe winter had killed off many of the cavalry horses and ponies were being used as substitutes. Ammunition was depleted and there was little food. Morale was low, and in March Bonnivet ordered a retreat towards the Alps to avoid a confrontation with an imperial force led by Charles de Lannoy, Viceroy of Naples, against the French force encamped at Abbiategrasso in the Po Valley.

An especially grievous defeat took place on 30 April, as the French army was crossing the River Sesia. A combined force of imperial soldiers and 10,000 *Landsknechts* attacked the French and inflicted hideous casualties upon them. The long-suffering Bonnivet had his arm shot to pieces by an enemy arrow and, after ceding command to the Count de Saint-Pol, had to escape over the Alps in a litter, and the Swiss mercenaries who had been aiding the French army during the retreat abruptly deserted them, citing a lack of funds. Perhaps most crushingly of all, the great warrior Bayard was mortally wounded by a Spanish marksman. A sentimental, but probably apocryphal, story has Bourbon finding his erstwhile comrade-in-arms dying underneath a tree, and commending his bravery, only for Bayard to reply, in his dying breath, 'I do not need your pity, who am dying like a gentleman – but you need it, who are serving against your King, your country and your oath.'[8]

What remained of the French army eventually descended the Alps, but they had suffered a catastrophic defeat. Of the 1,500 cavalrymen who had left France, less than a quarter returned. Milan remained an imperial possession, and the two French garrisons at Lodi and Alessandria were forced to surrender. Francis distracted himself in early March by attempting to have Bourbon condemned to death in absentia by the *parlement*, but they refused to pass the sentence, saying that he must be put on trial in person. The only consolation was that his property was forfeited, along with his various titles, meaning that it could all be sold off again to the highest bidder.

Francis and Duprat were appalled that the lands of the other conspirators whom the court had sentenced had not been confiscated for similar profit, but the *parlement* held firm, refusing a judicial review. Three other rebels had received almost comically light sentences: they were to be released and their lands returned to them. The sole punishment meted out was that they would have to remain for an initial period in a town chosen by the king. Furious, Francis ordered that the three offenders be kept in custody, which the *parlement* complied with, but in all other respects it was clear that his royal power was considerably less far-reaching than it had been, overseas or domestically.

As for Bourbon, rather than return to the French court and face an almost certain sentence of death after extensive torture, he decided instead to support Henry VIII's imminent campaign to acquire the throne of France on 25 June. Bourbon, who had once been the second most important man in the country, was now committing himself to a venture that sought to place an English king on the French throne. His fee was 200,000 crowns, to be paid equally by Charles V and Henry, who had drawn up a new alliance in late May. Although, as a small gesture of residual loyalty, and possibly inculcated by centuries of Anglo-French warfare, Bourbon avoided formally recognising Henry's claim to the throne of France, he agreed to leave it to the emperor to act on his behalf.

In early July the duke once again returned to France, with an imperial army of 20,000 men. His forces moved across the Var towards Provence, where the local towns were soon occupied. After Aix surrendered on 7 August Bourbon could, with a certain grim irony for a man who had abandoned his other titles, now call himself Count of Provence. Had Henry supplied the agreed forces he might well have been successful in his aim of once again capturing the French throne, but Wolsey believed, correctly, that the local population remained loyal to Francis, and persuaded Henry to wait and see how matters developed before risking an English army in northern France. Suffolk's lack of success the previous year was still fresh in recent memory. Meanwhile, the bulk of Charles V's imperial army was still stuck in Catalonia and its commanders showed no sign of moving to the north.

Nonetheless, Bourbon pressed on. He began a siege of Marseilles on 19 August, perhaps reflecting as he bombarded the city's walls that its fortifications had recently been repaired at Francis's instructions. The assault continued into September and managed to break through a section of the city's northern wall, but Marseilles refused to surrender. This was partly due to pride, but a garrison of 8,000 men, together with a citizen militia of the same number, proved formidable opponents, as did the firepower of the French navy anchored in the harbour nearby. A letter from Francis informed the city's residents that he would 'remember their services for evermore', and rumours circulated that he himself was heading to relieve the siege with a mighty army of 40,000 men. Bourbon's *Landsknechts* told him that they wanted to withdraw, and he knew that the siege could not succeed. At the end of September he started to retreat in a chaotic and disorganised fashion. By 1 October 1524, the French army had regained control of Aix.

Although Bourbon's claims to his titles and lands were supported by, in one historian's words, 'all reasons of law and equity',[9] he had estranged himself from his king and country for ever over the dispute. (Louise's claims, meanwhile, could only be sustained by an arbitrary and selective interpretation of the documents.) Although the immediate danger was past, Francis was unable to feel any great relief. Milan was lost, along with the Italian lands; his country was as poverty-stricken as before; and he had suffered a series of cruel personal blows throughout 1524. His second daughter Charlotte had died of measles on 18 September at the age of seven. She was cared for in her final illness by her aunt Marguerite, as her father was fighting his territorial wars, her grandmother Louise was sick herself and her mother had died less than two months before.

Queen Claude saw her husband for the final time in July 1524, as they parted before he headed off on his Italian campaign. She had suffered ill health for some time, including gout and ever-worsening tuberculosis, but had continued to produce royal children, including Madeleine in 1520, Charles in 1522 and Marguerite in 1523. Yet it was common knowledge throughout Europe that she was approaching the end of her life. Francis believed that she would live until his return in the autumn, but in fact her illness was more advanced than anyone had suspected and she died on 20 July 1524 at Blois, shortly after saying her farewells to the king.

Despite her unprepossessing appearance and less than regal

stature, her kindness and gentleness had endeared her to Francis and
to his kingdom. The Bourgeois de Paris spoke for many by mourning 'the very noble and very good lady', and Fleurange described her
as 'one of the truest princesses that ever walked the earth and the
most beloved by everyone great and small'. As for her husband, he
responded to her loss with a very sincere and humble grief, telling
Marguerite that 'Could I buy her life with mine, I would do it with
all my heart. I never thought that the bonds of marriage, ordained
by God, could be so hard to break.'[10]

In his own way he had loved her, and the loss was a terrible one
to bear. Yet the events of the coming months meant that the death
of his wife, tragic though it was, would be insignificant compared
to the disaster that Francis, and France, was to face.

CHAPTER 11

Nothing Remains Save Honour

Character is fate. In the case of Francis, this old saying could hardly be more accurate. His genius and folly as king were inextricably intertwined with his personality, which had, in the near-decade that he had ruled France, been displayed in all its aspects. He was bold, daring and decisive in a way that few of his predecessors had been, and his natural warmth and charisma made him comfortable with his monarchical role, which he had more than ably fulfilled. It helped that he was a natural man of action, happiest when hunting or leading his men into battle, despite his intellectual and artistic interests. On the other hand he was reckless, short-sighted and impetuous, happy to risk everything on repeated gambles played for the highest of stakes. And, as every gambler knows, if you play too long the house always wins. Francis's downfall was the more regrettable as it was entirely of his own making. A willingness to pause, consider and trust the advice of others would have led to an entirely different outcome, and a seismic change in the history of sixteenth-century Europe.

In late 1524 Francis needed to recover his momentum; valuable time had been lost due to his unsuccessful attempts to discover and punish Bourbon's treachery. Once again, Milan and the Italian north fired the king's imagination. He believed that he had an excellent opportunity: the imperial forces that had been protecting Milan were being redeployed to other areas. Bonnivet had made a good recovery from his wounds and was keen to recover his reputation on the field of battle. Surely, Francis mused, this was a unique opportunity to reclaim the prize, and along with it France's standing amidst the great powers of Europe; if he had to fight Marignano again, so be it. Reports of his decision reached Louise, who could see its inherent folly. Alarmed, she hurried south to Avignon in order to counsel her son against so rash a venture. But she was too late: three letters that she sent to Francis were ignored. On 5 October 1524 the forces had moved on from Aix. By the middle of the month Francis left his kingdom at the head of the French army and crossed the Alps. Louise assumed the powers of Regent of France; once again, she feared the worst.

Francis arrived at Milan on 24 October. If he had expected a grand battle along the lines of the conflict of 1515, he was to be both disappointed and relieved; the city was riddled with plague, making a full invasion impossible. Therefore, in a desperate bid to regain momentum, he decided to besiege nearby Pavia, a small town approximately twenty-two miles away. The garrison there consisted of 6,000 Spanish and German troops under the command of Antonio de Leyva, one of Charles V's best generals, albeit one suffering from debilitating gout at the time of the attack. On 6 November the French army began to lay siege to Pavia, and after a great barrage of artillery fire they broke through the massive wall that surrounded most of the city. A small band of Spaniards who had attempted to defend a tower that guarded a strategically important bridge were hanged, 'for daring to resist the King's army in a pigeon-loft'.[1] It was a clear and ruthless message that Francis was not in a lenient humour towards those who opposed him.

However, the imperial army was prepared to continue the resistance, until the last man if necessary. They constituted a force that included 5,000 *Landsknechts* under the command of de Leyva. Following the arrival of reinforcements sent from Milan, the defenders mounted a vigorous counter-attack, which inflicted heavy casualties on the French and forced them to retreat. During the next stage of the onslaught the French repositioned themselves to the south of the city, where the River Ticino formed a natural boundary between Pavia and its rural environs. Francis and his troops found themselves unable to advance, as the city's defensive system lived up to its reputation for impregnability – largely thanks to the constable's valiant efforts in 1516.

Throughout the rest of the winter Francis's army, encamped beyond the city walls, engaged the enemy in a number of fruitless skirmishes. Frustrated by the lack of progress and forced to live in the open, where they were beset by mud, wet, cold and sickness, the French soldiers grew increasingly restless. Yet the king insisted, desperately, that the imperial defence would eventually be ground down. In order to strengthen morale and engage in decisive action, he decided to send 6,000 of his men to southern Italy in late November. This force, commanded by the Duke of Albany, was intended to invade Naples, while an equivalent number of Swiss *Landsknechts* arrived to replace them at the siege. This move has subsequently been described as 'the maddest of all the strategic errors for which he and his two predecessors have been responsible'.[2] Yet at the time it seemed to make excellent sense, as Albany expected to conquer Naples without difficulty.

Despite the lack of progress, Francis's spirits remained high. He was especially buoyed by the knowledge that the new pope, Clement VII, had sent him a message indicating that he wished to form a secret alliance, and that he had high hopes that the Florentines and the Venetians might be persuaded to join an increasingly grand Franco-Italian union. Clement undertook not to support Francis's enemies and Albany's troops were therefore granted the right to march through the papal territories of central Italy towards Naples. Both audacity and cockiness can be detected in the message that Francis sent to Clement at this time: 'I hope soon to occupy Pavia. I have taken all the necessary measures . . . and my troops are paid. I have not crossed the Alps in person nor invaded Italy with 30,000 good infantry and the support of a fleet with 6,000 or 7,000 troops on board to stop now. I want nothing less than the entire state of Milan and the kingdom of Naples.'[3]

Unfortunately, Albany was a more easily distracted leader than Francis. Rather than heading directly towards the Neapolitan kingdom's northern border, he became bogged down in Siena's factional disputes, a task with all the military glory of a cold bath. His lack of leadership did little to raise French spirits. Things were no more glorious at Pavia, where the expeditionary force lacked any clear military plan other than sitting, waiting and hoping that providence would deliver a breakthrough. The regular bulletins dispatched to the French court could not disguise the fact that the campaign, embarked upon with such élan, was becalmed. However, when, in early January 1525, it was publicly revealed that an alliance of sorts had come about with Clement, the effective bestowal of a papal blessing on that campaign provided a much-needed boost to morale. The small print was, perhaps, less of a cause for celebration: Francis not only promised to cede Parma and Piacenza to the Holy See, but also offered his support for Medici rule in Florence. As the pope was himself a Medici, they were therefore his natural allies. In time, Catherine de Medici would become a crucial presence at the French court, just as Francis had wished for her when she was an orphaned baby.

The military stalemate at Pavia continued to frustrate both sides during January. It was undoubtedly true that the town was an especially difficult trophy to capture; for some decades it had enjoyed a reputation as an urban fortress like no other, with sophisticated and well-maintained defences that had been repeatedly tested and never defeated. Charles V's military engineers were reckoned to be some of the best in Europe and Pavia's fortifications benefited from their considerable professional expertise. This apparent impermeability tested the resolve and military strength of those armies foolhardy enough to approach the city walls.

Francis's decision to besiege the enemy therefore went against both received wisdom and his own strengths. His greatest abilities as a warrior king included audacity on the field of battle, thanks to his quickness of thought and accurate calculation of his enemy's strength and tactics, and cool executive command, which included delegation to his most able lieutenants. As Marignano and other smaller conflicts had shown, he was at his best when the high-adrenaline demands of warfare meant that he must act quickly. If he was less impressive as a domestic ruler, it was because the subtle, insidious intricacies of in-depth negotiation often bored him to tears, unless they were combined with pageantry such as the Field of the Cloth of Gold. It was glory that Francis wished for, and glory was obtained or lost in a moment. He believed that, according to Renaissance kingship – for him, the standard by which sovereign princes should be judged – the monarch's role was predominantly to lead his people to military victory.

Yet, compared to the strategies of Charles and the empire, this view could be considered somewhat passé. The warrior king belonged to the past, and Francis's objective of winning acclaim by personally leading his campaigns marked him out as an old-fashioned monarch rather than a contemporary one. (The same could be said of Henry VIII, in many regards Francis's mirror image.) By the 1520s successful kings also needed to pay attention to bureaucratic procedures and mundane administrative tasks. Their average day did not consist of hunting, wenching and planning heroic invasions, but of banal meetings with counsellors, diplomats and ministerial servants of the Crown, accomplishing judgements and policies that reflected well on them. Diplomacy and careful planning were more important than charging into battle, sword held priapically to the fore.

The extent of Francis's military success as a young man, however, misled him into thinking that he knew better than the cautious counsellors around him. The decision to embark on a siege at Pavia was Francis's sole responsibility and blatantly repudiated over a century of established French military intelligence regarding the relative advantages held by the besieged and their antagonists; if appropriately provisioned, the besieged could simply take refuge inside a castle or town for a number of years. Thus the men and equipment conducting the siege could not be used elsewhere. Francis's decision to embark on the siege was therefore both anachronistic and foolhardy. The fact that nobody publicly questioned Francis's actions was a tribute to his own charisma and well-known impatience. It also proved wholly regrettable.

At the beginning of January 1525, France's enemies were beginning to amass. A rejuvenated Bourbon, set on revenge, obtained 6,000 *Landsknechts* and 500 cavalry from Germany with the financial aid of Charles V, and headed to Pavia with his allies. Together they had a force of around 17,000 men and 1,000 cavalry. They were bound for the scattered French troops surrounding the old city of Pavia. The main encampment stood to their east and a substantial force, including Francis's field headquarters, had also occupied Mirabello, a country house situated to the north and within whose walled park French cavalry horses grazed. It also had the tactical advantage of being guarded by the River Vernavola, meaning that the enemy had to content themselves with taking opportunistic shots from the opposite bank.

For weeks a phoney war of sorts existed as both sides tried, with little success, to break the stalemate. The imperial army attempted a hoax by suggesting a planned withdrawal, fooling Francis and his generals into believing that they instead wished to attack Milan, thus luring them into the open. The stratagem failed and Francis, writing to Louise, commented: 'According to the view I have always held, I think the last thing our enemies will do is fight because, to be frank, our strength is too much for them . . . Pavia will be lost to them unless they find some means of reinforcing it, as they have now tried everything in attempting to hold it to the last gasp.'[4] He went on to speculate that the besieged must be starving and would be only too willing to throw open their gates and receive the French, if only the imperial army would withdraw. What he did not mention was that, by that stage, the French army was itself as besieged as the imperial troops manning the defensive systems at Pavia.

The imperial feint having failed, a further stalemate lasted throughout the first three weeks of February. On the fourth of the month a detachment of the imperial army tried to force its way through the gates of the park at Mirabello. The French swiftly repulsed the attack, which entailed no real realignment of ground forces. However, on 20 February events quickly changed. Francis's military fortunes had often reflected, for both good and ill, the strength and decisions of his Swiss mercenaries. Bored and weary, some 5,000 Swiss troops, predominantly drawn from the Grisons canton, had left the French army in order to defend their region against an imperial attack. The offensive capacity of Francis's artillery and infantry divisions suffered accordingly, and a demoralised 2,000 German troops deserted en masse. Francis's army was now down to less than 20,000 men. While the king believed that the mercenaries' perfidy was the main reason for the eventual outcome, the arrival of a further imperial contingent in mid-February proved highly significant. Its troops were carrying a substantial amount of gunpowder, which they delivered to the garrison. The besieged force within the city now possessed a substantial quantity of fire-power, giving the imperial army an added edge.

Francis, for perhaps the first time since he became king, felt fear. Consulting his generals, he suggested that he was prepared to retreat, given that the odds seemed to have become insurmount-able, and this no longer seemed a battle that he could win. Most of his generals, including the Marshal de la Palice and Marshal de la Trémouille, agreed with him and counselled a withdrawal. Yet it was Bonnivet who swayed him. The old admiral, aware that this might be his last campaign, wished to depart his command gloriously and appealed to Francis's bellicose side. Speaking to an increasingly convinced and moved audience, he chided his prede-cessors for the timidity of age and scornfully said: 'We Frenchmen never refuse battle, are not used to waging war by little stratagems, but instead show forth our banners proudly, especially when we have for general a brave king who can make even cowards fight.' To cheers and applause, the veteran soldier ended by saying: 'Sire, give battle!'[5] They were fine, noble sentiments, meant sincerely, and they achieved Bonnivet's desired effect. Francis had plenty of time to reflect upon them a few days later.

The long-awaited endgame began on 23 February 1525. Late in the evening, the main body of the imperial army left its encampment, aided by a bombardment of artillery directed towards the French troops. It proceeded to march under cover of darkness in battle for-mation and in a northward direction; the only way that the soldiers were able to recognise one another was by the white shirts that they donned over their armour. By midnight Charles's army had arrived at Mirabello's unguarded eastern wall, which they began demol-ishing in a systematic fashion in three separate places with picks, shovels and battering rams. It was ironic that Charles's troops had once used their engineering ingenuity to maintain the walls; now the same technical skill was used to destroy them instead. It was difficult work, but they knew that the results could prove decisive; the sappers had finished their labours as dawn broke. The French had had no time to prepare a defence; Francis had spent the night with his troops, not realising what was taking place nearby until just before midnight, when he was warned of the impending attack.

In the early morning of 24 February, on the feast of St Matthew, three columns of imperial troops invaded Mirabello under the command of the Marquis del Vasto. The French occupiers were taken unawares, although Francis had hurriedly drawn up his army within the park in defensive formation, and therefore the Battle of Pavia's opening shots were fired by French troops as they sought to defend themselves against the advancing enemy. While del Vasto's men hurtled towards the house, the main body of the imperial army moved across the park southwards. Their object of attack was the French base camp, which the defending force would die to protect. Francis's men opened fire; the imperial force were taken by surprise and retreated, intent upon regrouping within the park.

At this point Francis could have won the day in a decisive victory. Although his troops were in disarray, with the Swiss on his left and the Germans on his right, he was a better military leader than his opponents and managed to inspire his troops with chutzpah and daring. Never someone to hang back when there was fighting to be done, he charged at the head of his cavalry, but his advance meant that the French guns had to be silenced since he and his horsemen were now in their direct line of fire. This proved his greatest error, although it did not seem so at the time; instead, to both forces it was a scene of French bravura and success as Francis's heavily armoured men-at-arms fell on their opponents and tore them to pieces. The Marquis of Sant'Angelo, commander of the imperial cavalry, was thrown off his horse and killed. Francis was exultant, believing himself minutes from another legendary triumph. 'Now I really can call myself Duke of Milan!'[6] he shouted. Charles de Lannoy, an imperial general, agreed with the French king, grimly saying, 'There is no hope but God' as he made the sign of the Cross.

But the tide of battle was about to turn. Not only were the French infantry slow and disorganised, out of formation and thus easily attacked by the imperial forces, but the French cavalry were about to experience catastrophe. It came in the form of the arquebus, a primitive blunderbuss that could be unreliable, unwieldy and slow, but was fatally efficient at dispatching large quantities of the enemy at close range. Early-sixteenth-century aristocracy tended to be dismissive of portable guns as an element of warfare. Their use in battle was deemed to be unchivalric and the arquebus was regarded as a particularly uncouth means of waging war. It was also lethal, which endeared it to those who saw conflict as something to be won, rather than played at with style and courage.

Francis and his horsemen, having gained their earlier advantage against the imperial cavalry, were now exposed to the firepower of no less than 1,000 Spanish arquebusiers under the command of the Marquis of Pescara. As the clear, cold morning wore on, the Spaniards revealed themselves from the trees and bushes in which they had been hiding, and took aim against the French forces.

It was an unequal contest from the beginning. As the French died in their droves, cut down by tactics and technology that they could not understand, it was nothing less than the triumph of mechanisation and portable weapons over the traditional 'death or glory' ethos of the French. As the Spanish marksmen took aim and reloaded over and over again, wounded men-at-arms fell to the ground, helpless in their heavy armour against their opponents. As they writhed like fish caught on a line, the imperial foot soldiers, armed with daggers, grimly dispatched their foes with clinical efficiency.

Many of the greatest generals in France either died or fled. Francis's brother-in-law the Duke d'Alençon, who was in charge of the rearguard of the army, retreated when he saw the extent of the defeat, destroying the bridges behind him as he turned tail and ran. Several of his men jumped in the river to save themselves and drowned in the process. The Marshals of France, la Palice and la Trémouille, who had earlier counselled caution and prudence, had their warnings justified in the most unfortunate way, as both were cut down without dignity. And Bonnivet, who had been so instrumental in persuading Francis to fight this battle, saw to it that this would be his own last engagement. The noble admiral purportedly cried: 'I must die – I cannot survive such disaster, such destruction for anything in the world!' The only small consolation was that he died by his own hand, cutting his throat rather than being butchered by the enemy. An unsympathetic Bourbon later found his corpse and hissed: 'Wretch, you were the cause of France's ruin – and of mine!'[7]

Inevitably, Francis fought on to the last. Clad in a silver surcoat with plumes sweeping over his shoulders, his enormous form could be seen battling all his foes, wielding his sword aloft. His horse was shot beneath him and he continued to fight on foot. Several Spanish officers lost their lives to his pell-mell attacks but, even as Francis tried single-handedly to save the day, there was little to be done. He began to tire, and sustained wounds to his arm, right hand and above his eyebrow. Eventually he was ignominiously struck to the ground, and a lowly Spanish infantryman prepared to administer the *coup de grâce*, without knowing who his victim was. Francis might have prepared for death, but he was saved by the intervention of Bourbon's lieutenant, the Sieur de Pompérant, who recognised him. Intervening, he asked for the king's surrender to Bourbon, only to be told by Francis that he would never surrender to a traitor. Even in the greatest adversity he retained his regal dignity. Therefore it was de Lannoy who, pushing his way through a curious mob of soldiers, knelt before Francis, kissed his hand and received his sword, as protocol demanded, while a crowd of exultant Spaniards crowed 'Vittoria! Vittoria! España! España!' Francis I, King of France, hero of Marignano and one of the greatest leaders in Europe, was now a prisoner.

The rest of the French troops were finished. The Swiss, having arrived late at the battle, found themselves in an impossible situation and decided to flee the bloody scene. By midday on 24 February the Battle of Pavia was over. The imperial army could declare itself victorious and attention immediately turned to what was to be done with Francis. He was a pawn without peer for his captors; he could be ransomed at great cost, or his liberty might also be brokered as part of a diplomatic deal that might extend or confirm the victor's territorial gains. Imperial triumph could be declared, and French recriminations began. Many of the greatest knights were either dead or captured, including Fleurange, Henri d'Albret and the artillery captain Jacques Galiot. Eight thousand French and their mercenaries had perished on the field of battle. And the greatest of all France's lords, Bourbon, had allied himself with the victorious enemy. It was a defeat as shocking and total as the French had ever known; not since Agincourt had so many gallant and high-born aristocrats been slaughtered in battle.

For all his gallantry and leadership, the loss was due to Francis himself. His initial cavalry charge was elegant and spectacular, but the extent of the subsequent trap into which he led his men marked him out as an anachronistic warrior. Not only had the siege been time-consuming, expensive and ill conceived, but its resolution was the inevitable result of two forces meeting, one with new technology and one without. There were other difficulties: some of Francis's 25,000 infantry, dogged by limited mobility and the ability to respond to the call to arms, failed to get to the scene of battle at all. Yet it barely mattered. Pavia was a defeat like no other, an unmitigated catastrophe.

In the afternoon of the dreadful day, the king's captors removed him to a Carthusian monastery on the road to Milan a few miles from the battlefield. As Viceroy of Naples, de Lannoy's authority ranked second only to that of the emperor himself, and it was deemed appropriate that he should be entrusted with the task of looking after so eminent a prisoner. The viceroy, aided by the Duke of Bourbon, served Francis at lunch in the monastery's refectory. It was an accepted international code of conduct that a king retained his rank at all times, even when defeated and imprisoned, and, according to the courtesies of the time, must be treated with the respect due to a monarch. The presence of Bourbon, however, was a cruel humiliation; Francis simply ignored him. It soon transpired that his wounds were largely superficial, in no small part because his suit of armour, designed according to the latest standards of military technology, had protected him well despite the intensity of the battle.

Francis's injuries were to his pride and honour, rather than his body. After the battle the French king sat down and wrote to two crucial people. The first was Charles V, acknowledging the emperor's total superiority. As he said, 'I have no comfort in my plight other than in my esteem for your kindness. I pray you decide in your own heart whatever you may be pleased to do with me, certain that the great good pleasure of such a prince as you can only be joined with honour and magnanimity. You may be sure, should it please you mercifully to offer the ransom which the imprisonment of a king of France warrants, that, instead of acquiring a useless prisoner, you will turn a king into your slave for ever.'[8] Only a few hours earlier, and in the heat of battle, he had felt the likelihood of victory. Now, in the bitter aftermath of defeat, he had to compose an even more difficult letter: to his mother. It bears reproduction in full as an insight into his psyche.

Madame,
   To let you know the extent of my misfortune, nothing remains to me but my honour and my life which are safe. And so that news of me may be of some small comfort to you, I have begged to be allowed to write this letter, which favour has been given to me freely. I beg you not to lose heart but to employ your usual good sense, for I have confidence that in the end God will not desert me. I commend unto you my little children, who are also yours, and beg you to hasten the bearer of this on the road to and from Spain – he is on his way to the Emperor to enquire how he wishes me to be treated. And I recommend myself humbly to your kindness.
   Your very humble and obedient son, Francis.[9]

Ambition had laid him low. Even as he wrote 'nothing remains to me but my honour and my life', he knew that his reputation as a *chevalier*, once so bright and alluring, had taken a blow from which it would never recover. Perhaps nothing remained for him, not even honour. His torment can only be imagined.

CHAPTER 12

The King Without a Country

In the aftermath of the defeat at Pavia one European king, at least, was happy. Upon hearing the news from an envoy, Henry VIII leapt out of bed, informed the surprised bearer of good news that he arrived 'like St Gabriel announcing the coming of Christ', and demanded wine in celebration. He was particularly thrilled at the death of Francis's ally Richard de la Pole, a member of the house of York who had long been a pretender to the throne of England; de la Pole, the so-called 'White Rose', had died fighting in battle, alongside many thousands of others, and so an irritatingly persistent problem was laid to rest. Although Henry had not been directly involved in Francis's defeat, England having withdrawn from an active part in the campaign in 1524, the thought of France weakened and its charismatic leader neutralised was invigorating and more than merited a call for alcoholic refreshment first thing in the morning. Henry then announced his intention to write to Charles V to demand drastic action, saying: 'Now is the time for the Emperor and myself to devise means of getting full satisfaction from France. Not an hour is to be lost.'[1]

As for Charles, his response to his enemy's downfall was more considered. Although the battle had taken place on his birthday, he was in Spain on 10 March 1525 when news of his victory and of Francis's capture arrived. Rather than throw himself into wild celebrations he took the news quietly, and retired to pray. Later, he arranged for thanksgiving services and requiems for the dead to take place, but forbade any public displays of jubilation. His naturally pensive character was to be tested by the circumstances in which he found himself; as de Lannoy had stated, 'God sends to every man in the course of his life a good crop. If he does not harvest it well, he loses the opportunity for ever.'[2]

Although both Henry and Charles's brother Ferdinand argued that Francis should be made an example of, with his country sacked and then partitioned between its allies, Charles ignored their entreaties. He wished to pursue his desired ends by legal means rather than becoming further embroiled in an expensive and lengthy military campaign; if nothing else, he had learnt from Francis's mistakes. Therefore there were to be no further hostilities, although the formal outbreak of peace had to wait for negotiations to take place. Ironically, the defeat at Pavia had indeed brought about the end to the fighting that all parties had looked for over the previous years.

While Charles decided on the best course of action, albeit from a position of considerable strength, there was the question of what to do with his kingly captive. The emperor instructed de Lannoy to take good care of Francis and to ensure that his period in captivity, which would last a little over a year, was not one of privation. After a few weeks at the Charterhouse monastery he was taken to the castle of Pizzighettone, near Cremona, where a Spanish captain, Fernando de Alarcón, proved to be a humane custodian. It came as some small comfort to the king that he did not have to endure captivity alone; his fellow prisoners at Pizzighettone included Anne Montmorency, Philippe Chabot de Brion, valiant defender of Marseilles against Bourbon's forces in the summer of the previous year, and Philibert Babou de la Bourdaisière, a senior royal treasurer. All had previously encountered one another under happier circumstances.

As Francis paced about like a caged animal, Louise found her regency prolonged indefinitely. She replied to her son on 8 March 1525 by thanking God for his deliverance and his continued honour, life and health, before saying: '[as] you are content to bear bravely everything God pleases to send you, as Montpezat [her messenger] tells me, that I too for my part can endure whatever your fortune and your desire may ordain . . . I will never give you further cause

for sorrow.'³ Upon hearing the news of the defeat at Pavia she acted
decisively, advised as ever by Chancellor Duprat; she remained at
the monastery of Saint-Just near Lyons, as she did almost entirely
throughout the period of Francis's captivity. Du Bellay described
how this 'woman of fine quality . . . considered carefully how to
make best use of what was left, and to this end summoned to her
side those princes and lords who had stayed in France'.⁴ She negotiated with European rulers in Francis's stead, flattering and cajoling
where she could, and always with the intention of representing
her country and its king in the best light, at a time when Charles's
power seemed unassailable.

One major difficulty in arranging her son's release from captivity was that this could only take place once both sides had agreed
on a diplomatic solution to the Franco-imperial rivalry in northern
Italy. Louise, aided by her loyal council of ministers, sought to keep
the kingdom on a war footing along its eastern frontier. She raised
a small army and, thanks to the money that she had accrued from
her careful husbandry of the treasury, ransomed many others who
had been captured. One who returned of his own volition, Alençon,
found no warmth in his welcome. Stories of his cowardice soon circulated, and he died two months after Pavia, possibly by his own
hand. A scapegoat for the defeat had to be found, and he was as
worthy of blame as any other.

Louise's swift actions not only secured France's immediate
future, but retained the loyalty of those who might have considered
Francis an embarrassment. However, her diplomatic skills were
tested not by Charles's careful, if opportunistic, courtesy, but by the
bumptious adventurism of Henry VIII. The resolution of the Pavia
siege had excited the Tudor king's *folie de grandeur* and he began
to see himself as a second Henry V, preparing to invade France.
Throughout the spring and summer of 1525 he acted as if he really
believed that the French kingdom could be carved up, with its com-
ponent parts then being allocated to the relevant regional claimants.
His plan, such as it was, would be to reduce Francis to no more
than a territorial duke, like his father had been, with the present
line of succession to the French Crown abolished. Henry himself
would then sit on the throne of the much-diminished kingdom as

monarch of both England and France. Despite the lack of support, Henry, in bellicose humour, believed that he stood on the brink of achieving all that had frustrated his Plantagenet predecessors. English diplomats were thereby dispatched to Madrid with orders to prepare the ground for an Anglo-imperial alliance whose army would invade France before the end of the year.

For all Henry's grandiosity and self-aggrandisement, he might have succeeded had he launched an attack, whether in collaboration with Charles or through his own agency. The condition in which France found itself while Francis remained a captive suggests that Henry's militancy had its roots in the weakness of the impoverished and demoralised country. French military defences and civilian government suffered tremendous strain throughout 1525 since the Italian campaigns and Francis's lack of interest in domestic affairs had drained the treasury of much-needed cash, just as the plethora of casualties had undermined the army's fighting strength. It did not help that a good deal of military hardware, useful in terms of keeping the peace domestically as well as in a military campaign, had been seized by the enemy. Adding to the country's woes, many troops quartered in the northern garrison towns had been dismissed without pay because of the near-empty exchequer. It was not long before they became bands of embittered, impecunious vagabonds roaming the countryside. Largely reduced to violent scavenging, the former troops posed a particular threat to Paris, which afforded them rich pickings. Had an English emissary offered them money in exchange for their defection, it is likely that many would have taken it.

By the end of April Albany's substantial army, having retreated across the Alps, had returned to southern France, and the troops required payment. Understanding the peril that the country faced, Louise and her advisers raised enough money, by dint of cutbacks on household costs, to allow for a reasonably well-ordered disbandment of at least 5,000 of Albany's men. This still left a large number of unpaid soldiers, meaning that, while the wholesale destruction of the entire French monarchy remained unlikely, it was not inconceivable that Normandy, together with some of the coastal towns in the north, might once again become dependencies of a predatory English Crown.

Louise might have been suffering from gout, advancing years and shock at France's predicament, but she exhibited dauntless courage and resolve throughout the difficult circumstances of her second regency. She worked closely with the *parlement*, especially with Jean de Selve, president of the Parisian branch, who was appointed to the regency council and became a valued intermediary between the two institutions. She was also aided by Charles V's doubts about Henry VIII's reliability. Over and over again the English king had promised action and then failed to deliver on his grand words. Charles saw little reason to believe that Henry's tendency to equivocate had diminished with the passing of the years, meaning that an Anglo-imperial alliance remained improbable.

As his mother did her best to keep his country together, Francis's captivity continued glumly. He was not entirely divorced from the business of royal affairs, since his fellow prisoners were allowed to move regularly between Pizzighettone Castle and the regent's much-reduced court. Nonetheless, he was a man who was happiest in the pursuit of action, and, with this taken from him, he sank into a depressed and embittered state. A letter written to Louise on 4 March 1525 by Jean de la Barre, another nobleman imprisoned with Francis, reveals something of the king's mental state at this time. He fasted for two days a week and as far as possible confined his diet to fish. De la Barre believed that the king was ill suited to such a sparse regime; presumably the punishing semi-fast was to admit a degree of penitential rigour into a life previously devoted to the pursuit of pleasure. On 22 March, in reply to her concerned entreaties, Montmorency assured Marguerite that Francis was being well looked after and recommended that she should write to her brother regularly. In a subsequent letter Marguerite counselled Francis to stop fasting and instead take comfort from the Epistles of St Paul, a copy of which she enclosed: an unusual remedy for loss of appetite. His reaction to her well-intended but perhaps inappropriate pieties is not recorded.

The papal nuncio visited the king on 27 March, and he wrote an account of the monarch's circumstances. Surrounded by a large number of Spaniards, Francis headed to the castle's chapel in the early morning each day, clad in the same ash-coloured tunic that he had donned after being divested of his armour on the first day of his captivity. During the celebration of Mass Francis appeared composed, although this was to be expected given that he was on public view. The nuncio was then granted a brief private audience, and found the king alternately melancholic and animated. He expressed his concern about Albany and appeared astonished to learn that the duke, together with his army, had recently left Italy. Francis was also anxious to discover the fate of Giovanni de Medici, the most daring and successful *condottiere* of his day, who had entered his service to fight at the siege of Pavia; unbeknownst to the king, de Medici had been wounded during a skirmish on 17 February and withdrew with his men to Piacenza, thus missing the battle altogether. Francis was relieved that de Medici would, unlike himself, be able to return to the field imminently.

Nonetheless, the nuncio did not shy away from telling the king the grave news that all seemed to be lost. To this, a woebegone Francis replied that nothing else could reasonably be expected and, in response to the nuncio's final enquiry, stated that he had no message for the pope, save that he wished to be recommended to Fortune. After this elliptical remark, Francis left the room without looking at the nuncio. In his formal report the papal envoy described what he had seen as 'a pitiable sight . . . for he does not seem a prisoner of the emperor and his captains, so much as of his guards, who all claim a right in him. He behaves courteously . . . and jokes with them, thinking it no less a virtue to accommodate himself to fortune than to command a kingdom.'[5] He was all too aware that he would remain confined to his not-so-gilded cage for some time, while Charles and his advisers debated how to deal with Europe's most famous prisoner. All Francis could do was to hope that Fortune returned him to his kingdom, and in the meantime embrace a stoic acceptance of this newfound purgatory.

In March 1525 Franco-imperial peace negotiations formally opened, with the unspoken primary intention of dealing with the king. If any of the assembled negotiators had underrated Charles V, they now viewed him in a different light; the emperor not only saw himself as the defender of Christendom, but also gave a clear indication that his main interest lay in expanding his territories. This came as a blow to the French representatives, whose initial hopes were that Francis would be released forthwith in exchange for a suitably generous cash payment. Money was, of course, one of Charles's demands, but it was less significant than his belief that the defence of a Christian and European empire could prove to be entirely compatible with the pursuit of Habsburg Continental hegemony. Nonetheless, Francis still clung to the chivalric code and hoped that, by personal appeal as one regal knight to another, he might soften the most extreme demands that Charles now insisted upon.

The emperor was not in a mood to be conciliatory. He began by informing a surprised Francis that he himself could, if he so wished, assert a claim to the French kingdom as a whole. That dynastic right had been inherited from Charles's father Philip le Bel, Duke of Burgundy, but in order to demonstrate magnanimity in victory the emperor was prepared to set aside, at least for the moment, his right to the French Crown. Having thus displayed a token attempt at generosity, the emperor set out his demands. The duchy of Burgundy's return to the Habsburg territorial domain was his chief goal. Burgundy had been seized by the French in 1477 after the last duke, Charles the Bold, had died without a male heir, and Charles V could claim descent from him via the female line. Nonetheless, it was his political calculation rather than dynastic pride that drove his Burgundian claim. Were this rich and fertile duchy, stretching along his western borders, to be incorporated into the empire, it would pose an alarming and perpetual strategic threat to the French.

There were many other demands as well; so many, in fact, that it might have been easier for Charles simply to have demanded the French throne *in toto*. Tournai and all the lands and towns that were under French occupation in Artois were to be restored; this area, including its capital Arras, had come under French rule as a result of the military campaigns waged in the region by Francis and his predecessors, and Charles's demand that these territories be returned to Habsburg control demonstrated his determination to entrench his own dominant position in the aftermath of Pavia.

The imperial wish-list lengthened as the emperor's requirements became increasingly extravagant, even absurd. It is possible that he was making a deliberately outlandish series of requests, in the expectation that even to achieve half of them would be a remarkable accomplishment. Provence should be detached from the French kingdom and awarded to the Duke of Bourbon. One can imagine the incredulity of Francis's response to that particularly galling provision. Dauphiné, in south-eastern France, was to become an imperial possession, and Toulouse must belong to Aragon. Francis was told to pay the imperial debts due to Henry VIII, who would also have whatever lands belonged to him by right restored. All French claims to Milan and Genoa would have to be surrendered in perpetuity and Charles expected the king to accompany him to Rome to attend on his person during the forthcoming imperial coronation. For this splendid event, French troops should be made available to the emperor at Francis's expense. All those French subjects who had been implicated in Bourbon's treachery were to receive a royal pardon. Finally, a proposed marriage between the dauphin and Mary of Portugal, the emperor's niece, would provide a symbolic affirmation of Habsburg-Valois amity. While Habsburg dynastic expansion was Charles's primary goal in the peace negotiations, Christendom's needs were not entirely neglected. The treaty should, he considered, contain a clause committing himself and Francis to the leadership of a crusade against the Ottoman Turkish armies.

One imagines, after this series of demands, Charles sitting back, his arms literally or metaphorically folded, and looking at Francis, keen to see how he responded to terms that bordered on insolent. While the French king was far too proud to accept the conditions, he was also aware that he was not in a position to engage in horse-trading if he ever wished to see his country again. Nonetheless, with his back against the wall, the king's response to the imperial requests managed to blend prevarication with resistance. Arguing that Burgundy was not his to yield, he suggested that the question of who should be its legitimate ruler ought to be decided by a body of independent arbitrators. In the event of the adjudication going against him, Francis offered an ingenious, and face-saving, proposal. A royal marriage would, he agreed, be a splendid way of demonstrating the crucial spirit of cooperation for Europe's two greatest dynasties. Alliance at this level of significance, however, ought to involve those of the very highest rank. The dauphin's marriage would certainly be a diplomatic event but Francis, in what was either optimism or simple cheek, suggested that his own betrothal to Eleanor, the King of Portugal's widow and the emperor's sister, would surely be of far greater importance.

This might have sounded ludicrous, but there was a measure of sensible calculation behind it. After all, if Charles was to agree to the match, Francis's second bride was still young enough to bear children and the future son of this marriage would, he suggested, become Burgundy's next ruler if the peace treaty meant that the French Crown had to surrender the duchy. Regarding Arras, however, he remained stubborn. The town was central to the French Crown's strategic interests on the north-eastern borders and there could be no question of handing it over. As for Tournai, Francis asked, with almost wilful *faux-naïveté*, how he could possibly order an evacuation from a town that had become an established and constituent part of his kingdom. The people, he seemed to suggest, would miss him, and in his role as father of the nation he could not allow that.

Perhaps realising that he was in danger of pushing matters too far, and reminded that he remained a prisoner, he was considerably more accommodating when he responded to some of the other imperial demands. He agreed that the French Crown's Italian claims would be abandoned and also offered his troops to Charles, as long as the emperor was able to pay their monthly wages. Although it no doubt stuck in his throat to say the words, Francis agreed that Bourbon's lands would be returned to him and Louise would therefore have to suspend the lawsuit that sought to affirm her legal title to the contested lands that the duke had inherited from his late wife. However, he was unable to let this go entirely without comment, adding 'let him never be seen'.[6] Finally, Francis concluded by telling Charles that an enormous, if unspecified, ransom would then be paid in order to get the King of France back to his kingdom. It was a counter-offer that combined accommodation with provocation, and indicated that Francis, despite everything, believed that he remained a king.

It is impossible to know whether he was sincere about any of this. Certainly, it was extremely doubtful that the king seriously contemplated yielding any of his rights and possessions on any permanent basis. As he himself justifiably pointed out, it was unreasonable to expect a sovereign prince to negotiate the terms of his own release from captivity, and the constraints of his imprisonment were an inevitable impediment to the exercise of rational judgement. The future of his country was at stake, and it could only be decided upon by those who were not negotiating from a glorified prison cell. In this he echoed his mother, who rejected Charles's demands, saying that only a king in his kingdom could hope to have any influence over his subjects.

Therefore, Francis declined to participate further in what felt close to a charade, instead surrendering overall responsibility for the peace treaty to Louise. The regent, for her part, peremptorily rejected all the imperial demands, citing the question of French public opinion; she argued that the empire was proposing a fundamental diminution of the French monarchy's territorial possessions and diplomatic standing. These claims, she pointed out, were bound to be unpopular among the king's subjects and could only be arbitrated by a French king from his own throne. While this prevarication continued, she appointed Francis de Tournon as her personal representative in the peace talks at the end of April, which was seen as yet another delaying tactic. As de Tournon continued to refuse to yield any French territories to the empire, the lack of resolution continued into May 1525.

As the negotiations continued, Francis's captors became uneasy about his security and were concerned that he might escape; his fellow captive Henri d'Albret, King of Navarre, had already done so, and the castle's location close to the French border in an exposed position made it particularly difficult to defend. It was not inconceivable that the French might launch a military expedition that could move swiftly across the border, attack Pizzighettone and liberate the king. Therefore, it seemed safer to continue Francis's confinement in Spain. On 31 May Francis was escorted to the

harbour at Genoa where fifteen Spanish galleys were anchored, and
told that he was travelling to Naples. However, the intention was
to ensure that he could not be captured en route, and once the fleet
set sail it was joined by six French galleys at Portofino on 8 June.
Equipped with Spanish crews, the French galleys were there to act
as hostages and deter a possible attack and rescue by the French
Mediterranean fleet, headquartered at Marseilles. If there had been
a daring scheme to abduct Francis and bring him back in glory to
France, it came to nothing, although he had earlier broached the
idea to his mother in a secret letter of 12 May.

By 17 June the flotilla had arrived at Palamos on the Catalan
coast, and two days later Francis was in Barcelona. De Lannoy,
acting on the powers delegated to him as viceroy, had decided that
the transfer was the right move, and Francis, who had warmed to
his captor, gave him his support. A move to Spain carried with it
greater access to the emperor and Francis was convinced that a
personal dialogue between the two sovereigns – acting on their
own and without too many intermediaries present – would provide the most effective way to achieve a peace agreement. Despite
his shattering and humiliating experience of defeat, Francis had
not abandoned his nostalgic preconceptions about the courtesy of
kings, nor his belief in cutting through tiresome protocol in favour
of a handshake and a binding agreement. Had he remembered the
various ignored or discarded treaties that had originated in just such
a way, he might have been less keen on his Spanish sojourn.

Besides, Francis was able, for the first time since Pavia, to feel
that he was a king once more. As he travelled through Spain the
monarch was received by cheering crowds shouting acclamations
that befitted his royal status, and once more he was clad in his finery
astride a magnificent horse. He might even have thought, momentarily, that he had been triumphant and that the previous months
had been nothing more than a disappointing dream. A Mass that he
attended at Barcelona Cathedral on 19 June was a particularly magnificent affair; as he emerged into the sunshine, the people roared
with excitement at the sight of this still-glamorous king. One of the
reasons for the warmth of his reception was the widespread belief
that he could cure the afflicted, regardless of their nationality; he

laid his hands on, or 'touched', a large number of the sick who had travelled to Barcelona expressly to benefit from his healing powers. One Venetian observer even commented: 'He bears his prison admirably . . . [and] he is well nigh adored in this country.'⁷

While Francis was pleased by his reception – and might have wryly reflected that he was offered an adulation that the less charismatic figure of Charles V was not – he knew that he remained a king out of his own country, and that the crowds who surrounded him were there as much to gawp at the exiled monarch as they were to celebrate him. Renewed concerns for his safety led to Francis's removal from Barcelona to Valencia at the end of June, and in the weeks that followed he was taken to a variety of country houses as negotiations continued in earnest.

The early summer found Charles at his Spanish court in the then capital of Castile, Toledo, the spiritual epicentre of Iberian Catholicism, and it was hither that Montmorency travelled in order to convey messages between Francis and the emperor. The king wished for a truce to be declared while the peace negotiations were in progress and he also wanted an assurance that his sister Marguerite, who would subsequently play an important role in those discussions, would be granted safe passage while travelling from France and across Spanish territory. Francis also requested that he himself, while playing no formal role in the negotiations, have regular meetings with the French representatives. Charles granted the requests but preliminary discussions between the two sides were in other respects unpromising. On 17 July the emperor held a meeting with two French ambassadors, Tournon and De Selve, in which he explicitly stated that it was absurd to think that a person as significant as the King of France could be released in exchange for a ransom.

When Louise's chosen proxy Philippe Chabot, who would represent her at the truce negotiations, arrived in Toledo, the discussions began in earnest. It was always clear that Charles would hold the upper hand. The major obstacle to a mutually agreed peace settlement remained the future of Burgundy, and any concessions on this issue, on either side, would be seized upon as examples of weakness. The imperial chancellor Maercurio di Gattinara maintained that Burgundy had been annexed unlawfully by Louis XI and remained an imperial possession by right; he went so far as to announce that there could be no peace between the two as long as Burgundy remained in enemy hands. For the French, however, there was no doubt that the duchy had come into the possession of the French Crown legally and by right of inheritance, following the death of Charles the Bold. A stalemate ensued, underpinned by the cessation of hostilities brought about by a Franco-imperial truce.

In late July Francis left Toledo, after another regal progress through Spain during which he saw bullfights and visited the famous university of Alcalá de Henares. He was ultimately bound for the less *simpático* surroundings of a tower in the Alcázar fortress in Seville, which had originally been built by Muslim invaders in the late ninth century and had since become the royal palace. This was where Francis was accommodated, in unexceptional fashion. If he had forgotten over the previous weeks that he was a prisoner, the place soon reminded him of his situation; one visitor wrote of the king's new surroundings that 'the room was not big, and had only one door through which one entered. It was made a little larger by an embrasure on the right as one came in, facing the window . . . it had a double iron grill, strong and stiff which was welded into the wall.' In other words, it was a cell like any other, and even the addition of 'chairs, coffers, a few tables and a bed'[8] could do little to obscure that fact.

It was perhaps not entirely coincidental that a few days after he arrived, Francis told the French ambassadorial team that he would never yield Burgundy, and revealed to his inner circle on 16 August that he had no intention of negotiating in good faith. If a treaty were signed, he made it clear that he would have acted solely under duress. As a treaty was only valid if its signatories acted of their own free will, the king felt entitled to conclude therefore that he was not honour-bound to abide by a treaty whose terms included the secession of Burgundy. Nonetheless, there had to be a clear distance between his private and public views; his official position, communicated to the peace negotiators by his ambassadors in late August, was that the Parisian *parlement* should decide the Burgundian question. Unsurprisingly, this was immediately rejected by Charles's diplomats.

For all his scheming and desire to remain king-in-captivity, Francis's health and mental state were, understandably, not at their peak at this time. For a man used to vigorous exercise and outdoor (and indoor) activity, he was frustrated by being limited to nothing more exciting than an occasional mule ride, and that while being closely watched by armed guards in case of any escape attempts. Although the king had been remarkably self-contained in his demeanour since his capture, he found the situation that he was in both compromising and frustrating, to say nothing of personally humiliating. He might have written: 'The body conquered, the heart remains the victor',[9] but inwardly it seemed as if all was lost.

Superficially he seemed to have adapted well enough to his imprisonment, especially when he was being lionised in the Spanish streets; but a king forced to obey others was a freakish phenomenon in the sixteenth century and Francis had become a spectacle. He was used to leading his life in public, but as a monarch; his new existence rendered him little more than a prisoner, even if his gaolers were civilised men who understood the aristocratic code of manners and behaved impeccably in the royal presence. His forced participation in these public events, with the crowds following him at close quarters, had been going on for some three months when, on 11 September, the king collapsed at the Alcázar, suffering from a high fever and a nasal abscess. It was believed that this was caused by a combination of lack of exercise, poor diet and mental distress, and Francis passed into a near-death state, unable to see, hear or show any signs of life. His doctors thought that he was dying; if they had been correct, it would have been an ignominious end to a reign that had begun so promisingly.

Yet, just as hubris and arrogance had led to his downfall, unexpected events would see his star rise once again.

CHAPTER 13

A King Restored

As her son progressed from despondency to despair and, ultimately, to near-death, Louise was doing her considerable best to ensure that the regency continued as successfully as possible. After her immediate actions had ensured that no threat was posed to France, the regent, whose personal deviousness dovetailed with her country's and her son's advantage, realised that a certain amount of intrigue could both discomfit the empire and actually benefit the French cause. Despite the joy with which Henry VIII had greeted the news of Francis's downfall, it soon became clear that a treaty between England and France was key to Louise's strategy. It was of considerable help to her that many English diplomats were concerned that a Franco-imperial peace treaty would leave England out on a limb.

Therefore the Treaty of the More, signed with much pomp and ceremony on 30 August 1525, saw Anglo-French relations restored to somewhere near the heights of the Field of the Cloth of Gold, even if one participant languished a considerable distance away. Henry agreed to campaign actively for Francis's release and, in exchange, Louise promised to pay him a total of two million gold *écus*, spread in equal annual amounts over the next twenty years. France also promised not to ally with any Scottish territorial ambitions, thus thwarting any forays into northern England. The treaty was an anti-imperial ploy but it was put together with some discretion; it would not do to aggravate Charles unduly. Nonetheless, Louise had spent a great deal of 1525 canvassing assistance throughout Europe. In June she had proposed a new coalition to the papacy and to

Venice that would seek to eject imperial forces from Italian soil. The only money on offer was a tiny monthly subsidy, and there was no serious French military commitment, which indicated that Louise was testing international support rather than proposing a serious policy. Even with these strictures in place Venice was still prepared to support the French initiative; the papacy rejected it, however, and the proposal only strengthened Charles's suspicion of French diplomatic skulduggery, which hardly made him more amenable to the idea of releasing Francis on any lenient terms.

Louise also ventured into international negotiations in a considerably more significant area. Hitherto, the idea that any European Christian ruler might enter into dialogue with the Ottoman Turks, as opposed to launching a crusade against them, was inconceivable. The Christian–Islamic divide was regarded as unbridgeable, given the radical differences between their entirely opposed religions. Francis would place his country's national interests first in future years and treat with the sultan if that was where France's advantage lay, but his mother had arrived at this conclusion long before him. One of Louise's first acts after the disaster at Pavia was to send an ambassador to Constantinople. Upon receiving the envoy, Suleiman I – also known as 'The Magnificent' – was duly informed that soon the Emperor Charles could legitimately call himself 'master of the world', a state of affairs that would surely imperil the sultan's own position. Louise therefore suggested that Suleiman should raise an army that would liberate western Europe from imperial tyranny. It was a move that might have worked in the short term, but threatened to have significant consequences; however, in the event the sultan made only the most token nods towards military action and did little more than write sympathetic letters to the royal prisoner. Nonetheless a new precedent had been set, and with it a reminder that France's self-interest could trump the existing order of things.

Throughout 1525 Louise found herself at odds with the *parlement*. While they were happy to assist her when it came to military matters, they were opposed to her views on religion, and saw Francis's incarceration as an opportunity to promote their own policies. Shortly after Francis had been taken into custody the Parisian lawyers sought to take advantage of his absence, and the *parlement* delivered a series of official protests to Louise on 10 April 1525, on matters including the toleration of heretics, who now found themselves whipped, branded and burned alive. The *parlement* also launched an attack on the French Crown's traditional liberties, and the way in which the Crown's administration of justice, together with its methods of raising revenue, constituted a subversion of due process. They demanded that the Gallican Church be restored to its former independence, that the judiciary also become independent and that the royal finances should be subject to an audit.

The final provocation was the nomination of Duprat for two particularly rich and desirable benefices, namely the archbishopric of Sens and the abbacy of Saint-Benoit-sur-Loire. After the death of his wife, Louise had decided that her long-standing ally would be cheered both by his ordination and then by these lavish gifts; he now became known as Archbishop of Sens and a Titular Abbot, among his many other offices. Given the avaricious reputations of Louise and her chancellor, it was felt that action was needed, especially as Duprat had taken matters into his own hands and announced that the monks from Saint-Benoit would be forcibly expelled unless they accepted the chancellor as their lawful abbot; his emissaries had already forced entry and occupied the abbey.

At first the *parlement* opted for moderation, hoping that matters could wait until Francis's return, but Louise and Duprat would not budge. On 3 June the Crown's ministers, using the *Grand Conseil* as their judicial mouthpiece, declared all *parlementaire* judgements delivered in the previous two months to be worthless. A battle thus ensued between the *parlement*, defender of traditional French liberties, and the representatives of the Crown; even as Louise appointed a special commission, charged with the task of resolving the issues raised at Sens and Saint-Benoit, the *parlement* refused to recognise her authority in so doing. Nonetheless, she was the king's mother, so the *parlement* decided it would be far easier to go after the unpopular Duprat alone. His personal greed, aided and abetted by the regent, had led, in the view of the lawyers, to a perversion of justice. It did not go unnoticed that, in arraigning Duprat, the *parlement* also attacked Louise by association.

Justice did not come swiftly. Duprat, to the surprise of no one, ignored the *parlement*'s request that he appear in person before a specially convened session at the end of July, and no progress was made through the summer. As autumn brought the resumption of official administrative business, resolution remained as remote as ever. At the beginning of November the *parlement* wrote to Louise. As usual, the tone was nothing but respectful and polite, but steel tempered the compliments, with a clear reminder that their judicial independence lay at the heart of the French constitution. The letter stated that, while it did not seek to subvert Louise's actions, the *parlement* traditionally had the right to judge cases involving ecclesiastical properties and stipends. The intention was to drive a wedge between Louise and those of her ministers who disapproved of Duprat's autocratic style of government. This failed, partly because the ministers remained loyal to the Crown's authority, and partly because the issue of foreign policy was a more pressing one.

By the end of 1525 it had become obvious that there would be no invasion of the kingdom, and the renewed sense of security strengthened the regent's hand. After the initial shock of her son's defeat and imprisonment the regent, no political neophyte, had managed to secure her own power. When the *parlement* sent messengers to her in Lyons they were first made to wait six weeks, and then dealt with peremptorily; Louise informed them that they had behaved in a disgraceful manner, in a style unworthy of their honour as Frenchmen. Now that the hour of greatest danger had passed it was, she said, evident to all that *parlement* had sought to benefit from the threat of a foreign invasion while she herself had behaved impeccably and patriotically. By the end of November the *parlement* had already begun a strategic retreat, and both Louise and Duprat managed to walk away undamaged. It was a telling reversal, but a continued demonstration of the power of both Louise and of Duprat, while the *parlementaires* could do little more than examine the dents to their dignity and bleat about how their sole intention had been the preservation of the kingdom's unity and good government. If it had been an attempted coup, albeit of the most timid nature, it had failed utterly. Besides, other matters were occupying both sides by the end of 1525, not least the imminent return of Francis from captivity.

*

After his collapse, there was a steady rush of people heading to Madrid in the belief that the French king's death was approaching. Charles, who had ignored his royal guest since Francis's arrival in Spain, was now filled with panic at the thought of his most valuable bargaining chip's demise, and hurried from Toledo to his bedside in Madrid to press the enfeebled regal flesh and wish him well. When he finally arrived on 18 September, the emperor embraced the barely conscious king, although any affection on Charles's part was checked by the fear that his long-desired objectives might not be achieved were his captive to die.

A more welcome visitor for Francis arrived the following day in the form of his sister Marguerite, who had travelled at speed from Barcelona. Medical opinion, a speculative science then as now, had concluded that Francis was indeed dying, and she wished to pay her farewells. Dressed in white mourning attire for her husband the Duke of Alençon, it seemed as if she was about to lose an even more important man in her life. Mass was said, and the last rites for Francis's soul pronounced. On 22 September 1525, as he languished in an intermittent coma, the end seemed near. And then, entirely unexpectedly, the nasal abscess that was the source of his affliction burst of its own accord and Francis regained consciousness. The priest who had been ministering to him, Father de Selve, informed the *parlement* on 1 October that he was recovered, and had been cured while in the act of receiving the sacrament. As he wrote, 'From this time onwards, he has improved steadily, and, thanks be to God, he is now rid of the fever that had gripped him for twenty-three days without respite. Nature has performed all its functions, as much by evacuation above and below as by sleeping, drinking and eating, so that he is now out of danger.'[1]

When news of the king's sickness and subsequent recovery reached Paris the reaction was characteristically mixed. Some malcontents and rumourmongers roamed the city bemoaning the king's demise and accusing the regent's government of a cover-up. Four men dressed as royal messengers travelled through the streets spreading lies, claiming that 'the king was dead and that madam the regent was in great pain; that as wise men were concealing the truth, madmen had to proclaim it'.[2] Francis was no longer the popular and beloved figure of a few years before, especially after the English near-invasion of Paris, and there was a general feeling of recrimination and rebellion in the air. Other dissidents stated that the king, though alive, had proved himself unfit to rule and should now be deposed. It was also said that many of his ministers and other leading figures should be executed. A great deal of this talk emanated from the students, who enjoyed causing trouble as sport; as punishment they were banned from participating in the traditional Epiphany celebrations in December, in order 'to prevent wickedness taking advantage of such games to spread words which would carry serious consequences'.[3] Nonetheless, these Parisian murmurings showed that the French monarchy, if it were to survive in its present form, depended upon the king's imminent return.

Francis might have recovered his health, but his liberty was still in the balance. During the autumn, peace negotiations resumed in Toledo, and French brinkmanship came to the fore. A plan was mooted to bring about Francis's escape from prison; his choice of disguise might have raised eyebrows, as he wished to festoon himself in the garb of a black servant. This scheme was organised by an Italian captain named Emilio Cavriana, but one of the king's servants, Clément Champion, blew the whistle on the plot, fearing that, if it were unsuccessful, it would jeopardise any chance of an amicable settlement and result in Francis's indefinite imprisonment. Even if it had succeeded the likely consequence would have been military action, which the French could ill afford at that time. Thus the unlikely disguise remained an idea and no more.

Initially Marguerite led the peace delegation, but as Charles dismissed her proposals on the grounds that her suggested terms were unacceptable, she temporarily abandoned the negotiations on 11 October. She withdrew to Madrid for the next month, only returning to Toledo on 14 November with a new offer for the emperor: her brother would be released in exchange for a ransom of three million gold *écus* and betrothed to Eleanor of Portugal, the emperor's sister. Charles once again rejected these offers, and by the end of the month Marguerite had returned to France, leaving her brother a small dog as a companion and token of her affection. On

her journey home she wrote to Francis several times urging him
not to despair. She was wasting her time, as he had already formed
a plan that would result in his much-desired release.

After his grave illness, the king had regained both his self-
confidence and a desire to return to his own country as monarch, as
if his confinement had been little more than an irksome distraction.
He made a provocative move by drawing up a deed of abdication
that would have allowed his son, the dauphin, to inherit the throne;
it is unlikely that he ever meant to enact this, but it nonetheless
showed that he was ready to act. Previously, his refusal to negotiate
had caused enormous frustration on both sides, keen as they were
to reach an agreement. It irritated Charles, who wanted his territorial ambitions met, and irked the French, who hoped that the king
would end the impasse and secure a return to stable government.
Francis also felt extreme concern over his mother's health, as she
was now physically exhausted by the demands of her regency. Even
her obstinacy could only last so long; personal circumstances and
public need combined to persuade her that Burgundy had to be
sacrificed in order to maintain the country's integrity. France's territorial monarchy, she explained in a memorandum, would survive
the duchy's departure; worse had been lost before, most notably
when Edward the Black Prince had captured Poitiers in 1356. For
the sake of peace, she suggested, Francis must accept the emperor's
terms. Otherwise France would suffer irreparable damage and his
future status as king would be uncertain.

Francis's seemingly meek acceptance of his mother's decision
was not mere filial obedience; the contrived and somewhat tenuous argument he had prepared for this eventuality would soon
be revealed. Only *force majeure* could possibly compel him to cede
Burgundy, and a contract agreed to under duress could not be considered legally binding. Francis's consent to the Treaty of Madrid,
signed and agreed on 14 January 1526, was therefore given without
any belief or commitment and would subsequently be withdrawn
with similar dissimulation. Had Charles known the true character
of his kingly captive, it is doubtful that he would ever have considered his intentions honourable.

The treaty that Francis signed was theoretically humiliating

RIGHT An active monarch, especially in his youth, Francis took great delight in participating in hunts and jousts.

BELOW The salamander, a typically Renaissance humanist symbol, was Francis's personal emblem. Its motto was 'Nutrisco et extinguo', meaning 'I nourish the good and extinguish evil'.

VERBO·DIC·TM· ·ET·SANABITVR·

LEFT Francis's mother, Louise of Savoy, had high ambitions for her son, even before his birth. Many considered her ruler in all but name. This miniature shows her symbolically guiding the rudder of state.

RIGHT Marguerite of Angoulême, Francis's devoted and brilliant sister, was known for her intellectual and artistic gifts.

RIGHT This flattering portrait of Queen Claude ignores her unsightly appearance, which included a squint and hunched back.

LEFT Claude's seven children included the later Henri II of France, Madeleine, queen of James V of Scotland, and Francis III, Duke of Brittany.

RIGHT Anne de Pisseleu d'Heilly was Francis's most notable mistress, but made many enemies at court with her entitlement and extravagance.

ABOVE The costly meeting between Francis and Henry VIII of England at the Field of the Cloth of Gold offered fine pageantry, but achieved little else.

LEFT Charles V, the Holy Roman Emperor, became Francis's most notable adversary and nemesis, in a power struggle that lasted over two decades.

RIGHT Suleiman the Magnificent was the most feared ruler in the world. Francis's relationship with him was accordingly both cautious and opportunistic.

LEFT Henri II had a strained relationship with the king, who openly preferred his brothers Francis and Charles, and father and son were never fully reconciled.

BELOW The marriage of Catherine de Medici to Henri was soon marred by the unexpected death of her uncle, Pope Clement VII.

LEFT Diane de Poitiers, mistress of Henri II, was a powerful and shrewd figure who would become one of the most important women in France.

RIGHT The unprepossessing Catherine was treated with enormous sympathy by Francis. She eventually became a surrogate daughter to him. Helped by his patronage, she become the most powerful woman in the country after her husband's death.

ABOVE Château de Chambord was constructed for Francis as a hunting lodge,
and it is possible that da Vinci was involved in its original design.

BELOW Château de Fontainebleau was Francis's favourite, and extensively rebuilt in his reign.
He referred to it as 'Chez moi', and considered it his home.

in the extreme, both in his concessions to the emperor and in the conditions contained therein. Burgundy would be abandoned, as would French claims in northern Italy and Artois. Henri d'Albret, King of Navarre, was expected to surrender his rights to more than half his kingdom, which had been captured by Ferdinand of Aragon in 1512. The treacherous Bourbon and his accomplices could enjoy their liberty in all perpetuity and be assured that they would regain the legal titles to their estates. It seemed as though everything that Francis had ever fought for, even while a prisoner, was being taken away from him without his putting up any more than token resistance. An observer might have considered that he had been beaten down by the combination of his captivity, recent ill health and general fatigue.

This reading, while true to the circumstances, underestimated both Francis's essential cunning and Charles's *naïveté*. The months that Francis had spent away from his country had not been entirely wasted; he had come up with a stratagem that inspired him to make two key demands before he would sign the Treaty of Madrid. He convinced Charles that ceding Burgundy was bound to lead to uproar, and that he should therefore be allowed to return to France before all the treaty requirements had been met. Only a king living in his own kingdom could win the day and persuade his subjects that handing Burgundy to the emperor was the right thing to do. Charles allowed himself to believe that victory was almost within his grasp and assented, perhaps ignoring the obvious likelihood that, once returned to his domain, Francis had no motivation to honour such a demeaning part of the treaty.

He also repeated his desire to become betrothed to Charles's sister Eleanor. This was out of simple revenge rather than a desire to find a wife to follow Claude. His hatred of Bourbon was implacable; he conveniently viewed him as the agent of his downfall, a simplistic yet seductive view. Knowing that the duke had already been promised Eleanor's hand in marriage, Francis saw an opportunity to usurp his loathed enemy, not least because, in granting his wish, Charles ran the risk of alienating Bourbon, who had been such a vital part of the imperial cause. However, a king was always a more impressive match than a duke, regardless of how far the reputation of the former had fallen. The proposed marriage also appeared to demonstrate the seriousness of Francis's intent when it came to fulfilling the treaty. Charles believed that, once the various claims had been settled, the match would show the strength of the French ruler's commitment to the Valois-Habsburg rapprochement.

Charles's closest counsellors gave him varying advice. His viceroy, de Lannoy, who had been charged with guarding the king during his captivity, had grown to like Francis, whom he mistakenly regarded as an honourable and decent man who wished to do right by his country, even if it meant acceding to a treaty of this kind. Therefore de Lannoy vouched for his honesty, stating that he believed the king would abide by the treaty. The more wordly lawyer Gattinara, by contrast, was both a pragmatist and a cynic; aware that Francis could not be trusted to fulfil his end of the bargain, especially to a treaty that seemed so obviously weighted against him, he suspected that the prisoner was planning a stratagem. He therefore advised Charles to release the French king unconditionally, and hope that his generosity earned his respect and gratitude, or otherwise keep him imprisoned indefinitely.

Faced with a stark choice, the emperor weighed up the advice of his counsellors and eventually decided to proceed with Francis's release. He also inserted a further provision, one which would have tested the king since he had signed the Treaty of Madrid in bad faith; Dauphin Francis and his younger brother Henri, Duke of Orléans would be handed over as hostages and their release could only take place once the French had fulfilled their obligations. As Francis had signed a secret agreement of his own two days earlier, nullifying the surrender of Burgundy, this placed his sons in a potentially grim predicament. Yet the king viewed this as a risk worth taking if it ensured his release. His gambling instincts remained intact, even after the catastrophic loss at Pavia, but he also knew that his country needed its king to return. He therefore placed France before the welfare of his two eldest boys.

Francis's health remained fragile throughout January 1526, and he did not leave Madrid until mid-February, long after he had signed the treaty. During the last few weeks of his confinement he was officially betrothed to Eleanor by proxy on 20 January, and did not fully recover his strength until the end of the month, when, on 29 January, he finally declared that he was fit and well enough to hunt again. Charles visited Francis on 13 February, and the two men spent a few days together; each tried to understand his opponent under cover of diplomatic niceties. During this period, Francis was introduced to Eleanor in person for the first time, at nearby Illescas. Physically Eleanor had most of the unfortunate Habsburg traits and could not be considered anything other than tolerable-looking. A moment of potentially embarrassing diplomatic intimacy occurred when she, as tradition dictated, curtseyed and made to kiss Francis's hand; he, much to the surprise of the Habsburg siblings, embraced her as intimately as though he were already her husband. This ostentatious gallantry utterly charmed the dull, devout and decent widowed queen, who promptly fell in love with Francis. She could hardly believe her good fortune when the treaty was finally agreed.

The two rulers parted at Torrejón on 19 February. Charles was bound for Seville for his own arranged marriage with Isabella of Portugal, while Francis travelled under guard, through Madrid, Burgos, Vittoria and San Sebastian. As he journeyed across the Spanish countryside he seized every opportunity to enjoy the hunting that he had been denied since his capture the previous year. As his travels brought the king close to the agreed meeting point with the French delegation, de Lannoy planned the complex protocol required for the exchange of hostages; the exchange would take place on the River Bidassoa, near Fuenterrabía, and all troops, local people and the king's household would be kept away. Before the transaction occurred, Francis distributed generous gifts to those who had been his gaolers in captivity, most of whom had grown fond of their charming and regal prisoner. Had they known his intentions, their tears might have flowed less freely at the king's imminent departure.

Finally, on 17 March, a poignant sight could be observed near Fuenterrabía. A few weeks earlier, Louise had been informed of Francis's imminent release. She had been concerned as no news had been forthcoming from Spain since the end of 1525. When the tidings were announced, she informed the *parlement* that she would soon step down from her regency to return the throne to her son.

After this she offered prayers and intercessions for his good health, and travelled from the Loire Valley towards Amboise. Here she collected the two royal princes before going on to Bayonne. She was accompanied by the English ambassador, John Taylor, who noted that 'the king's godson [Henri] is the quicker spirit and the bolder, as seemeth by his behaviour'.[4] Before they departed she had explained to the two young boys, then aged eight and six, that they were about to be sent on a mission of national importance, one that would save both France and their father. The recently motherless children, who had become accustomed to the absence of both their parents, took the news quietly and with dignity, but the brothers looked pale and were noticeably silent throughout the rest of their journey, which took place in appalling weather.

On the allotted day of exchange, following the usual elaborate protocol, two rowing boats left their moorings from opposite sides of the river at an agreed signal at seven o'clock in the morning and the passengers alighted on a pontoon anchored in midstream. One noblewoman seemed especially moved by the boys' plight, particularly that of Henri; this was the twenty-six-year-old Diane de Poitiers, who would later occupy a central position in his life and affections. The king and his sons were reunited, but only briefly, as Francis tearfully embraced and blessed the dauphin and Henri while promising them a safe and speedy return to France, before making the Sign of the Cross over them. Having exchanged the hostages, de Lannoy declared: 'Sire, your highness is now free; let him execute what he has promised!' As Francis vowed 'all shall be done',[5] each boat returned to their original moorings, leaving the monarch once more a free man.

While he might have wished for the pomp and pageantry of earlier in his reign, Francis's return to French soil was an unpretentious affair. Lautrec and a few attendants were anxiously waiting for him at the riverbank, fearful that they might be the victims of some late ruse, but his safe arrival soon reassured them. As the small party galloped off, a jubilant Francis could be heard to shout: 'I am King! I am King again!'[6] Upon his arrival in Bayonne a few miles away, Louise, Marguerite, a few close friends and senior counsellors waiting there expressed their joy and relief at his deliverance, and an artillery salvo greeted him. To further celebrate the happy scene, on 20 March a service of thanksgiving was held at Bayonne Cathedral, attended by the French king, Marguerite and Louise.

Francis was free at last. Yet he had not been released unconditionally, and despite his faithless intention to break the Treaty of Madrid almost immediately, he knew that his sons were hostages and that an angry Charles would feel no obligation to deal with them leniently. As for the task ahead of him, it must have seemed breathtakingly immense. The king had to restore faith in the monarch's authority, re-establish France as a European power to be reckoned with and then – and only then – contemplate taking a much-longed-for revenge. How he would accomplish these aims would preoccupy courtiers, officials and the royal family itself for the foreseeable future, perhaps even the rest of his reign.

CHAPTER 14

A Reversal of Fortune

Francis was free. Yet, rather than take advantage of his newfound liberty to seek military glory, or even to set about mending the divisions within his country, he was initially more interested in enjoying himself. Even as Louise took care to keep him informed of the events that had taken place in his absence, not least those that concerned Duprat and the *parlement*, he was less concerned with dispensing justice than in visiting his favourite parts of the country, which he must once have believed that he would never see again. There were grim duties that could not wait, not least replacing many of the noblemen who had died at Pavia; the ever-faithful Fleurange was rewarded for his constancy by becoming Marshal of France. As Francis travelled through Bordeaux, Cognac, Angoulême and Amboise he sought to cheer himself by resuming his previous activities. He hunted, he danced and he sought the attention of beautiful women, perhaps to console himself after the death of Queen Claude. His recent betrothal to Eleanor of Austria did not seem to inhabit his thoughts, despite the gallantry of his behaviour when first introduced to her. Others now took his interest instead.

Chief among these was the eighteen-year-old Anne de Pisseleu d'Heilly, whom Francis first encountered in March 1526. She had arrived at court in 1522 aged fourteen; the daughter of a Picardy nobleman, the Seigneur de Pisseleu – a name meaning 'worse than wolf' – she understood the milieu that she inhabited. Her position as a junior lady-in-waiting in Louise's household gave her access to the most important person in the kingdom both before and during the regency, as well as a great deal of influence. It helped her cause that Louise was desperate to oust Françoise de Foix, Madame de Châteaubriand, and have Anne succeed her as the king's acknowledged mistress; Louise detested Françoise for her open meddling in her son's affairs and the influence she had over the king. Instead, she desired a more malleable companion for her son.

Anne was a blossoming young beauty, with flowing golden hair and a voluptuous figure, but she was no innocent. She had witnessed many of the dramatic political events that preceded the battle at Pavia, and held an insider's knowledge of the political instability visited upon France following the king's defeat. Serving as a member of Madame de Vendôme's household had given her additional experience of public affairs, and she had a keen interest in the arts, developed in her time as a lady-in-waiting; she was certainly no *ingénue*. By the spring of 1527 she had already consolidated her position in Francis's household and was a well-respected member of 'la petite bande' of ladies who would travel with the king on hunting expeditions. These excursions, which combined killing with amorous sport, were described by the ambassador Sir Anthony Browne to Henry VIII. Browne did not write without a touch of envy, even if the final description of Anne was disingenuous: 'The king's bed is always carried with him, when he hunts; and anon, after that the deer is killed, he repairs to some house near at hand, where the same is set up, and there reposes himself three or four hours, and against his return there is provided for him a supper by some nobleman, as by Monsieur de Vendôme, Monsieur de Guise or other; whereunto, a great number of ladies and gentlewomen used to be in his company be sent for, and there he passes his time until ten or eleven o'clock, among whom above others, as the report is, he favours a maiden of Madame de Vendôme, called Hely, whose beauty, after my mind, is not highly to be praised.'[1]

Françoise was less than impressed by her putative replacement and, upon first hearing of her rival's place at court, travelled from Normandy to upbraid and belittle her. She described Anne as nothing more than a 'fuzzy chit', a strangely ineffectual insult that nevertheless gave Francis the excuse that he and Louise had been looking for to sever relations with her. The king wrote an admonitory letter to his erstwhile mistress in which he explained that he no longer had any affection for her, and desired that she left court and instead returned to her husband's estates; he also called her a 'rabid beast'. Anne, irritated by the existence of golden ornaments engraved with love messages to Françoise, demanded that Francis ask for their return. The displaced lover melted them down into ingots and sent them back to the king, who, impressed, said, 'She has shown more courage and generosity than I would have expected from a woman.'[2]

When he was not occupied with dealing with his mistresses past and present, there were other matters that called for his urgent attention. Familial duties, some of them distinctly sorrowful, had to be performed before the year was out, not least the burials of his wife Claude and their seven-year-old daughter Charlotte. The queen's funeral had been postponed as a result of Francis's absence during the recent Italian campaign and could not take place while the king was imprisoned. At last, Francis's return provided an opportunity to do justice to the memory of his late consort. Nonetheless, private grief took second place to the expected rituals of public mourning. Any sorrow felt by Claude's widower on the occasion of her funeral and burial would have been concealed beneath the artifice of the day.

Louise and Marguerite, along with the Duke and Duchess of Vendôme and Marshal Lautrec, were present among the mourners when Claude and Charlotte's bodies were transported from Blois to Paris. Here, the funeral service was held at Notre-Dame on 5 November 1526, before their burial at Saint-Denis on the following day. This was a great public occasion attended by the dignitaries of the French Church and nobility, along with representatives of the *parlement*. The king, who had immeasurably benefited financially from his marriage to the late queen, to say nothing of her forbearance in all personal matters, stayed away. Although it is uncertain what his emotional state was, the grief that he displayed when he heard of her demise was probably an accurate indication of the turmoil that he felt. On the days of the funeral and burial Francis chose to busy himself at Vincennes. He only visited Saint-Denis on 8 November, when he took the sacred relics from their place on the high altar, where he had laid them before embarking upon his ill-fated Italian adventure. He then joined Louise, Marguerite and the rest of the court at Saint-Germain-en-Laye, west of Paris, in the weeks leading up to Christmas 1526.

After a year of relaxation and sport, work once again had to begin. Queen Claude, for all the pomp and ceremony of her funeral, would become a forgotten detail of dynastic history that winter. On 26 December the recently widowed Marguerite announced her betrothal to Henri d'Albret, King of Navarre, and a national hero following his daring escape from the castle at Pavia. On 30 January 1527 the couple were married and Marguerite would then divide her time between court and her husband's tiny kingdom in the Pyrenees. The wedding ceremony, conducted at Saint-Germain-en-Laye, would later have profound consequences for the future of the French monarchy, as Jeanne d'Albret, the couple's daughter, would give birth to the future King Henry IV of France.

With Francis's return came a series of innovations and changes. He turned his back on the Loire Valley, concentrating his energies and interests on Paris. There he demolished the great keep of the Louvre in order to make the palace a more arresting and contemporary place to live. Although he knew that the Parisians had hostile feelings towards him, he decided to make the city his home, and began building a great château in the Bois de Boulogne; in what he called 'our delightful wilderness' he aimed to make a grander and more impressive version of the château at Blois. Parisians, lightly mocking their king for what they perceived to be influences acquired from his Spanish sojourn, described it as 'Madrid-en-Boulogne'.

His homecoming could be described as a second accession of sorts, not least because it represented Francis's chance to turn the page on what had been a disastrous previous couple of years and once again prove that he was fit and able to rule. The consolidation of his, and the rest of the royal family's, power could be discerned in the series of public appointments that were made in the months immediately following his return. The apparatus of government had survived his absence, but a regency could never be the same as a monarch's personal rule. This was especially true of Francis, who could be capable both of providing strong public leadership and of bringing about much-needed reform. He was eager to assert his authority in questions of state and, as recent events had left a large number of senior offices to be filled, this gave him an opportunity to remake the government in his preferred style and image.

Many of those who benefited from his largesse were trusted friends and comrades-in-arms, such as Anne de Montmorency, Marshal of France and a boon companion since childhood. On 23 March 1527, Montmorency became Grand Master in succession to the king's uncle, René, the Great Bastard of Savoy, who had died of wounds inflicted at Pavia. Montmorency was thirty-four years old, a member of one of France's oldest and richest aristocratic families and unfailingly loyal. As a reward for his steadfast service, he also became governor of Languedoc, an office previously held by the Duke of Bourbon, whose loyalty had proved anything but reliable. As Grand Master, Montmorency's elevation to his new office gave him an important role in governmental circles, to which he brought the same detailed and careful eye he had always displayed as a military commander. Montmorency was an unswerving supporter of royal authority, a trait that endeared him to Francis. It was little wonder that the king was an ardent advocate of his marriage in January 1527 to the late René of Savoy's daughter Madeleine, which brought him closer into the royal circle.

At the same time that Montmorency was honoured, Philippe Chabot was promoted to the position of Admiral of France, replacing Bonnivet. Like Montmorency the admiral had been a childhood companion to the king, and in January 1528 his union with Françoise de Longwy, the king's niece, also drew Chabot into the monarch's extended family. Appointed gentleman of the bedchamber at the start of Francis's reign, Chabot had long been his close confidant. The post of Admiral, together with his appointment to the governorships of Burgundy and of Valois, was a clear recognition of his crucial role in the king's restoration. It was no coincidence that these men, and others chosen for promotion to higher office, came almost entirely from conventional aristocratic backgrounds and had been part of Francis's inner circle for many years. By acting this way, Francis conformed to a well-established code of conduct that maintained that a sovereign's court should consist of aristocrats, soldiers and a few churchmen, as well as mistresses and retainers. While it was traditional across Europe for governments of the royal household to contain clerks, non-clerical scholars who were adept at such tasks as the drafting of legislation, Francis had little understanding of or desire to promote the role of clerks in his administration, and thereby ensured that the usual cheerful aristocratic insouciance would be represented at the highest levels of government. It was to be business as usual, for good or ill.

There were also those who had to be dealt with harshly. The most notable of these figures was Jacques de Beaune, Baron de Semblançay, formerly a key figure in the royal administration before Francis's imprisonment, but who had fallen foul of the king due to perceived corruption and misappropriation of royal funds. The cynical might have noted that the king was looking for a scapegoat to blame for his financially insecure position, and the opportunity to castigate a rich man publicly and then to seize his property was one not to be missed. Therefore, after a rigged trial in which the evidence was either ignored or falsified, Semblançay was condemned to death and executed on 11 August 1528, after the cruel humiliation of being forced to wait six hours. While it was hoped that the public execution would show Francis as a strong and decisive ruler, the kangaroo court and the eighty-year-old financier's dignity turned sympathies towards the accused. One chronicler wrote that 'he was much pitied and mourned by the people, who would have been pleased if the king had seen fit to spare him'.[3] Nonetheless, his execution had a macabre epilogue. After his body disappeared in mysterious circumstances, his great nemesis Duprat, who was largely responsible for his downfall, demanded that the corpse be found and then publicly hanged once more. The body was eventually discovered in a graveyard, allowing for the burial that Semblançay deserved. Francis, meanwhile, found that his erstwhile friend's death meant that a debt of over a million *livres* was now cancelled: nothing more than a coincidence, of course.

*

Yet an even harsher and more cynical side would manifest itself in this new regime, both in Francis's political outlook and in his treatment of allies. Even Duprat, in time, would find that his influence and power would wane. By the end of the decade he would concentrate on his recently adopted clerical duties rather than his legal and administrative career. In the summer of 1528, however, he remained a figure of central importance. His considerable diplomatic talents, to say nothing of his abilities in skulduggery, were amply suited to the unenviable task of convincingly explaining to an unimpressed Charles V why the King of France was about to renege on a peace treaty that he had signed in January of that year.

For all the apparent trust between Francis and the emperor, the French king had never deviated from the view formed during his imprisonment that the demands made upon him were outrageous. Although the details had been readily conceded, and indeed formalised in the Treaty of Madrid, Francis now believed that, given that he was once again free and in his own country, he was no longer bound by terms he considered no less than a personal insult. After all, he reasoned, no country gives up its territories lightly – hence the military expeditions that he had undertaken at enormous personal cost – and no King of France should be treated in so cavalier a manner. Memories of his imprisonment and the humiliations that he had endured still rankled.

However, he was intelligent enough to know that his personal feelings were not sufficient reason to renege on his agreement and so, containing his anger, he ensured that France's failure to ratify the treaty could be explained by technicalities. Initially, on 17 March 1526, the imperial ambassador who had been dispatched from Spain to collect the king's ratification of the treaty was sent away on the grounds that he had not been granted the right degree of authority. When these powers were granted by Charles on 27 March, yet another excuse was found: the document could only be validated once affixed with the Great Seal. The original seal had been lost at Pavia and the engravers were still working on a replacement. He hoped that excuses such as these, though scarcely believable, would obscure the real issue.

It did not take long for Francis's public position to harden from simple obfuscation to something more adversarial. On 2 April he angrily complained that the treaty had already been published in Rome, Florence and Antwerp. This was a minor technicality, but Francis argued that the rush to publication was improper and the news about the surrender of Burgundy had enraged the king's subjects, who were especially angry that foreigners had been informed before the French. This was, of course, untrue, but it was a useful excuse that Francis now exploited, claiming that French subjects demanded a chance to express their opinions in advance of the treaty's ratification. The appeal to 'public opinion' was spurious: Francis was not a proto-democrat, but a monarch who regarded his own judgement as the true source of authority in French public life, the only people he needed to consult being the nobility, senior clergy and members of the provincial *parlement*. The fake consultation merely provided another ruse to give him more time and build up alliances to support his military position. Nonetheless, the stratagem worked. The imperial negotiators allowed the king time to explain the situation to his subjects – time that could well be used in other ways.

Despite the glee that Henry VIII had felt when he initially heard of Francis's downfall, Anglo French relations were once again amicable, not least because the English king feared that Charles would become a threat if he were to control Burgundy as well as the rest of the Holy Roman Empire. Francis therefore decided that the safest course of action with Henry was to flatter him, praising him for his generosity both in resisting the temptation to invade France while her king was absent, and for the (largely non-existent) role he had played in securing his release. These compliments were diplomatic ploys rather than realistic statements, but they worked. It was also true that Henry regarded Francis's imprisonment as a hideous breach of monarchical etiquette, and publicly said so. Even if the treaty negotiation owed nothing to English diplomacy, it was convenient for Henry to imagine that he had played a part in Francis's release. Francis was therefore pleased to ratify at least one treaty, namely that of the More, which he had agreed on 15 April 1526. This was largely symbolic, but nevertheless strengthened the

at times tenuous Anglo-French détente, as it stated that Henry and
the French monarch could now meet at any time, with good feeling
between the two. To add to this sense of intimacy the English ambassador, Sir Thomas Cheyney, was allowed to become one of the
gentlemen of Francis's bedchamber, meaning that he would have
the same access to the French king as he would to his own. It was a
potentially risky piece of licence, but also served to create trust. Its
success could be seen by a further bilateral agreement, which was
signed on 8 August and tightened the screws on Charles. England
and France now agreed to cooperate as a single foreign policy entity
and neither country would negotiate on its own with the empire.

Other allies pressed their cases. An initiative led by Venice and
the papacy arrived in France at the end of March with the intention of eliciting Francis's support for the so-called Holy League,
which was already well under way. Its primary aim was to eject the
imperial armies from northern Italy, but its intent to recover and
affirm Italian freedoms also gave it both a political and a cultural
dimension. Northern Italy had endured repeated invasions, and the
consequent ravaging of its countryside and urban settlements, for
two generations, and Francis had been one of those responsible. If
he felt any sense of guilt, then it was at least an opportunity to atone
for his past actions. On 20 April he agreed to join the Holy League,
stressing that he took the decision not out of self-interest but for
the cause of liberty in Italy. He might have been disingenuous, but
any ally that he could summon in his current predicament was a
welcome one.

As for Charles, he was as subject to the vagaries of chance and
luck as any other monarch. If he believed that his victory at Padua
and subsequent imprisonment of Francis had settled his reputation
and power in Europe beyond doubt, he was soon to be disabused
of the assumption. Not only was his adversary a considerably less
honourable monarch than he had initially believed (or hoped), but
he was faced with his own difficulties. He was desperate for the
French king to ratify the treaty, not just for the territorial advantages that it would give him, but to settle the question of his own
authority. As Francis had found, a great victory had its own cost,
and throughout 1526 Charles's unpaid troops trickled disconsolately

through central and northern Italy. Although a total breakdown in discipline seemed inconceivable, there was a great deal of bitterness on the part of those who had been dispensed with to save money. He might even have believed that Pavia had been a victory too far and that his treatment of Francis could unite a mighty alliance against him.

It was therefore with decidedly unimperial desperation that Charles continued to cajole Francis to fulfil his obligations. The emperor knew that Francis had a high regard for de Lannoy, who had after all been responsible for saving his life at Pavia, and so entrusted him with a special diplomatic mission. He was dispatched to the French court, which had assembled at Cognac in early May. On a personal level de Lannoy was delighted to see his friend, but had no illusions about his trustworthiness; although he had initially supported Charles in his decision to release the king before the ratification of the Treaty of Madrid, he had also consistently warned the emperor since then that it was inevitable that Francis was bound to renege on their agreement with him.

De Lannoy was to be proved correct on 10 May when the King's Council, meeting in formal session, announced that Francis would not hand over the duchy of Burgundy. The initial reason given was that, as the king had been a prisoner when the treaty was drawn up, his assent was obtained by force, and therefore not legally binding. Francis and his council also informed the incredulous de Lannoy that, whether they had wanted to cede Burgundy or not, an outraged public had shown their displeasure with such vehemence that they had effectively tied the king's hands.

Therefore Burgundy would remain in French hands, and the only offer that the council was prepared to countenance was a cash ransom as, by rejecting one clause of the treaty, the whole thing was invalidated. Unsurprisingly, the imperial delegation rejected any idea of a ransom, the only option left to them being one of military conquest. It did not help that, on 4 June, Burgundy's representative estates held a conference at Dijon and informed the king's representative and governor of the region, Philippe Chabot, of their unanimous view that they wished to remain subjects of the French Crown and that the Treaty of Madrid stood 'contrary to all reason and equity'.[4] The possibility of Charles imposing a new regime in Burgundy following an armed intervention could best be described as remote; like so many other military leaders, he was extremely short of funds.

Nonetheless, Chabot decided to leave little to chance and ordered tight security in Burgundy; this included the introduction of a network of spies, as well as the requirement for all Burgundian adults to swear public oaths of allegiance to the French Crown. This made a mockery of Francis's statement that he was acting purely on behalf of 'the people', given that deference to public opinion was not his natural state; pro-imperial commentators ridiculed him for his hypocrisy. Francis did not take any notice, instead forming the League of Cognac at Angoulême in June 1526, alongside the papacy, Venice, Milan, Genoa and Florence. Henry VIII, while described as its 'protector', did not hold any formal role within it. Although the league ostensibly described its aim as being 'to ensure the security of Christendom and the establishment of a true and lasting peace', its primary purpose was once more to liberate Italy from imperial control; the unspoken secondary aim was that of revenge for any slights committed against the royal person. Francis again repudiated the Treaty of Madrid, citing the ill treatment that he had received when imprisoned in Spain as one of the reasons for his unwillingness to go along with the agreement. As he said, entirely disingenuously, 'How many times did I not warn him that it was not in my power to dismember the kingdom?'[5]

For Charles, who now faced a military and diplomatic alliance formed against him less than three months after he had released Francis, it was an unsettling and miserable time. After his stunning victory in Pavia – in many respects the equal of Francis's at Marignano – he had been able to survey his domains in Europe with a degree of equanimity. His achievement was especially satisfactory since it had been delivered at the expense of the French sovereign, a rival whose poise and charisma showed how a powerful monarch could enjoy such widespread appeal throughout Europe. Compared to Francis, who had a winning combination of personal charm, political intelligence and savvy opportunism, Charles seemed distinctly second-rate as both a man and a ruler, and he cursed his folly and gullibility in allowing his prized captive to slip through his fingers and repudiate his promises almost immediately. Yet such behaviour was entirely true to Francis's character. He believed that his duties to himself and to his kingdom were unambiguous. His crown carried with it a sacred trust to maintain the security of his country's borders, to sustain the peace and to defeat her enemies. Any action that he undertook thus went beyond simple questions of trust and honour; his interest, and that of France, always came first.

As for the emperor, the humiliation that he now felt was brewing with anger. He did, however, have one form of revenge at his disposal, and he lost little time in taking it. After he was invited to join the League of Cognac in exchange for various demeaning terms, he responded by ordering that the retainers who had waited on Francis's two sons should be sent to the galleys as slaves, and that the boys should henceforth be closely guarded by Spanish gaolers at a castle near the town of Valladolid. This was a far cry from their earlier 'honourable captivity' at Vitoria in Castile, where they had stayed with their stepmother-to-be Queen Eleanor with an entourage that included as many as seventy attendants, servants and governors. Now they were little better than prisoners, kept captive in the most demeaning conditions.

The French ambassador Calvimont, alarmed by this turn of events, offered a generous ransom for their release, but an outraged Charles responded with indignant anger, saying: 'I will not deliver them for money. I refused money for the father: I will much less take money for the sons. I am content to render them upon reasonable treaty, but not for money, nor will I trust any more the king's promise, for he has deceived me, and that like no noble prince. And where he excuses that he cannot fulfil some things without grudge of his subjects, let him fulfil that that is in his power, which he promised by the honour of a prince to fulfil; that is to say, that if he could not bring all his promises to pass he would return again hither into prison.' He even declared that, in the event of an attempted rescue by the French, he would engage Francis in hand-to-hand combat, wildly claiming that 'Would to God, that he were content, in the avoiding of Christian blood, to try the right with me, hand for hand, I would, upon confidence of my right, take it on me, which I trust in the righteousness of God should defend me.'[6]

For all his brave words and defiance, Charles was facing a series of considerable difficulties. The Treaty of Madrid had been entirely superseded by the formation of the League of Cognac, he was out of money, his territories in Hungary were under attack by the Turks and his German lands were torn with religious strife. An English envoy of the time described him, evocatively, as 'full of dumps'.[7] Even as he repented of his anger and offered to discuss the release of Francis's sons, he felt that the tide of fortune had turned against him.

For the French king, meanwhile, it seemed as if an appallingly poor hand had been turned to his advantage through careful alliances and good fortune, and the fact that his opponent's strength was considerably less than he had believed. Yet Francis's position remained unsure. There were many domestic difficulties to deal with, not least a rebellious *parlement* to take in hand. His sons remained captives in a foreign country. And his new allies all possessed their own agendas, which were of less benefit to him than the initial union had been. His struggle to exert his own supremacy would lead him into some strange alliances, and the gambling monarch was, once again, preparing to bet his kingdom on events that only the most confident of rulers might have predicted.

CHAPTER 15

Violent Beginnings and Peaceful Ends

Fortune had favoured first Francis and then Charles, and a curious compromise had developed between the two in which neither was triumphant nor entirely defeated. A similar kind of stasis also existed for the Duke of Bourbon, whose initial discontent had indirectly led to Francis's defeat and capture. With the French king once again restored to the throne, it looked as if Bourbon's imperial ambitions were to be frustrated. As he lingered in Italy with no clear idea as to how he should act, he began to fear that his pact with Charles was unlikely to withstand a potential peace treaty. Knowing how much Francis despised him for his perceived treachery, he realised that there was no possibility of a reconciliation with his former king, even if such an outcome were desirable. Instead, drastic action had to be taken that would redefine the new set of alliances that now existed after the League of Cognac. Bourbon would march on Rome, and lead his ragged army to a glorious and era-defining victory which would make Marignano and Pavia look puny in comparison.

By early 1527, Bourbon had descended into a frayed state both mentally and physically. He commanded a motley band of *Landsknechts* who roved the countryside, robbing and sacking where they could. Their leader was scarcely a more impressive figure. The duke had metamorphosed from a self-assured and elegant nobleman whose vast territories dominated central France into a semi-feral warlord who lived in the woods. He had been driven to a state of near-insanity by paranoia and frustration. Once, he might have been able to sue for peace, but this had become impossible. Even if he had been able to come to an accommodation with Francis, his troops, who had not been paid for months, would not allow their leader to return to the status quo ante. Such a state of affairs meant that his only option was to act decisively against a new enemy, in the form of Pope Clement VII, and thereby deal a crippling blow to the League of Cognac.

By the end of 1526 Clement had become a diminished figure, if he had ever had any stature at all. Although he had been an outstanding right-hand man to his cousin Pope Leo X, he suffered from acute indecisiveness and consequently ended up in the worst of all situations. He made not had much impact within the league ever since an attempt to blame his early Italian military misfortunes on the French had been dealt with by the usual mixture of dismissal and contempt. At the end of July the secretary of the embassy informed him that 'you have no idea what things are said about us by persons of high standing in the Curia on account of our delays and our behaviour hitherto'. The secretary ended, with characteristic sardonic condescension, by remarking that 'the language is so frightful that I dare not write it'.[1] It was not long until Clement, tiring of the hostility from his supposed allies and the cost of the apparently endless war, decided that his best option lay in signing a declaration of truce with Charles; he duly did this on 21 September, albeit for the relatively short period of four months.

Had he been a more significant figure on the international stage, this might have been a shocking moment of destabilisation. Clement's relative impotence, however, made him easy prey for his various enemies, who included the *Landsknechts* invading Mantua, to the north of the papal states, and the forces of the Colonna army attacking from the south. As de Lannoy, who was prepared to ignore any truce that existed, landed with 9,000 troops in a Tuscan port on 28 November, one chronicler described Clement as resembling 'a sick man [on] whom the doctors have given up'.[2] When the pope renewed the truce with Charles at the beginning of 1527, blaming the non-arrival of a promised French subsidy, Francis prepared to turn against his former ally, telling a papal nuncio that 'I hope to act in such a way that the Emperor will not succeed in his aim of subordinating everything to tyranny, but I will leave those who have fallen into servitude through their own baseness and fear.'[3]

If his intention had been to shock Clement into action, he succeeded. The papal army engaged the imperial forces at Naples shortly afterwards, leading Francis once more to offer substantial assistance to his ally. Yet the strength and conviction of de Lannoy's forces meant that Clement, never a natural military leader, was unable to hold off his attackers for long. On 15 March 1527 he signed yet another peace treaty with Francis's former captor in a desperate attempt to maintain the status quo. This proved successful, as de Lannoy was a fair and reasonable leader, and one who kept his troops in good order. No such accommodation could be reached with Bourbon, however, and his cold, hungry and increasingly mutinous army could only be placated with one promise: that Rome awaited them with her arms and legs wide open. Bourbon declared to the soldiers that he was no longer their leader, but their brother-in-arms, and the predominantly Lutheran forces under his command relished the opportunity both to avenge themselves on the hated papists and to loot the city's treasures and indulge their carnal appetites.

Bourbon's army, which consisted of around 20,000 men, had its ranks increased by various bandits and deserters who joined it as the throng progressed southwards through Italy in the early months of 1527. The ragtag assembly did not attack Florence, which would soon be torn apart by a revolt against the Medici, but, after they had sacked towns including Arezzo, Acquapendente and San Lorenzo alle Grotte, the greatest prize of all awaited them on 5 May.

Clement had decided, erroneously, that these adversaries were not men with whom he could bargain. Theoretically they marched under the banner of Charles V, but the fierce and unstoppable band of mercenaries and desperados who were heading to the walls of his city would not be prepared to countenance a peace without substantial financial compensation. This was not something that the disorganised and indecisive pope would offer, even as the price rose with each mile that they advanced. He attempted to come to another agreement with the league, which he rejoined on 25 April 1527, but it was too late. Even if men and arms had been forthcoming, no relief force large enough to save Rome could reach the city in less than a fortnight. Likewise, Clement's vacillating and inconstant behaviour had meant that, even if his erstwhile allies had wished to save him – and it is likely that Francis sought personal revenge against Bourbon – they saw no benefit in facing a feral fighting force at enormous risk and expense. The pope stood alone, with only 5,000 or so militiamen, a couple of hundred papal Swiss Guard and the hope that God would protect the hitherto inviolable capital of Christendom against its enemies. It was to be a vain wish, as the Eternal City looked all too transitory.

On the morning of 6 May 1527, the Sack of Rome began. A last-minute appeal to the loyalty of the city's inhabitants to take up arms against the invaders produced little success. Of the 55,000 people living in Rome when the attack started, no more than 500 pledged themselves to the fight. It did not matter; as the imperial troops attacked the walls from the Vatican and Janiculum hills, the assault was conducted with the bare minimum of restraint or order. What little discipline there was came entirely from the command of Bourbon who, for all his degradation, still retained the respect and standing due to a brilliant and daring military leader.

His flowing robes were in the traditional white of his dynasty, with the intention of showing his ragtag army that he was their commander and the figure to follow into battle. This, unfortunately, had the same effect of marking him out to the enemy: as the sack began he was struck by a bullet from an arquebus and fatally wounded. Legend has it that he was the first fatality. The marksman was unknown, although a twenty-seven-year-old goldsmith and musician would claim credit for the shot: none other than a man who would become one of Italy's greatest artists, Benvenuto Cellini. Whether or not this leading Renaissance figure had indeed killed the erstwhile Constable of France, Bourbon's death, and the subsequent secession of authority to the less competent second-in-command, Philibert de Châlon, meant that any possibility of a negotiated peace was at an end. Rome was doomed.

The ensuing chaos and bloodshed represented a nadir in sixteenth-century human behaviour; seizing on Bourbon's death as the most spurious of pretexts, the assembled men threw themselves

into chaos, shouting, 'Kill, kill, blood, blood, Bourbon, Bourbon.'[4]
For all the apparent sophistication of the French and Italian civili-
sations in the Renaissance, the barbarism beneath the surface was
sharply exposed in the days and weeks that followed. With no chain
of military command in place to check the wildest excesses of the
mutineers, they were able to cause a literal orgy of devastation. The
population of Rome, who had refused to assist in the defence of
their city, were now tortured, defiled and murdered. The violence
proved a great leveller, as everyone, from churchmen to common
ers, was treated with the same brutality. Churches were sacked,
nuns raped, cardinals butchered, sacred relics thrown into cesspits
and holy buildings treated no better than gutters.

One of the few to escape this slaughter was Clement, thanks
to a heroic last stand by the Swiss Guard. Led by their captain
Kaspar Roïst, they knew that they would not be able to hold off the
legions of their attackers for more than a few moments, but their
acts enabled the pope to escape. As the vast majority of his men
were butchered on the steps of the basilica, the pontiff fled down
the Passetto di Borgo, a secret corridor between the Vatican and
the Castel Sant'Angelo. Clement might well have been unworthy of
such a sacrifice, but he remained pope, and so it was for the office,
rather than the man, that the 150 soldiers gave their lives.

Even the arrival of a seasoned military commander in the form
of Cardinal Pompeo Colonna on 8 May 1527 did little to quell the
bloodshed. Colonna, who had always despised Clement, could not
control the forces running rampant through the city, although he
did discreetly ensure that some of the leading figures were accom
modated in his own palace – at least, those who had survived the
opening massacre. The Vatican Library was mercifully saved because Philibert had his headquarters there, and it was from there
that, on 9 May, he gave the order that the sack should cease. He
might as well have been speaking in tongues for all the attention
that his order received. Chaos had infected Rome like a plague, and
nothing could happen until the disease had run its course.

It was not until the beginning of June that the violence came to
an uneasy end, and that only after a failed attempt by the Duke of
Urbino to retake the city on 1 June. Five days later, Clement finally

agreed a surrender that could not have been more humiliating if it had involved his being paraded through the streets naked. He was required to pay an enormous ransom of 400,000 *ducati*, to cede six towns including Parma and Modena to Charles and to remain a prisoner until the conditions were fulfilled. The emperor, all too aware of what had happened after Francis had been released, had no intention of repeating his mistake. As he agreed the terms, Clement was able to reflect on the damage that had been wrought upon his city. As many as 12,000 Roman men and women had been murdered in the weeks of pillage, and the imperial troops – real or spurious – remained in the city until February 1528, continuing to cause acts of violence and theft. Their departure was only occasioned by the outbreak of plague, caused by the rotting bodies littering the streets that nobody had dared bury.

Charles and Francis reacted to the news of the atrocities in different ways. Although it was nominally an imperial victory, the destruction of the capital of Christendom appalled Charles, not least because he knew that the responsibility for not paying his troops and therefore triggering the chaos lay with him. When he learnt of the unwelcome events, he ceased the celebrations that he had ordered for the birth of his son Philip, dispatched ambassadors to Rome with letters stating his continued friendship of the city, and let it be known to allies and adversaries alike that he could neither have foreseen nor prevented the destruction, and that he deplored the outcome. These fine words, however well intentioned, did not stop him from using Clement as political capital. He blamed the pope for his own shifting alliances, and regarded him less as a worthy adversary than as an inconstant, vacillating blunderer who deserved the blame for all that had ensued.

Francis, meanwhile, greeted events with equanimity. Although Clement's actions had irritated him as much as they had Charles, it was still an unfortunate situation to see an erstwhile ally reduced to the status of a prisoner, as well as an uncomfortable reminder of his own recent captivity. Likewise, the destruction and violence that had laid waste to Rome was hardly an isolated occurrence. He remembered that it was simple good fortune that the same fate had not befallen Paris in 1523. The death of Bourbon did not quell

Francis's loathing of the traitor, whom he blamed for many of the events of the previous years, not least the continued imprisonment of his sons. On 26 July 1527 a posthumous trial began in the Great Room of the *parlement* during which, after the dead duke was solemnly summoned to appear by an usher, a series of commands were passed which saw Bourbon's property surrendered, his coat of arms defaced and his name ritually condemned, as he was found guilty of treason, a lack of regal respect and rebellion. Had it been possible, a royal edict would have been passed for Bourbon's name to become synonymous with wickedness. Some might have seen this as overkill, but it was a satisfying and symbolic way of burying the man whom Francis had never managed to defeat in combat.

Another legacy of the horrors of Rome was a closer diplomatic relationship between France and England, both to create a military alliance that would not allow a great city to be so crudely desecrated, and also to enable Wolsey to recalibrate the basis of European power. Rather than a simple imperial hegemony, he saw the opportunity to bring about a mutually beneficial understanding between the two countries. When the cardinal met Francis at Amiens on 16 August 1527, he made it clear that he would offer diplomatic support for the release of Francis's sons, but neglected to mention Henry VIII's longed-for divorce from Catherine of Aragon, which could only be granted by the pope. The latter, while remaining a reluctant guest of Charles, would be unable to turn his mind to such affairs.

Francis was on resplendent form, dressed in a suit of purple satin appositely adorned with a silver lining, and the relationship between the two men was as cordial and warm as before. Even a disagreement between Duprat and Wolsey, potentially jeopardising the rapprochement, was dealt with by Louise, ever the premier diplomat, who intervened 'so discreetly and wittily'[5] that matters were soon resolved. As before, there was hunting, this time of 'perilous wild swine', and Francis distinguished himself with his usual prowess. A treaty of perpetual peace signed two days later agreed a match between Mary Tudor and the Duke of Orléans, that neither king would attend a General Council of peace as long as Clement remained a prisoner, and that Henry would formally waive any objection he had to the marriage between Francis and Eleanor. The two kings exchanged honours to symbolise their renewed friendship. Henry received the order of St Michael and Francis, in turn, had the Garter bestowed upon him. As Louise exclaimed delightedly that the rulers were 'under one clothing . . . [and] in one mind and heart',[6] the old amity of the Field of the Cloth of Gold was restored, and no suggestion of the strife between them was mentioned.

Francis's energy and drive continued throughout the remainder of 1527. Freed from the privations and humiliation of his imprisonment, he exhibited both a newfound boldness and a greater cynicism about power and kingship. As he resumed his Italian campaigns in the autumn, invading Naples and Parma, he still wished to appear regal in his lofty aims, even though these broke his treaty with Charles. To this end he convened the so-called 'Assembly of Notables', which included the nobility, clergymen, politicians and leading citizens, at the *parlement* in Paris on 16 December. The purpose of the assembly was to lend legitimacy to his decision to go against the Treaty of Madrid, as well as to raise a sum of money with which to ransom his sons, or to wage war against Charles should he refuse the offer. Francis made an effective speech in which he claimed that his aim had always been peace, rather than belligerence, but that his actions had been forced upon him through duress and treachery, most notably that of Bourbon. Therefore, he asked the assembly for their views, knowing that the result was a foregone conclusion. Although he suggested that he might be liable to return to prison for breaking his oath, he knew that even the most foolhardy noble or cleric would not assent.

After a few days of token consideration, the delegates' response came on 20 December. Unsurprisingly, the assembly unanimously agreed to all of the king's demands. The Treaty of Madrid was declared invalid, the League of Cognac supported as a means of placing pressure on Charles to abandon his claim to Burgundy, and the renewed French alliance with England declared an excellent diplomatic idea that emphasised the image of the emperor as being isolated within Europe. When it came to raising the funds to release the princes, the representatives could not have been more accommodating. Francis announced that he required two million *écus*, which was immediately ratified. Raising it from the clergy and nobility proved to be a considerably harder task, however, and one that would not be accomplished until 1529, and only then after considerable pressure and the introduction of new levies upon such goods as wine. As before, the king also had to resort to loans extended to him from the holders of the great offices of state, many of whom might have recalled what had happened to Semblançay and hesitated before pressing too hard for the return of their money.

The actions at the Assembly of Notables could only be construed as an obvious snub to Charles. Given the circumstances in which it had taken place, his only response was to continue to refuse to release the dauphin and his brother, leading to a stalemate between the two rulers. War was declared, but the emperor now found himself faced with an Anglo-French alliance. On 28 January 1528, in a formal nod to the chivalric tradition of old, two heralds appeared before Charles to announce the grounds on which war had been declared, which included the undignified treatment of Pope Clement. Charles was justifiably unimpressed by this declaration, arguing both that a state of war had existed between him and Francis for years without any need to mark it, and also that Clement had left his captivity on 6 December the previous year.

Nonetheless, the obviousness of the pretext did not go unchallenged. The emperor still held the ultimate trump card: he retained Francis and Henri as captives and so, as a direct result of the declaration of war, he decided to see to it that the boys had an even less pleasant time than at present. Their remaining servants were dismissed, they were removed to an austere fortress near Segovia and treated as common prisoners. This caused a great deal of distress to the women who cared most deeply about the young princes; Eleanor of Portugal was said to have retired to a monastery in shock and unhappiness, while Louise used Wolsey's considerable diplomatic skill in an attempt to elicit more appropriate treatment for her grandchildren. Even the cardinal, however, was unable to intercede, and the boys remained in uncomfortable captivity.

By now Charles was beginning to feel that the situation was likely to result in an endless stalemate, and so he demanded a duel with Francis, repeating a challenge that he had made in 1526. Francis's previous claim that 'gentilhomme is the principal title that I bear and the one I esteem [the] most' made no impression upon Charles who, justifiably given recent events, knew that Francis was dishonourable and unworthy of being regarded on an equal level. After all, the French king had blithely signed a major treaty without the slightest intention of honouring it. Nonetheless, after the challenge was received, on 28 March 1528, Francis issued a formal acceptance. It looked for a moment as if the longed-for duel would take place, and Charles suggested that they face one another on the banks of the River Bidassoa. However, Francis managed to frustrate matters once again. The next stage should have involved a formal rendition of Charles's grievances against him, read out by a herald in an echo of the French king's declaration of war two months before. But Francis's courtiers detained the herald for over a month before the king refused him an audience, leaving the messenger little choice but to return to Madrid. Charles, angered and embarrassed, declared at the Council of Castile that no European sovereign, indeed no *gentilhomme*, had ever demonstrated such craven scorn for chivalry, and that Francis had once again proved his untrustworthiness.

If the French monarch was congratulating himself on running rings around the emperor, his army was soon to be humiliated once again on the field of battle. In February 1528, Lautrec seemed unstoppable as he swept through Italy. Following his conquest of the Romagna, he invaded the northern border of the kingdom of Naples a week later. It was not long before the inhabitants of the Abruzzi thronged to acclaim the French marshal as their liberator, just as Apulia fell to him without any apparent effort. It seemed as if Naples, too, might be conquered by the end of April; before long his troops were encamped outside the city walls, while his ally Filippino Doria commanded a fleet blockading the city's port. Naples could not withstand this onslaught for long.

Yet, just as victory appeared certain, an act of treachery saw to it that glory was cruelly snatched away. As often with European rulers, the roots lay in poor financial management. Filippino's uncle Andrea, who had conquered Genoa and had captured Philibert, Prince of Orange, the previous year, felt dissatisfied with what he saw as double-dealing on the part of the French king. Once he had received the substantial ransom, Francis had failed to pass the money on to his captor. He would pay dearly for his short-sighted attention to such a trifling financial advantage.

In June 1528, shortly after a great French victory had seemed assured, Andrea retreated from Genoa and within a few weeks had enrolled himself in the emperor's service. He commanded that his nephew do the same, and Filippino obediently withdrew his fleet. As a result, Charles's naval commanders, rejoicing at what seemed like a divinely ordered deliverance, could now direct their ships, carrying essential supplies for the city's imperial defenders, into the port of Naples without fear of further attack.

As if to compound the hopelessness of what had occurred, Lautrec's army, which was still impotently encamped outside the city walls, fell prey to a fast-spreading epidemic of cholera. Although Lautrec was urged to retreat to the nearby hills and thereby save himself from infection, he refused to abandon his men and, like so many of them, succumbed to the disease. He died on 17 August 1528 with the miserable knowledge that his army had been reduced by two-thirds. One of the most gifted of Francis's commanders, as well as the brother of the king's erstwhile mistress Françoise de Châteaubriand, Lautrec died in vain, sacrificed to his ruler's opportunism and greed.

The Marshal of France's death had a number of consequences, all of which were unfortunate for the French. The total collapse of the enemy army in Naples saved Italy for the imperial cause, and it was not long before Genoa reasserted its independence, in September 1528. It was also unsurprising, given the circumstances, that Pope Clement might declare: 'I have quite made up my mind to become an Imperialist, and to live and die as such.'[7] On 29 June 1529, Clement and Charles signed the Treaty of Barcelona, the terms of which committed the emperor to provide all military assistance needed in order to restore the Medici rule in Florence, as well as to secure the return of Ravenna and Modena to papal control. As a quid pro quo, Clement agreed to officiate at Charles's long-delayed coronation as Holy Roman Emperor. He was also required to offer absolution to all those who were involved in the Sack of Rome. The latter request would undoubtedly have caused Clement some personal difficulty, as he remembered how close he had come to an ignominious end at the swords of the marauders. Nonetheless, he could not afford scruples, nor to bring up the past. As they signed the agreement, neither the pope nor Charles could have known that this would be the last papal coronation of a Holy Roman Emperor. Nor could Clement have predicted that his actions would directly lead to the Reformation in England, and an irrevocable breach with Rome. Such were the unforeseeable consequences of any treaty in Renaissance Europe.

Francis, meanwhile, felt a mounting sense of unease. Not only were his territorial ambitions once again frustrated, but his sons remained Charles's captives, with no release in sight. However, towards the end of 1528 a new opportunity to negotiate peace with the empire arose. This unexpected development came about as a result of the friendship that had developed between Charles's aunt, Margaret of Austria, and Louise, her sister-in-law. The two had always enjoyed a close relationship since they had grown up together at the court of Anne, Madame la Grande. Reappointed by Charles as Regent of the Netherlands in 1519, Margaret's formidable administrative skills drew great admiration from her nephew. In 1528 she had signed a truce with England and with France, and a recent commercial treaty with the English, negotiated by Margaret, had provided a much-needed boost to the Flemish cloth industry.

In December 1528 Margaret's private secretary visited Paris, and during a meeting with Louise discreetly informed her that a peace treaty between France and the emperor was hugely desirable. Charles, although he had had the best of the recent fighting, was growing weary of a seemingly unending conflict, not least because he did not have the money to prolong the war. When Louise first raised the possibility of peace negotiations, Margaret was able to suggest that they would be greeted with suitable accord. Her envoys were duly dispatched to Paris, and before long Margaret agreed to meet Louise in person at Cambrai. As news of the negotiations became commonly known, Francis's Italian allies grumbled that he was more interested in saving himself than in helping them, but he did his best to reassure them, saying: 'I would rather sacrifice my life and the lives of my children than abandon the confederates.'[8]

Those who had watched the ease and frequency with which Francis had broken his earlier promises might have been sceptical about the veracity of this apparently heartfelt claim.

The talks began at Cambrai on 5 July 1529 and ended a month later. Francis, knowing that he was regarded as a diplomatic liability, announced that he would not be attending. His absence proved a clever ploy as it meant that none of his allies, either Italian or English, were involved directly, and also gave him the possibility of a veto on any treaty with which he was not content. However, Louise represented her son more than ably. Assisted by members of the King's Council, she ensured that a daily series of dispatches by fast courier kept Francis informed about the progress of the negotiations, as he amused himself by hunting.

The Treaty of Cambrai was known as the 'Treaty of the Ladies', on account of those who had been instrumental in its agreement. It was signed on 3 August 1529, and was celebrated in Francis's presence at Cambrai Cathedral two days later. It represented the best compromise that Francis could have expected; he agreed to surrender Arras, Lille and Tournai, as well as any sovereignty over Flanders and Artois. As his Italian allies might have expected and feared, he left them defenceless by renouncing all his claims on the peninsula. A detail that must have aggravated him was the agreement that Bourbon's confiscated property would henceforth be restored to his heirs, though a long legal battle would delay the fulfilment of that provision. However, Francis did manage to secure one crucial victory, namely that Burgundy would remain French, in return for a payment to Charles of two million *écus*. Upon receipt of the money, the emperor agreed to return the two princes to France, and his sister Eleanor's marriage to Francis would finally be ratified.

The agreement of Cambrai was neither a victory nor a defeat for either ruler. While the French monarch was disheartened by the financial terms that he had been placed under, which would require another round of near-punitive taxation, he could delight in the knowledge that he would finally be reunited with his sons; such was his joy that he gave orders for heralds to distribute gold and silver coins among the waiting crowds, who promptly lit bonfires to demonstrate their exultation at the settlement. It was an action more befitting a great victory than a small compromise, and a typical piece of showmanship from a king who never ceased to be aware of the value of appearances. Besides, the gold would soon be collected again.

Nonetheless, despite the compromises and revelry, Charles remained understandably suspicious of Francis, both because of his previous broken vows and his fear of an Italian uprising backed by French support. He therefore formed his own league of Italian states, supported by the pope, at the end of 1529, during which he forced Venice to return Ravenna to papal control, and Francesco Sforza once again became the Duke of Milan. Those who murmured that this role did little more than make Sforza an imperial puppet were correct. Charles knew as well as Francis the value of ostentation, and the formation of the league, combined with the parlous French financial situation, persuaded him that French intrigue in Italy would be a remote possibility, at least within the foreseeable future.

Besides, on a personal level Francis was keen to be reunited with his sons, and was intelligent enough to realise that agreeing to this treaty in a sincere fashion was the only way in which the reunion was likely to become possible. In September 1529, when Louise sent her usher, Monsieur Bodin, to visit the boys, he was shocked at the hardship and solitude Henry and Francis had to endure. The boys were kept in a small, dark cell with walls ten feet thick and iron bars that prevented escape, with shabby straw mattresses providing the only furnishings. They were in a pathetic and bedraggled state, which caused Bodin to weep when he encountered them. The two princes feigned a stratagem, claiming to their gaoler that, because they had been away from France for so long, they no longer understood the French tongue, but upon realising who Bodin was, and that his mission was to bring them home, they eagerly fired a series of questions at him concerning their family and friends. The Spanish, meanwhile, forebade Bodin either to measure the boys' heights or give them new clothes, suspecting that he would attempt to use some sorcery to liberate them. By the time the distraught courtier left, he hardly dared report the extent of the ill treatment of the young princes.

When Francis heard of the difficulties that his sons faced, any thought of dissembling left his mind. Accordingly, the treaty was ratified on 20 October 1529, before the trusted courtiers Montmorency and Tournon were appointed to supervise the royal handover the following March. Finding the considerable funds required for the ransom had been difficult, not least because, when the correct amount of *écus* had finally been collected, it was discovered that unscrupulous officials had clipped some of the coinage, so further appeals for funds had to be made. The date of exchange of the prisoners, which was originally intended to be 1 March, had to be continually postponed, until at last a new date of 1 July 1530 was agreed upon, with just as many strict protocols in place as the release of Francis had required. A mutually satisfactory transfer was to take place across the River Bidassoa. The two princes, together with their future stepmother Eleanor of Portugal, would travel in one direction while enormous sacks of gold were dispatched to the riverbank opposite.

There was a last-minute hiccup on the part of the boys' gaoler, the Constable of Castile, who perceived a slight of some kind to his honour and stopped proceedings, at which point an exasperated Montmorency challenged him to a duel. The latter declined, but demanded and received a formal apology before the transfer was granted. Afterwards all went as planned on the day. The two princes were already showing clear signs of their distinct characters; when the Spanish constable offered his good wishes for the future and a formal apology for any wrongs that might have been visited upon them, the Dauphin Francis accepted these in the spirit in which they were offered, but Henry turned his noble backside upon his erstwhile gaoler and farted in his face.

By the time they eventually returned to France, they had been away in captivity for four and a half years and spoke more Spanish than French; the privations and indignities of their ordeal would affect them both throughout their lives. The boys did not come back to the affectionate welcome that they might have wished for. They had no mother, and their father was soon bored by his two eldest sons, whose understandable lack of *joie de vivre* irritated him. The youngest, Charles, who had not been incarcerated, most enjoyed Francis's affection and attention, not least because of his strong resemblance to his father in both manner and looks. Brantôme wrote that 'the King berated them for not behaving as true French-men, for he did not care for dreamy, sullen, sleepy children'.[9]

As for Francis, his personal role in the treaty was to marry Eleanor, and, although they had already been wed by proxy, Charles wished to ensure that all the aspects of the treaty were fulfilled. Although, as Burgundy remained a French possession and the two princes were back in their home country, there was little to stop Francis reneging on the marriage deal, the king atypically decided that, whatever he thought of the union, he felt duty-bound to go through with it. On 7 July 1530 the King of France and his bride were married in the chapel of the Monastery of Beyries, making Francis and Charles, the two long-standing foes, brothers-in-law, and finally sealing the peace of a protracted and bitter campaign.

Yet it would be foolish for his adversaries to believe that the king would be satisfied with mere retirement.

CHAPTER 16

A Trio of Marriages

Marriage to Francis I was not an easy affair. As Queen Claude had discovered, the priapic monarch was seldom able to restrain his attention from wandering for any length of time, and the substantial tally of royal lovers and other amusements grew appreciably during his reign. Nonetheless, he had loved Claude, in his fashion, and made a point of sleeping with her whenever they were under the same roof. Consequently, he had been devastated by her death. Eleanor might therefore have hoped that the unorthodox basis of their marriage would not preclude a greater affection and understanding growing between the two of them, in time. In this she would be disappointed.

The new queen, although not favoured in good looks, at least boasted an impeccable bloodline. Before her marriage she was a princess of the highest rank, the daughter of Duke Philip of Burgundy and his wife Joanna (ungallantly but accurately nicknamed 'The Mad'), who had inherited the Crowns of Aragon and Castile from her parents Ferdinand and Isabella. Eleanor's marriage to Francis was not the first time that she had been used as a bargaining chip in the European marriage market. After Charles V acceded to the thrones of Castile and Aragon in 1517, he decided to implement a matrimonial agreement between his sister and King Manuel of Portugal in 1518. This had the aim of minimising Portuguese interference in the domestic politics of Castile, where the Habsburg dynastic inheritance was being contested by the local aristocracy. Yet the marriage did not last, as Manuel died of plague in 1521. In

1523 she was betrothed to Bourbon, as part of Charles's campaign against Francis; the widowed duke was reportedly enthusiastic about the match, and correspondingly disappointed when it did not come to pass. Her betrothal to Francis, arranged in 1526, had a sense of shoddy compromise about it, a view apparently shared by all parties, although the ever-optimistic Montmorency declared that Frenchmen should give thanks to God for the bestowal of 'so beautiful and virtuous a lady'.[1]

Although he was not generally an unkind or cruel man, Francis felt an incompatibility between his new consort and himself and had taken a strong and intense dislike to her. This manifested itself in near-immediate adultery. After her coronation at Saint-Denis in March 1531, Eleanor made her official entrance into Paris, as the streets teemed with cheering masses. As the new queen graciously nodded to her subjects, acknowledging their welcome, the whispers began as to the king's whereabouts. He could be seen at a prominent window, supposedly watching the proceedings. Immediately before him stood his mistress, Anne d'Heilly, with whom he was shamelessly engaging in sexual activity, which led one observer to comment that the king was 'devising with her for two long hours in the sight and face of all the people'.[2] It was said, with commendable understatement, that people 'not a little marvelled' at his behaviour.

Given Francis's lack of interest in concealing his antics, word soon spread internationally about his flagrant disinterest in fulfilling his marital duties. The English ambassador to Henry VIII, Sir Francis Bryan, explained that 'being both in one house they lie not together once in four nights; another he speaks very seldom unto her openly; another, he is never out of my lady's chamber, and all for Hely's [sic] sake, his old lover . . . he has also divers times ridden six or seven miles from the Queen and lain out four or five days together, as it is said, at the houses of his old lovers'.[3]

The betrayal was all the worse for Eleanor's apparent infatuation with her new husband, although she consented to the marriage in part because it offered a means of escape from her brother's dour court. Although she was not physically unattractive, at least compared to the other Habsburgs, Francis found it impossible to conceal the repugnance he felt for his new wife. Matters were made worse by the fact that Eleanor, at least in the early years of their marriage, seems to have been highly sexed. Pressed by the Duke of Norfolk in 1533 for an explanation as to why the marriage remained distasteful to the king and why no children had resulted from it, the king's sister Marguerite proved unusually forthcoming. She told him that, for the past seven months, 'he neither lay with her nor yet meddled with her'.[4] A further explanation came when she informed Norfolk that 'When he doth lie with her, he cannot sleep; and when he lieth from her no man sleepeth better.' Warming to her theme, she added: 'The queen is very hot in bed and desireth to be too much embraced', before concluding a damning description of her carnal interest by laughingly comparing her own marital situation, saying: 'I would not for all the good in Paris that the king of Navarre were no better pleased to be in my bed than my brother is to be in hers.'[5] It was made clear to Eleanor that her worth, such as it was, was to be no more than a diplomatic conduit between her husband and brother; if she expected more, she would only be disappointed.

The new queen might have hoped that her relations with her mother-in-law would be harmonious, but again Louise sided with her son and treated Eleanor with contempt. This, at least, proved to be a short-lived feud, thanks to Louise's extreme ill health. Although she had competently performed her offices as regent while her son had been incarcerated, and had continued to act as confidante, mentor and ambassador, she was worn out by her long standing gout and general decrepitude; since the time of Francis's imprisonment she had barely been able to walk. The woman whose scheming and careful brinkmanship had established her son on the French throne finally died of tuberculosis and gout at Grez-sur-Loing on 22 September 1531, at the age of fifty-five.

It was a tragedy for both mother and son that the king was not at her deathbed, as state business had taken him away to Chantilly. When she knew of his absence, Louise cried: 'Oh, my child, I will not see you! You will fail me at the last! I must leave this earthly place without kissing you for the last time.'[6] It is more likely that Francis had not attended because he did not want to be there. Nonetheless, when he heard of her end, the grieving son ensured that his adored mother's funeral rites at Notre-Dame, followed by the burial at Saint-Denis on 19 October, observed the very grandest royal ceremonial traditions, including having a wax effigy of her body displayed at the Abbey of Saint-Maur-des-Fossés, where she was taken after her death. It was an ostentatious and pomp-laden farewell to a woman who had at times literally ruled the country, and at others might as well have done; it was also uncomfortably clear that she would not easily be replaced.

Shortly after she died, the details of her estate became public knowledge. Although it had been widely assumed that she had feathered her nest, the extent of the riches that she left astonished most observers. Her personal possessions alone were valued at the enormous amount of 150,000 *écus*, and the territories she owned extended across great swathes of the kingdom; these included Anjou, Maine Bourbonnais, the Auvergne, the Forez region and the county of Marche. Louise's will specified that all these lands were to be bequeathed to her son and they were therefore absorbed within the French royal domain, strengthening Francis's position at a precarious time. The bequest was all but inevitable since Louise had lived entirely for her son. The circle of female adoration that had surrounded and captivated Francis since childhood had experienced its first and greatest loss. His new wife was not to be a fitting replacement, nor could she expect to be.

As Francis married and mourned, the recovery of his country's prestige and international standing continued to be his primary objective. This was partially accomplished by a lavish tour through France in the autumn of 1531, in which the king made a great show of thanking his servants for their loyalty and forbearance as wine flowed through fountains in the great cities, but also by means of baser plotting. Despite the peace treaty agreed at Cambrai, it was inconceivable that royal ambition would be checked, and his *idée fixe* had remained unchanged since his accession: the acquisition of Milan as a French territory with the intention of expanding into Italy in due course. There were several compelling reasons for him to pursue this strategy, not least because Italy's political landscape had stabilised since Charles had become Holy Roman Emperor. An imperial hegemony now prevailed from Florence up to Milan in the north, while in the south Charles's right to rule as King of

Naples was uncontested. Nonetheless, the emperor considered the situation in Italy to be inherently unstable. He believed that Francis was an inveterate meddler in matters that did not concern him and that, despite recent events, he would continue to stir up trouble for the empire.

Charles was right, although he barely understood the complex reasons why. Francis's ambition to capture Milan was no fleeting quirk of character or some kind of monarchical whim. His Milanese ambitions were shared by the French power elite in all its forms, and had obsessed the kingdom's policy-makers for well over a generation. Conquest had become a defining feature of French kingship, meaning that Francis would not be in a position to abandon it even if he had wanted to. Had he done so, it would have led to a feeling of betrayal and a dereliction of duty far greater than his capture and imprisonment; the ethos of the day was that a territorial claim, however tendentious, must be pursued at all costs. Therefore he had to plan his campaigns, and his alliances, with diligence and care.

As Francis entered into a royal marriage with the utmost reluctance, so Henry VIII attempted to extricate himself from his own. The English king had been married to Catherine of Aragon, who happened to be Charles V's aunt, since his ascent to the throne in 1509, but two decades later Henry had grown dissatisfied with his wife, primarily because she seemed incapable of bearing him the son that he wished to become his heir. With this in mind, he cast about for someone suitable with whom he could have an illegitimate child. His offspring would, he intended, be legitimised and able to inherit the throne of England. His eye soon alighted on the sister of his mistress Mary Boleyn, Anne, with whom Francis had had a long acquaintance. It was this personal relationship that he could rely upon in acting as a go-between and broker in what would become one of the most notorious schisms of the past 500 years.

Anne Boleyn first appeared at the French court in the early autumn of 1514 when she became a member of the royal household of Mary Tudor, Henry VIII's sister, who was intended to marry King Louis XII in October that year. The daughter of the English diplomat Sir Thomas Boleyn, Anne was only thirteen, but had already lived an eventful existence which had included spending the previous year in the Netherlands, where her father had been the ambassador, and where she had followed an educational curriculum prescribed for her at the court of Margaret of Austria, Charles V's aunt. Although Margaret was herself childless, she delighted in the company of the young and took pleasure in acting as a mentor to a number of young women who were destined for a life in royal service. Anne learnt many of the aristocratic refinements at the French court, where she would spend slightly over seven years.

Although Mary returned to England in the spring of 1515, when Louis XII died after just three months of marriage, Anne wished to remain in France and was asked to join the household of Queen Claude. It was during this time that Francis probably first came across the lively, cultured and thoroughly Francophone member of his wife's retinue. Anne's sister Mary had also become a royal attendant accompanying Mary Tudor. During her time she had acquired something of a licentious reputation, which might even have included a sexual relationship with Francis, who supposedly described her as being 'una grandissima ribalda et infame sopra tutte', or 'a great whore, infamous above all'. The Boleyn family were undoubtedly at the centre of events at the French court. Thomas Boleyn, as Henry VIII's ambassador, oversaw preparations for the Field of the Cloth of Gold, and it was to him that the French monarch confided his desire to become Holy Roman Emperor, regardless of the cost. Meanwhile, Anne's literary and religious interests were developed within the rarefied milieu that she inhabited, thanks to Marguerite's circle of Humanists. By the time that Anne returned to England she had acquired a reputation as a spirited, if at times doctrinaire, intellectual.

It was Anne and Mary's brother George who was entrusted with a mission of the utmost delicacy by Henry in the summer of 1529, namely to approach Francis and ascertain the possibility of his supporting the English king's much-desired divorce. At the time, the negotiations in Cambrai and Francis's wish not to offend Catherine of Aragon's nephew rendered this impossible. Nonetheless, Francis saw to it that a statement of support by the leading theologians of Paris in July 1530 declared that no pope had the right to issue a dispensation allowing a man to marry his deceased brother's wife, meaning that Henry's marriage to Catherine had therefore contravened canon law; this was a significant endorsement of Henry's case, and paved the ground for closer collusion yet, which duly followed at a time when Francis needed to form as wide a coalition of support as he could.

In the autumn of 1532, the opportunity arose for the English and French monarchs to find a mutually agreeable cause. Henry had by now dismissed Wolsey and was using Cardinal Tournon, the French ambassador to the papacy, to present his case for a divorce to Pope Clement. Meanwhile, the perennially impecunious Francis needed English financial help to assist France's anti-imperial allies in Germany. An Anglo-French conference, held in Calais and Boulogne during the third week of October, brought the two kings face to face in order to discuss matters of common concern. This was no roistering occasion in the vein of the Field of the Cloth of Gold; the mood was prudent and serious, as the two kings embarked on a discussion of how they might frustrate Charles V's planned return to Italy and continued dominance there. Francis's endorsement of Henry's divorce plans, though tacit, seemed substantial enough and Anne Boleyn attended the conference as a guest of the French king. Eleanor judged it prudent not to be present. An exchange of gifts, traditional on such royal occasions, included a diamond worth 15,000 écus that Anne received from Francis, and Henry's remittance of 300,000 écus, part of the overall debt owed to him by the French monarchy, meant that Francis could send financial aid to Germany. Although the two kings once again disingenuously claimed that their meeting was to pledge themselves to an anti-Turkish campaign, it was in the English divorce and the anti-imperial strategy that their interests and concerns tallied.

The days that the men were together proved rewarding and a useful reminder of how old loyalties might be revitalised. Although neither man jousted, not least because Henry was altogether stouter at forty-one than previously, there was much revelry and feasting, with guests dining on wild fowl, venison and fish in Calais. After this Francis danced with Anne, who was masked in 'apparel of strange fashion' of gold and crimson satin. She had attracted a great deal of attention from the English for being, as one put it, a 'goggle-eyed whore',[7] but Francis offered her conspicuous signs of gallantry and favour that might have confirmed his deep affection for her to any onlooker.

Like Francis, Henry held orthodox and unexceptional religious views, being neither especially devout nor an unbeliever. Certainly, although he was desperate for a son and heir – and showed conspicuous interest in Francis's boys, who in turn thanked him for what help he had offered with the king's release – he did not wish to estrange himself and his country from the papacy. To this end, he believed that keeping the emperor out of Italy would be the best way of restoring Clement's independence, which, in turn, would lead to a grateful pope granting him a dissolution of his troublesome marriage. This underestimated the gratitude that Clement felt towards Charles, to whom he would remain a constant ally, and simplified a complex series of alliances into something that would benefit both kings. Nonetheless, Clement was regarded as malleable, and both Francis and Henry were convinced that, if he was presented with the marriage as a *fait accompli*, he could do little but accept it.

Therefore the Cardinals Gramont and Tournon were sent to Bologna in order to negotiate with the pope. They arrived on 3 January 1533, and initially all seemed to proceed as they might have wished. Clement agreed to meet Francis at a suitably grand state occasion and he also gave his formal blessing to the marriage of his niece Catherine de Medici to Francis's son Henri, which the French king believed would be a sure route back to Italian conquests, an opinion Clement did nothing to discourage. The pope, who seemed anxious to oblige the two kings' wishes, also issued the papal bulls required in order to confirm Thomas Cranmer's appointment as Archbishop of Canterbury. Perhaps excited by what seemed to be his complete dominance of the situation, Henry acted decisively, and rashly. On 25 January, in a private ceremony conducted by Cranmer, he married Anne Boleyn. In March George Boleyn was once again dispatched to the French court, this time officially to communicate the news to Francis.

This revelation might not have been a great surprise; Henry would later claim that Francis had urged him to take command of the situation by marrying Anne. Certainly, the assertion is not entirely implausible. Ever the gambler, Francis realised that the marriage's most obvious and immediate consequence was a deep rupture between the emperor and Henry, which could only benefit him in the role of power-broker. He also knew that he had read too much into Clement's diplomatic response to the French cardinals, but had no desire to alienate the pope, given his own connection with the marriage of Catherine and the English king. However, the final responsibility for the match lay with Henry, who was increasingly desperate for matters to be resolved. Anne was due to give birth in September, meaning that it was all-important that the marriage be validated long before then, whatever the consequences.

On 23 May 1533 Archbishop Cranmer declared the king's second marriage to be lawful and on 1 June he crowned Anne Queen of England. It was inevitable that Clement was obliged to condemn the marriage, which he duly did on 11 July. The pope gave Henry a deadline: either he must annul the new marriage and take back Catherine as both his wife and queen, or he would be excommunicated. Nonetheless, when September came Francis persuaded Clement to stay his hand and Henry was given more time to consider his options.

Francis and Clement's summit coincided with the marriage of Catherine de Medici and Francis's son Henri, Duke of Orléans in October 1533 and, as usual, saw further concessions and deals. Clement created four French cardinals, an action that allowed Francis to claim a tenth of the French clerical tithe. Emboldened, the French monarch suggested a plan for a Franco-papal alliance whose aim, inevitably, would be the recapture of Milan. This was impossible, given the pope's alliance with Charles. Likewise, the issue of the royal divorce remained contentious. Francis, acting on Henry's behalf, asked for another six months' extension before the excommunication came into effect. Clement offered a single month's delay but he did agree to Francis's proposal that the entire issue be submitted to a specially convened Franco-papal commission which would meet at Avignon. Had it taken place, it could well have gone in Henry's favour, but the English king's impetuosity scuppered this outcome. On 7 November 1533, while the pope was still in

Marseilles, Henry's emissary Edmund Bonner forced his way into
Clement's chamber and all but threatened him, announcing that
only an adjudication of the General Council of the whole Church
would now satisfy the English.

Although Francis was not a king who was normally affected
by diplomatic niceties, Bonner's behaviour angered him, leading
to a strain on relations between the two kings. The pope, after
all, had been in Marseilles as Francis's guest; had anything happened to him, the rules of hospitality would have dictated that it
would have been the French monarch's fault. Yet Henry suffered
a fit of pique, believing that Francis and Clement were parties to
a secretive anti-English alliance; when a messenger was sent to
England with a formal protest, Henry kept him waiting for four
days before granting an audience. Without Francis's diplomatic
efforts excommunication was inevitable, and duly followed on 23
March 1534, paving the way for Thomas Cromwell to publish the
legislative statutes that would make the English Church independent of the Roman jurisdiction. Despite this royal schism, Henry
could not afford to become estranged from Francis. His excommunication amounted to an expulsion from European Catholic
Christendom and the French king remained his only champion,
a state of affairs that Francis exploited in the shape of generous
financial concessions from Henry. Nonetheless, the English
king's unruly behaviour had caused difficulty; by acting in haste,
he had destroyed any possibility of another grand anti-imperial
alliance, as well as estranging himself from the papacy for all
perpetuity.

On a happier level, Francis was present at the marriage of his son
Henri to Catherine de Medici. It had been decided that the union
between the two clans should be hugely ostentatious in true Renaissance fashion, both to demonstrate the continued influence of the
papacy and to show that Francis, the restored monarch, was once
again in charge of his kingdom and his domestic affairs. A marriage contract had been drawn up that stated that Clement should
'at his own discretion, furnish his illustrious relative with clothing,
ornaments and jewels'.[8] With the assistance of the so-called 'First

Lady of the Renaissance', Isabella d'Este, Catherine was clad in an outfit made of 'three pounds of gold, two pounds of silk and two pounds of silver';[9] it was so lavish and expensive that Alessandro, Duke of Florence, levied a tax on the Florentine people of 35,000 écus, supposedly to pay for the reinforcement of the city's defences but in fact to pay for Catherine's impressive wedding finery. These were complemented by some of the finest jewellery that could be found in Europe, most notably a casket of rock crystal created by the master of precious stone-cutting, Valerio Belli Vincentino. The casket's twenty-four panels depicted religious scenes, set in silver gilt. Such was the extravagance and financial cost of the bride's dowry that Clement was obliged to borrow 50,000 écus in order to fund it; he might have reflected that, once again, Francis had engineered an advantageous situation through a mixture of cunning and diplomatic skill.

Catherine had left Florence on 1 September 1533, travelling with a large retinue that included not only her various noble relations but also seventy gentlemen sent by Francis. The original intention had been for the wedding to take place at Nice, but the plans were thwarted by the Duke of Savoy – a vassal of the emperor – and Marseilles was substituted. Shortly after Catherine's departure from Florence, an emissary of Francis arrived bringing her jewellery as a wedding gift; among this was a splendid diamond and a sapphire. If they were not quite of the same standard as her Italian accoutrements, it still meant that the French king was in a delighted and accommodating temper.

By the time that Catherine arrived in Marseilles on 11 October, the most extravagant preparations for her arrival had taken place, organised by Montmorency, who was putting as much effort and concentration into the reception of the royal family, the pope and his niece as he had into any military campaign or stratagem. An entire quartier had been blown up in order to make way for a temporary palace of wood, as befitted the city's exalted visitors. When the Medici armada arrived in the dock, there was as much excitement and anticipation as if conquering heroes had come to relieve the populace; 300 cannon fired off welcoming salvoes to the accompaniment of 'hautbois, clarion and trumpets', and order was given that the church bells should chime in anticipation of the glorious wedding, as the people were giddy with glee.

Clement made his state entrance on 12 October, with all the trappings of grandeur and expense that a papal visit should entail, and Francis arrived in Marseilles the next day. It was agreed that he should lodge at the palace of the Comtes de Provence on the Place-Neuve, where an enormous chamber had been built that could simultaneously serve as a magnificent reception room and allow for secret meetings between the king and the pope without any observers being able to pry. Francis made a suitably grand first appearance of his own, with 200 soldiers, 300 archers and his velvet-clad Swiss bodyguard. After some politicking, and of course the obligatory homage being paid to Clement by Francis, it was time for the most impressive moment of all the pageantry thus far: the official entrance of Catherine into Marseilles on 23 October 1533.

As befitted a girl who would one day be a queen, she was preceded by six horses, five decorated in silver and gold, and one grey charger in silver cloth led by her cousin Ippolito's pages. She wore an outfit of gold and silver brocade and, with her fine dress and brilliant skill at riding, she impressed the crowd immensely. Among her train rode twelve demoiselles with a royal and papal guard, followed by a coach draped in black velvet with two pages on horseback. When she arrived at the audience chamber at the pope's temporary palace, Francis and Henri stood watching as Catherine curtseyed to Clement before kissing his feet; the humility of the gesture pleased the French king, who lifted the young girl to her feet, kissed her and then bade his son do likewise.

The usual days of revelry and great banquets then preceded the wedding, during which Catherine was able to see something of the character of the boy she was about to marry. Unlike his father, Henri was both taciturn and awkward, and had to be cajoled and leant on by Francis to make a good impression. He was at least good-looking, tall and muscular, without his father's conspicuous nose; Catherine herself was no great beauty, but her intelligence and fine clothes, to say nothing of her youth, helped to offer an impression of agreeability and charm. One historian described a portrait of her as displaying features 'which, though strongly marked, are not irregular'.[10]

On 27 October the signing of the marriage contract took place, before a fanfare and a great ball entertained the assembled guests. The wedding proper took place the following day, beginning with Francis collecting Catherine from her chamber. The king looked as if he could have been the bridegroom, so lavishly was he attired in his white satin embroidered with fleur-de-lys and a cloak of gold cloth covered with pearls and precious stones. Catherine, meanwhile, dazzled in her ducal robes of golden brocade with a violet corsage of velvet encrusted with gems and edged with ermine. Her hair was dressed with precious stones, and a ducal crown of gold – a gift from Francis – completed her attire. After a nuptial Mass, Catherine found herself crowned Duchess of Orléans.

After the solemnity came the celebrations, which it is likely that Francis enjoyed a good deal more, so vigorously and wholeheartedly did he throw himself into them. After another banquet came a masked ball, in which Francis danced in only the most token of disguises and which descended into a raucous orgy. A famous Marseilles courtesan, brought in to add spice to the proceedings, removed most of her garments before dipping her breasts into the goblets of wine on the tables and offering them to the delighted men around her. Not to be outdone, many of the great ladies of court indulged in similar behaviour, leading one observer to comment that 'their honour was wounded'.[11]

In contrast to this lewd and unseemly behaviour came the consummation of their marriage. Catherine was led into the royal bedchamber by Queen Eleanor before Henri entered; the nuptial loss of virginity for both parties was, as was customary, publicly witnessed by a group of onlookers which included Francis, who approvingly claimed that 'each had shown valour in the joust'. The compatibility of the union was greeted with similar relief by Clement, who saw the broad smiles on the faces of the couple in bed the next morning when he entered the room to bless them. This did not take place out of voyeuristic pleasure, but as part of the fulfilment of a diplomatic deal, performed before those who had an investment in the success of the alliance.

After duty had been done, the two courts prepared to travel home, although not before a ritual exchange of gifts. Francis presented Clement with a Brussels tapestry depicting the Last Supper and the pope, not without a certain wry humour, gave the French king a gold-mounted 'unicorn's horn' (in all likelihood a narwhal's tusk) which was reputed to ward off poison. Francis and his entourage left Marseilles on 13 November 1533, Clement delaying his own journey by a week due to rough weather. Before he left he was said to have whispered, 'a spirited girl will always conceive children' to Catherine. The success, or failure, of the Franco-papal alliance now lay in her power.

As Francis had predicted, Catherine would soon become an integral figure in the French court, offering a combination of charm and amiability, especially in her dealings with Marguerite and the other courtiers. Yet her likeable presence would soon be thrown into relief by the dealings of her father-in-law with some of the leading figures of the day. One would end up betraying France; the other would bring about an understanding between countries and religions that few could ever have predicted.

CHAPTER 17

Allies of Necessity

During Francis's wedding-peace summit with Pope Clement in 1533, his suggestions of a full Franco-papal alliance against the emperor were politely rebuffed. According to Clement, who later made a full report of his conversations with the French king to Charles, Francis then suggested that 'Not only will I not oppose the invasion of Christendom by the Turk, but I will favour him . . . in order . . . to recover that which plainly belongs to me . . . and has been usurped by the Emperor.' This might have seemed like mere bravado, but in fact represented an unguarded allusion to what would soon become the Franco Ottoman alliance between Francis and Suleiman I. Compared to Suleiman, no European ruler – not even Charles – could be described as great or impressive. Yet his Islamic faith, military might and opaque attitudes towards his western compatriots meant that if one supped with Suleiman, like those who dined with the devil, one would need an extremely long spoon.

The first treaty of sorts between France and the Ottoman Empire came in 1500, signed by Louis XII and Sultan Bayezid II. This so-called 'Capitulation' made various trade and diplomatic concessions between the two states, but did not offer any kind of formal alliance. When Suleiman took power in 1520, at the age of twenty-five, Francis, who was actively searching for an ally who would strengthen his power and influence throughout central Europe, began making overtures of peace. These then intensified in 1525, after Francis's defeat at Pavia and subsequent imprisonment. After an initial expedition was unsuccessful, with the participants ambushed, robbed and killed by the Pasha of Bosnia, Louise sent a second secret mission, led by John Frangipani, to Constantinople in December 1525. The intent was both to create a military alliance between the Ottomans and the French against the Habsburgs and, more immediately, to attempt to bring about Francis's release from prison, by force if necessary.

Suleiman's response was a masterclass in careful diplomacy. He first restated the facts: namely that 'you have informed me that the enemy has overrun your country and that you are at present in prison and a captive, and you have asked aid and succors for your deliverance. All this your saying having been set forth at the foot of my throne, which controls the world.' If Francis had hoped for assistance, he was to be disappointed; although Suleiman allowed that 'your situation has gained my imperial understanding in every detail, and I have considered all of it', he also believed that 'there is nothing astonishing in emperors being defeated and made captive', and urged Francis: 'Take courage then, and be not dismayed. Our glorious predecessors and our illustrious ancestors . . . have never ceased to make war, to repel the foe and conquer his lands. We ourselves have followed in their footsteps, and have at all times conquered provinces and citadels of great strength and difficult of approach. Night and day our horse is saddled and our saber is girt.' If this fell considerably short of what Francis had hoped for, it still represented an encouraging move towards an entente between the two rulers. Suleiman's influence was such that the pasha was encouraged to return the goods that he had purloined, and the understanding remained that Charles could not be allowed to become all-powerful.

Francis contacted Suleiman again in 1528, shortly after his release, this time to enquire about the protection of Christians in the Ottoman Empire, and to ask for the return of a mosque to its former state as a church. While Suleiman politely declined the latter request, citing Islamic law that did not permit a mosque to alter its function, he was prepared to guarantee the protection of all Christians within his states, as well as continue to renew the privileges of French merchants which had been granted in Egypt in 1517. As he put it, 'No one will molest those who remain there during our just reign. They will live in tranquillity under the wing of our protection . . . they may retain in complete security all the oratories and other buildings which they occupy at present, without anyone being permitted to oppress them or to torment them in any way.'[1]

When Suleiman led an attack on the Habsburg stronghold of Vienna in 1529, he wished for a sympathetic ally within western Europe who might be interested in forming a partnership against the loathed Holy Roman Empire. Francis therefore found himself treading the line between public adherence to his Christian faith, both celebrating the Turks' retreat from Vienna in October 1529 and continuing underhand dealings. If pushed, he might have claimed that his interest lay in protecting Christians in eastern Europe, but this would simply have been a ruse. Informal talks took place between the French and the Ottomans during 1530 and 1531 which came to the attention of many throughout Europe. Thomas Cromwell remarked that no Christian scruple would deter Francis from bringing the Turk and the devil into the heart of Christendom, if it would ultimately enable him to recapture Milan.

This was an exaggeration, but only barely. As Francis stated to the Venetian envoy Giustinian in March 1531, 'I cannot deny that I keenly wish to see the Turk powerful and ready for war, not for himself – for he is an infidel and we are all Christians – but to weaken the power of the emperor, to compel him to make major expenses, and to reassure all the other governments who are opposed to such a formidable enemy.' The ideal outcome for the French king would have been for Suleiman to attack Charles within Italy, weakening the emperor to the point where Francis would have been able to invade, with guaranteed success, and to present himself as a defender of the Christian faith into the bargain.

Thus, as Francis made much of allying himself with the pope against the infidel, he continued sending his ambassadors to meet with Suleiman. One of these, Antonio Rincón, headed to Belgrade in July 1532, where he presented the sultan with an expensive and grandiose four-tiered tiara. Rincón professed himself impressed by the Ottoman camp, saying that it possessed 'astonishing order, no violence. Merchants, women even, coming and going in perfect safety, as in a European town. Life as safe, as large and easy as in

Venice. Justice so fairly administered that one is tempted to believe that the Turks are turned Christians now, and that the Christians are turned Turks.' Rincón arrived in Belgrade at a time when intelligence suggested that the sultan was preparing to attack Habsburg territories in central Europe. Francis contemplated his options, knowing that, while a Turkish assault of that nature would benefit him in the short term, it would also solidify Habsburg support. He therefore sought an alternative strategy.

When the news came that Suleiman was planning another attack on Austria, Francis was ready with his alternative scheme of an Ottoman invasion of Italy, which was the purpose of Rincón's embassy. This strategy might have worked, but by the time Rincón arrived at Suleiman's camp the Turkish army was already advancing through the Danube Valley and a change of direction was logistically impossible. However, the Ottoman army was met with defeat, meaning that, as Charles V made a triumphal entry into Vienna at the head of his army in September 1532, the plot's details were common knowledge. As a result, Francis's claims to be regarded as 'The Most Christian King' could now justifiably be mocked by his enemies, who instead made much of his alliance with the dreaded Turk and now called him 'The Executioner of Christendom'.

This did not go unnoticed by the Ottomans, most notably the potentate Kheir-ed-Din Barbarossa, chief admiral of the navy and a belligerent figure who struck fear into the hearts of his enemies; he was said to have strangled the Sultan of Algiers with his own turban in 1516. Nonetheless, in 1533 the admiral's thoughts turned to potential alliances, including that of France. In July of that year Barbarossa dispatched an embassy for a meeting with Francis, which took place on 19 July at Puy-en-Velay. The Ottoman delegation, led by the interpreter and ambassador Janus Bey, brought with them an exotic menagerie of animals, including the so-called 'lion of Barbarossa', and 100 Christian prisoners as a gesture of good faith. In the presence no doubt of surprised English ambassadors, various treaties were agreed, such as a three-year trade agreement and a 'declaration of mutual friendship between the Kingdoms of France and Algiers'. In a showy but effective symbolic display, the chains of the Christian prisoners were broken and they were released. An unlikely gesture of unity was therefore made, much to the horror of Charles V, who feared the possibility of his two greatest enemies uniting to lethal effect.

By mid-1534, Francis seemed to be in an enviable position. Henry VIII remained unstable, both as a man and as a king, but the Anglo-French alliance continued. Catherine de Medici's marriage to the Duke of Orléans meant that a Franco-papal league, while by no means definite, seemed a good deal more possible than had been feared during the immediate post-Cambrai period. Meanwhile, much as a treaty with Suleiman would appear directly to counter the possibility of a papal entente, it would also suggest that France's power could, in time, dwarf that of the Holy Roman Empire or any other European country. However, these calculations, along with Francis's other, reasonable, expectations, were thrown into disarray when the news arrived from Rome of Pope Clement's demise on 25 September.

Clement had been a sickly man at the time of his niece's wedding in 1533, and had never recovered his health. He had been a poor pope, his authority having been destroyed by his capitulation to Charles after the Sack of Rome, and his inability to keep Henry's ambitions in check resulted in Parliament declaring the Act of Supremacy on 3 November 1534, proclaiming the king 'the only supreme head on earth of the Church of England'. When the sixty-six-year-old Alessandro Farnese was elected Pope Paul III on 13 October, he made it clear that he had no intention of honouring the enormous dowry that Clement had promised Francis, meaning that the *mésalliance* of his son and Catherine was now treated with horror. The Medicis had always been sneered at for their bourgeois roots, and only their connections to the papacy had led to their advancement. As the French king lamented, 'The girl has come to me stark naked.'[2]

With the tentative papal alliance at an end, Francis had all the more cause to search for a new comrade-in-arms, and Suleiman and the Ottoman forces continued to seem the most suitable match, not least because Barbarossa's conquest of Tunis on 16 August 1534 from the imperial sympathiser Muley Hasan meant that much of the Mediterranean was now controlled by the Ottomans. Therefore, when a second embassy arrived at Marseilles in October 1534, accompanied by the French ambassador Rincón, it was with the explicit intention of furthering a Franco-Ottoman alliance for an offensive the following year. The exotic appearance of the sultan's elite infantry, the janissaries, caused a stir, leading the writer Valbelle, an eyewitness, to comment: 'They were circulating through the city as if they were in Constantinople. It is so new to see Turks like this, something that was never seen before.'[3] It went unremarked upon that Barbarossa had earlier tried to kidnap Duchess Giulia Gonzaga, widely believed to be the most beautiful woman in Italy, to be given to Suleiman for his harem. Nonetheless, it is unlikely that Francis would have cared had he known; he was credited with the apocryphal saying, 'When wolves fall on my flock, it is necessary to call upon dogs for help.'

These so-called dogs travelled across the country to see Francis at his court in Châtellerault but, initially at least, they found the monarch distracted by what became known as the Affair of the Placards. This took place on 18 October, and consisted of a series of anti-Catholic placards being placed around Paris, each of which had as its subject 'True articles on the horrible, great and insufferable abuses of the papal Mass'. These placards, which had been written by Antoine Marcourt, a Protestant Frenchman exiled in Switzerland, were designed to indicate opposition to Rome; at a politically sensitive time when a new pope had been elected, it caused a febrile and dramatic response. Wild rumours circulated that a Protestant mob were on the verge of burning churches and massacring Catholics celebrating Mass. It soon became clear that what had happened in Paris was no isolated incident, but part of a wave of intimidation that had spread to provincial centres including Amboise, Blois, Tours, Rouen and Orleans.

That many of these towns had links to Francis himself was no coincidence. One placard was discovered on the king's own door, something, chroniclers noted (albeit with likely exaggeration), that threw him into such extreme anger that 'he vomited rage through his eyes and mouth'. Consequently, he announced there and then that he would 'exterminate everyone'.[4] In rapid response a series of death sentences were pronounced, which pleased the king, who on 9 December told Duprat in a letter that 'the diligence . . . has given me much pleasure and nothing would satisfy me more than that it should continue so that the damned and abominable sect may neither set foot nor take root in my kingdom'.

For a man who was engaged in discussions with 'the infidel', Francis took the Affair of the Placards, and the apparent insult to his country's religious credentials, extremely seriously. A second round of placards appeared in Paris on 13 January 1535, which caused the normally good-natured king to react with even greater fury. This led to an authoritarian display of strength that had scarcely been seen, if at all, since the beginning of Francis's reign: all new books were banned 'under pain of the gallows',[5] anyone even suspected of involvement with the plot – there were as many as 200 – was arrested, and numerous dissenters, from booksellers to drapers, were burned at the stake.

It seemed clear to the king that he would have to engineer a public show of unity and so, on 21 January 1535, Francis organised a 'general procession' in Paris. This was an unprecedented display of religious fervour and civic strength that featured the country's most sacred relics, including the Crown of Thorns from Sainte-Chapelle, being solemnly marched through the city as Francis followed behind, bareheaded, black-clad and holding a candle aloft. The procession, featuring thousands of the city's worthies from all walks of life, including the courts, trade guilds and *parlement*, headed from Saint-Germain to Notre-Dame, to the accompaniment of shouting and cheering from the spectators, as well as occasional weeping when the monarch paused to pray. After lunch at the bishop's palace – because even a ruler in the act of penitence could not be expected to forego his victuals – Francis addressed the populace and railed against heretics. He demanded that all his people should be vigilant, and commanded them not to flinch from denouncing friends and family if they were believed to be guilty. Finally, another half-dozen malefactors were publicly burned at the stake.

That evening the king made another speech, in which he attempted to set out his religious beliefs and convictions publicly. He was aware that his recent alliances had caused murmurings about a lack of adherence to the country's Catholic faith. He proclaimed that 'I do not speak to you as King and master but as subject and servant to those who with me are subjects and servants of the same King, the King of Kings and Master of Masters, which is almighty God.' His orthodox opinions thus confirmed, Francis then spouted invective against the 'wicked and unfortunate persons who wished to spoil [France's] good name, sowing damnable and execrable opinions', beseeched his listeners to return to 'the way of the Holy Catholic Faith', and reached a stirring peroration when he announced: 'Our fathers have shown us how to live according to the doctrine of God and of the Holy Mother Church, in which I hope to live and die ... I would see these errors chased out of my kingdom and no one excused, in such sort that if one of my arms were infected by this corruption, I would cut it off. And were my children stained by it, I myself would burn them.' These were fine, passionately delivered words, and the sentiment inflamed many of those who heard them. Whether the audience included a delegation from Suleiman, who had been present throughout the day, can only be speculated.

The persecution and fury unleashed by the placards continued until the summer of 1535, when it became embarrassingly clear that the perpetrators had either been executed or fled the country. Parisian reactionaries, in both the university and *parlement*, might have rejoiced inwardly that the Placards Affair had at last persuaded Francis to behave as a 'Most Christian King' ought, but the disproportionate violence of his response had sent his country into a panic-stricken state. The bloodshed had done little more than turn the French into a frightened and fearful people, a state of affairs that not even the king's imprisonment had managed to bring about.

It was during this crucible of terror that an agreement was formed to coordinate military action between France and the Ottoman Empire, the desired result being that both sides would further their military dominance. Their aims included a revolt of pro-French factions in Italy; an Ottoman attack on Apulia and Calabria; a strike by Barbarossa from Tunis on Sicily, Naples and Tuscany, as well as the launch of hostilities by England, Scotland and Denmark against the Low Countries. It was a plan of overarching complexity, and giddily ambitious in its aims, but the new French ambassador to the Ottomans, Jehan de la Forest, was believed to be equal to the task. De la Forest was handed clear instructions by Chancellor Duprat, acting directly on behalf of Francis; these, which he was given on 11 February 1535, stated that:

Jean de la Forest, whom the King sends to meet with the Grand Signor [Suleiman the Magnificent], will first go from Marseilles to Tunis, in Barbary, to meet Sir *Haradin*, King of Algiers, who will direct him to the Grand Signor. To this objective, next summer, he [the King of France] will send the military force he is preparing to recover what is unjustly occupied by the Duke of Savoy, and from there, to attack the Genoese. This king Francis I strongly prays Sir *Haradin*, who has a powerful naval force as well as a convenient location [Tunisia], to attack the island of Corsica and other lands, locations, cities, ships and subjects of Genoa, and not to stop until they have accepted and recognized the King of France. The King, besides the above land force, will additionally help with his naval force, which will comprise at least 50 vessels, of which 30 galleys, and the rest galeasses and other vessels, accompanied by one of the largest and most beautiful carracks that ever was on the sea. This fleet will accompany and escort the army of Sir *Haradin*, which will also be refreshed and supplied with food and ammunition by the King, who, by these actions, will be able to achieve his aims, for which he will be highly grateful to Sir *Haradin*.[. . .]

To the Grand Signor, Monsieur de La Forest must ask for one million in gold, and for his army to enter first in Sicily and Sardinia and establish there a king whom La Forest will nominate, a person who has credit and knows well these islands which he will retain in the devotion of, and under the shade and support of the King [of France]. Furthermore, he will recognize this blessing, and send tribute and pension to the Grand Signor to reward him for the financial support he will have provided to the King, as well as the support of his navy which will be fully assisted by the King [of France].

The plan of campaign required great trust between the French and
their new bedfellows, but the so-called 'Sir Haradin', or Barbarossa,
was felt to be a stalwart and courageous ally, and so Francis placed a
great deal of faith in de la Forest. The embassy arrived in Marseilles
on 3 April 1535 and departed eight days later, bound for Tunis, where
Barbarossa had armed a special galley to transport de la Forest to
Constantinople. A close and all-encompassing relationship between
the French and the Ottomans might have given cause for embarrassment, but Francis, knowing that Charles had belligerent intentions
towards the Barbary pirates of North Africa, could pretend that his
actions did not stem from warmongering but from defence. As he
put it, with knowing bluster, 'The engagements entered into with
me are not kept at all. If the emperor arms, I cannot but do the
same.'[6] A more moderate or temperate ruler might have offered
a less truculent response; the papal nuncio was sufficiently taken
aback by Francis's attitude to claim that 'he seems to make it his
business to provoke the emperor'.[7]

Charles V had indeed commissioned some new ships, but the
aim was to attack the pirates who endangered Spanish shipping in
the western Mediterranean. Still, reports of an imperial rearma-
ment programme were undoubtedly a suitable pretext for going
to war, and when the emperor launched a naval campaign against
Barbarossa's corsairs, he offered the French a splendid opportunity.
Charles set sail from Barcelona on 10 June 1535 with an impressive
navy and by the middle of July he had seized La Goletta, a fortress
guarding the entrance to Tunis that had also served as a naval base
for the pirates. Tunis itself fell soon afterwards, although the wily
Barbarossa managed to escape before he was executed or captured.
Shortly afterwards, on 22 August, Charles arrived in Sicily after a
relatively easy campaign through the Italian south. For the time
being his fortunes again seemed to be in the ascendant.

An angered Francis, fearful at the prospect of his rival seizing
European glory, might have taken this moment to strike. However
he did not, much to the chagrin of Admiral Chabot, head of the
French navy, who believed that the emperor's absence from Spain
should be exploited. Francis's motivations were partly dictated
by Montmorency, Constable of France, who saw himself and his

king as honourable men, and thought that this was not how gentlemen should behave. Francis had promised Charles's ambassador
to France that there would be no opportunistic moves against his
master during the latter's absence from Spain, which provoked an
angry rebuke from Chabot. Behind the smokescreen, the pragmatic
truth was that a Franco-imperial war was impossible while the
French forces were yet recovering their strength. Francis was still
attempting to assemble a competent fighting force as late as July
1535. Nor was his health as strong as it had been, perhaps a lingering result of both his captivity and his military adventures. He was
forced to remain in Lyons during the early autumn with 'a fever,
flux of the belly and stomach pain'.[8] The once-almighty leader was
proving that he, too, was no second Hercules.

In addition, following a long period in which Francis had viewed
the new pope, Paul III, with suspicion, it was now necessary to
make peace with him. This was doubly difficult as the pope also
distrusted Francis and wished to prevent him from declaring war.
Therefore, in June 1535 he issued an interdiction for Christians not
to fight between themselves during the time Charles was engaging
the Ottomans, effectively precluding Francis from launching any
offensive if he wished to attract papal support. It is perhaps not coincidental that de la Forest became the official French ambassador
to the Ottoman court, with the aim of negotiating military and
commercial treaties.

Yet, inevitably, the faint sound of military alarums could be
heard as 1535 wore on. Although Francis realised that he had no
grounds on which to go to war, it had never stopped him from
engaging in past conflict, and Chabot's fighting spirit appealed to
the king; the admiral gained in influence during those summer
months, as hawks around him bewailed the king's apparent inac-
tivity. The death of Francesco Sforza, Duke of Milan, on 24 October
introduced a further and familiar element to the Franco-imperial
rivalry: the perennially vexed question of who would succeed to
the northern state. As Francesco had no male heir, it was Charles's
responsibility, as the duchy's overlord, to decide who would be his
successor. Unsurprisingly, his arch-enemy was quick to throw his
hat into the ring once again, but this time with a twist, suggesting

that Charles's former captive, Francis's son Henri, Duke of Orléans, be invested as Duke of Milan.

It is likely that this suggestion was made out of provocation and mischief rather than genuine expectation, as Charles had no intention of allowing a French return to Italy. Henri's marriage to Catherine de Medici had placed him in a potentially threatening position for any land grabs upon the peninsula. To play for time, Charles suggested that Milan might, eventually, become the property of Francis's third and favourite son, Charles, but this was unacceptable to the French king, who acted decisively. He signed an agreement known as the Capitulations with Suleiman, which covered both military and commercial matters, and meant that French citizens in Suleiman's kingdom would be essentially autonomous, answerable only to the French ambassador at Constantinople and to the French consuls at Damascus and Alexandria. This not only gave Francis a greater degree of influence throughout the Mediterranean, but also, by association, linked France and the Ottoman Empire – an alliance few might have expected. His next move was another surprise attack, although based on a long-standing family schism.

Francis's invasion of Savoy in February 1536 initially achieved the intended effect. However, it soon became clear that there was a dynastic reason for his action, namely his uneasy relationship with the local magnate, his uncle, Charles III, the ruling Duke of Savoy. Francis's trumped-up claim that the duke was wrongly occupying his late mother's territory represented a classic opportunistic land grab, one that had been foreshadowed by the king's spurious sabre-rattling as far back as December 1535. The campaign was a fitting memorial to Louise in that it was efficient, based on an extremely dubious pretext and had a greater strategy in mind – the continued disconcertion of Charles, who watched Francis's movements with enormous disquiet. The king's unblushing claims that he acted only in self-defence and to regain territories that were rightfully his were treated with the contempt that they deserved.

Chabot led the French invasion force and did a typically excellent job, pushing his advantage and marshalling his troops to great effect. By the end of March the city of Turin, Savoy's capital, had fallen. French occupying forces were once again in a position to be used to mount an attack on Milan, should Charles continue to ignore the French king's demands. The emperor, cautious as ever, made no immediate counter-attack, but instead offered an apparent willingness to compromise and responded constructively during the negotiations that followed. His atypically emollient tone could be explained by the fact that the emperor occupied southern Italy at the time of the invasion, and he, too, was playing a waiting game while preparing his troops.

Once his army was ready, Charles made an about-turn with a swingeing rebuttal of the expected peace treaty. On 17 April the emperor's official response came in the unusually public form of a speech, which he delivered to the pope and members of the College of Cardinals. It was uncompromising. He stated that there were no circumstances under which Henri, Duke of Orléans, could lay claim to the duchy of Milan. The only hint of an agreement was the suggestion that Francis's youngest son Charles, being further removed from the French throne, could be invested as Duke of Milan at some unspecified date. He also repeated, almost as a joke, his previous proposal to Francis that, were the two rulers unable to come to a decision, the matter might be settled in a perfectly honourable fashion by a duel fought in single combat. This was quickly vetoed by the pope, who considered the suggestion ridiculous. In the meantime, the emperor concluded that the French must withdraw from Savoy immediately before any new peace agreement could be considered.

A fractious process of negotiation, urged upon the two parties by Paul III, led nowhere. Neither side was prepared to modify its case and, diplomacy having failed, on 11 June the imperial ambassador was informed that he had to leave France. It did not help that Barbarossa had begun a vigorous series of raids of Habsburg possessions across the Mediterranean, indicating that the long-feared spectre of a Franco-Ottoman alliance had finally materialised. With this in mind, and fearing total annihilation, Charles finally acted in a manner becoming a supreme warlord. On 13 July 1536 he gave the order to invade Provence, and officially triggered the next round of Franco-Italian Wars.

CHAPTER 18

Friendships Old and New

While Francis had previously liked to view himself as commander-in-chief, it was becoming increasingly clear to the forty-two-year old king that he no longer possessed the vigour or the youth to mastermind lengthy and draining campaigns alone. Aware of his tendency towards impetuosity and rashness, he realised the importance of recruiting a lieutenant who was both martinet and military supremo. Therefore it was time to summon Anne de Montmorency back to court, and place the army on a suitable footing for what threatened to be a lengthy war.

Montmorency had left court in disgrace the previous July after being criticised for what was seen as excessive caution by the more hawkish elements surrounding the king, including Chabot, the new Chancellor Antoine du Bourg and Cardinal du Bellay. Du Bourg's predecessor Duprat had died in July 1535, his bloated body finally worn out by gangrene caused by his excessively lavish lifestyle of unrestricted gluttony and avarice. It was noted that his sole visit to the cathedral of Sens, of which he was nominally bishop, was when it became his final resting place. Du Bourg, an old friend of Francis's and fellow-captive after Pavia, was tough and able, but lacked the Machiavellian guile that his predecessor possessed. It is likely that Duprat would have advised against conflict, which would have made him an anachronism in this harsh and chaotic world inhabited by Charles and Francis.

If any man still retained a sense of honour and decency, it was Montmorency. As he had pledged his word to the imperial ambassador that Francis would not embark on a campaign during the emperor's absence, he found himself shamed by the actions of the pro-war party. Consequently he withdrew to his great château at Chantilly, attracting much harsh and unfair criticism of his actions. Nevertheless, as Grand Master he remained *en poste* as the royal household's chief administrator, and continued to act as governor of the province of Languedoc, a role that he assumed in October 1535. From the spring of 1536 onwards, however, Montmorency's return was keenly sought, and on 14 July France's greatest soldier was appointed the army's 'lieutenant-general', or supreme commander, placing him at the centre of decision-making both civilian and military. He took command of an army of 40,000 men, including many of the dreaded *arquebusiers* who had inflicted such damage on the royal forces at Pavia, and proceeded to use his powers to negotiate with the emperor, as well as directing military operations.

Although Francis himself would play no direct part in the forthcoming war, taking the advice of his councillors to remain behind the lines so as not to run the risk of having to answer Charles's challenge of single combat, he had at least learnt one important lesson from the debacle of Pavia. Francis believed that the emperor intended to lead his army into Provence while another imperial contingent, under Henry of Nassau, would attack France at its north-eastern frontier. If they wished to invade, the king would make their arrival as difficult and time-consuming as possible. Montmorency gave an order that would demonstrate his ruthless leadership brilliantly: 'Destroy Provence.'

The great military leader knew that the town of Aix lacked sufficient defences to withstand the forthcoming imperial attack, and decided that it should be evacuated. The inhabitants were instructed to destroy anything that might assist the enemy. This command soon spread throughout the region, as farms and towns were burned to the ground, livestock were slaughtered and food and drink deliberately spoilt. While this led to thousands of peasants dying from starvation, it also meant that Francis's arch-enemy faced a country that seemed barely worth invading.

In his vain quest for supremacy, Charles soon saw the human cost. On 24 July 1536, shortly after crossing the border, the emperor

and his 30,000 men found that southern Provence had been subjected to a scorched-earth policy. With the rural population having
been evacuated en masse the landscape was deserted, and Aix was
little more than a ghost town. Montmorency and Francis's decision
was unprecedented in the annals of military history. Over a mil-
lennium before, the commanders of Rome's legions had done the
same, with devastating consequences for the enemy. An army stuck
in unproductive terrain would be unable to feed its soldiers, and
in these circumstances disease spread rapidly. There had been one
apparent gesture of generosity: Montmorency's decision to leave
the fruit trees and vines intact. In fact this was another piece of military strategy, as his hope was that the rotten fruit would poison the
starving enemy. He was not to be disappointed. By the beginning
of September a combination of famine and dysentery had killed off
more than 8,000 of Charles's men, including his principal lieutenant, Antonio de Leyva.

It soon became clear that the emperor's preferred target of Marseilles was all but impregnable. Any attack on the heavily fortified
city was doomed to failure, not least because of the difficulty of an
invasion by sea. Hence the choice of Aix, where, to Montmorency's
grim satisfaction, Charles and his troops found themselves in severe
trouble. As he directed his 60,000-strong army from Avignon in the
north, Montmorency had already decided that, unlike in previous
campaigns, there would be no grand set-piece battle, let alone
a *mano a mano* duel between Francis and Charles. Instead he had
determined upon a form of guerrilla warfare; he believed that he
might undermine the imperial army to the greatest effect with a
series of skirmishes and unpredictable hit-and-run raids. It proved
to be a terrible August for the emperor and his men, riddled with
death, illness and poor morale.

Matters worsened when the news from the north proved equally
disastrous. Henry of Nassau's forces had fled back over the border
into Flanders. Their adversary, the Duke of Vendôme, had proved
an implacable foe and prevented the imperial army's anticipated
victory. By the second week of September, Charles's soldiers were
in full retreat, plundering and butchering as they went. A fortnight
later the emperor was aboard a ship of his fleet bound for Spain. He

had spent a fortune, lost many of his men and achieved nothing. His boast that his retreat had been a textbook example of its kind, accomplished in a strong and stable fashion, rang as hollow as his coffers.

Francis did not take his enemy's defeat and retreat with the delight that he had derived from earlier successes. On a purely personal level, the humbling of Charles and the destruction of his army gave Francis immense pleasure, but he knew that he had played no part in the conflict or its military strategy. Instead, the victorious defence of Provence was solely attributable to Montmorency's skilled soldiering. The king's lack of involvement in the campaign can be seen in his geographical distance. He was based at Valence, seventy-five miles to the north of Avignon – considerably removed from the imperial humiliation taking place in southern Provence. Although Francis was in regular contact with his army on the north-east frontier, it was generally believed that, had he found himself nearer the front line, the monarch might have meddled and caused difficulty. Francis was not the only Frenchman who remembered the bitter lessons of Pavia. There was a general cynicism towards the king by now on the part of his soldiers, who considered him a totem of bad luck.

Instead it was Montmorency who once again showed his mettle in the summer of 1536. Charles and his advisers had decided that the French army would be unable to fight simultaneously on two fronts, but Montmorency's forces had proved him wrong. Once the necessary technology and soldiers had been obtained, at some cost, the French had successfully repelled the imperial army, reducing the chances of another invasion dramatically. Yet once again it remained a Pyrrhic victory. Provence had been devastated by the scorched-earth policy that Montmorency had adopted, and the costs of the conflict also showed the expense of contemporary warfare. When the French had invaded Savoy in February 1536, the government kept some one and a half million *livres* in its reserves, thanks to another round of punitive taxation. Yet by the end of the year the enormous cost of the war had claimed that entire sum, and more.

Thus, even as Charles retreated to Spain, Francis was unable to press home his success. A few years before there would have been a stirring cry of 'To arms, my countrymen!' and a pursuit of the imperial forces, which may well have resulted in the decisive victory for which both sides had hoped since Pavia. Charles, enfeebled and impoverished, was extremely vulnerable, and a French victory would have ended the war and secured peace for a generation. Additionally, it would have led to a resumption of the Valois dynastic rule over Milan, and Francis might possibly have enjoyed subjecting his imperial foe to his own humiliating captivity.

However, there were not enough men to engage in a tenacious pursuit of the retreating imperial army, nor was there money to pay them. Both the king and Montmorency understood that the soldiers serving in the army had not been recompensed. With the catastrophic events of the Sack of Rome still a recent memory, paying foreign mercenaries before domestic soldiers was considered a priority, as sell-swords exhibited their displeasure at not being paid by going off on an indiscriminate rampage. A quarter of the 60,000-strong force consisted of mercenaries, and the government was obliged to borrow from the banks of Lyons, then a major financial centre, to settle its debts. The unfortunate unpaid native soldiers were quartered in garrisons in Piedmont; draconian army discipline kept them in line more effectively than any deserved compensation might have done.

For Francis, the early summer of 1536 was a time of public triumph and private regret, which by mid-August had turned into deep personal sorrow. On 10 August his eldest son, the Dauphin Francis, had collapsed and died suddenly at Tournus. The boy had been the opposite of his father in terms of temperament and appearance, being reserved, often clad in dull black and, taking after his mother and aunt, more interested in books than in soldiering. He was described as 'sombre and bizarre'[1] by one courtier, but he and Francis were nonetheless close and, to his father's pride, the boy already maintained a fine mistress, one Madame d'Estranges. The dauphin's death was a catastrophic blow to all at court. The loss of his eldest son devastated the king, who tearfully prayed: '[God] you have afflicted me by humiliating my kingdom and my army, and now you have taken away my son. What else remains save to destroy me utterly? When it shall please you to do so, at least warn me that it is your will so that I do not rebel.'[2]

With some urgency, given the king's desolation, a scapegoat needed to be produced. After all, whispers and rumours were the currency of every royal court, and it seemed impossible that the royal prince could have met his end so young of apparently natural causes. In fact his death was probably caused by pleurisy or tuberculosis, brought about by the unseemly and dank environment in which he was detained during the latter phase of his Spanish imprisonment. Had Francis wished to take revenge for his son's death, the obvious step might have been finally to accept Charles's challenge of single combat.

Nonetheless, the unfortunate who faced the king's wrath was one Sebastiano de Montecuculli, the dauphin's young tutor, and Page of the Sewer. The Italian had previously been in the emperor's service. He was accused of the murder of the dauphin on only the flimsiest of evidence. These trumped-up charges included his possession of a scholarly treatise on poisons, and of having given the dauphin a cup of iced water after a game of tennis. Nonetheless, Montecuculli was subjected to lengthy and horrendous tortures in order to obtain a confession to acting as an imperial agent, and that he had also planned to murder the king. As often in Renaissance Europe, the cruel and protracted method of extracting this information from the victim was useless, not least because Montecuculli subsequently withdrew his confession. He knew that he would receive the death penalty and reasoned that he might as well die with his conscience intact, if not his body. As additional punishment, he was sentenced to a startlingly gruesome end, that of écartelage. Following a perfunctory trial, Montecuculli was taken to the Place de la Grève in Lyons, where the court assembled to observe his punishment. Here he was tied to four horses, which received the lash and galloped away, each in a separate direction. This proved to be a lengthy torment, as even strong horses took their time to rip their victim to pieces; the deeply unfortunate Montecuculli endured more agonising pain before he died. Even his execution was not the final indignity that he suffered, as the mob of onlookers played a crude game of football with his severed head. Unsurprisingly, an appalled

Charles delivered an official protest against both the barbarity of the death and the outlandish nature of the allegations made against his government. The murder of royal heirs was hardly the refined emperor's *métier*. Even on the verge of victory, Francis's paranoia showed the degradation of his former character.

The dauphin's death had many consequences, both personal and political, but one stood out in importance. Henri, Duke of Orléans, was now heir to the throne, but he lacked even the little charm his brother had possessed. Tall, dark and repressed, it was said that he never laughed and seldom spoke. His official mistress, Diane de Poitiers, was the only person whom he regarded with anything approaching affection. This indifference was reciprocated by his father, who regarded him as a disappointment.

Instead, Francis transferred his affection to his youngest son, Charles of Angoulême, who was now second in the line of succession. This meant that the emperor's suggestion that he might become Duke of Milan and inherit the French throne simultaneously had evolved from being fantasy into a real possibility; he stood only a step away from the Crown. Unsurprisingly, the idea of a French king as Duke of Milan appalled imperial sensibilities, and the potentate reacted angrily to accusations of complicity in the dauphin's death. Charles announced yet again that he would meet Francis in single combat. At the same time, the snide imperial suggestion that responsibility for the dauphin's death lay closer to home, with his brother Henri and his wife Catherine de Medici, did nothing to alleviate difficult relations between both parties.

There were also happier distractions. Francis left Lyons in mid-October and, while returning to Paris, he had an unexpected introduction to the twenty-four-year old King of Scotland, James V, in the Loire Valley. He greeted the king, saying that he had 'come to see Your Grace and to comfort you'.[3] This charming and handsome man, with a red beard 'like fine shining gold' and a hedonistic love of women, laughter and pleasure, reminded Francis of his own days as a carefree younger man. James managed to keep in touch with his people by disguising himself in rags in an attempt to understand their concerns and fears. History does not record whether he tried to seduce them once he had revealed his identity.

He was also vehemently anti-English, blaming them for the death of his father James IV at the Battle of Flodden Field in Northumberland in 1513. The young prince had been a year old at the time. As a result, he and Francis shared an antipathy towards Henry VIII. Their burgeoning friendship meant that the king felt no affront when James made it clear that he was not interested in a proposed arranged marriage to Francis's adopted daughter Marie de Vendôme; he apparently found her 'hunchbacked and misshapen'. The unfortunate girl was later said to have died, from a heart broken by embarrassment at such a public rejection.

Instead James asked for Madeleine, Francis's favourite daughter by Claude, and was given her hand in marriage. She had been smitten from the first encounter, and it was said that 'from the time she saw the King of Scotland, she became so enamoured with him and loved him so well that she would have no man alive to be her husband but he alone'. It might have been a love match, but Francis was delighted at the prospect of a marital union between the house of Stuart, a successful Scottish dynasty, and that of Valois, which strengthened the current Franco-Scottish special relationship.

Unfortunately for all parties involved, Madeleine suffered from tuberculosis, and was not thought able to bear children. Her doctors warned that if she were removed from France and taken to the colder climes of Scotland, it might prove fatal. Francis attempted to persuade James to marry his younger daughter Marguerite instead, but the Scottish king was as obstinate as he was charming. A barely affordable dowry of 100,000 gold coins was settled on Madeleine, and on 1 January 1537 a splendid marriage, as befitted the union of a princess and a king, took place in Notre-Dame. It was the first time that a royal daughter of Francis's was married. All the usual lavish ceremonies and entertainments were observed, not least a great feast with orchestras playing and a fortnight of tournaments and jousting. Yet there was sadness behind the dancing and frivolity, not just because Francis had found himself paying James's (far from inconsiderable) expenses. Madeleine, who had worn a dress of white and gold damask with a jewelled collar for the religious ceremony, had grown weaker, and Francis feared for her wellbeing upon her imminent departure for Scotland. When he took his leave of the newly married pair, with gifts of ships and horses for James and gold and jewellery for Madeleine, it was with deep foreboding.

Madeleine and her new husband arrived in their kingdom in May 1537, after a tempestuous five-day journey. Their entourage included a twelve-year-old page, Pierre de Ronsard, who would later become one of France's greatest poets. Upon her arrival Madeleine was surprised not to find a cultured and civilised country such as the one that she had left, but a cold, half-barbaric place. Although her blissful marriage meant that she was happy enough with the situation, the miserable climate only made her tuberculosis worse. She was dying before she left France. James believed that taking her to Balmerino Abbey in Fife might ameliorate her situation, but this proved useless. Repeating the words, 'Alas, I wanted to be Queen', she was confined to the sick-room. Although Madeleine, in an attempt at optimism, wrote to her father that she was cured, on 7 July 1537 she died at the royal palace of Holyrood in Edinburgh. Ronsard, who had been present, wrote: 'She died without pain in her husband's arms.'[4] She had only been queen for forty days, and was known as 'the summer queen'.

Unlike most other marriages of the day, that of James and Madeleine had been a genuinely affectionate one, and the Scottish king was devastated by the death of his wife. After he made a noble but pointless attempt to kill himself with his sword, which was wrestled out of his hands by his courtiers, he wrote to Francis to inform him of the tragic news. In his heartfelt letter he declared that 'Triumph and merriness was [sic] all turned into dirges and soul masses, which was very lamentable to behold . . . [I write to tell you of] the death of your daughter, my dearest companion.'[5] When Francis, who was himself lying ill at Fontainebleau, received the news, he felt stunned by grief. The revelation was delayed for some time until his health partially recovered, for fear that the shock would prove fatal. From the heights of his triumphs against Charles the previous year to the depths of his despair at the loss of his beloved daughter, it seemed as if his life had been summed up in microcosm by the reversals of fortune that he now faced.

Yet Francis had not managed to remain King of France for the previous two decades by being a sentimentalist. Despite his personal feelings, he knew that a sense of 'business as usual' had to be maintained. Accordingly, he let his former son-in-law know that the alliance between France and Scotland had to be maintained, and thus the following year James married Mary of Guise, daughter of Francis's trusted counsellor Claude of Guise and Antoinette of Bourbon. Unfortunately, although Mary gave birth to two sons shortly after her marriage, both of them died at birth. James then became ill, again due to his country's poor climate, but, despite his sickness, he managed to impregnate his wife one last time. On 8 December 1542 Mary of Guise gave birth to a daughter. Six days later James V died, leaving his wife Queen Consort of Scotland. It was his last wish that the girl be named after her mother. Their infant daughter Mary would later become known as Queen of Scots, and her own life, loves and death have become the stuff of legend. Had Francis still been as engaged in such matters as he was earlier in his reign, he might have seen the potential difficulty of a rival family establishing their scion in this way, but his attention lay elsewhere. Once again, his solution to personal sorrow was to go to war.

The grief-stricken king decided to distract himself with a bold initiative. Accordingly, he proceeded with the annexation of the counties of Flanders and Artois, which he had been forced to yield at the Treaty of Cambrai in 1529. Montmorency was charged with the execution of the military campaign, and the opening stages in March and April 1543 saw many French successes. It was therefore a surprise to many people that Francis, as if on a whim, suspended what promised to be a hugely successful offensive on 6 May 1537 and instead moved his soldiers from the Netherlands border to Piedmont. Had they known about his continued connections with the Ottomans, it might have been easier to explain.

As a trusted ally of Suleiman, Francis had been secretly informed that the Ottoman Turks intended to launch a major military offensive against the kingdom of Naples. With his cooperation, there now seemed a chance that a Franco-Ottoman alliance could control the entirety of Italy, and destroy Charles's influence and power for ever. This was a seductive but dangerous idea for Francis; much as he longed for military supremacy, he also knew that his choice of bedfellows was a dangerous one, and that the Ottomans were no more trustworthy than Henry VIII or Charles V. Despite the apparent warmth of his relations with them, there was no guarantee that France would not be turned on by an increasingly all-powerful army.

Thus Francis prevaricated before offering his full support. Initially he prepared to leave for Lyons, which had served as an assembly point for so many French armies bound for an invasion of Italy, with the hope that history might once again repeat itself. However, his latest Italian expedition was delayed when the emperor proceeded to besiege Thérouanne. The city had been seized weeks previously by Francis in order to bring the area back under French control. The emperor's representative, the ruler of the Netherlands, feared that a long and gruelling campaign was imminent and therefore called for a truce, which was signed at Bomy on 30 July. It was a strangely lacklustre effort on the imperial side. Not only were the French allowed to keep most of their territorial gains, but the truce only applied to the fighting in the north of France, not elsewhere, making it useless for any longer-term hope of peace.

Yet, if there had been a suggestion that further glory would be achieved with the aid of the Ottoman army, it did not last for long. The perennially impecunious king was unable to supply the army that would have been vital to a combined invasion of Italy, which meant that the Ottomans diverted their attention away to Corfu. This was both a manageable land mass and an island whose inhabitants could be colonised with comparative ease. While Francis's failure to implement the Franco-Ottoman alliance in military terms had momentous consequences, not least his inability to vanquish the impoverished and disorganised Charles, as well as to seize total control of the Italian peninsula, this was not due to military incompetence on the part of Francis or Montmorency. Instead, it was a further demonstration of how the French administration simply could not produce the money needed to attain its military goals.

Nonetheless, the French campaign in Italy had to go on, led by the indomitable Montmorency. Months after the failure to seize Italy with a coalition army, he led his army across the Alpine passes in early October. He was there to conquer and, in cahoots with the dauphin, he took the allegedly impregnable pass of Susa within days of his arrival. He acted pitilessly and efficiently, executing and laying waste as he went; by the end of October 1537 virtually the entire region of Piedmont was occupied by the French. Both sides had run out of money and a three-month truce, agreed on 16 November 1537, led to peace talks designed to resolve the question of Milan.

Francis held the upper hand, and so the imperial negotiators reluctantly agreed that Charles of Angoulême might indeed acquire the title Duke of Milan at some future date. They hoped that this would in turn lead to jealousy between the dauphin and his younger brother and a schism within the French royal family, which would cushion the blow of a Valois prince ruling Milan. Imperial intelligence had noticed the contrast between the Dauphin Henri's glum, reserved manner and his brother's more lively and boisterous personality. Charles had proved to be far more similar to his father in terms of temperament. A difference of approach might perhaps, with imperial connivance, translate itself into a state within a state. But in 1537 neither side could reach agreement on the details of how the duchy ought to be governed until the Duke of Orléans could be installed as its ruler, so the precarious treaty was extended until 1538.

That a peaceful, even friendly relationship between Francis and the emperor could ever exist seemed impossible. Mutual hostility, if not naked personal hatred, between the two had dominated European politics for over twenty years and the consequences, visible on many a battlefield, had been both bloody and expensive. The idea that the two might again converse, let alone form any sort of alliance, would have appeared impossible to all but the most optimistic, or godly, of men. Thus it became an evangelical mission for Pope Paul III to bring the two long-standing adversaries together in what he regarded as a crucial alliance. Convinced that a crusade that expressed Christendom's Catholic unity was the only way of stopping the Ottoman expansion, he believed that this goal could not be achieved if Francis and Charles persisted in never-ending war. That Francis might have been reluctant to embark on a crusade against his erstwhile ally seemed unimportant compared to the greater good that might be accomplished.

The papal peace treaty was immeasurably assisted by Montmorency. His military success had been compromised by the parlous state of the French finances. He rightly believed that he had accomplished a great deal; Savoy and Piedmont were now French-occupied areas, as were Turin and other towns recently acquired on the north-eastern frontier. It was a position of strength that indicated French military superiority, but it was not one of total supremacy. Careful negotiations and an open-minded attitude towards what had seemed unthinkable just a few months before hinted at the possibility of an advantageous peace treaty.

Francis, as ever, proved the sticking point. In January 1538 he reluctantly agreed to attend a peace summit, arranged by the pope, which was due to be held in Nice that summer. However, as the date of the colloquy drew near he made impatient noises about rejecting any further papal mediation, claiming, bizarrely, that he was more interested in talking to Charles directly. Given the tension and difficulty between the two men, this was an unlikely outcome. Charles, unsurprisingly, continued to wish that the pope would act as a mediator, and so the king had to accede to these undesirable terms. Unsurprisingly, when the Nice peace conference was convened on 15 May it was doomed, all the more so because Francis, despite his brave talk, had refused to meet the emperor in person. All the negotiations were therefore conducted via the pope as intermediary.

Pope Paul III was, however, an impressive figure. Unlike his predecessors, he had the air of a venerable and godly man, and dealt with the feuding rulers with a mixture of good humour and stern decisiveness. Rather than allowing Francis to offer the traditional greeting of a kiss upon the papal toe, he embraced him in a manly fashion, showing his commitment to being an interventionist figure rather than a mere wittering prelate. Although neither party could agree on a date for Charles of Angoulême's induction as Duke of Milan, meaning that no concrete achievement arose from the summit, it was announced on 20 June that the Franco-imperial truce would now be extended for another ten years – something that would have appeared impossible only a matter of months before.

Yet, compared to what then ensued, this breakthrough would

seem almost insignificant. Due to the intervention of Queen Eleanor, Francis's wife and Charles's sister, on 14 July the two men were finally prevailed upon to put their considerable differences aside and meet in person, at the port of Aigues-Mortes on the coast of Languedoc. Here the king and the emperor came face to face once more when Francis stepped onto Charles's galley. The atmosphere was one of tension and uncertainty among the courtiers; the antipathy between the two had by now become legendary. It seemed possible that one would attack the other, necessitating a return to war.

And yet, when the two men met again, a strange kind of chemistry seemed to emerge. They had dominated each other's lives for so long that they might have known one another better than even their own families did. The hours and days that each had spent plotting the downfall of the other meant that they had placed themselves in each other's skin countless times, and the period that Francis had spent in captivity under Charles's yoke had brought about an intimacy, rough-hewn and reluctant though it was. Therefore, when Francis embraced the emperor, it was with a generosity and openness that few could have anticipated. Both men, perhaps overwhelmed by unexpected warmth, seemed to feel a sense of euphoria at meeting, and the French king, in a theatrical flourish that surprised and delighted those around him, announced: 'My brother, I am your prisoner once again!'

The apparently impossible finally seemed to have occurred. A legendary enmity at last seemed buried. Yet the last decade of Francis's life would be bedevilled by friction and conflict. Even new friendships, after all, have an unfortunate habit of souring.

CHAPTER 19

God Governs the Hearts of Men

The new entente between Francis and Charles bemused observers as much as it delighted them. Although the end of an expensive, gruelling war seemed a desirable outcome, the back-slapping and apparently sincere warmth between the two rulers made a mockery of the previous decades of conflict. As one onlooker, carefully picking his words, put it: 'It seems that what we are seeing is but a dream, considering all that we have seen in the past. God is letting us know that he governs the hearts of men as he pleases.'[1]

Yet the accord seemed a genuine one. The day after their initial meeting the emperor left his ship, and his second encounter with the king took place on French soil: a considerable risk if Charles had believed that the remotest chance of abduction or physical threat existed. Yet the bonhomie continued and, in a testament to their reconciliation, the two rulers agreed to serve the common interests of Christendom. If there was anyone who was responsible for the new understanding between the two it was Montmorency, who had successfully persuaded Francis that a meeting of this nature was both desirable and overdue. He was greatly pleased with their encounter and wrote, somewhat optimistically, that the two rulers could begin to regard their affairs as interchangeable from then on. His continued influence could also be seen in the treaty signed at Compiègne by Mary of Hungary, Charles's younger sister and Regent of the Netherlands,* and Francis on 23 October 1538. This

---

* Margaret of Austria, the previous ruler of the Netherlands, who had been responsible for the Treaty of the Ladies with Louise of Savoy, had died in 1530.

both settled territorial disputes along the French border with the Netherlands and saw Francis solemnly promise not to assist any of the imperial rebels in the area. Just a few months before, an accord like this would have been unthinkable, not least because Francis would have benefited from assisting such a rebellion.

Given the present strength of the two men's friendship, Montmorency was eager to ensure that further and more extensive peace talks followed. The terms, as put forward by the French, amounted to a general settlement: Francis would join a crusade against the Ottomans and cooperate with the emperor in order to defend European Christendom. To cement relations, the Duke of Orléans would marry either the emperor's daughter Maria or his niece Christina of Denmark, and Charles V's son Philip would marry Francis's daughter Marguerite. Francis would return the disputed territory of Savoy and the majority of Piedmont. On 22 December 1538, to great rejoicing, Charles agreed to all of these terms, which saw the two great enemies bound together in what amounted to an alliance: a previously unimaginable state of affairs. It was hugely popular in France, as the country was sick of war and invasion. Once again Francis had managed to present himself as a monarch who seemed to listen to his people and act on their behalf.

There was an element of wish-fulfilment in this apparently utopian deal, however. The sceptical noted that Milan had yet to be handed over. Likewise, given the French king's reputation for agreeing to alliances and treaties and then breaking them the next day, even the pope believed that his handiwork was unlikely to lead to his long-cherished crusade. Although Charles, who was perhaps less sure of the integrity of the treaty, made some discreet enquiries as to Francis's intentions, he was reassured when his ambassador informed him: 'I can certify to your Majesty, under pain of being reproached as the lowest wretch in the world, that any promise made here will be completely fulfilled.'[2] It seemed as if the peace would last for years, possibly even decades.

With this in mind, Francis had to act in as diplomatic and cautious a fashion as possible. He felt it was important to reassure Henry VIII that, despite having promised to abandon him in the pre-Christmas 1538 pact, he remained on friendly terms. Nor did he have any intention of siding with Pope Paul over his erstwhile ally, even if the English king was about to be excommunicated. Thus, for all the talk of a Franco-imperial alliance against Henry, it never came to pass. Relations between the two men were friendly enough for Francis to send Henry, in 1540, a suitably carnivorous Christmas gift of terrine made from the largest wild boar ever hunted in France. Likewise, the French monarch felt that it was prudent to maintain friendly relations with Suleiman, meaning that his commitment to a crusade seems to have been similarly specious. Although they now, by necessity, had to be more circumspect, French dealings with the Ottoman government continued to be close. Suleiman even invited Francis as a guest of honour to the celebrations for his son's circumcision in September 1539, a sign that only the closest of the sultan's allies had made the cut.

Nonetheless, a balance had to be struck between honouring existing friendships and diplomatic alliances and celebrating new ones. During the winter of 1539–40, it was with this in mind that Charles, at Francis's explicit invitation, travelled in state through France on his way to the Netherlands. There had been a rebellion in Ghent, and the French king saw the opportunity to further his friendship with the emperor by allowing him to pass through his country with his men. Charles also suffered from excruciating piles, and the shorter journey would curtail his suffering. Reassurances had to be made once again that there would be no attempt by the French king to use the emperor's presence in his country for his own ends, most notably the question of Milan. Montmorency, in particular, stressed that Charles had to be treated in an open and honourable fashion, as otherwise any concession extracted from him was liable to be nullified as soon as he left the country.

A warm exchange of letters followed between the two monarchs, who referred to each other as 'brother'. Neither side asked for any hostages or guarantees, indicating the degree of trust that had grown between them, before the emperor, accompanied by his men, arrived in Bayonne on 27 November 1539. Although Francis was suffering from ill health and was unable to ride to meet his guest, he organised a succession of resplendent *entrées joyeuses* that followed at Bordeaux, Poitiers, Orleans and Fontainebleau. One chronicler described the excess of the lavish welcome: 'rooms, chambers and galleries were so richly hung with tapestries and decorated with such costly and beautiful pictures and statues that no mortal man could describe them or give a true account, for it seemed more like paradise, the work of gods rather than human hands'.[3]

The emperor's journey was not without incident. Francis was keen to show him the treasures of his various châteaux, and took him to Chambord and Amboise. At the latter, a flaming torch set an unfortunate courtier alight, and the conflagration spread rapidly through the tunnels; it was with great haste that Francis diverted his imperial guest elsewhere. At nearby Blois a beam came crashing to the floor, striking the emperor with a glancing blow; he was nearly asphyxiated at Bordeaux; and at the bridge of the Tournelles the young Duke of Orléans seized an alarmed Charles in a bear hug from behind and said: 'Now, sire, you are my prisoner!'[4] The emperor's presumable great discomfort at these events was well concealed.

This was all but preamble to the culminating and grandest reception of them all, in Paris, where the emperor arrived on a black horse beneath a golden canopy. At each city Charles was allowed to set prisoners free and was given expensive gifts, although one of these, a life-sized silver statue of Hercules between two pillars, was described by Francis as 'the ugliest work of art that he had ever seen'.[5] Nonetheless, the aesthetic of the rest of Charles's visit was carefully designed to represent France at its best, as he visited the great châteaux, resided in the modernised Louvre and attended a banquet at the Palais in Paris. Charles, unused to strong drink and rich food, was frequently ill, and spent his nights in prayer rather than revelry, despite the lavishness of the chamber in which he was sequestered. One notable example was a bed covered in crimson velvet and festooned with pearls and precious stones. If anyone had observed the Holy Roman Emperor being feasted and feted, they might have assumed that he was a long-standing friend of France rather than the man who had been its bitterest foe for years.

*

It was Montmorency's prevailing intelligence that had conceived and planned the imperial welcome and his personal power base seemed positively all-encompassing as a result. After the revolt and subsequent downfall of Bourbon, France had a vacuum at its heart for a leading noble who could operate on a scale to rival the king. Certainly, Montmorency was a rare combination of wealth, power and, thanks to his military success, popularity, despite Brantôme's claim that men trembled in his presence 'like leaves in the wind'.[6] Both the dauphin and his mistress, Diane de Poitiers, regarded him as a confidant and he enjoyed the backing of the Parisian *parlement*. He also had managed to retain the friendship of Queen Eleanor and the king's major mistress, Madame d'Étampes – a delicate balancing act that he nonetheless managed with some aplomb. It went without saying that he was a boon companion of Francis; the Venetian ambassador said of him: 'he rules everything, for himself and just as he pleases'.[7]

He was even, initially at least, fortunate in his choice of enemies. The Constable of France, as Montmorency was created on 10 February 1538, had earned the enmity of Admiral Chabot, his former comrade and colleague, who resented his own exclusion from the recent high-level French negotiations. This seemed a matter of little consequence, however, since Chabot, following the revelation that he had accepted bribes from French merchants, was dismissed from public office in February 1541 and imprisoned at Vincennes. Rumours that Montmorency was directly involved in bringing the evidence of this bribery to the king's attention circulated, but the popular constable was not implicated in any shenanigans. If anything, his whistle-blowing seemed proof of his integrity and honesty. This was also exhibited in his implacable loathing of heretics, which appealed greatly to Francis; it was the constable who ensured that a list of prohibited books was kept at court, with heavy penalties for anyone found possessing them.

Yet in Renaissance France, the most secure of courtiers could be removed from their post without warning, and Montmorency was in no better a position than anyone else if the delicate relationship between Charles and Francis were to collapse. The pageantry and expense of the French reception of the emperor had been intended to act as an incentive for Charles to name the day when Milan would be handed over to the French. Yet once he had returned home, by some miracle safely, from his travels, it became increasingly obvious that the emperor was every bit as untrustworthy as Francis, and that he had never had any intention of allowing his old adversaries back into Milan.

Charles played for time, talking airily of bringing about a formal peace settlement, but he continued to prevaricate. When pressed, he claimed that his business suppressing a revolt in Ghent kept him from attending to matters with the French, but rumours soon circulated that the treaty between the French and the empire was precarious at the very least. Montmorency, who had as much as anyone to lose should the entente not hold, angrily denied the tittle-tattle, and swore that relations between the two powers were as strong as ever. Privately he believed that Charles would have to accede to a treaty surrendering Milan as he could ill afford a major rupture with the French; his territories in the Netherlands were slipping into ever-deeper religious crisis and the imperial financial situation remained parlous. Therefore, Montmorency reasoned, the emperor needed to come to heel.

The constable was anything but a stupid man, but unfortunately he had placed too much trust in an essentially fragile accord, and one made impossible by the fraught Milanese situation. Charles offered the Netherlands and various other concessions, but refused to agree to cede Milan. He was happy to lie to the French and to pretend to offer solutions while playing for time, but it was ultimately useless. By June 1540 peace talks between the emperor and the French had collapsed, and the apportioning of blame would swiftly follow.

At court there was at least one significant voice raised against the constable, who had made more enemies on his ascent to power than he might have considered possible. 'He is a great scoundrel', announced his former friend Madame d'Étampes, 'for he has deceived the king by saying the emperor would give him Milan at once when he knew that the opposite was true.'[8] A lesser man would have been unable to bear the weight of opprobrium that was now being visited upon his distinguished head, but he retained at least one crucial supporter in the king, who said to him, not without humour: 'I can see only one fault in you, and that is that you do not love those whom I love.'[9] Yet the constable's influence waned throughout 1540. He continued to attend the King's Council with all the trappings of a trusted adviser, but his presence there was a largely token one. Real power instead resided with Madame d'Étampes, described by the imperial envoy as 'the real president of the king's most intimate and private council',[10] which allowed for a splendid double entendre as well as an accurate description of where influence lay. The ambassador also noted in his letter to Charles that she felt 'angry feelings' towards the emperor on account of how 'you did not make so much of her as she expected'; clearly, she was a woman who would not be satisfied unless she was at the epicentre of attention. Therefore, given that Montmorency was no longer of any use to her, she would happily contrive his downfall.

This came in stages, but was precipitated on 11 October 1540, after Charles V invested his son Philip as Duke of Milan, finally resolving the question of who would assume power in the duchy. Although this did not mean the immediate end of Montmorency, the first period of his greatest influence now drew to a close. He offered his resignation, but Francis showed magnanimity and had no wish to humiliate a soldier of such brilliance, especially one who had done 'the state some service'. Montmorency retained his offices but was no longer invited to the crucial meetings. Finally, he was humiliated by his involvement in the marriage of Marguerite's twelve-year-old daughter Jeanne to Francis's would-be ally William of Cleves, which involved him literally bearing the reluctant princess to the altar on 14 June 1541: a task that he considered entirely beneath him.

As a result he left court the next day, and did not return during his former patron's reign. Francis responded to the snub with a circumlocutory punishment, namely stripping all the provincial governors of their powers before reinstating them, save Montmorency. Like Bourbon, he had been cast into the wilderness from his position of highest influence, but unlike the troublesome royal duke Montmorency felt too weary and exhausted to attempt any sort of revenge. By the spring of 1542 he was barely visible in French public life and became an all but forgotten figure. The final twist was that his former adversary Chabot, who had Madame d'Étampes on hand to plead for him, was released from Vincennes, granted new lands and titles and, in March 1542, absolved of all the previous charges against him. The only consolation for an increasingly bitter Montmorency was that Chabot died of a heart attack in 1543, ensuring that he would not inherit his own position.

Yet if the constable's decline was a predictable one, it seemed a premonition of the fate that would befall Francis. The king had been beset by ill health and a sense of his own mortality since his imprisonment and near-death in 1525, and he had never fully recovered. The emperor's ministerial council, fearful for his safety should the king die during Charles's period on French soil, had insisted that the formal invitation be in the name of the dauphin and of the senior government ministers as well as that of the king. And it was for this reason that it was decided that Montmorency and Francis's sons would welcome Charles in the name of the French monarchy after he crossed the southern border towards the end of November. The king later recovered his old *joie de vivre* in Paris, but it was an altogether more difficult process than it once had been. At the age of forty-six, Francis was growing old.

There were, of course, rumours about the causes of the monarch's evident physical decline. Many who had cause to dislike Francis, whether because of his buccaneering lifestyle or his harshness towards Protestants, were only too keen to deliver their own medical judgement, namely that he had contracted illness as a result of his unchecked sexual adventurism. This rumour, which would have been unthinkable in public discourse a decade before, had become common currency. The idea that Francis had developed syphilis was first advanced during his own lifetime at the tables and courts of European aristocrats, with a combined mixture of exaggerated horror and prurient delight that the pleasures of a sybaritic king had to be paid for. The legend spread that the husband of one of his mistresses, 'La Belle Ferronière', had deliberately contracted the disease in order to revenge himself upon his lecherous monarch. It was further suggested by those who were particularly interested in Francis's handling of public affairs that he had been subjective and wayward when he came under the influence of female admirers. An amorous ruler, with uncertain judgement, was of a piece therefore with the king whose disease bore the fatal consequences of being 'fondly overcome by female charm'.

This was a suitably malicious piece of tittle-tattle, but it ignored one key detail. Those who suffer from syphilis usually experience a severe mental collapse in the latter stages of the disease, reducing them to incapacity before they eventually die. Francis, despite his physical decline, was invariably mentally alert and his illness was not allowed to impede the conduct of public business. It is possible that he suffered from some mild sexually transmitted diseases, which he was said to have first contracted as a young man as far back as 1512, but these would not have been terminal. Instead, they are likely to have caused him little more than discomfort and inconvenience.

As the military and diplomatic entanglements of the autumn of his reign continued to cause Francis irritation and grief, he at least took comfort in the way that his status as a patron of the arts continued undiminished by the international situation. By 1540 he was more likely to be found hawking or wandering with his chosen courtiers than riding horses pell-mell towards an unfortunate target. He continued to associate with artists and writers (at least those whose books he had not banned), and in 1538 was painted in absentia by Titian, who was based in Venice at the time. The artist was obliged to work from a medallion of the king, but managed to produce a splendidly regal portrait of him, clad in a feathered hat and with a golden chain around his neck. The impression given is of a vital, healthy man who has achieved a vast amount.

Titian flattered his patron, who received the painting from Pietro Aretino, saying it was one that 'magnified the honour of man'.[11] The reality was that, the following year, the king was severely ill with an abscess below his stomach; although the truth was concealed due to the potential for diplomatic embarrassment, it was believed that he was in danger of dying. Although he recovered, his previous good humour and love of activity had been impaired and were never to recover. He was not as grotesquely obese as Henry VIII, nor given to the delicacy of Charles V, but Francis's long and tiring reign had taken its toll on his impressive bearing.

In an attempt to distract himself, he continued to act as an inno-vator in art and architecture. He was especially close to the painter Francesco Primaticcio, whom he commissioned to act as his agent on a number of visits to Italy. During the course of these, paintings and other *objets d'art* were first identified and then either brought back to France or models were commissioned of them. These in-cluded some of the great works of antiquity, such as *Marcus Aurelius*, the *Laocoön* and the *Capitoline Horse*. Primaticcio was also closely involved in Francis's expansion of Fontainebleau, which began in 1540; the French king saw the great château, which he referred to as 'Chez moi', as his legacy. Using land on the east side of the château purchased from a nearby religious order, he began to build a new square of buildings around a large courtyard. Its reputation was such that a jealous Henry VIII decided that he would build his own palace, and attempted to emulate Francis's grand vision at Nonsuch in Surrey. It proved to be an endeavour too far for the English king, who was never able to build such a grand monument to his own, questionable, magnificence.

It was at his own masterpiece, Fontainebleau, that Francis in-creasingly spent his time. He had begun to reside there as often as he could from December 1529 on account of the excellent hunting that it offered, and one courtier, the architect Androuet du Cerceau, wrote that 'he liked it so much that he spent most of his time there . . . all that he could find of excellence was for his Fontainebleau, of which he was so fond that whenever he went here, he would say that he was going home'.[12] It was here, in such grand spaces as the so-called 'King's Chamber', that Francis was able to display his gran-diose murals and sculpture, painstakingly acquired from all over Europe during the course of his reign. Sir John Wallop, the English ambassador, reported at least one surprising feature of his design. Although he praised the royal bedchamber as 'very singular, as well with antique borders, as costly ceiling and a chimney right well made', he was astonished to find that the priceless paintings that the king took such pride in were displayed in his baths. Wallop noted that 'these being warm and reeked so much, like it had been a mist, that the king went before to guide me'.[13] Francis's taste might have been excellent, but his choice of display left a great deal to be desired.

Nonetheless, artists were a treasured group at Fontainebleau, and had been since Francis had begun to employ Italians such as Giovanni Battista Rosso and Primaticcio. Rosso, in particular, did exceptionally well under Francis. Not only was he appointed First Painter, but he was given a substantial salary, lavish rooms and a Parisian house, and general indulgence to behave in any way that he saw fit. It was remarked by the artist Antonio Mini, not without envy, that Rosso led the life of a wealthy aristocrat, complete with horses, servants and the finest silk garments. He and Primaticcio were the founders of what became known as the first School of Fontainebleau, although much of the work was crudely executed by apprentices and underlings. This was at least in part because Rosso, having embraced a lifestyle filled with hubris, accused a friend of stealing a huge amount of money from him in November 1540. His allegation proved to be false and, riddled with shame and guilt, he killed himself on 15 November. When Francis heard the news, Vasari wrote that 'it caused him indescribable regret, since it was his opinion that in losing Rosso, he had been deprived of the most excellent artist of his time'.[14]

Others also flocked to Fontainebleau. Although a tapestry workshop that was established in 1540 produced little of lasting value bar a set of six hangings, a more valuable association came about between Francis and the Florentine goldsmith and sculptor Benvenuto Cellini. It was he who had also reputedly been responsible for killing the French king's nemesis, the Duke of Bourbon, in the Siege of Rome in 1527. Nonetheless, it was for his artistic skill rather than his occasional military prowess that Francis summoned him to his court. His initial visit to France in 1537 proved of little use, as Francis was distracted with war against Charles V, but he returned in 1540 for a five-year visit; during this time he caught the attention of the French king, later writing in his autobiography that 'one morning at his dinner the King called me. He began to talk to me in Italian, saying that he had it in his mind to execute several great works, and that he would soon give orders where I was to labour, and provide me with all necessaries.'[15]

Unfortunately Cellini initially had a disagreement with Francis over money and left the court, before being summoned back on pain of imprisonment. Thankfully for their harmonious working relationship, financial terms were agreed – the same as da Vinci had been offered – and Cellini made his base in the Petit Nesle in Paris, opposite the Louvre. Here he began to undertake a series of works in gold and silver for the king that included a silver statue of Jupiter, a bronze relief of the *Nymph of Fontainebleau* and a salt cellar, which was completed to Francis's enormous satisfaction in 1543. Upon first seeing it, 'he uttered a loud cry of astonishment and could not satiate his eyes with gazing at it'.[16] Yet other, greater, work remained unfinished, such as designs for statues of satyrs and a colossus at Fontainebleau. The king was dissatisfied with Cellini's attitude and expectations, telling him: 'You show your greatness only through the opportunities we give you . . . you ought to be a little more submissive, less arrogant and headstrong.' Francis ended with a threat that showed that his admiration for art was somewhat greater than his affection for its practitioners: 'Do your utmost to obey my commands, for if you stick to your own fancies, you will run your head against a wall.'[17]

Although Cellini grovelled and bowed to 'the most admirable prince who ever blessed this earth', he was uninterested in serving so demanding a king. He left for Italy in 1545, never to return to France in Francis's reign. During his time in Paris his perceived arrogance had made him many enemies, among them Madame d'Étampes, who did her best to sabotage the sculptor's work, not least the grand presentation of his statue of Jupiter. He was also attacked in the streets, probably by men hired by her. After he departed France it was Francis who regretted the loss of the great artist, instructing one of his treasurers to send him the enormous sum of 6,000 *scudi* as an apology in an attempt to lure him back to finish his magnum opus, the colossus. Cellini, perennially impecunious, was tempted by the money, but unfortunately Francis died while negotiations were still continuing for his return. The Italian artist nonetheless looked back on his time in France as having been hugely influential in his career and life, writing in 1556 that he was 'in part immortal, since the French king set me on the path of sculpture'.[18]

Others also gave the court a sense of aesthetic accomplishment. The great satirical writer Rabelais orbited the king, although he was never given official status, perhaps because his verses were far too risqué and near-the-knuckle for him to be brought into the court proper. Nonetheless the king had enjoyed his work, ever since he had asked for Rabelais' *Chronicles* to be read to him to discover whether they carried the fatal taint of heresy. He was both relieved and amused to find that they were far more diverting than that, and pronounced afterwards that there was nothing disreputable or disagreeable about them at all. He may have particularly appreciated Rabelais' low opinion of monks; he himself was said by Brantôme to have described them as 'useless people, who are good for nothing except eating and drinking, visiting taverns, gambling, making cords for crossbows and ferret nets, catching rabbits and whistling down linnets – those are their exercises, as well as the debauchery their idleness brings in its train'.[19] As a list of insults this might strike the modern reader as somewhat eclectic in its accusations, but it was no doubt meant sincerely.

It is unclear as to whether Rabelais' early work could be found in Francis's great library at Fontainebleau, but by the Ordinance of Montpellier of 28 February 1537 the king was to be sent a copy of every book published in the kingdom, a collection which was housed at Fontainebleau in May 1544. His early library consisted of nearly 2,000 volumes as well as curiosities such as a large globe and a crocodile's head in a leather case; many of his books were rebound in goatskin adorned with gold and silver, embroidered with his coat of arms. Eventually they would become the basis of the national collection of France, the Bibliothèque Nationale, which befitted Francis's self-description as 'the father of letters'. The king's printer, Robert Estienne, offered an insight into Francis's intentions when he said in 1542 that 'far from grudging to anyone the records of ancient writers which he at great and truly royal cost has procured from Italy and Greece, he intends to put them at the disposal and service of all men'. Although Estienne was speaking thus to maintain royal favour, there was no doubt that Francis throughout his reign had an abiding love of the arts, inherited largely from his mother. He spent a great deal of time and money promoting them, albeit usually insofar as they reflected his own interests.

Yet Francis had also heard the chimes at midnight, and in the remaining years of his reign he returned to military, rather than aesthetic, pursuits. Even as his recent alliance with Charles turned to ashes, he would find a new and unlikely confidante at court who would become the dominant figure in his final years and beyond.

CHAPTER 20

'In Spite of These Wretched Backbiters'

Following Pope Clement's death in September 1534, matters had been left unfinished. When Francis discovered that Catherine of Medici's dowry had been only partially paid and the pope's territorial promises left unfulfilled, his response was one of anger and his people shared his dismay. It is unlikely that the Venetian ambassador exaggerated when he wrote that the marriage 'displeases the entire nation'.[1] Catherine, above everything a practical girl, knew that she could change neither her birth nor her unexceptional looks, but was determined to use her formidable willpower and intelligence to overcome her misfortunes. Knowing how unpopular she was, she decided that the only option available to her was to cultivate the most important people at court and hope for their protection.

Francis was her first, and most obvious, conquest. Despite his disappointment at the comparatively meagre dowry that she came with, he had protective feelings towards this young and seemingly vulnerable girl. It helped that she, an astute judge of character, had quickly realised that the king placed his personal pleasure above all else. As one of his ministers remarked, 'Alexander [the Great] attended to women when there was no more business to attend to; His Majesty attends to business when there are no more women to attend to.'[2] It was because of the king's extraordinary love of female company that he had founded 'la petite bande'. They were a hard-riding, hard-gossiping group who could laugh at the king's bawdier sallies and still look decorative. Entrance to this salon was vetted with great diligence by Madame d'Étampes, but Catherine's status as Henri's wife ensured that her indifferent appearance did not bar her access. She soon became popular with the king, for she had a knack of amusing him, whatever his humour; she enjoyed 'honest exercise like the dance at which she showed great skill and majesty', hunted with as much aplomb as any man and generally endeared herself to Francis. As Brantôme said of her, 'Her role was not to have one unless it were to sue for the king's favour.'[3]

Another key figure with whom Catherine took great care to ingratiate herself was the king's sister, Marguerite, Queen of Navarre. One of the cleverest and wittiest women at court, she also enjoyed unparalleled access to Francis, meaning that her familiars were guaranteed royal favour. The royal entourage moved from one château to another, as the king visited the various building works that were being conducted at his palaces. Catherine found herself especially taken by the Château of Madrid in and around the Bois de Boulogne, although Francis remained more interested in Fontainebleau. After his death Catherine would finish the work at Madrid, and occasionally used the palace herself. When she accompanied the king on his visits, she absorbed his love for fine Italian craftsmanship, as well as his prodigious spending on rare books, paintings and sculpture.

It did not escape Francis's notice that, despite the high esteem Catherine had managed to recover at court, she had a strained and distant relationship with her husband Henri. Although Henri offered her a cold civility in public, he was indifferent to her, as he did not feel any sexual attraction to her and resented the absence of the promised dowry. She had also made a decision to foster favour with Madame d'Étampes, which in turn aroused her husband's enmity. He was obsessed by her rival, Diane de Poitiers, whose deserved reputation for virtuous and graceful behaviour did not stop her becoming close to a married man nineteen years her junior. It had begun when the king asked her to tame the unpolished and silent boy shortly after his release from Spain, and soon led to an unforeseen intimacy between the two. Although no adulterous liaison took place, at least not initially, it represented a potential threat to Catherine's influence, to say nothing of her marriage.

When the dauphin died on 10 August 1536,[*] Henri and Catherine automatically became Dauphin and Dauphine, with the expectation that they would in turn become King and Queen of France. Indifferent towards his least favourite son, Francis gave him a stern lecture, saying: 'Do all that you can to be like he was, surpass him in virtue so that those who now mourn and regret his passing will have their sorrow erased. I command you to make this your aim with all your heart and soul.'[4] Henri, smarting at the humiliation of knowing that his father openly preferred his younger brother Charles, saw to it that his unloved wife would suffer with him. A vicious whispering campaign, begun by the agents of the emperor, suggested that it might have been the dauphin and his wife who were responsible for his elder brother's murder, as they were the only ones who had anything to gain by his death. While Francis ignored the rumours, the hints of Catherine's involvement were personally damaging; her supposed expertise as a poisoner was considered practically an Italian birthright. It did not help that, after three years of marriage, she had not become pregnant; if she failed to produce children, repudiation as dauphine seemed inevitable.

Conceiving a son and heir was especially difficult because Henri compelled his father to allow him to serve in the war against the emperor. During the conflict he became close to Montmorency, whom he worshipped. He later wrote to him: 'Be sure that whatever happens, I am and shall be for my life as much your friend as anyone in the world.' Another object of affection, of a rather less platonic kind, was Filippa Duci, his groom's daughter, by whom he fathered a child. Henri triumphantly announced that this proved without doubt that the lack of issue from his marriage was Catherine's fault rather than his. It was therefore with a great deal of ceremony and pomp that Filippa eventually gave birth to Henri's first child, a girl named Diane de France – in honour of Henri's now *maîtresse en titre* Diane de Poitiers – in 1538. The child was duly legitimised, the mother paid off and allowed to retire to a convent, and Catherine suffered the humiliation of being sidelined at court, as Diane was entrusted with her namesake's upbringing.

* See Chapter 18.

She knew that she would not last long if a child was not produced, as the love affair between her husband and Diane was conducted without discretion. She was also in danger of being repudiated by her former allies, such as Madame d'Étampes, who wished to see Diane's position destabilised by the arrival of a new bride for Henri. Ironically, this threw Diane and Catherine together, as his mistress plotted to prevent her usurpation by an eligible foreign princess. As a result she brought her considerable influence to bear on the dauphin, impressing upon him his wife's many good qualities, such as her gentleness, her good nature and, implicitly, her tolerance of their affair. The result of this interjection was to leave Henri in a neutral position, ensuring that he would not press for a divorce.

The ultimate decision lay with Francis, who was torn between his affection for Catherine and the knowledge that he had to leave France with the assurance of a king for at least the next two generations. Therefore Catherine gambled everything on a peerless show of feminine submission to a man who, for all his own philandering, liked to be known as 'the first gentleman of France'. She quite literally prostrated herself at his feet, weeping piteously, and told the king that she accepted that she must renounce her title and stand aside in favour of a more fertile woman, but only asked to be allowed to remain in France and serve the fortunate lady who would replace her, in whatever lowly and humble capacity the king would permit. It was a bold move; had it been unsuccessful she would have found herself ejected from court and left with nothing.

Yet her sorrow and obvious humility were so moving that Francis was unable to do anything other than champion her cause, perhaps against his own better judgement. Unable to bear the sight of any woman in tears, especially one whom he had come to regard as a surrogate daughter, the monarch, deeply moved, declared: 'My child, it is God's will that you should be my daughter, and the wife of the Dauphin. So be it.' The king had spoken. There was now no question of a replacement bride for the young prince, provided Catherine overcame her barrenness. If that did not happen, then the whole vexed question would rear its ugly head once again.

Catherine's unyielding determination to become pregnant resulted in increasingly frantic attempts to become a mother. She was prepared to go to unparalleled lengths to preserve both her place as Henri's wife and, even more crucially, her role as the future Queen of France. In this she was helped by Francis's explicit support, which meant that she received encouragement from those who might formerly have been opposed to her. If she enjoyed royal favour, went the rationale of the ever-mutable flatterers at court, and the king wished Catherine to remain dauphine, then so did they. The Venetian ambassador, Matteo Dandolo, spoke for many when he wrote that 'there is no one who would not willingly give their own blood to give her a son'.[5] Even the dauphin, sensing the mood at court had shifted, offered his wife greater affection than hitherto. His aunt Marguerite, who had remained a consistent supporter of Catherine, wrote to her to say: 'My brother will never allow this repudiation, as evil tongues pretend. But God will give a royal line to Madame la Dauphine when she has reached the age at which women of the house of the Medici are wont to have children. The King and I will rejoice with you then in spite of these wretched backbiters.'[6]

Yet for all the fine words and prayers that accompanied Catherine's rehabilitation at court, there was no doubt that, in order for her to maintain her place there, it was necessary for her to conceive a child, and quickly. She first turned to traditional medicine, which offered little success. Prayers and devotions to the Almighty were similarly fruitless. Diane banished Henri from her bed and urged him to perform his husbandly duties, aided by potions and philtres, but the whole process proved useless. Even as Catherine showed her determination and gumption by drinking large draughts of mule's urine –believed to be a form of inoculation against sterility – and by applying foul-smelling poultices made up of ground stag's antlers and cow dung to her 'source of life', nothing happened, despite astrologers all over the kingdom being consulted. It was a strange echo of the events of half a century before, when Louise of Savoy had been assured that she would give birth to a boy, and that he would be King of France. Now, with the certain knowledge that any son born to Catherine would inherit the throne, the pressure could not have been greater.

Perhaps unsurprisingly, given the lack of success that conventional and unconventional means alike had elicited, Catherine became convinced that, being sexually inexperienced, she was making grievous errors in the performance of her conjugal duties. She felt especially envious of Diane, who was cavorting with her husband in a more effective way. According to popular legend, Catherine had holes drilled through her floor at Fontainebleau that allowed her to look down into the bedchamber inhabited by her husband and his mistress, so that she might watch their antics and learn from them. Her ladies-in-waiting, horrified at the idea of their mistress demeaning herself in such a way, attempted to dissuade her, but Catherine took herself in hand and prepared to watch Henri making love to another woman. Although she was devastated when she actually saw the coupling, she was also sufficiently self-assured to realise that the two were doing something different to what she and her husband did.

A doctor, Jean Fernel, was called, and after an embarrassing and invasive examination of both the dauphin and dauphine, he found that their reproductive organs were slightly abnormal, and counselled a method that he hoped would overcome this abnormality, namely having intercourse from behind. As a result, Henri was able to perform his marital duties to a satisfactory level, and in the early summer of 1543 Catherine finally became pregnant. In a surviving letter to Montmorency, who had given both her and her husband advice on the best ways to start a family – a strategy no less difficult than the defence of France she informed him with joy: 'Mon Compère, as I know well that you desire children for me as much as I do, I wished to write to tell you of my great hopes that I am with child.' Finally, on 19 January 1544, the dauphine went into labour, appropriately enough at Fontainebleau, and to the joy and delight of all around her she was delivered of a healthy boy. The couple named their son Francis; his proud grandfather stood beside Catherine at the delivery, having spent a considerable amount of time consulting French and Roman astrologers. His dedication to the birth was such that he even insisted upon examining 'all that came out with the baby'.[7]

The birth of Henri and Catherine's son proved a blessed relief amidst the ructions of the last years of Francis's reign. Knowing that the

French monarch's life was drawing to an end, ambitious courtiers jockeyed for position, leading to a marked increase in factionalism from at least 1542 onwards. But while Francis lived there was no question of his being regarded as anything other than a supreme monarch. Despite the many rises and falls in his fortunes over the previous decades, the king's charisma and force of personality still retained its allure. No courtier, no matter how senior, could afford to forget that Francis had the final say in all executive decisions, both civilian and military. It would be a severe mistake to assume that an aged king was an impotent one. Nonetheless, because of Francis's recent bouts of ill health, his officials worked on the assumption that his death would come sooner rather than later, which meant that it was important to plan for his heir's succession in an orderly and harmonious fashion. When a king died, inevitably a new king lived. As the diplomat Philippe Pot had said the previous century, 'Kingship is the dignity, not the property, of the prince.'[8] Yet, as Francis knew all too well, it was not certain who this king would be. The obvious successor was, of course, Henri, but the king had always disliked his second boy. Charles of Angoulême was a very different character; the impetuous and likeable young prince had built up a strong public following.

Henri resented the extensive, and at times laborious, campaign to secure the dukedom of Milan for Charles, and remained unenthused by his own title as Duke of Brittany. Although he knew that it would be difficult for him to be allowed to rule in Milan as well, he wished to do so, and the dispute revolved as much around the hurt pride of a spurned son as it did political realities. His case was complicated by his glamorous mistress Diane de Poitiers, who supported her lover's claim. At court her influence counted for much in the allocation of patronage, as she remained an anti-Protestant religious conservative and the face of the future as well as a source of contemporary influence. This jockeying for influence was anything but subtle. In August 1546 Nicholas Wotton, the recently arrived English ambassador to France, concluded that 'the Court everywhere is the Court, that is to say, a place where is used good shouldering and lifting at each other.'[9] No stranger himself to 'good shouldering and lifting' in pursuit of his own interests at the court of Henry VIII, Wotton recognised the same pattern of behaviour in France, at a time when anxious placemen guarded their backs for fear that a gilded and ornate stiletto might be delicately slipped in.

It did not help that Francis had dragged the country into his final conflict. Mindful of how many years they had been at war with the Holy Roman Emperor, most of his courtiers and ministers had regarded Charles V with suspicion even in times of peace. His defeats of Francis, both in the electoral process and at Pavia, had diminished some of the young king's aura of glittering success and had begun something of a downward spiral for the young Caesar. Despite the brief rapprochement between the two rulers, the emperor, the French believed, dissembled because that was his nature. Equivocation, manipulation and downright deceit were his preferred options at all times rather than an occasional strategic necessity. Even if some influential figures, such as Montmorency, argued that Charles ought to be trusted and used as a powerful ally rather than confronted and opposed, they remained largely unheard in the belligerent circles in which they moved. Conflict seemed to be the desired outcome for everyone.

It was therefore inevitable that, in the early 1540s, Charles would once again come to be regarded as Francis's and the nation's greatest enemy. The brief interlude of peace and unity seemed never to have occurred. It might be speculated that he performed a singular service to French interests at a period when the court was riddled with ambitious men, and women, plotting their own paths to glory. Whatever their individual circumstances, the overwhelming majority of them considered the emperor to be a malign influence and a determined opponent of French national interests, to say nothing of their own. Charles's return to traditional form as an ogre and villain also carried with it, therefore, the possibility of a diminution of courtly treachery. Observers and courtiers alike hoped that a declaration of war against the empire would remind all parties and factions of their common patriotic cause, and that a shared hatred of the emperor might put aside the bickering at court and end Francis's reign on a high note.

The obvious reason for war, namely Charles's installation of his son Philip as ruler of Milan on 11 October 1540, did not lead to an immediate resumption of hostilities. Indeed, the truce agreed between Francis and the emperor held, after a fashion, for another nineteen months. There were several reasons for this unusually pacific state of affairs. Francis did not wish to be seen as an aggressive truce-breaker, and publicly continued to avow his new friendship with Charles. However, he was also slyly looking for a pretext to justify a declaration of war, not least because he was interested in re-establishing his previous alliance with the Turks. Discomforting the emperor by consorting with his enemies had been a tactic beloved of French diplomats, most notably Francis's ambassador in Istanbul, Antonio Rincón, to say nothing of their king.

As for Suleiman and his countrymen, despite their dismay at the Franco-imperial peace they had continued to maintain back-channels of communication, mainly through Rincón, who had busied himself re-establishing their good relations in 1540–41. It was therefore both a blow and an opportunity that Rincón was murdered by imperial troops on 4 July 1541, while travelling in north-eastern Italy during his return to Paris from Istanbul. Although Charles, perhaps spuriously, denied any involvement and ordered an enquiry, Francis could now claim that Charles had broken the truce and justify this as an excuse for action.

War was not declared immediately, however. Charles, unlike Francis, had taken up the pope's call to arms and was preparing to lead a crusade against the Muslims in North Africa. The French king, perhaps amused at his enemy's hapless and expensive occupation, declared showily that he could not possibly declare war while the emperor was engaged in so noble a cause. Delaying their own conflict by a few more months also gave Francis the advantage both in raising money and in finding a wider range of allies. Charles's involvement in the crusade proved disastrous: after autumn gales damaged the imperial fleet, destroying most of the ships and half the troops, the humiliated emperor was forced to abandon his siege of Algiers and was back in Spain by November 1541. Perhaps fittingly, some extremely good news for Francis came from Istanbul in the early months of 1542, with a deal brokered by Baron de la Garde, Rincón's equally able successor as French ambassador to Turkey. The alliance that he had so eagerly sought was offered to him: were he minded to declare war on the empire, he would be provisioned with extensive Ottoman reinforcements for both the army and the navy. On 12 July 1542 a singularly confident Francis declared war against the emperor, having agreed to an alliance that no other European ruler would have countenanced. His proclamation was that the murder of Rincón was 'an injury so great, so detestable and so strange to those who bear the title and quality of prince that it cannot be in any way forgiven, suffered or endured'.[10] It was read out across the country, quite literally to the sound of trumpets.

Given Francis's age and indisposition it was no longer practical for him to ride to war, and so his sons conducted the conflict in his stead. The dauphin laid siege to Perpignan for six weeks while Charles, Duke of Orléans, successfully captured Luxembourg to the north of France, before losing his nerve and heading down to Perpignan to join the siege. In his absence Luxembourg was soon retaken by the imperial forces. As the assault on Perpignan proved unsuccessful, 1542 ended with the French army in a far less auspicious position than might have been expected. The emperor, aware of this, decided to play a final trump card that might have been the end of France. Once more, an Anglo-imperial alliance was declared.

In January 1543 the English ambassador to France, William Paget, informed Henry VIII that Francis had become an enigmatic and elusive figure, and that it was extremely difficult to fathom his intentions. 'This king', he wrote, with exasperation, 'never sojourns two nights in one place, disposing himself as the report of great [hearts] is made to him, and continually removing at an hour's warning so that no man can tell where to find the Court.'[11] It was little wonder that Henry, tiring of his sometime friend and ally's quicksilver loyalties, decided that an alliance with the reliable emperor was more desirable. Therefore, after signing a secret treaty with Charles on 11 February, Henry formally declared war on 22 June. Francis was appalled at the news, realising that his chances of victory against the emperor were drastically reduced if his forces were to be split against him and the King of England. In desperation he said to Paget that 'if my good brother will join with me, tell him I will stick upon no money matters; he shall rule me as he list'. It was too late. Before July was over, an English army under the command of Sir John Wallop had invaded northern France, indicating that this alliance was no mere arrangement of words. A greater plan was soon hatched for an Anglo-imperial offensive, the so-called 'Enterprise of Paris'. This would entail a full-blown English invasion from Calais, with Charles marching from his territories in the Low Countries, before both parties converged on Paris.

Yet the prospect of a serious challenge to the French Crown was less imminent than Francis might have feared, and before long it was hoped that all parties would cease hostilities. Henry had attained his real objective of proving to Francis that he was still a foe to be reckoned with, and Charles, who might well have wished to continue the conflict, was too cash-strapped to be able to fight a war of this nature with any guaranteed success. As for the French king, he had mired himself in a succession of skirmishes and conflicts on too many fronts, and soon found that he had exhausted both his funds and his men. He occasionally enjoyed small successes, as in the recapture of Luxembourg in September 1543, but more often he was forced into his own unlikely alliances.

The pre-eminent force in Europe at that time was almost certainly Suleiman the Magnificent. He lived up to his epithet with a series of bold and daring assaults, in cohorts with the wild Barbarossa, which threw a figurative grenade into the world of European diplomacy. Perhaps Suleiman found a kindred spirit in Francis, or saw him as a useful intermediary in his attempt to rid the world of the Holy Roman Emperor, but he was a powerful, if intemperate, ally. His value was proved beyond measure in the summer of 1543 when Barbarossa, with a 110-strong armada, raided the coasts of Sicily and Italy before sailing for Marseilles, where he was joined by a French fleet of forty ships. Emboldened by the presence of the Turk, the combined Franco-Ottoman force headed for Nice, which collapsed under their attacks on 22 August. The population were sold into slavery; this enraged civilised Europe, which cavilled at the spectacle of 'the protector of the faith' enabling the infidel to carry out his atrocities upon his supposed allies.

The demonic Barbarossa could never be considered the most constant of friends. The first indication of trouble came in early September 1543, when the great pirate threatened to remove his ships unless he was given a naval base. Cowed by this inarguable threat, Francis ceded the town of Toulon to Barbarossa. He banished the port's inhabitants and oversaw the establishment of traditional Muslim institutions such as a mosque, a slave market and holy men clad in flowing golden robes. It was rather more exotic than anyone in France might ever have imagined; 'a second Constantinople' was all that people could describe it as. It housed around 30,000 Turks, including soldiers, captains, servants, slaves and all the accoutrements of an invading force. Yet, belying their bellicose appearance and actions, they behaved with strict and efficient discipline, and the feared outbreak of violence and pillage never occurred. It was not to be a second Sack of Rome.

Nonetheless, Francis watched the endgame of his courtship of the Turkish forces with unease. His image as 'The Most Christian King', as he had enjoyed styling himself, did not accord with the large and potentially dangerous Muslim population that so quickly flourished within his own country. He did not trust Barbarossa, who he correctly surmised was essentially ungovernable; the violence that he had visited upon his enemies was by no means controlled. Therefore he dragged his heels when it came to sanctioning the full military alliance that the Turks expected, much to their fury. Barbarossa was said to have 'showed himself very angry and made acid and sneering remarks'.[12] It was inevitable that this strange and doomed partnership would come to an end, which it duly did in May 1544. After being bribed to leave Toulon, Barbarossa and his men departed, although not before ransacking five French ships in the harbour to reprovision his own fleet. He then headed to Italy for an orgy of chaos and bloodletting, before eventually returning to Turkey on 10 August. Suleiman received his erstwhile protégé with all the good grace that a bloodthirsty buccaneer might deserve.

Perhaps as a result of his brief flirtation with the unthinkable, Francis chose to pursue conflicts that he stood a better chance of winning. There had been some good news earlier in the year, when Francis of Enghien, a prince of the blood and a royal cousin, had won a notable victory at Piedmont. Yet even this advantage could not be pressed as an imminent invasion from the Low Countries, led by Charles, meant that troops had to be redirected to where they were needed. It did not help Francis's equilibrium that Charles invaded Champagne armed with a ragtag assortment of 30,000 German soldiers and 7,000 cavalry, just as a 40,000-strong English army arrived in Calais in June, invading Boulogne on 19 July 1544. It began to look as if the ageing king had met his match at last in the form of the Anglo-imperial alliance, not least when the strategically important town of Saint-Dizier, under the command of the Count of Sancerre, surrendered to the emperor on 17 August 1544. It was said that Sancerre only gave in when he received a forged letter purportedly from the Duke of Guise ordering him to lay down his arms, a piece of trickery that was atypical of the usually straightforward Charles. It seemed as if the emperor was determined to crush his great adversary for ever. On 21 August he called a council of war, with the aim of deciding whether to march on Paris or retreat. Some advisers suggested caution, even withdrawal, but Charles decided that it was too late for half-measures. Therefore he finally began to march on the capital, with a view to settling matters once and for all.

Once, a belligerent Francis would have rode out to meet his old enemy in full battle regalia at the head of his troops. Now, ageing, ill and beset by anxiety, Francis retreated to his bed, fearing that his kingdom was about to be riven by destruction and carnage. He was said to have prayed, 'Oh, my God, you are making me pay very dear for a kingdom which I once thought you had given me freely enough. May your will be done!'[13] As he asked his ever-faithful sister Marguerite to pray for a resolution that would not end in the destruction of his people, he announced wildly: 'I am determined to go out and meet him and fight – I pray God to give me death in battle rather than make me endure another captivity!'[14]

Panic gripped the nation, as if in reaction to its king. One Venetian wondered: 'Who ever would have thought that the French would allow the invaders free passage and let them devastate their country?'[15] As Charles and his empire continued on their largely unchecked advance, Francis wrote to the Parisians to offer notional reassurance, saying: 'The enemy has been reduced to such straits that it is impossible for him to escape destruction', boasting emptily that 'I will save you from harm – I do not know the meaning of fear'. This apparent confidence was not reciprocated by the inhabitants of the city, who frantically held Masses and prayed for peace, even as those who could get up off their knees fled the capital. One chronicler reported that the city's roads were blocked with handcarts and terrified people, retreating 'for fear of the army of the Emperor which was drawing near.'[16] It seemed, at long last, as if Charles was to have his vengeance for all the innumerable slights and humiliations that had been visited upon him. It appeared inevitable that Paris would burn, and that Francis, like Priam, would gaze out upon his city and weep at the implacable enemy taking their long-awaited revenge.

CHAPTER 21

Salvation and Redemption

It was a consistent feature of Francis's reign that, when all seemed lost, a sudden stroke of good fortune would redeem matters, just as, poised at the moment of greatest triumph, he would manage to ruin his own success. And so it proved at the time of what threatened to be a notorious defeat. As Charles advanced on Paris, and fears of a second Sack of Rome terrified the population, the city's organisation had crumbled to the point where justice could no longer be administered, particularly as the city's lawyers had already fled. Panic spread, and Charles waited for Henry VIII to join him in administering the *coup de grâce*.

The English king never came. Finding the situation in Boulogne unexpectedly rewarding, he made the decision to turn his efforts from a potentially costly and dangerous expedition to a less ambitious but more personally lucrative achievement. He eventually accomplished this on 13 September. As a result the emperor, who at the beginning of September 1544 seemed to be on the verge of a truly peerless victory, came undone. He was not helped by the dauphin's ruthless adoption of a scorched-earth policy towards all the lands around Paris; bridges were destroyed, food and wine despoiled and anything that might have given help or succour to the invading army was laid waste. As a result, the imperial troops' mood changed from belligerent aggression to insubordinate mumbling. By 11 September it seemed clear that there would be no invasion of Paris. Charles's greatest opportunity was lost.

A week later, the Peace of Crépy was agreed between Charles and

Francis. The emperor, tiring of Henry's unwillingness to commit to a full invasion of France, decided that it was best to come to an agreement with his adversary. Accordingly, he signed a document that was of a surprisingly conciliatory nature, given the slaughter that had narrowly been avoided. Francis agreed to withdraw his troops from Savoy and Piedmont and to join in a crusade against the Turks. One can only imagine the French king finding this condition grimly amusing. A further clause in the agreement stated that Francis would marry his son Charles either to the emperor's daughter or to his niece, and as a result would receive either the Low Countries and Franche-Comté or, at long last, Milan as her dowry. In return the duke would be given the important duchies of Angoulême, Châtelleraut, Bourbon and Orléans.

Given the circumstances, it appeared to be the best that Francis could have hoped for. Queen Eleanor, relieved at the restoration of relations between her brother and husband, openly rejoiced at the treaty, believing it to be the work of God. Madame d'Étampes, who had masterminded the alliance, was also delighted, seeing it as a public display of her power. Her skilful manipulation of the king gave her every reason to believe in her continued security after Francis's death. It is even possible that she had committed treason by passing state secrets to the emperor. Others were less delighted, not least Suleiman, who, upon hearing that his former ally was now joining a crusade against him, had to be restrained from impaling the French ambassador who brought him the bad news.

Chief among the malcontents was the dauphin, who felt, not without reason, that the events at Crépy represented a weak capitulation both to the emperor and to his own brother, who seemed to be about to rule Milan while he was restricted to the less exciting duchy of Brittany. Francis had never made any secret of the preference he felt for his younger son, and Henri believed, with some justification, that the last years of his father's reign had seen him increasingly sidelined. He was also aware from whisperings at court that, once Francis died, he might potentially find himself facing an imperial-Orléanist alliance, with the emperor using Charles as a means of increasing his own influence. At the very least his brother would be as powerful a figure as he himself, leading to a significant power split at court. France was only just beginning to unite as a country after the factionalism that had plagued it for so long, and this had the potential to revive a dangerous and divisive situation.

On 12 December 1544 the dauphin took the unusual step of making a formal complaint about what he saw as the unfairness of the treaty; the accord that had so delighted his stepmother came crashing down. Although he had signed the treaty out of 'fear and reverence for my father',[1] he proceeded to cover himself by writing a secret denunciation of it, especially the manner in which it gave away inalienable Crown properties to three close members of his circle – Francis of Guise, Antoine of Bourbon and Bourbon's brother, the Count of Enghien. He was soon joined in his protest by the *parlement* of Toulouse, and it was likely that only Francis's repeated personal intervention with the Paris *parlement* saw its ratification. The treaty was without doubt the most foolhardy political act of the French king's reign, as it trusted in the harmonious marriage of Francis's son and a descendant of the emperor; given recent events this seemed, and indeed proved, impossible.

Had the dauphin been able to predict the outcome, he might have worried less. After the announcement of Charles's forth-coming marriage to the emperor's niece, Anna, and subsequent elevation to the duchy of Milan, Charles headed to Boulogne to join an expedition to relieve the siege that the city was under. Although there was an outbreak of illness, the duke behaved with typical sangfroid, saying: 'It makes no difference [to me] . . . no royal son of France ever died of plague.' In an abandoned village he even entered houses of the recently dead, for he believed himself to be above such trivialities. Unfortunately his hubris proved fatal and his history faulty, as he fell ill with plague and died on 9 September 1545. Although there were rumours that he had been poisoned by the jealous dauphin, who had accompanied him on campaign, there was no attempt at recriminations, as Francis was overwhelmed with sorrow at the death of his youngest and dearest son. The imperial ambassador witnessed the king's grief and commented: 'He wept for a long time, crying loudly and shedding tears in great quantity.'[2] The emperor wrote a letter of condolence to his erstwhile enemy, to which the king responded that '[he prayed] God will be so gracious to you so that you may never need such comfort nor feel what pain it is to lose a son'.

Both men knew, despite the formal pleasantries of the letters, that the death of Charles, Duke of Orléans, had also killed the peace treaty. The dauphin, who sincerely mourned his brother's death, was now Francis's only surviving child. The king attempted a much-needed reconciliation with his son, and from this time on tried to build a closer relationship. Henri refused the blandishments and offers of presiding over council meetings and other duties, commenting that 'everything goes ill at present'. The underlying implication was that, if anything was to go awry, he would not be the one who was blamed for it. Besides, he was all too aware of his father's declining health. He calculated that the old king had a matter of a few years to live, and he had no wish to see his inheritance compromised by any ill-fated decisions arrived at in haste, especially those influenced by Madame d'Étampes and her circle. Better to wait and see what he could accomplish in his own time.

This was not always handled as discreetly as it should have been, especially after wine had been taken. One night Henri and his familiars were sitting around discussing affairs of state. Believing that he was among friends and unattended, the dauphin announced that 'when he was King, he should name such and such persons marshals or grand-masters . . . [adding] that he should recall the Constable'.[3] His friend Francis de Vieilleville, who would later become a Marshal of France, later recalled that he was frightened that this loose talk might be overheard, and told Henri that he was 'selling the skin before the bear was killed', then prudently absented himself. Despite his years at court the dauphin had not learnt that there were spies at every corner, and in this case the sharp ears belonged to the king's fool, Briandas, who had been hiding in an alcove by a window in the dining room. Briandas wasted no time in heading to his master to inform him of Henri's plans, telling him: 'Francis de Valois, you are king no longer . . . you will soon see the Constable here, who will put you in prison where you will have to learn how to play the fool. Run away – you're a dead man!'[4]

The consequences were predictable. Francis, outraged by the presumption of the son whom he had never liked, decided that he should act with decisiveness and speed, and dispatched armed men to the dauphin's apartments. Thankfully for Henri's head, he had been tipped off about his father's wrath and made a narrow escape. When Francis discovered what had happened he flew into an even greater rage. Finding himself amidst the remains of the dinner abandoned by his son and his friends, he smashed furniture, crockery and cutlery against the walls, throwing them at unfortunate servants and generally creating havoc. Many of his frightened staff threw themselves out of nearby windows rather than run the risk of being injured or even killed by the king in a furious outbreak of temper. Henri did not return to court for over a month; some of the young nobles with him that night were banished for the remainder of Francis's reign. This was a heavy price to pay for some ill-timed gossip and boastfulness, but it proved an important lesson for the dauphin and his cronies.

In one regard at least, Henri was acting propitiously. Francis was dying. The last years of his reign had been dogged by outbreaks of ill health, but these were worsening in impact, as they had done ever since his collapse in 1539 when the emperor visited France. An especially unfortunate attack came at the beginning of 1545 while the king was at Fontainebleau, consisting of a fever brought about by an abscess in 'his lower parts'. This might or might not have been caused by the pox. After doctors cauterised the painful abscess, releasing a 'plentiful quantity of vile pus', Francis was prescribed a treatment of 'Chinese wood', a root traditionally used to cure syphilis, along with quicksilver, or mercury, a remedy suggested by his former comrade-in-arms Barbarossa. It was little wonder that, although on 7 February 1545 Francis pronounced himself fit and well again, the great lover had to admit that he was 'dead in respect of the ladies'.[5] None other than Marshal de Tavannes thought that 'ladies more than years caused his death,'[6] and it seemed at last that he was defeated by his own carnal exertions. He continued to make occasional forays into the bedchamber, normally without satisfactory results. His abscesses continued to burst throughout the course of the year; in January 1546 the imperial envoy declared in irritation that 'if the game lasts much longer, he may yet cease to play altogether'. At the age of fifty-one, the end threatened to come before the king had made his peace with either God or man.

Yet although Francis was approaching his death, he maintained the vigour and self-assurance of a younger man. He was still hunting in 1546, prompting the courtier Cavalli to say: 'Without knowing that he is the king or having beheld his portrait, there is not a foreigner who, seeing him, does not say "This is the king". He has an excellent complexion, a hale and hearty constitution . . . he eats and drinks very well, sleeps even better, and, what is more important, thinks of nothing but living joyfully without too many cares.'[7] Even allowing for the hyperbole of one who wanted to believe the best of the French monarch, there could be little doubt that, even in his decline, Francis still presented a formidable figure.

Yet Cavalli's description of his monarch living without care was pure fantasy. There had never been a point during Francis's long reign when he had been able to abandon the concerns of kingship, and so it proved, even towards the end. Ambassadors had to be liaised with, plots uncovered or laid and powerful courtiers checked. Ambition was a national pursuit, follwed by all the great and the good, and few were unwilling to argue their own case. A sense remained that, for a country so accustomed to Francis's reign, a great question mark hung over the future. It seemed as if what might be the final years, even months, of his influence represented the last opportunity for many to establish themselves, beyond the king's death and into the reign of his successor.

This fear was just as true for the various royal mistresses as for their lovers. Henri's lack of standing with Francis was mirrored by that of Diane de Poitiers. Although she had once been a favourite of the king's, she was banished from court in the autumn of 1544 at the explicit request of Madame d'Étampes. She sulkily retreated to her château at Anet, followed by an equally aggrieved Henri. If this proved that Francis's mistress still held the greatest sway at court, and would use it to both good and malicious ends, it also meant that Catherine of Medici, freed from the humiliation of having to play second fiddle to her husband's paramour, was able to come into her own. In particular she formed a relationship of great warmth with the king. Despite his lack of any sexual interest in her and his ill health, he was one of the few who saw her best qualities, and knew that she would make an excellent Queen of France after his death. He therefore offered her many signs of favour, not least the present of a ruby and diamond each worth 10,000 *écus* at Christmas 1544 to celebrate her pregnancy. It was a relief for him to find a bright and loyal woman who never showed her true feelings in public, and when she gave birth to her daughter Elisabeth on 2 April 1545, the king's rejoicing was as great as if it were his own child.

It was telling that, as Francis's reign drew to its close, Catherine became a far greater presence in his life than either his wife or his sister. Eleanor had no illusions that she would ever match Madame d'Étampes. Marguerite, meanwhile, spent most of her days in the intellectual pursuits that she considered most satisfying, not least the composition of her collection of stories, the *Heptaméron*, which she began in September 1546. It was a task that would occupy her for the rest of her life, and they would be published posthumously in 1558. It was around this time that the war with England would finally come to an end. Henry's stomach for conflict had declined just as prodigiously as his appetite for food and drink had grown, not least because of the unexpected loss of his flagship, the *Mary Rose*, on 19 July 1545. The great vessel had been overloaded with men and ordinance before an excess of sea water sank it, killing nearly everyone on board. As a result, the Anglo-French war that had been pursued without any great enthusiasm by either side began to splutter to a halt, not least because the emperor, unsurprisingly given the previous behaviour of both the French and the English, showed no interest in forming an alliance with either of them. As a result, on 7 June 1546 a peace was signed by which England agreed to hand back Boulogne in eight years' time, for a sum of between 800,000 and two million *écus*, to be paid in eight instalments.

At last, war was over. The conflict between England and France, which had dragged on for four years, became the most expensive of Francis's reign, costing in excess of thirty million *livres*. At a time when the exchequer was inundated with demands, raising money proved to be a difficult business. Yet the work of the nation had to continue, and in autumn 1546 Henri and Catherine embarked upon their first official royal progress together, to the eastern borders of France, to inspect the defences in case of any further attack. Catherine, who had recently given birth to two children, fell seriously ill during their journey, and Henri halted their progress and saw to it that she was taken to his castle at Saint-Marc and allowed time to recover. It was an unusual gesture of kindness and concern from her husband, who cared for Catherine with tenderness, and she was soon well once more; unlike many others, she was possessed of a sufficiently strong constitution to recover without incident.

Yet the spectre of death hovered over Francis and those around him as the decade wore on, enemies and former allies alike. The most significant was that of Henry VIII on 28 January 1547. This was giddily announced at court in early February by Madame d'Étampes, who ran into Queen Eleanor's bedchamber in the early hours of the morning and shouted: 'News! News! We have lost our chief enemy, and the King has commanded me to come and tell you of it!' Eleanor, correctly believing that the general perception was that France's chief enemy was her brother the emperor, was deeply upset, but soon recovered upon hearing the true facts.

She was to be alone in this. Although Henry and Francis had spent many years at war, it was largely without the personal enmity that had poisoned the French king and Charles V's relations. Had the emperor died, there would have been far greater rejoicing and relief, of a sincere nature. The French king's attitude towards the death of his counterpart was contradictory. On the one hand he was said to have been seen 'laughing much and enjoying himself with the ladies'[8] on the day that he learnt of Henry's death, but he was also reported, given his own progressively declining health, to have been much moved by the loss of a man who, for all the conflict and difficulty between them, had been 'a good and true friend'.[9] To hear that a king who was his mirror image in many regards had predeceased him left Francis 'more pensive than before', given that 'he feared that he might soon follow him'.[10] His woes were not assuaged by the story that, shortly after Henry's death, he received a message allegedly sent by the English king from his deathbed, reminding Francis that he, too, was mortal. Understandably, given the posthumous warning, the king fell into a depression and took to his bed.

It was a time of morbidity. The Count of Enghien was killed during a snowball fight at a château near Mantes, where the court was temporarily sequestered. Francis had organised the fight between two sides, one led by Henri and Francis of Guise, the other by Enghien, whom he regarded as a protégé of sorts. It was, typically, a rough, rude mock battle, and during it Enghien felt exhausted and momentarily paused for breath, sitting down beneath an upstairs window. It was later reported that 'some ill-advised person threw a linen chest out of the window, which fell on the Sieur d'Enghien's head and . . . he died a few days later'.[11] Although there were rumours of foul play, the truth was more prosaic: the consequences of excitable mock violence, often instigated by the king himself, could be fatal. The tragic demise of Enghien was the *coup de grâce* for Francis; it seemed that the end of everything was at hand.

In mid-February 1547 the monarch attempted to recapture the energy that had typified his reign for so many years. Gathering his court around him, he moved restlessly from château to château, travelling from Saint-Germain to Villepreux, Dampierre and Limours. Francis was keen to hunt, but his indisposition meant that, more often than not, he could do little other than be carried in a litter. Yet his ambitions continued to outstrip his physical abilities. He intended to head to Henry's memorial service in Paris, which he saw as an opportunity to pay homage to an old adversary and friend, but, as so often at this time, his body failed him. At the Château of Rambouillet he collapsed, and this time would not recover. The feverish fifty-two-year-old king was taken to a chamber, and all around him knew that he lay upon his deathbed.

The cause of Francis's final illness still remains unclear. Although it has traditionally been held that he suffered from syphilis, he remained lucid and comprehensible up until the moment of his death. It is more likely that he had contracted gonorrhoea from his extramarital affairs, and that, left untreated, this had led to further infections of his bladder and urinary tract. Certainly, he also suffered from serious organ disease: his stomach, kidneys, throat and

a lung were all but wasted away, leading one physician to comment
candidly that 'the King's insides were rotten'.[12] Francis had led an
extraordinarily full and eventful life, but now it was limping to its
conclusion.

By 20 March 1547 the king knew that his illness was fatal, and so
sought to settle his affairs, both spiritual and temporal. According
to the imperial ambassador Jean de Saint-Mauris, who was present,
'he knew it was all over with him and for that reason he would
devote his mind to God and examine his conscience, ordering that
no one should try to speak with him on matters of State'.[13] After
hearing Mass, he took communion and made his confession; he
publicly admitted his sins, including breaking the commandments
frequently and often riotously, but prayed that he would be shown
divine mercy. He then spoke to Henri, who had arrived at his bedside, with great earnestness, telling him about the wrongs that he
had committed during his reign, and how his son had to avoid the
pitfalls and snares to which he had been prey. Over the next few
days, when he was conscious and able, Francis attempted to instil
all that he had learnt of kingship in his son. He urged him to act as a
good and just ruler, one who could honour his people and maintain
the country's pride, and to act in the name of God. Perhaps mindful
of his own mistakes when it came to women, he took especial care
to warn his son against being influenced by them, admitting that
many of his own errors had been caused by loving not wisely, but
too well.

There were other, more specific, edicts. Francis advised Henri
against recalling Montmorency and, remembering what had been a
long and troubled rivalry, urged him to beware of the Guise family,
saying that their aim 'was to strip him and his children to their
doublets and his people to their shirts'.[14] If he had seen Francis of
Guise pacing around, anxious for the old king to die, he would
probably have redoubled his warnings, not least because Guise was
heard to murmur angrily, 'The old gentleman is leaving.'[15] He asked
that his son take care of Queen Eleanor, admitting that he had ignored and neglected his unfortunate wife, and asked, more in hope
than expectation, that his son should offer Madame d'Étampes his
protection, although he tempered this by saying, 'She is a lady . . .

do not submit yourself to the will of others, as I have to her.'[16] When the royal mistress, who had been denied entry to the royal bedchamber since 29 March and had been confined to a nearby room, heard her name mentioned, she attempted to gain entry. After being denied, she shouted with vitriol: 'May the earth swallow me up!', and when this failed to occur, left for the nearby Château of Limours. She never saw Francis again – an ill omen for her later treatment by his son.

Yet, with Madame d'Étampes dispatched, a new serenity came over Francis. He asked for extreme unction and, as he spoke one final time to Henri, stated that his conscience was clear, and that he could think of no man whom he had wronged or treated unfairly. 'The Most Christian King', at the last, embraced religion with a fervour that he had never truly displayed during his lifetime or reign. He heard repeated Masses, spoke of visions of the afterlife that he had seen and forgave his enemies. When he was still conscious he spoke to his son, indistinctly but with great urgency, and at one point held him fiercely in a tight embrace from which he would not release him until the dauphin 'fell into a swoon'.[17]

On Thursday, 31 March 1547, the end came, between one and two in the afternoon. After hearing a final Mass, Francis spoke faintly of the heavenly crowd awaiting him, and, after listening to a homily by the scholar and theologian Origen, kissed a proffered crucifix. Unable to speak more than a few words, he mumbled: 'In manus tuas, Domine, commendo spiritium meum' ('Into your hands, God, I commend my spirit'), and finally breathed the word 'Jesus'. As his strength deserted him the maker of modern France, *le Roi Chevalier* and the Renaissance king breathed his last. All around him considered it to have been an exemplary death, and one that did honour to a complex, flawed but brilliant man. His physical body had finally expired. Now it was time for the legend to begin.

CHAPTER 22

'Tears and Continual Lamentations'

When Francis died, those around him reacted in entirely different ways. Henri, who now became king, sprang into action with a clinical efficiency that offered a hint of how he would reign. He made preparations for his father's funeral that would both honour his glorious reputation and offer the mourning populace an unforgettable spectacle. Catherine, meanwhile, collapsed to the ground, head in her hands with grief and misery. She had been a near-constant presence at Francis's bedside during his final days, and had seen the best of him then, just as she had been inspired by his kindness and patronage during his reign. For all of the former king's undoubted mistakes, he had inspired his young apprentice. When she eventually came to protect France and the monarchy alone, she would invoke the name and example of the man who had protected her and seen to it that she had the potential to rise to her later eminence.

Yet immediately after his death, the twenty-seven-year-old Catherine rightly believed that she had been supplanted by her husband's mistress, Diane de Poitiers. Freed from the necessity of at least feigning an element of discretion, Diane soon saw to it that she availed herself of the many benefits that came with the position of royal mistress. She acted with the inflated dignity and hauteur that she had always possessed, but the prospect of untrammelled wealth now led to an unsightly contempt for propriety that saw the less showy Catherine pushed out of the limelight. She was now turned into little more than a royal consort and mother of the king's children. It was her rival who was the true power behind the throne, and the unfortunate queen was not allowed to forget it. Nor was this affection kept private. The Venetian ambassador, who observed something of Henri shortly before his accession, noted that his relationship with Diane resembled 'that between mother and son', and, with Oedipal overtones, that 'the lady has taken it upon herself to instruct, correct and counsel him'.[1]

The ambassador had other opinions of Henri as well. Unlike his priapic father, he was said to be 'little addicted to women', other than Diane. Instead he was seen as a complete change, indicating that this was to be a new kind of monarchy. He was described as 'not very ready with his answers when addressed, but very decided and very firm in his opinions, and what he has once said he adheres to with great tenacity'. Although he was decried for his 'not . . . very keen intellect', he was compared to autumn fruits, 'which ripen late, but which are, for that reason, better and more durable'. His Italian ambitions were described as honourable ('he supports Italians who are discontented with the affairs of their country') and, in contrast to Francis and his financial extravagance, he was praised for spending his money 'in a manner at once prudent and honourable'.[2] The implication was clear: Henri was to be a new king for a new age, and the conflicted legacy of his father would soon be built upon or replaced as seemed appropriate.

The new monarch wasted little time in establishing himself. He gave instructions for a grimly magnificent triple funeral, that of his father, elder brother Francis and younger brother Charles, whose bodies had remained at Tournon and Beauvais since their deaths. He also acted with alacrity in dispensing favour and dismissals alike; ever since the Peace of Crépy, which he considered both ignoble and humiliating, he wished to punish those responsible, and now had his chance. The most notable of his enemies was Madame d'Étampes, who had remained at Limours in a state of 'tears and continual lamentations' since Francis's death. She was a deeply unpopular figure, whose arrogance and sense of entitlement had made her many enemies. It was believed that, had she been forced to appear in public, an angry mob would have stoned her to death within moments. However, Henri was not interested in petty revenge. Although she was made to return precious jewels that Francis had given her, and much of her property, it soon became clear that the threat of judicial violence was not to be used against her. Much to her relief, she was allowed to retire in obscurity to one of her châteaux, where she spent her last years in contemplation and occasional acts of charity.

Francis's wife and sister were dealt with in a faintly haphazard fashion. Neither had done anything that merited punishment, but Henri had never been close to either, and so therefore was not inclined to reward them. Queen Eleanor, although allowed to remain in France, preferred to follow her brother the emperor to the Netherlands and to Spain, where she would eventually die in February 1558. Marguerite, meanwhile, learnt of her brother's death in strange circumstances. Nobody had wished to break the news to her when she was staying at Navarre, but she dreamt that Francis's ghost appeared, moaning, 'My sister! My sister!' Frightened that this was a premonition, she soon came across a nun, rendered insane with grief, who confirmed the news; furiously, she turned on her ladies-in-waiting, saying: 'You have tried to hide the death of the King from me, but God has told me through the mouth of this madwoman.' Bereft, she continued to write mystical verse, and died on 21 December 1549, an anachronism in this new France.

As many departed the court, one well-known figure returned. Henri and Montmorency had been close friends throughout much of the younger man's life, and the king had regarded Montmorency as the epitome of all that he wished to be as monarch: a great warrior, a chivalrous and learned man, and the proponent of solidly conservative values that would benefit France. The young king had long viewed him as a second and truer father, and so the constable was recalled almost immediately, and on the most generous of terms. After his partial downfall in 1541 he had languished on his estates, banished in all but name. Yet on 2 April 1547 Henri recalled his mentor to Saint-Germain-en-Laye, and the two men sat together for what was presumably a very warm and emotional couple of hours. When they emerged, Montmorency was nothing less than the second most powerful man in the kingdom once more. He had been created President of the King's Privy Council, with responsibility for all government matters, and answered only to Henri in all military and civilian affairs. It was apt that he should install himself within the recently vacated apartments of Madame d'Étampes; the old order had replaced the new. He was also awarded over 100,000 *écus* in recognition of the income that he had not drawn since his banishment, in addition to an annual salary of 25,000 *écus*, and was given the king's signet ring in an explicit sign of unparalleled favour. Those who dared whispered that it was not clear whom Henri loved more, Diane or Montmorency.

This early sign of royal favour showed the new king at his best and his worst. His loyalty and consistency to a man who had done virtually everything for him, including helping free him from his long captivity in Spain, was admirable, but in many respects he had chosen the wrong person to shower with honours. Montmorency was a conservative, unadventurous man who, while adept at military tactics, seldom displayed the originality or flair that the role of Constable demanded. Instead, he had a pedantic, know-it-all attitude that ignored everyone beneath him, and he made great show of his closeness to Henri in his aim to maintain the security of France and the continued glory of its king.

Unsurprisingly, Montmorency's behaviour soon infuriated those who had to deal with this arrogant and unyielding man. The Italian ambassador of the duchy of Ferrara scoffed that 'he is more insolent than ever before and provokes the hatred of men and women, and everyone in general',[3] and the papal nuncio said of him, contemptuously: 'This man is the most French, in word and act, of any that has ever been known . . . Do not suppose that he will ever resign himself . . . to any course which is not the most advantageous to his King.'[4] For all his pomposity, Montmorency was unbendingly, uncompromisingly loyal to king and country, while many around him would have used the position as a way to enrich themselves and their intimates. Although he saw to it that his nephews benefited from his return to favour, with the brilliant Gaspard de Coligny becoming Colonel-General of the infantry and his brother Ôdet, Cardinal de Châtillon, receiving yet more benefices, his first priority remained his surrogate son.

Others fared less well. The men who had been responsible

for running the government in the last years of Francis, Admiral Annebault and Cardinal Tournon, were both demoted. Annebault retained his position on the King's Council, albeit in a less important role, and lost his salary for the role of Admiral. Tournon, meanwhile, was dismissed from court altogether; although he had attempted to prove his credentials by staging a display of grief over Francis's corpse that would have done credit to an actor on the stage, Henri was unimpressed by such lachrymose excesses and forbade him a place at his side. He eventually found himself a position in Rome serving the newly elected Pope Julius III. There were many more who did not find any preferment under Henri, including the head of the Bourbon, Antoine, Duke of Vendôme, Marguerite's husband Henry, King of Navarre, and Henri's former boon companion Francis, Count of Enghien. These slights were not forgotten, and would return to haunt Henri later in his reign.

Yet it was Diane who dominated all, single-handedly tarnishing the new king's reputation for calculation and fairness. It was said of her that 'when her name was mentioned, it connoted nothing but the fortune she had acquired',[5] and the way in which she was lavishly showered with everything from jewels and fine clothing to honours and estates, including most of those that had belonged to Madame d'Étampes, made a mockery of the country's debts. Henri, who clearly was his father's son in his apparent inability to think beyond a woman who had enraptured him, entitled her to receive a tax levied on all office holders throughout the country whenever a new king ascended the throne. Additionally, and controversially, she was allowed the right to *les terres vagues*, or property in which the owners had died intestate or where there was otherwise no clear title, including those that had been confiscated from heretics. Diane received countless signs of favour, but nothing seemed enough for her. She demanded Chenonceau, which Francis had speciously appropriated from the finance minister early in his reign. An inalienable property of the Crown, it was the only château for which Catherine made a timid request, but she was denied even this small pleasure.

Henri remained captivated by his lover, and was therefore wilfully blind to the envy and contempt with which the distribution of his largesse was greeted by the rest of his people. One contemporary said of Diane and her family that 'Nothing escaped their greedy appetites as little as a fly escapes a swallow. Positions, dignities, bishoprics, every good morsel were all greedily snatched.'[6] As Henri dealt with his queen with a distracted and vague kindness, elevating her cousins, the Strozzi, to positions of importance and granting permission that she might refurbish her preferred residence in Paris, the Château des Tournelles, she knew that she would never compare to her rival, 'Madame'.

Yet for the population of France, the greatest priority was for there to be a fitting funeral for Henri's father. The new king, mindful of the importance of acts of pageantry on the grandest scale, decided that it would be the most magnificent one that the country had ever seen, simultaneously celebrating his predecessor and demonstrating his own glory. Thus he commissioned a death mask of Francis almost immediately from the artist Francis Clouet, before the former king's heart and entrails were removed from his body, and the corpse itself was embalmed in preparation for its formal burial.

This took place with great ceremonial pomp and grandeur. On 24 April 1547 the king's wooden and waxen effigy, which wore state robes and the imperial crown, was laid on a bed of state at Saint-Cloud, watched over by heralds at all hours of the day and celebrated as if it were the living king himself. Meals were served as if Francis had been alive to eat them, after being tasted by the Grand Master, with the formal preparations underlined by the singing of psalms and the recitation of grace. The whole façade was designed to perpetuate the old tradition that the king never died, but was instead reincarnated in another equally regal form. Queen Eleanor was not required to spend the customary six weeks in gloomy isolation, for even had she miraculously been pregnant with a son, Henri would still have ascended the throne as Francis's eldest boy.

This solemn pretence lasted until 4 May, when the effigy was replaced by the king's coffin, on which were arranged the great trappings of kingship, including his crown, sceptre and hand of justice. On 18 May Henri was seen in public beside the coffin for the first time, allowing the public to regard him as the new king, although he was still officially only dauphin. After sprinkling his father's body with holy water, he gave instructions that the coffin should be borne to Notre-Dame-des-Champs, where those of the royal sons, Francis and Charles, awaited their father for a final re-union, which took place on 21 May. The three of them remained in the cathedral overnight, as a vigil was kept by Francis's closest com-rades and servants. The next morning the *parlement* was admitted, and the final procession began.

The funeral cortège travelled from Notre-Dame-des-Champs to Notre-Dame-de-Paris on 22 May 1547, with an impressively vast number of mourners. Among these were the parish clergy, Francis's former bodyguard of his archers, hundreds of the city's poor and the town watchmen. Pride of place was reserved for the royal of-ficers and knights, who carried effects of the late king including his gloves, shield, coat of arms and helmet. The Master of the Horse, the Marquis de Boisy, rode in front of the effigy of Francis bearing the ceremonial sword of France, and Admiral Annebault, still at this stage in the royal company, rode behind the effigy along with the cardinals, ambassadors and other noblemen. The main funeral service took place on the following day, 23 May. Pierre du Chastel, Bishop of Mâcon, delivered the grand oration before the last rites were celebrated at Notre-Dame. A sombre banquet followed and the entire procession then reassembled for the journey to the Abbey of Saint-Denis, the final resting place of Francis and the two sons who had predeceased him. The whole impressive affair was said to have cost more than half a million *écus*, a staggering sum for a country that could ill afford the expense of such pageantry. Yet Henri was determined to honour his father in the most grandiose and ostentatious fashion. If it had cost double or treble the amount, he would have borne the cost without blinking.

Nonetheless, the new king's attitude towards his father's funeral was deeply ambivalent. Rather than take part in the solemn pro-cession himself, he had arranged to watch the cortège pass from a window in the rue Saint-Jacques that overlooked part of the route; he had to remain incognito until after the burials, as only then would he be officially proclaimed king. It was telling that, as he saw the splendid coffins and their effigies pass by his window, Henri's reaction was not what those around him might have expected; he was said to be 'very troubled and deeply aggrieved, even to the point of tears'.[7]

One of his confidants, Monsieur de Vieilleville, attempted to cheer his master by lauding his father's strengths and achievements as king. When this did not work, he tried a low but effective psychological ploy, namely rubbishing his younger brother Charles to check his mourning. Firstly, he announced that there had never been a more pernicious prince of France in the past three centuries than Charles, and, casting any tact aside, he claimed (probably accurately) that 'he never loved or esteemed you'.[8] As Henri continued to mourn, Vieilleville, warming to his theme with a vigour and gusto that few would have dared exhibit, recounted how, after a boating accident in which it was believed that Henri and his elder brother Francis had drowned, Charles had rejoiced, believing that he would now inherit the throne. When it became clear that they had survived he was stricken with depression, remarking with great bitterness that 'I renounce God; I shall never be anything but a nonentity.'[9] This disparagement of his brother and the sight of his coffin had an unusually invigorating effect on Henri, who remarked, as Charles's remains were carried past, 'See, there is the nonentity who leads the advance guard of my felicity!'[10]

As the procession wore to its end, the next rituals had to be observed. On 24 May the last rites were repeated, the effigies removed and the three coffins taken to the Saint-Denis vault. Heraldic rituals were observed in punctilious detail: the royal insignia were placed on Francis's coffin, stewards of the royal household threw their wands into the vault, and the ceremonial sword of state and the banner of France were lowered so that they touched the coffin. A herald cried out, 'Le Roi est mort' three times before then uttering the acclamation which signified the continuity of kingship: 'Vive le Roi!' The sword and banner were then raised and the ceremonies were declared to be at a close. The king never died, after all; he had simply been reborn in another person.

Although Henri had little interest in following his father's example, he knew that various obsequies had to be performed, the most notable of which was the commissioning of a suitably splendid tomb for his father. He chose the architect Philibert de l'Orme to design one that was based on the traditional Roman model, complete with triumphal arch, and the sculptor Pierre Bontemps, a veteran of Fontainebleau, carved a suitably mighty depiction of the late king, complete with bas-reliefs of his great achievements, such as the Battle of Marignano. Henri also ensured that his father was represented in the Palais de Justice by a full-length statue clad in the robes of state and holding a sceptre and hand of justice. Despite the absence of any great filial affection, he had fulfilled his public duties admirably.

As befitted tradition, the new king's coronation was to take place shortly afterwards, and was duly held on 26 July 1547 at Rheims Cathedral, just as his father's had been before him. Henri had made his official entry into the city the day before, in a riot of colour and pageantry. Naked nymphs and men dressed as the most licentious of all fabulous figures – the satyr – cavorted in the streets, which were decked with banners and flowers. The king was accompanied by his pregnant queen, who would give birth to a daughter, Claude, on 12 November. She had no illusions that he would pay her the attention that his mistress Diane would receive, and, although he greeted her 'fort honorablement', it was clear to any onlooker where his interest and affection lay.

Catherine's hurt at her husband's lack of consideration for her is likely to have been exacerbated by the events at the coronation. Although, as befitted both her status and her condition, she was given a prominent position with which to view her husband's crowning, she was upset by a cruel favour that was displayed upon his tunic as he entered the cathedral; it was covered with the embroidered and interlaced letters H and D. Yet, as before, Catherine said nothing but simply smiled and watched as her husband performed his accustomed part of the ancient ritual with the distinction, devotion and nobility that would become his defining features as a ruler. The new king prayed for a conspicuously long time, so much so that Diane asked him afterwards what had so occupied him that he had to take such an opportunity to engross himself. He replied that he had asked God to make his reign a long one if he believed that it would be good for France, and a short one if he was unable to act as an adequate ruler. He would reign for a little over twelve years – an impressive enough time, although nowhere near the thirty-two that his father managed.

During his coronation he made an oath to uphold the Catholic Church, and to expel all heretics. He was determined that, unlike his father, he would live up to his dignified title of 'The Most Christian King'. He had decided that he would be a ruler who would combine the ritualistic marriage between God, King and country, and one of his first tasks would be to drive the heretics from his land, before settling scores with an old enemy. When the crown of Charlemagne was placed upon his noble head, the assembled congregation broke into spontaneous – as far as anything that took place in such a gathering could be considered so – cheers of 'Vivat rex in aternum!' Following another monarchical tradition, Henri ensured that he distributed large amounts of gold and silver, specially minted for the occasion. The cries of joy and shouts of 'largesse' were echoed by the triumphant sound of trumpets.

The sullen, detached Henri was given great impetus by his kingship. One Venetian ambassador, Matteo Dandolo, had written five years previously that he had never seen him laugh, but now, freed at last from the necessity of being in his father's shadow and finally overcoming his dreadful sojourn in Spain, he seemed a changed man. Dandolo wrote to his master that 'I ought to assure you that he has become gay, that he has a ruddy complexion, and that he is in perfect health . . . his body is well proportioned, rather tall than otherwise.' Pausing to note that he was 'much addicted to tennis', Dandolo concluded, approvingly, that 'personally, he is all full of valour, very courageous and enterprising'.[11]

Yet the king was unable to find peace until he had waged war against his, and his father's, oldest adversary, Charles V, who watched the accession to the throne of his former captive with a mixture of interest and fear. The pope sent urgent entreaties to Henri to ask for help to avenge the killing of his son Pier Luigi, who had been murdered by imperial agents. While the new king was keen for war, Montmorency, fearing both the cost and loss of life in such a conflict, counselled against it. Additionally, there was no obvious ally for the new ruler, who would have to use his skills in diplomacy to acquire a greater standing within Europe. A consistent feature of Henri's character, which was largely alien to his father's, was a grim and dogged determination to achieve his desired ends, regardless of how long it took him or the cost, financial or otherwise. He had always believed that he, his father's least-favoured son, was pre-destined for kingship. When his elder brother, the dauphin, died, this conviction was justified; he now knew that he was destined for greatness. He had suffered undignified privations, and realised that he would struggle to be as popular a figure to his people as his father had been. Yet, for the sake of accomplishing his goals, he was prepared to wait and bide his time. Nobody had ever exacted revenge with haste or bluster. His calculating nature would serve him well as he sought the opportunity that he longed for – to further the glory of France, and fulfil his own ends at the same time.

EPILOGUE

Metz, 1552

Onwards.

Henri II had an implacable loathing of the Holy Roman Emperor. It was not the animosity that his father had felt for his long-standing nemesis, which, when affairs of state were settled, was common enough among most sparring European rulers at some time or another. This was a visceral, man-to-man hatred, originating in his long captivity at Charles V's hands. Henri had suffered an indignity that no royal prince had ever undergone and survived, being treated no better than a common criminal. He felt the humiliation keenly, even after he was crowned king. It is likely that his cold, brooding demeanour stemmed mainly from the privations to which he had been subjected during his Spanish imprisonment. Once he became king, he was bent on revenge at all costs. He did not have long to wait until he was in a position to take action.

Onwards.

It was on 12 February 1552 that the first stage in Henri's vengeance began. As he formally declared war upon the emperor, he feigned concern for the German territories that he claimed were rightfully his, but all around knew that this was a mere pretext. As he prepared to lead a mighty army of 50,000 men across France and into Germany, he entrusted the regency of his country to his wife, Catherine. It proved to be an invaluable experience for her.

The first few months of the campaign proceeded seamlessly. By April, Henri, Montmorency and his men had taken possession of several major cities, including Metz, Nancy and Toul. Henri showed both determination and diplomatic intelligence in his actions, taking the young Duke of Bar, an imperial prince and great-nephew of Charles V, out of Nancy, against his mother's wishes, and sending him to the French court to be brought up as if he were his own son. His eventual intention was to marry him to his own daughter, Claude, creating a quasi-incestuous frisson that he hoped would lead to further humiliation on the part of the emperor.

Throughout the first half of the year he encountered next to no resistance, armed or political, to his advance. The German princes bore no love for Charles and were happy to accommodate Henri, but they continued to warn him that the emperor was not as passive or stupid as he seemed to believe. Henri treated his adversary with contempt, knowing that he suffered from gout and, like his father by the end, acted like a much older man, but he underestimated his enemy's pride. Francis had got the better of Charles through his stratagems and cunning; the emperor was damned if he was going to suffer at the hands of Francis's son. It was time, he decided, that the empire struck back.

Onwards.

On 10 November 1552 Charles began his counter-attack, with the initial intention of recovering Metz. He brought with him an impressive force of 55,000 men, 150 guns and the sense of outraged righteousness that he hoped would ensure that his troops would fight on his behalf with the anger and determination that they would need to win a just victory. He reckoned without a cunning and able enemy, led by Francis of Guise, the defender of Metz. Although Guise had far fewer men at his command, he could count on Camillo Marini, an Italian engineer, and Jean de Saint-Rémy, a mining expert, who were able to respond to any of the various attacks with swift and efficient assistance.

It also frustrated Charles's attacks that the people he was attempting to subdue – his former subjects – felt no great love for their erstwhile master. As a result, not only were they happy to assist the

French to repair Metz, but they repelled the attacks with vigour and determination. Before long Charles's army began to lose heart. As autumn turned into winter, his men became cold and hungry, not helped by his lack of resources. On 3 January 1553 Charles admitted defeat and humiliatingly slunk away, leaving Henri and his forces triumphant.

The young king was grandiloquent in his victory. There were thanksgiving services throughout the country, and Guise held a triumphal parade in Metz, where the Mantuan ambassador, much moved by the scale of what had occurred, declared that 'there is no one among those who was at Metz who does not praise the courtesy and good government of Monsieur de Guise so that he is adored today by the whole kingdom'.[1]

Technically it was Guise's victory. Yet there was no Frenchman who did not know that the credit lay with the king. Through bold and daring action, Henri had managed a great victory against Charles that avenged his captivity, that of his father and the many insults that had been directed towards France, since, one might argue, Charles had stolen the office of the Holy Roman Emperor from Francis. Although this was a biased and partisan misreading of history, it chimed with the new mood that the French victory had aroused. It was little coincidence that Charles, exhausted and humiliated by his defeat, began the slow process of abdication before his death from malaria, alone in a monastery, on 21 September 1558. It was noted that he was surrounded by clocks, as if he were trying somehow to recapture the time that he had lost.

The battle was won; what became the Italian War of 1551–9 was not. And Henri himself only outlived his enemy by less than a year, dying in a jousting accident on 10 July 1559. With his death another age arrived, that of his much-maligned and ignored wife, Catherine of Medici. She rose from her early years as a timid, put-upon girl to being the most powerful woman in sixteenth-century Europe; it was a remarkable and brilliant progression that Francis and Henri had begun but that she would finish, becoming a legend in the process.

Onwards!

NOTES

CHAPTER 1: *A Prophecy Fulfilled*

1 Desmond Seward, *Prince of the Renaissance: The Life of François I* (London: Constable, 1973), p. 14
2 Ibid., p. 15
3 Edith Sichel, *Women and Men of the French Renaissance* (London: Constable, 1902), p. 78
4 Robert J. Knecht, *Renaissance Warrior and Patron: The Reign of Francis I* (Cambridge: the University Press, 1994), p. 4
5 Seward, p. 17
6 Ibid., p. 21
7 Ibid., p. 18
8 Knecht, p. 8
9 Seward, p. 22

CHAPTER 2: *A Game of Thrones*

1 Julia Pardoe, *The Court and Reign of Francis I* (Cambridge: the University Press, 1849), p. 15
2 Seward, p. 21
3 Sichel, pp. 78–91
4 Martha Walker Freer, *The Life of Marguerite of Angoulême* (Cambridge: the University Press, 1895), p. 16
5 Voltaire, M. de, *Abregé de l'histoire universelle, depuis Charlemagne jusques à Charlequint*, in M. Gailliard, *Histoire de François I, Roi de France* (Paris: 1776–9)
6 Sichel, loc. cit.
7 Knecht, pp. 12–14
8 Fleuranges, Robert III de La Marck, *Mémoires du Maréchal de Florange, dit le Jeune Adventureaux* (Paris: R. Goubaux, 1913), p. 219
9 Pierre de Bourdeille, Abbé de Brantôme, trans. Alec Brown, *The Lives of Gallant Ladies* (London: Panther Books, 1965)
10 Seward, p. 34
11 Ibid.
12 Ibid.

CHAPTER 3: '*The King Never Dies*'

1 Erin A. Sadlack, *The French Queen's Letters: Mary Tudor Brandon and the Politics of Marriage in Sixteenth-Century Europe* (London: Palgrave Macmillan, 2011), p. 44
2 Seward, p. 35
3 J. Bacon, *The Life and Times of Francis the First, King of France* (London: Edward Bull, 1830), p. 113
4 Knecht, p. 16
5 Leanda de Lisle, *Tudor: The Family*

Story (London: Chatto & Windus, 2013), p. 142

6 Seward, p. 38

7 Walker Freer, p. 16

8 R. E. Giesey, *The Funeral Ceremony in Renaissance France* (Geneva: Libraire E. Droz, 1960), p 84

9 Ibid., p. 39

10 Knecht, p. 42

11 Ivan Cloulas, *Diane de Poitiers* (Paris: Fayard, 1997), p. 30

CHAPTER 4: *'Swimming in French Blood'*

1 Seward, p. 43

2 Knecht, p. 70

3 Seward, p. 48

4 Knecht, p. 72

5 Seward, p. 50

6 Ibid., p. 51

7 Ibid., p. 52

8 Ibid.

9 Ibid.

10 Ibid., p. 55

11 Ibid.

12 Ibid., p. 57

CHAPTER 5: *A Good and Honest Man*

1 Seward, p. 61

2 Leonie Frieda, *Catherine de Medici* (London: Weidenfeld & Nicolson, 2003), p. 15

3 Seward, p. 64

4 Ibid., p. 66

5 Knecht, p. 84

6 Seward, p. 64

CHAPTER 6: *A New King of France*

1 Knecht, p. 105

2 Ibid., p. 107

3 John Julius Norwich, *Four Princes: Henry VIII, Francis I, Charles V, Suleiman the Magnificent and the Obsessions that Forged Modern*

Europe (London: John Murray, 2016), p. 11

4 Seward, p. 103

5 Knecht, p. 153

6 Seward, p. 88

7 Ibid.

8 Ibid.

9 Ibid., p. 95

10 Ibid.

11 Charles Terrasse, *François I: le Roi et le Règne* (Paris: [B Grasset, 1948), vol. I, p. 221

12 Norwich, p. 10

13 Seward, p. 70

14 Ibid., pp. 69–70

15 Ibid., p. 73

16 Ibid., p. 104

17 Ibid., p. 74

CHAPTER 7: *The End of Ambition*

1 Seward, p. 77

2 H. N. Williams, *Henry II: His Court and Times* (London: Methuen, 1910), p. 8

3 Manuel Fernandez Alvarez, *Charles V: Elected Emperor and Hereditary Ruler* (London: Thames & Hudson, 1975), p. 30

4 Seward, p. 78

5 Frieda, p. 19

6 Ibid., pp. 19–20

7 Ibid., p. 14

8 Paul Van Dyke, *Catherine de Médicis* (London: John Murray, 1923), p. 7

9 Frieda, p. 14

10 Knecht, p. 107

11 Seward, p. 78

CHAPTER 8: *The Field of the Cloth of Gold*

1 J. J. Scarisbrick, *Henry VIII* (London and New Haven: Yale University Press, 1997), p. 74

2 Ibid.
3 Knecht, p. 170
4 Seward, p. 79
5 Ibid.
6 Ibid., p. 81
7 Ibid., p. 80
8 Ibid.
9 Knecht, p. 171
10 Seward, p. 82
11 Ibid., p. 84
12 Scarisbrick, p. 79

CHAPTER 9: *Consequences*

1 Seward, p. 114
2 Ibid.
3 Ibid., p. 116
4 Alvarez, p. 42
5 Knecht, p. 177
6 Ibid., p. 178
7 Ibid., p. 179
8 Seward, p. 117
9 Knecht, p. 179
10 Ibid.
11 Ibid., p. 180
12 Charles Terrasse, 'As Amorous As
   A Cat' (Paris: B. Grasset, 1945),
   p. 18
13 Ibid., p. 182
14 Seward, p. 118
15 Ibid.

CHAPTER 10: *The Enemy Within*

1 Knecht, p. 201
2 Ibid., p. 203
3 Seward, p. 120
4 Ibid.
5 Knecht, pp. 206–7
6 Ibid.
7 Seward, p. 126
8 Ibid., p. 127
9 Knecht, p. 209
10 Ibid., pp. 127–8

CHAPTER 11: *Nothing Remains Save Honour*

1 Seward, p. 128
2 Knecht, p. 216
3 Ibid., p. 218
4 Seward, p. 130
5 Ibid.
6 Ibid., p. 134
7 Ibid., p. 135
8 Ibid., p. 137
9 Ibid., p. 136

CHAPTER 12: *The King Without a Country*

1 Stewart MacDonald, *Charles
   V: Ruler, Dynast and Defender of
   the Faith* (London: Hodder &
   Stoughton, 2000), p. 75
2 Ibid.
3 Seward, p. 137
4 Ibid.
5 Knecht, p. 227
6 Ibid., p. 240
7 Raffaele Tamalio (ed.), *The Private
   Correspondence of Federico Gonzago
   at the Court of Francis I of France*
   (Paris: 1994) (cit. Frieda, p. 34)
8 Seward, p. 138
9 Alistair Horne, *Friend or Foe:
   An Anglo-Saxon History of France*
   (London: Weidenfeld & Nicolson,
   2004), p. 234

CHAPTER 13: *A King Restored*

1 Knecht, p. 245
2 M. Félibien, *Histoire de la ville de
   Paris*, vol. 2 (Paris: 1725), p. 973 (cit.
   Knecht, p. 245)
3 Ibid.
4 Williams, p. 38
5 Ibid.
6 Ibid., p. 39

CHAPTER 14: *A Reversal of Fortune*

1 *State Papers of Henry VIII* (London: 1830–52), vol. 6, p. 58 (cit. Knecht, p. 250)
2 Seward, p. 145
3 Nicolas Versoris, ed. G Fagniez, *Livre de raison de Me Nicolas Versoris, avocat au Parlement de Paris, 1519–1530* (Paris: 1885), p. 106
4 Knecht, p. 255
5 Jocelyn Hunt, *Spain 1478–1598* (London: Routledge, 2000), p. 66
6 *Letters and Papers, Foreign and Domestic of the Reign of Henry VIII*, ed. J. S. Brewer, J. Gardiner and R. H. Brodie (London: 1862–1910) (cit. Knecht, p. 257)
7 Frieda, p. 41

CHAPTER 15: *Violent Beginnings and Peaceful Ends*

1 L. von Pastor, trans. F. I. Antrobus and R. F. Kerr, *The History of the Popes* (London: 1891–1933), vol. 9, pp. 323-4 (cit. Knecht, p. 257)]
2 Ibid., p. 345
3 F. Mignet, *La Rivalité de François Ier et de Charles-Quint* (Paris: 1875), pp. 289–90) (cit. Knecht, p. 259)
4 Seward, p. 149
5 Ibid., p. 150
6 David Starkey (ed.), *Henry VIII: A European Court in England* (London: Collins & Brown, 1991), pp. 96–7
7 *Calendar of State Papers, Spanish*, ed. G. Bergenroth, P. de Gayangos and M. A. S Hume (London: 1864–98) (cit. Knecht, p. 279)
8 Terrasse, vol. 2, p. 116
9 Williams, p. 62

CHAPTER 16: *A Trio of Marriages*

1 Knecht, p. 289
2 Frieda, p. 46

3 *State Papers of Henry VIII*, vol. 7, p. 891
4 *Letters and Papers*, vol. 6, p. 682
5 Ibid.
6 Patricia F. and Rouben C. Cholakian, *Marguerite of Navarre: Mother of the Renaissance* (New York: Columbia University Press, 2005), pp. 200–202
7 Seward, p. 180
8 Ivan Cloulas, *Catherine de Médicis* (Paris: Fayard, 1979), p. 65
9 Ibid.
10 Ibid., p. 66
11 Ibid., p. 67

CHAPTER 17: *Allies of Necessity*

1 Norwich, p. 89
2 Cloulas, *Catherine de Médicis*, p. 54
3 Édith Garnier, *L'Alliance Impie. François 1er et Soliman le Magnifique contre Charles V* (Paris: Éditions du Felin, 2008), p. 7
4 Knecht, p. 318
5 Seward, p. 185
6 *Calendar of State Papers, Spanish*, vol. 5, part 1, no. 130
7 H. Jedin, trans. E. Graf, *A History of the Council of Trent* (London: Nelson, 1957–61), vol. 1, p. 300
8 M. François, *Le Cardinal François de Tournon* (Paris, 1951), p. 126

CHAPTER 18: *Friendships Old and New*

1 Seward, p. 191
2 Ibid., p. 192
3 Ibid.
4 Ibid., p. 197
5 Ibid.

CHAPTER 19: *God Governs the Hearts of Men*

1 Terrasse, vol. 2, p. 293

2 Knecht, p. 388

3 Seward, p. 221

4 Jack Lang, *François Ier: Ou le rêve Italien* (Paris: Perrin, 1997), pp. 398–400

5 Knecht, p. 391

6 François Decrue, *Anne de Montmorency à la cour, aux armées et au conseil du roi* (Paris: 1885), p. 167

7 Ibid.

8 François, p. 179

9 François Decrue, *De consilio regis Francisci I* (Paris: 1885), p. 341

10 Knecht, p. 395

11 Ibid., p. 445

12 P. Guilbert, *Description historique des château, bourg et forêt de Fontainebleau* (Paris: 1731), vol. 2, p. 262

13 *State Papers of Henry VIII*, vol. 8, pp. 482–4

14 Giorgio Vasari, *Vies des Artistes* (Paris: Bernard Grasset, 2007), p. 217

15 *The Life of Benvenuto Cellini Written by Himself*, trans. J. A. Symonds, ed. J. Pope-Hennessy (London: Phaidon, 1949), p. 264

16 Ibid., pp. 106–15

17 Ibid., pp. 142–4

18 Ibid., pp. 144–6

19 M. A. Screech, *Rabelais* (London: Duckworth, 1979), p. 182

CHAPTER 20: *'In Spite of These Wretched Backbiters'*

1 Frieda, p. 49

2 Cloulas, *Catherine de Médicis*, p. 56

3 Ibid., p. 57

4 Frieda, p. 54

5 Jean Orieux, *Catherine de Médicis ou la reine noire* (Paris: Flammarion, 1998), p. 115

6 Sichel, pp. 37–9

7 Cloulas, p. 71

8 Knecht, p. 41

9 Ibid., p. 497

10 G. Guiffrey, *Procès criminel de Jehan de Poytiers, seigneur de Saint-Vallier* (Paris: 1867), p. 392

11 *Letters and Papers*, vol. 18, p. 29

12 Seward, p. 235

13 Ibid., p. 238

14 Ibid.

15 A. Rozet and J.-F. Lembey, *L'invasion de la France et le siège de Saint-Dizier par Charles-Quint en 1544* (Paris:1910), p. 178

16 Knecht, p. 492

CHAPTER 21: *Salvation and Redemption*

1 Frieda, p. 63

2 Seward, p. 241

3 Williams, p. 164

4 Seward, p. 245

5 Knecht, p. 495

6 Seward, p. 244

7 J. Jacquart, *François Ier* (Paris: Fayard, 1981), p. 389

8 *Calendar of State Papers, Spanish*, vol. 9, p. 493

9 Knecht, p. 541

10 Frieda, p. 77

11 Williams, p. 169

12 Knecht, p. 544

13 Seward, p. 245

14 Williams, p. 171

15 Frieda, p. 69

16 Williams, p. 171

17 Frieda, p. 69

CHAPTER 22: *'Tears and Continual Lamentations'*

1 Williams, p. 168

2 Ibid.

3 Frieda, p. 72

4 Ralph Roederer, *Catherine de*

Medici and the Lost Revolution
(London: Harrap, 1937), p. 60

5 Ibid., p. 66

6 Frederic Baumgartner, *Henry II:
King of France 1547–1599* (Durham,
NC: Duke University Press, 1988),
p. 57

7 Frieda, p. 77

8 Williams, p. 191

9 Ibid., p. 192

10 Ibid., p. 193

11 Ibid., p. 216

Epilogue

1 Knecht, p. 218

BIBLIOGRAPHY

Adamson, John (ed.), *The Princely Courts of Europe 1500–1750*
     (London: Weidenfeld & Nicolson, 1999)
Alvarez, Manuel Fernandez, *Charles V: Elected Emperor and
     Hereditary Ruler* (London: Thames & Hudson, 1975)
Ariès, Philippe and Duby, Georges (eds), *A History of Private Life:
     Revelations of the Medieval World*, trans. Arthur Goldhammer
     (Cambridge, MA: Belknap Press, 1988)

Bacon, J., *The Life and Times of Francis the First, King of France*
     (London: Edward Bull, 1830)
Baldwin Smith, Laccy, *The Elizabethan Epic* (London: Panther Books,
     1969)
Baumgartner, Frederic, *Henry II: King of France 1547–1599* (Durham,
     NC: Duke University Press, 1988)
Bennassar, Bartolomé and Jacquart, Jean, *Le XVIe Siècle*, 3rd edn
     (Paris: Armand Colin, 1997)
Bergin, Joseph, *Cardinal Richelieu: Power and the Pursuit of Wealth*
     (London and New Haven: Yale University Press, 1985)
Bicheno, Hugh, *Vendetta: High Art and Low Cunning at the Birth of the
     Renaissance* (London: Weidenfeld & Nicolson, 2008)
Blunt, Anthony, *Artistic Theory in Italy 1450–1600* (Oxford: the
     University Press, 1962/1978)
Bourdeille, Pierre de, Abbé de Brantôme, *The Lives of Gallant Ladies*,
     trans. Alec Brown (London: Panther Books, 1965)
Bowen, Marjorie, *Mary Queen of Scots* (London: Sphere Books, 1971)

Bradford, Sarah, *Cesare Borgia: His Life and Times* (London: Weidenfeld & Nicolson, 1976)

Briggs, Robin, *Early Modern France 1560–1715* (Oxford: the University Press, 1977)

Calendar of State Papers, Spanish, ed. G. Bergenroth, P. de Gayangos and M. A. S. Hume (London: 1864–98)

The Cambridge Modern History, vol. 1, *The Renaissance*, ed. A. W. Ward, G. W. Prothero and Stanley Leathes (Cambridge: the University Press, 1907)

The Cambridge Modern History, vol. 2, *The Reformation*, ed. A. W. Ward, G. W Prothero and Stanley Leathes (Cambridge: the University Press, 1907)

Carroll, Stuart, *Noble Power During the French Wars of Religion: The Guise Affinity and the Catholic Cause in Normandy* (Cambridge: the University Press, 1998)

Cartwright, Julia, *Beatrice d'Este, Duchess of Milan 1475–1497: A Study of the Renaissance*, 2nd edn (London: J. M. Dent & Co., 1908)

Cartwright, Julia, *Isabella d'Este Marchioness of Mantua 1474–1539*, vol. 2 (Hawaii: University Press of the Pacific, 2002)

Castelot, André, *François Ier* (Paris: Perrin, 1983)

Castelot, André, *Diane, Henri, Catherine – le Triangle Royal* (Paris: Perrin, 1997)

Castiglione, Baldesar, *The Courtier*, trans. George Bull (London: Penguin Books, 2003)

Castor, Helen, *She-Wolves: The Women Who Ruled England Before Elizabeth* (London: Faber & Faber, 2010)

Cellini, Benvenuto, *The Life of Benvenuto Cellini Written by Himself*, trans. J. A. Symonds, ed. J. Pope-Hennessy (London: Phaidon, 1949)

Chastel, André, *French Art: The Renaissance 1430–1620*, trans. Deke Dusinberre (Paris: Flammarion, 1995)

Cholakian, Patricia F. and Rouben C., *Marguerite of Navarre: Mother of the Renaissance* (New York: Columbia University Press, 2005)

Clark, Kenneth, *Civilisation: A Personal View* (London: British Broadcasting Corporation & John Murray, 1971)

Cloulas, Ivan, *Catherine de Médicis* (Paris: Fayard, 1979)

Cloulas, Ivan, *La vie quotidienne dans les châteaux de la Loire au temps de la Renaissance* (Paris: Hachette, 1983)

Cloulas, Ivan, *Henri II* (Paris: Fayard, 1985)

Cloulas, Ivan, *Philippe II* (Paris: Fayard, 1992)

Cloulas, Ivan, *Diane de Poitiers* (Paris: Fayard, 1997)

Collis, Louise, *Memoirs of a Medieval Woman: The Life and Times of Margery Kempe* (New York: Harper & Row, 1983)

Cronin, Vincent, *Louis XIV* (London: Collins Harvill, 1990)

Davies, Robert C. and Lindsmith, Beth, *Renaissance People: Lives that Shaped the Modern Age* (London: Thames & Hudson, 2011)

Decrue, François, *Anne de Montmorency à la cour, aux armées et au conseil du roi* (Paris: 1885)

Dictionnaire de l'Ancien Régime: Royaume de France XVIe–XVIIIe Siècle, ed. Lucien Bély (Paris: Presses Universitaires de France, 1996)

Félibien, M., *Histoire de la ville de Paris* (Paris: 1725), vol. 2

Fleuranges, Robert III de La Marck, *Mémoires du Maréchal de Florange, dit le Jeune Adventureaux* (Paris: R. Goubaux, 1913)

Fossi, Gloria, *Uffizi Gallery: The Official Guide, All of the Works* (Florence: Giunti & Firenze Musei, 2004)

François, M., *Le Cardinal François de Tournon* (Paris: 1951)

Fraser, Antonia, *Mary Queen of Scots* (London: Panther Books, 1970)

Fraser, Antonia, *The Six Wives of Henry VIII* (London: Weidenfeld & Nicolson, 1992)

Frieda, Leonie, *Catherine de Medici* (London: Weidenfeld & Nicolson, 2004)

Frieda, Leonie, *The Deadly Sisterhood: A Story of Women, Power and Intrigue in the Italian Renaissance* (London: Phoenix, 2013)

Gallo, Max, *François Ier: Roi de France, Roi-Chevalier, Prince de la Renaissance Française 1494–1547* (Paris: XO Editions, 2014)

Garnier, Édith, *L'Alliance Impie. François Ier et Soliman le Magnifique contre Charles V* (Paris: Éditions du Felin, 2008)

Garrisson, Janine, *Les Derniers Valois* (Paris: Fayard, 2001)

Giesey, R. E., *The Funeral Ceremony in Renaissance France* (Geneva: Libraire E. Droz, 1960)

Giono, Jean, *The Battle of Pavia: 24th February 1525*, trans. and ed. A. E. Murch (London: Peter Owen, 1965)

Goubert, Pierre, *Initiation à l'histoire de la France* (Paris: Fayard-Tallandier, 1984)

Guiffrey, G., *Procès criminel de Jehan de Poytiers, seigneur de Saint-Vallier* (Paris: 1867)

Guilbert, P., *Description historique des château, bourg et forêt de Fontainebleau* (Paris: 1731)

Haggard, Lieut.-Col. C. P. Andrew, *Two Great Rivals: François I & Charles V and The Women Who Influenced Them* (London: Hutchinson, 1910)

Hall, Peter, *Cities in Civilization* (London: Weidenfeld & Nicolson, 1998)

Hare, Christopher, *The Most Illustrious Ladies of the Italian Renaissance* (London: Harper & Brothers, 1907)

Hook, Judith, *The Sack of Rome 1527*, 2nd edn (London: Palgrave Macmillan, 2004)

Horne, Alistair, *Seven Ages of Paris: Portrait of a City* (London: Macmillan, 2002)

Horne, Alistair, *Friend or Foe: An Anglo-Saxon History of France* (London: Weidenfeld & Nicolson, 2004)

Hunt, Jocelyn, *Spain 1478–1598* (London: Routledge, 2000)

Jacquart, Jean, *François Ier* (Paris: Fayard, 1981)

Jardine, Lisa, *Worldly Goods: A New History of the Renaissance* (London: Papermac, 1997)

Jedin, H., *A History of the Council of Trent*, trans. E. Graf (London: Thomas Nelson & Sons, 1957–61)

Johnson, Paul, *The Renaissance* (London: Weidenfeld & Nicolson, 2000)

Kent, HRH Princess Michael, *The Serpent and the Moon: Two Rivals for the Love of a Renaissance King* (New York: Touchstone [Simon & Schuster], 2004)

Knecht, Robert J., *Renaissance Warrior and Patron: The Reign of Francis I* (Cambridge: the University Press, 1994)

Knecht, Robert J., *The Rise and Fall of Renaissance France* (London: Fontana, 1996)

Knecht, Robert J., *The Valois Kings of France 1328–1589* (London: Hambledon & London, 2004)

Knecht, Robert J., *The French Renaissance Court 1483–1589* (London and New Haven: Yale University Press, 2008)

Koenigsberger, H. G., Mosse, George and Bowler, G. Q., *Europe in the Sixteenth Century*, 2nd edn (London: Longman, 1989)

Lang, Jack, *François Ier: Ou le rêve Italien* (Paris: Perrin, 1997)

Lebrun, François, *La vie conjugale sous l'Ancien Régime* (Paris: Armand Colin, 1998)

Leonardo: Art & Science, ed. Enrico Crispin (Italy: Giunti, 2005)

Letters and Papers, Foreign and Domestic of the Reign of Henry VIII, ed. J. S. Brewer, J. Gardiner and R. H. Brodie (London: 1862–1910)

Lev, Elizabeth, *The Tigress of Forlì: Renaissance Italy's Most Courageous and Notorious Countess, Caterina Riario Sforza de'Medici* (New York: Houghton Mifflin Harcourt, 2011)

Lisle, Leanda de, *Tudor: The Family Story* (London: Chatto & Windus, 2013)

Lotherington, John (ed.), *Years of Renewal: European History 1470–1600* (London: Hodder & Stoughton, 1998)

Lubkin, Gregory, *A Renaissance Court: Milan Under Galeazzo Maria Sforza* (Oakland, CA.: University of California Press, 1994)

MacDonald, Stewart, *Charles V: Ruler, Dynast and Defender of the Faith* (London: Hodder & Stoughton, 2000)

Machiavelli, Niccolò, *The Prince*, trans. George Bull (London: Penguin Books, 1999)

Maguire, Yvonne, *The Women of the Medici* (London: George Routledge & Sons, 1927)

Malaguzzi, Silvia, *Botticelli: The Artist and His Works* (Florence: Giunti & Firenze Musei, 2003)

Michon, Cédric, *Les Conseillers de François 1er* (Rennes: Presses Universitaires de Rennes, 2011)

Mignet, F., *La Rivalité de François Ier et de Charles-Quint* (Paris: 1875)

Miquel, Pierre, *Histoire de la France* (Paris: Fayard, 1976)

Murray, Linda, *The High Renaissance and Mannerism* (London: Thames & Hudson, 1977)

Murray, Peter and Linda, *The Art of the Renaissance* (London: Thames & Hudson, 1997)

Neale, J. E., *The Age of Catherine de Medici, and Essays in Elizabethan History* (London: Jonathan Cape, 1966)

The New Cambridge Modern History, vol. 1, *The Renaissance 1493–1520*, ed. G. R. Potter (Cambridge: the University Press, 1957)

The New Cambridge Modern History, vol. 2, *The Reformation 1520–1559*, ed. G. R. Elton (Cambridge: the University Press, 1958)

The New Cambridge Medieval History, vol. 7, *c.1415–c.1500*, ed. Christopher Allmand (Cambridge: the University Press, 1998)

Noel, Gerard, *The Renaissance Popes: Culture, Power and the Making of the Borgia Myth* (London: Constable, 2006)

Norwich, John Julius, *Four Princes: Henry VIII, Francis I, Charles V, Suleiman the Magnificent and the Obsessions that Forged Modern Europe* (London: John Murray, 2016)

Orieux, Jean, *Catherine de Médicis ou la reine noire* (Paris: Flammarion, 1998)

Pardoe, Julia, *The Court and Reign of Francis I* (Cambridge: the University Press, 1849)

Parker, Geoffrey, *The Grand Strategy of Philip II* (London and New Haven: Yale University Press, 1998)

Pigaillem, Henri, *Claude de France: Première épouse de François Ier* (Paris: Pygmalion, 2006)

Refuge, Eustache de, *Treatise on the Court: The Early Modern Management Classic on Organizational Behaviour*, trans. J. Chris Cooper (Boca Raton, FL.: Orgpax Publications, 2008)

Renaissance Quarterly, vol. LXI, no. 1, Spring 2008 (New York: The Renaissance Society of America, 2008)

Ridley, Jasper, *A Brief History of the Tudor Age* (London: Robinson, 2002)

Roederer, Ralph, *Catherine de Medici and the Lost Revolution* (London: Harrap, 1937)

Rosenthal, Margaret and Jones, Ann Rosalind, *The Clothing of the Renaissance World* (London: Thames & Hudson, 2008)

Rozet, A. and Lembey, J.-F., *L'Invasion de la France et le siège de Saint-Dizier par Charles-Quint en 1544* (Paris: 1910)

Sadlack, Erin A., *The French Queen's Letters: Mary Tudor Brandon and the Politics of Marriage in Sixteenth-Century Europe* (London: Palgrave Macmillan, 2011)

Scarisbrick, J. J., *Henry VIII* (London and New Haven: Yale University Press, 1997)

Screech, M. A., *Rabelais* (London: Duckworth, 1979)

Setton, Kenneth M., *The Papacy and the Levant (1204–1571)*, vol. 2, *The Fifteenth Century* (Philadelphia: American Philosophical Society, 1978)

Setton, Kenneth M., *The Papacy and the Levant (1204–1571)*, vol. 3, *The Sixteenth Century* (Philadelphia: American Philosophical Society, 1984)

Seward, Desmond, *Prince of the Renaissance: The Life of François I* (London: Constable, 1973)

Sichel, Edith, *Women and Men of the French Renaissance* (London: Westminster, Archibald Constable, 1902)

Simonin, Michel, *Charles IX* (Paris: Fayard, 1995)

Solnon, Jean-François, *Henri III: un désir de majesté* (Paris: Perrin, 2001)

Somerset, Anne, *Elizabeth I* (London: Fontana, 1992)

Starkey, David (ed.), *Henry VIII: A European Court in England* (London: Collins & Brown, 1991)

State Papers of Henry VIII (London: 1830–52)

Stemp, Richard, *The Secret Language of the Renaissance: Decoding the Hidden Symbolism of Italian Art* (London: Duncan Baird Publishers, 2006)

Tamalio, Raffaele (ed.), *The Private Correspondence of Federico Gonzago at the Court of Francis I of France* (Paris: 1994)

Terrasse, Charles, *Francis I, le Roi et le Règne* (Paris: 1948)

Tuchman, Barbara W., *A Distant Mirror: The Calamitous 14th Century* (New York: Ballantine Books, 1979)

Van Dyke, Paul, *Catherine de Médicis* (London: John Murray, 1923)

Vasari, Giorgio, *Vies des Artistes* (Paris: Bernard Grasset, 2007)

Versoris, Nicholas, *Livre de raison de Me Nicolas Versoris, avocat au Parlement de Paris, 1519–1530*, ed. G. Fagniez (Paris: 1885)

Voltaire, M. de; *Abregé de l'histoire universelle, depuis Charlemagne jusques à Charlequint*, in M. Gailliard, *Histoire de François I, Roi de France* (Paris: 1776–9).

Von Pastor, L., trans. F. I. Antrobus and R. F. Kerr, *The History of the Popes* (London: 1891–1933)

Walker Freer, Martha, *The Life of Marguerite of Angoulême* (Cambridge: the University Press, 1895)

Weir, Alison, *Children of England: The Heirs of King Henry VIII 1547–1558* (London: Pimlico, 1997)

Weir, Alison, *Elizabeth the Queen* (London: Pimlico, 1999)

Whittock, Martyn, *A Brief History of Life in the Middle Ages* (London: Robinson, 2009)

Wiesner-Hanks, Merry E., *Early Modern Europe 1450–1789* (Cambridge: the University Press, 2008)

Williams, E. N., *The Penguin Dictionary of English and European History 1485–1789* (London: Allen Lane, 1980)

Williams, H. N., *Henry II: His Court and Times* (London: Methuen, 1910)

ARCHIVES

Archives Nationales, Paris
Archivio Capponi delle Rovinate (Florence)
Archivio di Stato di Firenze
Archivio Storico Italiano
Biblioteca Nazionale Centrale di Firenze
Bibliothèque Nationale, Paris
British Library, London
Public Record Office, London

ACKNOWLEDGEMENTS

This book has been a very long time in the creation, having first occurred to me nearly two decades ago. Listing all of the people involved in its genesis would lead to an acknowledgements section the size of a telephone directory. Nonetheless, several of those responsible for helping me deserve to be singled out for particular thanks. It is the remarkable work and scholarship of Professor Robert Knecht to which I owe the greatest debt. I have felt as though I were 'standing on the shoulder of giants' when it came to following in Professor Knecht's footsteps, and remain grateful for his kindness and influence. I also owe my thanks to the late Ivan Cloulas, former Conservateur Général Honoraire at the Archives Nationales of Paris, a much-missed mentor and friend. His good-natured enthusiasm and generosity of heart have aided me immeasurably and I am sad that this book represents our final collaboration of sorts. Desmond Seward is the other great influence upon me. His work has untied many a knotty historical conundrum and I am humbly thankful for his scholarship.

In the research and writing of this volume, I have consulted countless institutions and museums. A few of the most notable are the Bibliothèque Nationale de France (which, of course, was first set up by Francis), the Louvre, the Biblioteca Nazionale Centrale di Firenze, the London Library, the British Library, the Royal Collection, the National Archives at Kew, Archives Nationales in Paris, Basilique Saint-Denis and the Bibliothèque de la Sorbonne. Of course, many of the châteaux built or expanded by Francis have been invaluable to my research, along with their wise and brilliant custodians. Fontainebleau, Blois, Chambord, Amboise, Clos Lucé and Chenonceau have been the most wonderful places to revisit.

Working with Weidenfeld and Nicolson, and the excellent Alan Samson, has been one of the great pleasures of my professional life. It was Ion Trewin who was my first editor, and I hope that the book is a fitting testament to him. My acknowledgements also must go to my agent, Georgina Capel, and her team. Of course, friends and loved ones act as the final spur in the last days of a project, not least the 'top kat' himself, David Davies. Andrew Roberts has been a huge source of advice and guidance, and the book has been written using the patented 'Roberts Rules of Writing'. Dan Jones, Saul David, Lady Antonia Fraser, Paul Johnson, Leanda de Lisle, Alison Weir, Count Niccolò Capponi, David Starkey, the late Lisa Jardine and Anne Somerset have all been wonderfully supportive and generous with time and advice for all my work, and this is no exception. The wonderful Alexander Larman has been both a muse and splendidly amusing, at times when I needed a boost. Alexandra Hazeldine kept my life in order, along with the wonderful Evie and Ro, and I can only offer them my loving thanks.

My mother deserves a special mention, as so many of our plans and expeditions have been sacrificed while I wrestled with this book, and I hope that we can now find the time to have them. And, as ever, thank you to my beloved children, Jake and Lil.

INDEX

ALSO BY LEONIE FRIEDA

THE DEADLY SISTERHOOD

A Story of Women, Power, and Intrigue
in the Italian Renaissance, 1427-1527

Available in Paperback

"An alluring and worthy study of the powerful
matriarchs at the helm of Italy's great
Renaissance-era dynasties." —*Publishers Weekly*

An epic tale of eight women whose lives—
marked by fortune and poverty, power and
powerlessness—encompass the spectacle,
opportunity, and depravity of
Italy's Renaissance.

CATHERINE DE MEDICI

Renaissance Queen of France

Available in Paperback and Digital Audio

"Vivid and entertaining . . . a convincing human
portrait against the backdrop of a brutal age."
—*Wall Street Journal*

Poisoner, despot, necromancer — the dark
legend of Catherine de Medici is centuries
old. In this critically hailed biography, Leonie
Frieda reclaims the story of this unjustly
maligned queen to reveal a skilled ruler battling
extraordinary political and personal odds.